THE AMERICAN WOMAN

Also by E. J. Dingwall:

Studies in the Sexual Life of Ancient and Mediæval Peoples
Ghosts and Spirits in the Ancient World
Artificial Cranial Deformation
The Girdle of Chastity
Racial Pride and Prejudice
Some Human Oddities
Very Peculiar People
Woman—an Historical, Gynæcological and Anthropological Compendium, by Ploss and Bartels. (Editor, English edition.)

BON VOYAGE BOAT IN NEW YORK HARBOUR
(1938)

THE AMERICAN WOMAN

A Historical Study

by

ERIC JOHN DINGWALL

M.A., D.SC.

GERALD DUCKWORTH & CO LTD
3 Henrietta Street, London, W.C.2

Printed in Great Britain by Richard Clay and Company, Ltd.,
Bungay, Suffolk

CONTENTS

ILLUSTRATIONS

The author's thanks are due to Mrs. Charles D. Gibson for kind permission to reproduce I–IV above, cartoons by Charles Dana Gibson originally published in *Life*.

PREFACE

THIS volume is an attempt to describe, briefly and without great detail, certain aspects of the sexual life of a significant number of American women of the upper and middle income groups, an attempt which, I think, may throw some light upon the general condition and position of women in the United States, and may help to clarify some of the statements so often made concerning them. It is, for example, repeatedly said that there is "something wrong" with the American woman, that she plays a dominant rôle in the social structure of the United States, and that, having gained so much, she is nevertheless profoundly dissatisfied, frustrated, resentful and neurotic.

Although numbers of books have been published dealing with the American woman in which the authors have attempted to diagnose what is assumed to be at fault, I am not aware of any that have traced the story of her development back to colonial days, and have shown how the present dominance of women in the United States can be directly connected with the tenets of Puritanism, the rise of industrialism, and the effect of female influence on the young of both sexes as seen in the American educational system. Moreover, it is precisely with those aspects of her life that are usually neglected or glossed over that I am mainly concerned. The conflict within the soul of many American women is, in my view, primarily a sexual conflict; and it is directly connected with their position in an industrial civilization where men are supreme in business and women in society. This strange dichotomy between the sexes is merely a part of those contradictions and paradoxes which are so often pointed out by American writers and which are the despair of the uninstructed foreign critic. As I hope to show, the riddles which American society presents can be solved only if attention be paid both to the historical roots from which the culture of the United States developed, and, above all, to those hidden springs of thought and action which are so clearly connected with the sexual life.

Few, I think, can doubt that the American people are a sex-obsessed people and that they harbour very peculiar ideas about the position of woman, above all of the Mother. Many of these notions seem to me clearly inimical to the happiness and contentment of women generally, and thus we may begin to understand that the gnawing restlessness and tension, which are all too common among women, are due, in great part, to that American Way of Life of which we hear so much. Moreover, the theory of American individualism, that is to say, the ideal of equal opportunity coupled with the idea that there is something almost sacrosanct about "private enterprise", has been the driving force in American culture for almost three centuries. Its effect upon thought and action can hardly be lightly dismissed. Here I am concerned mainly with some of the effects of American ideals upon the condition of women, and above all with the results of beliefs such as that prosperity is the reward of virtue or that sexual appetite in the female is something of which to be ashamed.

Finally, it must here be stated that this volume makes no attempt to be a scientific and objective study of "the American woman". It is, rather, an attempt to analyse the varied statements that have been made about her by native and foreign authors, to interpret the many views expressed, and to fit them into a general picture which may help to give us a better appreciation of those aspects of her sexual life without which, I am convinced, no proper understanding of American society is possible.

To all my friends, both in America and Europe, who have supported, criticized, and helped me, I herewith extend my most grateful thanks. But above all I am indebted to those American women, both young and not so young, who, in my travels in the United States, have confided in me, told me their troubles, their problems, their hopes and their fears, and from whose lips I have learned many of the facts which I have here so imperfectly tried to clarify and interpret. To these invaluable, but necessarily anonymous confidantes, I dedicate this book.

E. J. DINGWALL

I

PARADOXES AND CONTRADICTIONS

IT has often been said that the condition of women in a given
civilization is a fair measure of the progress of its culture. From
one point of view this may be true, but the phrase "the condition of
women" is too vague to admit of any rational discussion without
careful definition. Social and political historians are too apt to look
merely at superficial phenomena; and the foreign visitor, unless
already equipped with a sound background of accurate information,
is tempted to pick out those features alien to his own culture and
neglect those which, though they seem similar, may be very different
when viewed from another angle or at a different level. We are too
much inclined to examine a culture from our own standpoint, and to
assume that what seems good and desirable to us here and now is a
valid standard for others whose mode of life is very different and
whose social framework may be founded on customs and ideas wholly
foreign to our own.

In the following pages I propose to examine the condition of certain groups of American women and to suggest that many of those
features of American culture which appear inexplicable, not only
to foreign observers but often to Americans themselves, can be com-
prehended only if we understand more fully what is going on beneath
the surface and realize the nature of the driving forces which animate
and inspire what is generally called The American Way of Life.

Descriptions of any society, above all that of the United States,
solely in political and social terms, are apt to be misleading. Most
anthropologists have ignored the fascinating and important phenomena on their doorsteps, preferring to journey to so-called "primitive" cultures, while few historians and sociologists have thought it
necessary to consider the relevance of anthropological, biological and
psychological knowledge to their study of complex Western societies.
Most historians have regarded man and his institutions mainly as
material for descriptive analysis, and even in their chosen field have
tended to select only certain aspects of human behaviour for discussion. Indeed, most historians write as if women hardly counted
and the sexual life had no existence. Women, if mentioned, are to
them merely actors in the social drama, usually playing minor and

supporting rôles. This reluctance to discuss sexual matters has always exercised a cramping and hampering influence on any candid examination of the condition of modern Western society, especially of American society. For in America many women are, it seems, frustrated and thwarted creatures whose biological needs remain unsatisfied and, turned inwards and again outwards, have a profound effect on the society in which these women live. Another limitation on the value of the conventional historical approach is that many historical writers, when attempting to account for social changes, often seem to fail to realize that the reasons men give for their actions are in many cases mere rationalizations which spring from unconscious desires which are unacceptable to the conscious mind and are therefore held in abeyance.

In this connexion it is interesting to observe the effects upon subsequent writers that *The American Commonwealth* (1888) has doubtless had. The stately volumes of sonorous prose, which made the work classic and lifted Bryce to a position of prestige and authority, raise doubts and questions in the mind of the reader of today. For example, was it really true of the United States of 1888 to say that the average knowledge among native Americans was higher and the habit of reading and thinking more widely diffused than in any other country? Were the standards of truthfulness and general probity really higher than in any of the great European nations, and, even if this were so, how could Bryce ever have obtained this knowledge? Above all, what reliance can we place on Bryce's generalizations about American women? According to him, no country in the world owed more to its women than did America, especially through their contributions to what was best in social institutions and in the beliefs through which conduct was governed. The level of culture, he believed, was safe in female hands and, indeed, the world seemed to be at the feet of the American woman.[1] Such statements give us a glimpse of the narrow world in which Bryce moved, and we can realize the nature of the evidence on which he relied if we but read his account of Negro characteristics.

The paradoxes and contradictions of American life have puzzled and intrigued visitors to the United States for years. To some extent this is inevitable, since few visitors can see more than a tiny fraction of this vast land and many travellers lack the background of historical knowledge that would enable them to interpret what they do see. The causes and effects of these paradoxes, especially in relation to American women, will be discussed later in this book, but a few

[1] James Bryce, *The American Commonwealth*, 1888.

examples may be given here of some of the main inconsistencies that have puzzled Americans and foreigners alike. Why, for instance, is it that the country that prides itself on being the land of freedom and individualism has struck so many observers as exhibiting so drab a uniformity and so rigid a standardization? E. A. Mowrer, in his *This American World* (1928), stated that the mass of the population was compelled by the situation in which it found itself to stifle the individuality of its members, to conform to a standardized type, wear standardized clothes, eat standardized foods and behave in a standardized way, while *at the same time* the country set itself up as the land of freedom and individualism. Similar criticisms were made by Theodore Dreiser, who maintained that even the average college or scholastic institution was opposed to the development of an individualistic outlook in its pupils and who thought that the average college man was a standardized machine held fast by custom and convention. This loss of individual character in the United States has long been observed, although, as would be expected, there have always been some Americans who have strongly resented and resisted the charge, whether brought by their fellow-countrymen or by outsiders. Over a hundred years ago, A. de Tocqueville was saying that he knew of no other country in the world where there existed so little independence of mind and genuine freedom of discussion.[1] As the years went by the same opinion was expressed by numerous other writers, many of whom also noted the peculiar position of women in American society without, however, realizing that these two phenomena were closely connected. Writing of the later half of the nineteenth century, for example, Thomas Beer made his well-known scathing indictment of the American woman ("The Titaness") and also commented on the fact that individualism was feared as nothing else in university circles.[2] In the present century similar criticisms, and expressions of bewilderment at the paradox, come both from Americans and from visitors of many nationalities. Thus Adrien de Meeüs, in his *Amusante Amérique* (1938), admitted to frank incomprehension at the contradictions which he observed, calling the United States a charming country of crazy people,[3] while P. Hamp (i.e. Henri Bourillon) complained that what he disliked about the American was not so much the way that he chose to conduct his own life but the way in which he tried to compel others to do likewise, and added that it seemed clear that the Americans, half recognizing their lack of personal freedom, tried to liberate themselves through a

[1] A. de Tocqueville, vol. ii, p. 150. English ed., i, p. 337.
[2] T. Beer, p. 207.
[3] A. de Meeüs, p. 16.

mixture of cocktails and pietism.[1] In the collection of impressions of America contributed by fifteen foreign correspondents in 1939,[2] the Dutch writer, B. Person, noted the prevailing lack of individuality, although he praised the intelligent and high-spirited American women, while the French writer, Raoul de Roussy de Sales, found himself quite unable to account for many of the contradictions which make up the American viewpoint. Roussy de Sales is one of those foreigners who has never failed to show his astonishment at the American scene, as when, in his *What Makes an American* (1939), he says that the immigrant has to adopt a new *credo*, but soon finds that those amongst whom he has to dwell only pretend to listen to the teaching of the founders and in practice act very differently. Odette Keun is another critic and has some very unpleasant remarks to make about her own sex in America, saying, amongst other things, that the women of New York seem to her to be simply examples of mass production.[3]

It seems that the pleasure of conformity and the fear of being thought unusual begin very early in the life of the American child and are more firmly implanted than in other countries. The children grow up to a kind of fixed pattern, prettiness and poise being favoured in the girls and aggressiveness and a masterful attitude in the boys. It is thus that the teen-age girls grow up, dressing in similar standardized clothes, using similar cosmetics, going to the same kind of parties, swooning at the fashionable crooner and falling in love with the film star of the moment. This conformity is especially marked in the Middle West, where, as Graham Hutton remarks, more standardization exists than elsewhere and where also the people particularly pride themselves on their individualistic outlook and sense of keen competition.[4]

Some understanding of the principles underlying American civilization may be gained from reading the literature, the popular magazines and newspapers, from listening to the radio programmes (not neglecting the soap-operas, of which I shall say more later) and from personal observations. Such sources are likely to give a more balanced picture than do the volumes of social studies which pour from the offices of American educators, many of whom, for all they know of what is going on around them, might, it seems to me, be living on the moon. However, the main aid to understanding lies in the realization that much of human activity is a form of substitution; that is to say, many of the things we do and say are, in a sense,

[1] P. Hamp, p. 311. [2] B. P. Adams, *You Americans.*
[3] Odette Keun, p. 71. [4] Graham Hutton, p. 283.

substitutes for quite other actions and thoughts. In dealing with a civilization like that of the United States—a civilization which, I suspect, produces more neurotic individuals than any other—it is essential to have psychological insight into the underlying mechanisms operating within the society. Fortunately, the clue to two of the major underlying factors in the development of life in the United States is provided by American salesmen of culture. They make it quite clear, firstly, that the Americans suffer from a peculiar form of sex-obsession which is linked to a mother-worship of an unusual kind, and, secondly, that the notions of what they call liberty, equality, opportunity and free enterprise are absolutely essential ingredients of the American Myth.

It is the nature of these two dominating influences which makes America seem such a "foreign" country even to many of those Europeans who do not make the false assumption, pointed out by André Siegfried among others,[1] that American civilization is merely the civilization of Europe transported across the Atlantic. The strangeness and the difference of America is not primarily due to its size and variety but to the nature of the basic conceptions which form the foundations of its national life. Many of the contradictions in practice arise from the holding of incompatible ideas. For example, the gospel of free enterprise and opportunity for all, however much or little meaning there may be in these fine phrases, has led not only to a vast increase in material prosperity but also to the loss of many individual liberties and to the standardization already mentioned. Anyone acquainted with the history of American business is aware how, in a country which prides itself on being the land of private enterprise, many a small business man has been gradually squeezed out of what he believed to be his legitimate field by the great trusts and combinations which ever seek to extend their empires at the expense of less strongly entrenched competitors. The successes claimed by private enterprise in the past were made at a time when resources seemed limitless and when the frontier was still a living reality. But as opportunities began to decrease, so the great combinations began to close in, and individualism in business began slowly to show signs of withering. This was fully recognized by the czars of the great industrial empires, most of whom did not labour under the delusions cherished by so many of their countrymen. For example, in 1885 John D. Rockefeller declared that the great combinations would remain and that individualism had gone, never to return.[2] Similarly,

---

[1] A. Siegfried, p. 345.
[2] Quoted by Allan Nevins in *John D. Rockefeller*, vol. i, p. 622.

President Woodrow Wilson, speaking in 1910 before the American Bar Association, is reported to have stated that men were no longer units but fractions, cogs and pawns in the business game.[1]

The same tendency is observable in other quarters, and is especially to be remarked in those organizations which control, direct and influence public opinion. The Press is gradually being controlled from fewer and fewer sources; and some States have now reached a point where not one of the large cities has any newspaper competition whatever. In many cases block bookings of new material are sent out from a central source, such as the W.N.U. (Western Newspaper Union), and accepted by the local journals; and it is well known that sometimes nearly 50 per cent. of space is reserved by some popular journals for advertisements which offer for sale all those appurtenances to good living which are bought by the women of America, in whose hands lies much of the retail buying. A similar state of affairs can be seen in the radio and film industries, where a handful of executives control a vast staff, which Morris L. Ernst has well said exercises what can only be termed a kind of mental dictatorship.[2]

Apart from these curious paradoxes and contradictions operating in American society, many domestic and foreign observers have remarked that the United States seems to have a surprising number of men who remain adolescent and of women who play the rôles both of doll and of matriarch, and they have not always realized that this is part of the American cultural pattern and the result of the domination of society by women. The conflict in the American soul is an economic and a sexual conflict, and the American woman is, I think, at the heart of that conflict. It is women who set the stage and largely control the players in important sections of American life. America is a woman's world, a world in which, as a Chinese woman, Helena Kuo, remarked, women have succeeded in everything except in the art of being truly feminine.[3] In this lies the tragedy and the danger. It is the purpose of this book to try to see how the American woman has attained her position and how the whole of American culture is permeated by her influence.

The conflict that can now be seen within the American soul has its roots in the past, and its development can be traced to the days when the frontier was a vital influence in shaping the minds and behaviour of men and women. The early immigrants who came to America from the Old World did so for a variety of reasons; and many of the motives that inspired them can still be seen at work in

---

[1] Quoted by T. C. Cochran and W. Miller, pp. 193 ff.
[2] Morris L. Ernst, p. 245.   [3] Helena Kuo, p. 728.

the United States today. In the late sixteenth and early seventeenth centuries little was known of the vast Western continent, and some men, stirred by the love of adventure and the unknown, itched to explore and to discover new treasures. Others came to set up fishing or farming settlements, as did the Dorchester Company of Adventurers, the forerunners of the great Massachusetts Bay Company. Others again came of necessity and not of choice, like the younger people imported by the Virginia Company and the Negroes, of whom there were possibly nearly half a million in the middle half of the eighteenth century. Apart from the indentured servants, numbers of convicts and persons accused of various crimes entered Virginia and Maryland, and thus some elements of the mixed population had no intention of living according to the rules of conduct which were, in some parts of the country, laid down for them. Doubtless it was at the door of these people that a proportion of the crimes over which the Puritans used to lament can honestly be laid. But apart from these early settlers and some of the French, Spanish, Dutch, Swedish and other colonists, there were many who came primarily because of a desire to lead their own lives and follow their beliefs and customs unhampered by the restrictions that they found so irksome in the Old World. These were men and women of strong character and independent outlook, willing to suffer and even to die for what they conceived to be the truth. Rather than submit to any arbitrary or external dictation, they were willing and anxious to tear up their roots in their homelands and replant them in a soil more suitable for growth and development. Among these were the Puritans and Separatists, whose views had a profound influence on the American character, although, as we shall see later, much of what is supposed to be due to Puritanism would not have been understood by these early colonists, who were, in many respects, far from being ascetic spoil-sports, as is now often supposed.

Before passing on to a brief review of colonial conditions and the position of women in the colonial family, something must be said of the mentality of the frontier. It does not require much thought to see what must have been the main characteristics of a pioneer faced with a world to win, especially when that same pioneer was often filled with the fervent belief that God helped those who helped themselves and that prosperity was the reward of virtue. Above all, the pioneer was an individualist and, as R. Barton Perry has put it, a buoyant, self-reliant and resourceful individualist.[1] It was through

---

[1] R. B. Perry, Broadcast for the British Broadcasting Corporation, Dec. 8, 1947.

his own efforts and those of his family that the wilderness was made to bear fruit, that the rushing waters were tamed and that the virgin forest first yielded to the axe and the plough. Rewards came to him who strove for his own good: external interference was anathema: individual enterprise and personal initiative were not to be coerced by government meddling, and intrusiveness by such busybodies would be resisted with violence if necessary. It was only gradually, as the population increased and the settlements became less widely separated, that the desirability of some control began to be felt. The ideal of the squatter began to clash with the ideals inherent in democratic procedure. The conflict had already begun and was to be continued right up to the present day, when we can see in the modern industrialized United States men and women holding simultaneously incompatible ideas about "free enterprise" and "democracy".

The gregariousness and dislike of personal isolation, coupled with the opposing desire for self-reliance and self-assertiveness, are other characteristics of the modern American which can be traced to frontier days. Graham Hutton observed that in the Middle West these contradictory tendencies often exist simultaneously. In his *Midwest at Noon* he asked what it was that made so many people in the Middle West seem unable to relax and lose their inhibitions except when in company? Were they, he inquired, trying to escape from something and, if so, from what? Why did they dislike solitude and feel that the man or woman who treasured privacy, silence and the pleasures of contemplation must be a person up to no good, clearly abnormal and possibly immoral? In spite of such observations, however, Graham Hutton declared that the people of the Middle West were less inhibited in their lives than any other people he knew either inside or outside the United States. He admitted that the nervous restlessness that they exhibited somewhat belied their self-assurance and, like Professor R. B. Perry, found this a puzzling phenomenon, although less marked in the cities than on the farms. This feeling of loneliness, which John Gunther has stated to be one of the most important problems that America has to face,[1] is doubtless difficult to understand at first, since it is combined with precisely those qualities which, one might have thought, would make such feeling difficult to maintain. In earlier days the pioneers of the frontier, in their bold advance towards the conquest of new territory, had to rely almost entirely on their own efforts. Self-reliance and resourcefulness were to them a necessity, and with their manifold

[1] John Gunther, p. 909.

activities they had little time to be lonely. Yet how often at least a few of these hardy adventurers must have felt how small they were when faced with the magnitude of their undertakings. What was their boasting but a means of keeping up their courage? (And even to this day boasting among Americans is not unknown.) It seems that in the past feelings both of self-reliance and loneliness were by no means incompatible, since both were responses to actual situations, whereas today the reasons for that loneliness are no longer conscious and the basis for those inhibitions of which Mr. Hutton speaks are no longer understood. The frontier has gone but the frontier mentality remains.

Fears and inhibitions of this kind are not part of the inheritance of each child. They arise from factors which are set in motion very early in life and are often derived from early upbringing and training and in later life have to be explained away through rationalizations. Sometimes they become so burdensome that the sufferer is unable to live an active and useful life and becomes seriously neurotic. In recent years a considerable body of evidence has been produced by American psychiatrists to show the high incidence of neurotic complaints. This evidence cannot be fully described or discussed here but, even if it would be rash to draw too firm general conclusions from it, it does, at least, clearly show that a serious problem exists, and that in the Second World War it presented the American military authorities with grave and disturbing practical difficulties. For example, in 1945 Dr. J. D. Campbell stated that in the United States approximately 25,000,000 persons could be classified under one or the other of the borderline mental conditions.[1] (The population of the United States in 1945, including armed forces overseas, was estimated at about 139,934,000.) Examination of the draft for the Second World War disclosed some remarkable figures. According to Colonel Leonard B. Rowntree, chief of the medical division of the Bureau of Selective Service, speaking on October 30, 1942, 13 per cent. of the men who had been classified as 4-F had been placed there on account of mental or nervous disorders. This amounted to 6·3 per cent. of the total draft registrants who had been called up. In 1944 the Selective Service System disclosed that men were being rejected as mentally and nervously unfit at about seven times the rate recorded during the First World War, although the rate of hospitalization was almost the same. The Office of War Information added that the current rate of such rejections was over 20 per cent. In October 1945 it was stated that the total number of

---

[1] John D. Campbell, p. 298.

B

men mentally unfit for the armed forces had reached the figure of 2,300,000.[1]

These figures are a curious commentary on the mental condition of so many of the younger men in the United States and throw some light on certain social conditions there. The behaviour of many of those men who were not rejected from the armed forces also suggested, both to American and to foreign observers, a lack both of social responsibility and of emotional maturity. For example, General R. L. Eichelberger stated that in Japan in 1946 the drunkenness, rapes and thievery that were going on among the men would endanger the success of the occupation's mission. The military authorities had a hard task to discipline their occupation forces, in spite of efforts by men like General Joseph McNarney. In Germany the "Fräulein nights" were popular, while according to Hutton and Rooney in their *Conquerors' Peace*, civilians in some German towns were in real danger of being beaten up and robbed by drunken American soldiers. In Austria American culture was introduced and the Festspielhaus was turned into a cinema, and the young women who "fraternized" were soon taken at their true value and nicknamed "chocoladies". R. C. Kennedy also, in a paper in the *Christian Century*, made a violent denunciation of the behaviour of American troops in Europe, saying that they were regarded by English, French and even Germans as uncouth barbarians.[2] Although fortunately such strictures were by no means universally true, it was, however, clear that the mental condition of whole blocks of the male population seriously disturbed the medical military authorities, who cast about for an explanation of this unfortunate situation.

The explanation was not far to seek, and had indeed already been suggested in 1943 by the Dowager Lady Nunburnholme in her discussion of the homesickness of American soldiers in Britain, at the conference of the National Council of Women. These men, she said, "have been brought up by women and they have the mother complex". In 1946 the Americans learnt that one of their foremost authorities had come to very similar conclusions. In the *Saturday Evening Post* of October 26 appeared an article by Dr. Edward A. Strecker, chairman of the Department of Psychiatry at the University of Pennsylvania and a prominent medical consultant to the armed forces. It was followed by a book [3] on the same lines as the

---

[1] Cf. "The Psychiatric Toll of Warfare", *Fortune*, Dec. 1943, pp. 141 ff.; *New York Herald Tribune*, Feb. 19, 1944; D. L. Dumond, p. 289.

[2] R. C. Kennedy, p. 496.

[3] E. A. Strecker, *Their Mothers' Sons*. On the other hand, it is suggested in S. A. Stouffer's *The American Soldier* (1949) that the data do not seem to sup-

article, a book which, as the advertisements indicated, revealed a "startling, staggering situation". For Dr. Strecker's conclusion was that the person mainly responsible for this deplorable situation was none other than the American Mother. That sacred figure in the American Myth had become, as one blurb unkindly put it, "The Great American Mom—a juggernaut whose toll of crippled lives is greater than all our wounded in two World Wars". As has been said above, the roots of those neurotic conditions which prevent the normal social life of those suffering from them were to be found in childhood and in early traumatic experiences which left their mark on the developing personality. As Strecker realized, in seeking an explanation it was necessary to look into the past, to note the kind of early education that young Americans received and to see what persons were primarily responsible for influencing their minds during the formative years.

If Dr. Strecker be right in his surmise (and the evidence in favour of his thesis is fairly abundant, as I think the following pages will show), then this fact alone must be of considerable importance in any appraisal of the nature and pattern of American society. For if the influence of the American Mother be such that she is mainly responsible for turning thousands of young men into neurotics, what is her influence likely to be upon her daughters? Why, indeed, does she adopt this "cannibal" rôle, as Sidney C. Howard puts it in *The Silver Cord*, and whence spring the motives for her beliefs and actions? Moreover, can it be said that the condemnation of the American Mother by writers such as Strecker and Wylie [1] is generally justified, or ought it to be limited to certain social strata? Does it hold good, for example, for the mothers of factory or farm workers, or for Negro mothers? Does it apply to the foreign-born women, or only to the second and third generations? If we can judge from the figures presented by the U.S. military authorities, it would seem that the alleged influence of the American Mother was widely diffused among those drafted, although an analysis according to social standing might have disclosed considerable variations. It is possible that the unhealthy influences mentioned by Strecker, if such they be, are most widely spread among the more leisured classes, gradually weakening through the farming and industrial workers and thence to the more simple Negro families, where the matriarchal

---

port the prevalence of psychiatric breakdown in the army as traceable to maternal indulgence (vol. i, p. 136), but the point is rather maternal over-protection than "indulgence".

[1] Philip Wylie, *Generation of Vipers*.

influence, although sometimes strong, appears to be of a different type.

In order to inquire into the truth or falsity of the charges that are now being brought against the women of America by Americans themselves, it will be necessary to do more than merely describe feminine activity in the United States from colonial times to the present day. We shall have to examine the relations between men and women, husbands and wives, lovers and mistresses, boys and girls, prostitutes and clients. Attention must be paid to such matters as the control of the purse, the management of the home and the education of the children. We shall have to study the mysteries of "dating", the effects of the "petting party" and the relation it bears to "chastity", and the attempts to transform the American man into a protean creature according to the moods of the potent sorceress who rules him. We shall have to consider the American girl, both in her "glorified" and in her plain aspects, the American spinster and wife in their varied rôles, the American mother at home and in society, the American widow and divorcée.

It is the complexity of the American scene that so often baffles the observer. In the attempt to find a pattern one often seems to be trying to do a gigantic jig-saw puzzle of which the picture is unknown. One fits in one piece only to find that the next is at variance, and so both have to be scrapped and the work begun afresh. Gradually one realizes, however, that a pattern exists and that the paradoxes, the contradictions, the apparent cross-purposes and almost unintelligible mystifications are all essential parts of this pattern. The American is able to hold contradictory ideas at the same time because he is essentially ambivalent, and when one recognizes this ambivalence one sees that it is one of the most striking features of his character. He is almost like a man living within two worlds: the flesh is always at war with the spirit and the spirit with the flesh. His education leads him to believe in ideals which he sees being violated on every side. Yet these same ideals have been so firmly implanted in him that even if he no longer consciously believes in them, their traces remain in the unconscious and generate feelings of guilt and fear which wreck his peace of mind. It is interesting and not without significance that two recent and simultaneous bestsellers from New York to California have been Joshua Loth Liebman's *Peace of Mind* and the Kinsey report on sexual behaviour in the American man.

It may be said that the sense of fear and the desire for security and tranquillity are due to the dangers of the international situation

for the United States in the post-war world. Yet the restless energy
and urge to escape, so different from the normal wish for relaxation
after effort, was noted by observers of the nineteenth as well as of the
twentieth century. Alexis de Tocqueville said of the American that
he clutches everything but holds nothing fast and after a short time
loosens his grip in order to pursue some new gratification.[1] The
highly unpopular Captain Frederick Marryat (1792–1848) declared
that the Americans were a "restless, uneasy people", adding that
they always had to be doing something, since they could not sit still
and listen attentively unless, perchance, it were a question of politics
or dollars.[2] In the later years of the nineteenth century the same
characteristics were noted by the French critic Mme Thérèse Blanc,
who wrote under the pseudonym of T. Bentzon. She said that a
German physician who was at that time resident in the United
States had called this curious restlessness "americanitis", and that
the disease was so prevalent that people were seeking relief in Annie
Payson Call's *Power through Repose* (1891). This latter authoress
was not at all complimentary to her own sex, stating that a ladies'
luncheon-party was worse than a farmyard, so loud was the cackle,
and adding that the term "dry drunk" was used in colleges to describe the intense nervous excitement and want of control which
were apparent among some people at the time at which she was
writing. C. A. Bristed, in *The Upper Ten Thousand* (p. 51), stated
nearly forty years earlier that "repose is not a natural state" to the
American woman, and some years later Thomas W. Higginson,[3] the
writer, social reformer and linguistic genius, said that the "terrors of
nervous prostration" haunt men almost equally with women. In
the earlier years of the present century also, writers such as Rita
(Mrs. W. D. Humphreys) have said that in America one can do anything but rest,[4] while O'Higgins and Reede, in their interesting study
of the American mind, insisted upon the relationship between worry,
that pet psychological vice of the American, and the inner feelings of
guilt and "soul-fear" from which he longs to escape.[5] On the other
hand, there are those who maintain that the prevailing restlessness
is merely due to a superabundance of healthy energy, a view which,
in my opinion, is quite untenable if all the facts be considered. This
inability to rest, this scorn or even fear of leisure, is part of the com-
petitive system which is an essential ingredient of the American way

---

[1] A. de Tocqueville, *Democracy in America*, vol. ii, p. 120.
[2] F. Marryat, *A Diary in America*, pt. 2, vol. ii, p. 120.
[3] T. W. Higginson, *Women and Men*, p. 239.
[4] Rita. *America—through English Eyes*, p. 116.
[5] H. J. O'Higgins and E. H. Reede, pp. 8, 13 and *passim*.

of life and is itself, as R. B. Perry has pointed out, a product of the
Puritan urge which ever goads men on to fresh efforts, thus engender-
ing envy and embitterment among those who, often for reasons beyond their control, are left behind in the race.[1] Some of the most recent comments by British observers on the restless activity of
Americans come from the teams who visited the United States under
the auspices of the Anglo-American Productivity Council. For
example, the report on steel founding says, in its conclusions, that
"the Team has been aware of a widespread degree of productivity-
consciousness" and mentions also "the pressure exerted upon the
wage-earner by his womenfolk". It states that investigators of
conditions in the U.S. must confess to meeting continual contradictions which are traceable to the co-existence in American life
of two warring motives, and says, "It would be strange if there were
not violent contradictions to be found among a people who at one
and the same time hitch their wagons to the stars of individualism
and uniformity."[2]

Although writers in the United States, in Europe and elsewhere
have not attempted to differentiate the restlessness of men from that
displayed by women and vice versa, it is, I think, necessary that
some attempt should be made to do so. As we shall see later, the
position of woman in the United States is peculiar. But whatever it
may be, and however regarded, there is little doubt that it fails to
fulfil what is expected of it. Feminine restlessness in the United
States is, in my opinion at least, due primarily to a search for satisfaction, coupled with the constant feeling that that search is, and
seemingly must always be, unsuccessful. In men the situation is
somewhat different, and is complicated by the fact that the cares of
business and the strain of competition are added to the difficulties
which life in the United States compels every man to face. Sex
antagonism, which in America runs at fever heat, is an added irritant
to the restlessness of both men and women; and since the average
intellectual equipment is poor and the powers of concentration of
the average citizen nominal, he has little chance of being able to turn
from distracting business and personal affairs to the tranquil pleasures that await the cultured individual in the contemplation of
works of art or the meditation aroused by philosophical speculation.
The American's life is a perpetual round of strain, rush and worry.
Buoyant, optimistic, gay, he often surmounts his many difficulties,
but at what a cost !

[1] R. B. Perry, *Puritans and Democracy*, p. 319.
[2] See *Productivity Team Report*, etc., pp. 33, 35.

It was on my first visit to the United States, over thirty years ago, that I first became puzzled by these apparent inconsistencies in the American Way of Life. The contradictions between faith and practice seemed to me everywhere so apparent that it was hard to believe that my American friends were unaware of them. Attempts to discuss such differences were met by a resistance which showed that there must be a strong and deep-seated conflict within the minds of those from whom I sought enlightenment. At that time much of American civilization seemed to me merely a veneer beneath which simmered and seethed something sinister and, at times, a little frightening. The rush, the turmoil, the eternal hurry—all these were clearly symptoms of some malaise which I could not diagnose, although it seemed to be connected with a curious kind of delayed maturity on the one hand and with an even more curious and half-unconscious sense of fear and guilt on the other. Although I had been led to believe that the United States was the "land of individualism, free enterprise and opportunity for all", it was gradually brought home to me that these terms were used in a very different sense from that which I had been led to expect. Similarly, the passion for "law and order", which animated so many of my friends, seemed oddly out of place in a country where the scale of criminal activity was remarkable. Raymond B. Fosdick has just issued his *Crime in America and the Police*, and the figures he published were sufficiently startling to disturb the most complacent. The contrast between the criminal and the law-abiding sections of the community was but one example of the great gulfs which seemed to divide the different sections of the population. Many groups, such as those in some of the universities, seemed to live in a world altogether apart from that of the teeming millions around them. On the other hand, the world of higher education was itself divided; and many universities and colleges could be described as stores where technical knowledge was sold, later to be fed back to those industrial and business concerns which, to a certain extent, controlled such centres of learning. Americans who held the European idea of culture, and who, like Plutarch, thought that education should be the fountain and root of a noble life, were regarded with suspicion and often with open dislike by the many who thought that there could be no better educational symbols than a row of dollar signs, as Ted showed to Pop Babbitt after dinner.

The pursuit of the dollar is only one of the aspects of American activity which have been especially noted by foreign observers. The roar of New York's traffic, the blaze in the sky over the steel mills of

Pittsburgh, the clang of metal as the cars roll in endless streams off the lines in Detroit, the swish of the machines in the corn of Iowa, and the shouting at the cheese auctions in Plymouth, Wisconsin—all these are signs of that restless energy which is so prominent a feature of life in the United States. This energy seems sometimes to take on the characteristics of a compulsive obsession which conceals deep-lying neuroses and is clearly pathological. The desire to escape from something seems to me to be one of the most striking features of American civilization, although doubtless to many observers and to most Americans such a statement will sound odd or even prepos-terous. What is it that drives the business man in pursuit of more and more wealth, so that when it is attained and running over he still seeks more and never has the leisure, even if he has the capacity, to enjoy the rewards of his labour and his sagacity? What is it that makes the leisured women of the United States a prey to every new fad, fashion and cult, and what makes them betray so clearly their desire to escape from that "American Way", which they proclaim to the world to be so superior? Why, as serious Americans themselves have pointed out, was the behaviour of many of the American Forces in Europe so incompatible with professed American ideals? If, as R. C. Kennedy alleged,[1] the three main interests of many of the G.I.s in Europe were to fornicate, to get drunk and to go home, were these interests determined partly by the fact that they were reared in a country dominated largely by women and had been educated mainly by unmarried women school-teachers?

It may seem to some an impertinence that a foreigner should attempt to answer these and the many other questions that the American scene provokes. Yet it is perhaps desirable that a greater candour should exist between two great peoples as closely linked as Great Britain and the United States, with whose destinies the future of the entire world is interwoven. In dealing with a country as vast and as complex as the United States it has seemed to me best to rely mainly on American observers themselves and in the following pages an attempt is made merely to interpret and to suggest hypo-theses to explain the often bewildering variety of facts, praise and criticism that citizens of this country themselves offer. It is perhaps fortunate that the United States' publicity and information services have so little reticence in "selling" the American conception of civilized life to the world. Numerous information agencies, radio chains and similar organizations are plentifully supplied with news-papers and magazines, often at the expense of the American tax-

[1] R. C. Kennedy, *op. cit.*

payer. Such journals as the international editions of *Time* and *Life*, to name but two, bring to the nations of the world what must, I think, be considered as a fairly true and continuing account of what the United States is doing and thinking, and telling the world for what America stands and what the American people are. The importance of journals like these is obvious, just as is the appeal of such papers as the *Saturday Evening Post*, the *Ladies' Home Journal*, the *Nation* or the *New Republic*. In reading a paper such as *Time*, which has a large circulation in countries outside the United States, one can, I think, assume that those who control the paper aim at selecting information which will be regarded as news and as of interest to readers wherever they may be. What seems to the foreigner so interesting, and so odd, is the basis of selection, above all in the space given to petty details of sex life and of female anatomy. For example, in the issue of the Atlantic Overseas Edition of April 12, 1948, there is, under the section headed "Music", a column and a half about the adventures of a female crooner who had been sentenced to a reformatory. It describes the welcome given to her on her return by her fans, says that her voice, now a "petulant, sex-edged moan", is better than before, gives an account of her life in the reformatory, and adds the important information that at the age of fourteen she had "big breasts". The preoccupation of the American male with the breasts, and also with the buttocks, will be discussed later, but it may be said here that examples of breast fetishism can be found in almost every issue of every popular American magazine. The glossy products of the American Press, on news-stands from China to Peru, display the stereotype of the glorified American girl. In a sweater or a low-cut dress, she smiles from almost every page. She advertises bathing-dresses, films, brassieres, scents, lotions, soaps—but always and above all she advertises those charms the thought of which seems rarely absent from American consciousness. It cannot be wondered, I think, that in certain circles in the book trade best-sellers are called breast-sellers, for, as one advertising man is reported to have said, it is sometimes difficult to judge from looking at the wrapper of a book whether it deals with breast development or with land investment, with seafaring or with suckling.

It is very clear that the kind of "American Way" portrayed by the merchants of culture is not at all like the civilization of the United States as presented by Bryce and the long line of historians, sociologists and philosophers who came after him. For it is not only in the newspapers and magazines that the contrast may be perceived. Is the American scene as painted by Sinclair Lewis, by Steinbeck, by

Caldwell, by Farrell and by dozens more, a gross and monstrous libel on a great people, or is the world of Zenith like that in *Babbitt* and is Grand Republic really like the city featured in *Kingsblood Royal*? Or do these novels merely paint portraits of isolated communities, cities and townships that are not in the least representative? Are they malicious caricatures, drawn for some purpose we cannot understand? Certainly the Middle West of Sinclair Lewis is not the same as that of Graham Hutton, but as the latter's *Midwest at Noon* fails even to mention the existence of the Chicago *Tribune* (and what is the Middle West without it?), it may well be that Mr. Hutton has painted only one portion of the picture and that Mr. Lewis and his contemporaries have painted the other. However, I confess I find myself rather in agreement with Professor T. K. Whipple when he says in his *Spokesmen* (1928), p. 218, speaking of the novels of Sinclair Lewis, that hardly anybody could deny that this author's picture of the United States is what could be called a good likeness.

The high speed of life in the United States, the piling up of production, and the ever-increasing tempo of everyday existence are not the signs of a young and healthy people. They are signs and symptoms of some kind of psychological disturbance evidently arising from conditions obtaining early in life, and clearly anchored to a whole set of ideas and notions which are embedded in the core of the "American Way". This teaching is carried on through each generation by parental and school education and thus, like so many of the other puzzling phenomena in American society, must be closely linked with the position, power and influence of the American woman. It is to her that we must look if we wish to understand the strange and fascinating picture presented by the United States. It is through an understanding of her that we can, if I mistake not, fill in that multi-coloured and complicated jig-saw which is America.

II

THE COMING OF THE PURITANS

AMONG American writers who have expressed candid criticisms of the civilization in which they live, the majority have, so far as I am acquainted with the literature, put a great deal of blame upon the Puritans for any situation they deplore. Thus Henry B. Adams (1838–1918) ascribed the American views on sex and women, which he attacked somewhat intemperately, largely to the influence of Puritanism. He declared that the extraordinary nineteenth-century delusion that sex did not exist was one which the observer could only regard with mute astonishment. It seemed to Adams that this strange point of view, so different from that of previous ages, made woman not only a being of whom to be ashamed, but also one who was forced to be ashamed of herself. Thus the even more remarkable situation had developed in which the American man found himself in the unpalatable position of being looked on as without sex, while the American woman, on the other hand, was regarded as so sexual a creature as to offer a constant temptation to the innocent.[1] Similar criticisms and theories have been put forward by many other writers, as, for example, by E. A. Mowrer in his *This American World*. Mowrer maintained that Puritanism, with its distrust of pleasure and its suspicion of certain kinds of mental activity outside the ranks of the theocracy, was responsible for much of the distrust of intellectual pursuits and for the deplorable condition of sexual life in the United States. He thought that, generally speaking, conversation in its proper sense, which he considered the mark of a mature mind, was beyond the capabilities of the average citizen. Views were not exchanged and discussed; facts, culled from the latest newspapers, were repeated and stories heard in smoking-rooms or barbers' chairs were passed around. In his opinion, the nation was composed of what could only be called adult children, who were not wholly

---

[1] Henry B. Adams (2), pp. 384, 443 ff. I am not sure how far this point of view would meet with the approval of Elizabeth Hawes, who has recently lamented the forgotten females of the United States in her book *Why Women Cry; or Wenches with Wrenches* (New York, 1943). Declaring that females are often human beings, this author has come to the surprising conclusion that American women never receive any attention, and that modern methods of running the American home normally lead to the wife eternally crying and never attaining to her full strength.

unaware of their condition but who liked it and wished to continue as they were.[1] Similarly, Theodore Dreiser, in his *Hey, Rub-a Dub-Dub!*, contributed a stinging indictment of contemporary America, saying that the country was a victim to what could only be termed a deep-seated neurosis, as, since the conviction was everywhere prevalent that sex was in essence both degrading and evil, the extreme emotional interest it engendered caused a general fear to face reality; and by allowing teachers in the upper-class levels to inculcate such doctrines about sex (which in fact were widely disregarded) the country was made ridiculous not only to observers within its own borders but to the world outside.[2] As to the American woman, Dreiser expressed astonishment that the ideas regarding her could honestly be held by any rational person. But, he stated, Americans move in a world of illusion. To them woman is more than human and has become a goddess, a divine creative principle in whom no vice, error or weakness can be found. He went on to say that this fantastic delusion caused sex activity, as it were, to become a criminal offence, since it was through its expression that the paragon was violated.[3]

In order to understand the mechanisms underlying modern American culture, it is essential to study the nature of that Puritanism which not only imposed its ideas on early New England, but which has so profoundly affected the mental outlook of the whole of the United States. From what we know of the life and beliefs of the Puritans, those effects are very much what might have been expected. But before dealing with those effects it will be well to trace briefly the origins of Puritanism and its development in the United States.

When Queen Elizabeth came to the throne in 1558 she was faced with a number of thorny problems both in affairs of State and in matters ecclesiastical. The situation in the Church was difficult, since those who favoured the retention of the Roman Catholic doctrines and practices supported by Queen Mary desired to remain, while those who opposed them were vigorous in their denunciation of the Papal influence. Moreover, many of these men, who had been exiled in the previous reign, had fled to the Continent, where, in such places as Geneva or Zurich, they had been deeply affected by the

---

[1] E. A. Mowrer, *op. cit.* It was the late G. Lowes Dickinson who, after his tour of the United States, pointed out that it seemed to him that the Americans he met never thought but only calculated, that they invented but never discovered, and though they talked they never conversed (see G. L. Dickinson, p. 102).

[2] T. Dreiser, pp. 131, 136. Cf. L. Lewisohn's *Expression in America*, pp. 477, 483.

[3] T. Dreiser, *op. cit.*, pp. 272 ff. Cf. Christina Stead's *Letty Fox: her Luck*, p. 133.

teaching of Calvin, and on their return to England were determined to purge the Anglican Church of any traces of Rome, such as vestments, the observance of days dedicated to certain saints, the use of the sign of the cross and even the custom of wearing a surplice. Between these two extreme schools lay a third and more moderate section to which the Queen herself lent some support and which, while rejecting the tenets of the Roman Church, still wished to preserve what was good without slavishly adhering to the rigid and austere Protestantism which the reforming zealots had brought over with them from the Calvinistic strongholds in Switzerland.

On their arrival in England these reformers began to agitate for the purification of the English Church. Their propaganda was well directed, ingenious and extremely troublesome to the authorities. Their objections to the prevailing forms of belief and ceremonial were much more radical and intolerant than merely wishing for the removal of a few ornaments or refusing themselves to wear a surplice. What they demanded in essence was that the English Church should be brought into line with the Protestant Churches in Europe, and that this change should affect not only doctrinal points but also details of organization and disciplinary measures.

The methods adopted by these Puritans, as they were called, were the use of serious sermons, books and exhortations, and also pamphlets like the Marprelate tracts, which combined a simple style with caustic wit and invective which, together, created an appeal which was both persuasive and amusing. English bishops naturally did not like to have such terms flung at them as the "Beelzebub of Canterbury", and the ecclesiastical authorities began to lose patience with their vigorous and well-organized assailants.

When James I ascended the throne, the Puritans at first believed that their great day had arrived. The new King had been reared in a Calvinistic atmosphere in Scotland, but he was not prepared to carry out what the Puritans asked and they soon discovered that their demands were not going to be met. A further and much deeper disappointment greeted them on the accession of Charles I in 1625. The King did not favour the outlook of the Puritans; and in the growing struggle between the King and Parliament they found themselves more or less allied with the Parliamentary group in opposition to the Royal party. Moreover, with the rise of William Laud to the bishopric of London the prospect for the Puritans grew ever more gloomy. Laud was a vehement opponent of the whole Calvinistic system of philosophy and ecclesiastical discipline, but his methods lacked statesmanship and annoyed the Episcopalians almost as much as the Separatists. He punished the misdemeanours of the more wealthy classes as severely as he did those of the poorer people; and his work in the Star Chamber, which was at that time becoming increasingly unpopular, made him become little by little a detested figure and one whose influence over the King was considered by many to be disastrous.

It must have been about this time that the leading Puritans in England came to the conclusion that their hopes of a radical reformation were not likely to be fulfilled in the near future and that it would be better to seek a new home elsewhere than to attempt a futile struggle to carry out their doctrines and practices at home. New England would obviously be the place to which their thoughts would be directed, since the group of Separatists from Holland and England had already arrived in December 1620 and had set up congregational churches on the usual self-governing model. Once the scheme was mooted, plans were rapidly made for its fulfilment. With the support of such prominent men as John Winthrop (1588-1649), the son of Adam Winthrop of Groton Manor in Suffolk, the little group met in 1629 to discuss plans, and in the Cambridge Agreement it was arranged that the migration to New England should be speedily effected, provided that the government and patent of the Massachusetts colony be transferred to them.

Plans went well, and in 1630 the party, including many prominent members of Puritan families, sailed for New England. At last they could do what they had wanted to do for so long. Religious freedom for themselves was clearly within their grasp, although they had little intention of allowing the same freedom to be extended to others. The Puritans *knew* they were right; and so it was clear that those who differed from them were in error, and therefore not to be tolerated. To imagine, as so many in Europe do, that the Puritans emigrated to the New World to set up a free and democratic community is a delusion of the first order. They were neither tolerant nor democratic, and the wish to set up their own religious state was not divorced completely from the natural wish to better their material condition. What forced the Puritans to be more tolerant was not the fact that they wished to be so, but that they were compelled to extend a measure of liberty by reason that business had to be carried on and the influence of the religious bodies in the southern colonies could not be wholly ignored. It was an unwilling conciliation that was wrung from them. Their lives were dominated by what amounted to a series of fairly rigid rules, a break in which, if condoned and forgiven, might end in weakening the whole structure on which their system of thought depended. Let us glance at the main characteristics of that system, since without understanding for what the Puritans stood it is impossible to estimate how far they fell short of their ideals and how far those ideals were carried forward and made an integral part of the American credo. It is only by so doing that we shall be able to decide whether a novelist like Mr. Sinclair Lewis is right when, in *Bethel Merriday*, he describes the influence of Connecticut Puritanism on one of his characters as a system whereby anything that she wished to do was wicked.

Perhaps the two most important features of the Calvinistic creed were, firstly, the belief in the supreme sovereignty of God, who must therefore be the absolute ruler over all His creatures, who must strive above all to know Him and do His will. Secondly, submission was sought to the proposition that since the fall of Adam, man was utterly sinful and corrupt and that this depravity extended even to the infant, since, although the seed within it had not yet thrown up the blossoms of sin, yet the potentiality was there, and consequently accursed. Through the incarnation, death and resurrection of Jesus Christ man had been redeemed, but since some were predestined to eternal life and some to everlasting death, it was essential to the elect to recognize the signs made manifest within them, so that they could fulfil God's commandment, eschew evil and do good so as to be certain to avoid the fiery torments reserved for those not so lucky in the divine scheme. This, then, in barest outline, was the kind of guide to life here and hereafter which was held with a sincere tenacity by the Puritans in the New and the Old World. It may well be, however, that the English Puritans, or at least some of them, did not go to the extremes to which many of the Swiss Calvinists were led through the logic of their beliefs. Winthrop and his band had not separated completely from the Church, as the earlier group had done. They were still a part, even though a disgruntled part, of the English Church, and so were still under the influence of the milder and more broad-minded views of the party from which they had not yet seceded. The deep influence of Calvinism, however, was to be perceived in all their writings. To them, as to the Swiss reformer, God came first. Everything must be subordinated to that one overruling and overriding consideration. Man was responsible before God: he was an individual in whom the seeds of sin were always liable to sprout, but the responsibility was his if he failed to listen to the divine prompting and permitted the lesser goods of this life to overshadow and usurp the place that belonged to God alone. The alternative was clear; eternal damnation was certain for many, and thus fear of the hereafter, coupled with a sense of personal guilt before God, became a constant element within the Puritan conscience. Mundane pleasures, although good and right as far as they went, were suspect. Health, beauty and the natural bodily appetites were to be enjoyed, but—and here was the snare—only provided that they made no encroachment upon the supreme good and were kept always entirely subordinate. The very fact that man desired such pleasures made them suspect. The devil well knew the value of such snares and knew, once they had been enjoyed, temptation towards renewal became ever more difficult to resist. Thus the seductions offered by good food, strong drink, beautiful women and the delights of the dance were dangerous, as it was impossible always to guarantee that such enticements would be enjoyed with sobriety, moderation and the realization that everything must be done in such a way as to redound to the glory of God. Learning, far from being discouraged by the Puritans, was regarded with favour, and science was rarely looked upon with suspicion and condemned. Men like Winthrop and Cotton Mather were keenly interested in the new scientific discoveries that were being made and, as their knowledge increased, they began quietly to drop many of the more common superstitions, such as the belief in the baleful influence of comets, which were often regarded as signs of the divine displeasure. It is possible that they sometimes felt that this gradual sapping of the beliefs that they had cherished for so long was destined to weaken their own positions of prestige and authority, and so, when the sudden interest in the supernatural was ushered in by Increase Mather's *An Essay for the Recording of Illustrious Providences*, it suggested to them an alternative which they seized upon with avidity. Sorcery and the malign influence of demons were not likely, they may have thought, to be explained away by advancing knowledge, in spite of the highly sceptical tone which some writers openly expressed, like the merchant, Robert Calef, in his fascinating *More Wonders of the Invisible World*. They were right. Our knowledge of these matters in 1956 is little more than it was in 1684.

It must, I think, be repeatedly pointed out that the Puritans were not people who tried to withdraw from the world in order to escape from its allurements. They were fighters, who wanted to live in the world, and live in it fully, as long as what they did in worldly things was always kept within the bounds that they had set. Such ideas were advanced in many Puritan manuals and popular commentaries, as in the exposition of the Decalogue by John Dod (d. 1645), whose comment on the "wantoness in immodest dancing" is typical, and

which may be compared with the discussion of the same subject by
William Ames, who spoke of the "common revellings or sportly
dancings" between the two sexes which were altogether to be condemned.[1] The position that the Puritans adopted as regards dancing
was, from their point of view, so logical and simple that it is worth
more than passing notice, as it leads directly to the Puritan view of
woman, which is of great importance when considering the position
of women in the United States. In broad outline the Puritan position
to the dance was that the rhythmical movements, the proximity of
the bodies of the partners, the necessary touches, etc., had, as Increase Mather so well put it, "a palpable tendency to that which is
evil".[2] Similarly, Cotton Mather, in his charming *Ornaments for the
Daughters of Zion*, utterly condemned "promiscuous dancing",
where people "leap and fling about" and where so many of the nine
snares enumerated by Ames might be present that one was liable to
break "all the Ten Commandments of God".[3] It is true that all
dancing could not be wholly condemned. As Increase Mather wrote,
such "Pyrrhical or Polemical Saltation" as of men vaulting in armour
might be tolerated. What was abhorrent was the "gynecandrical"
dancing, where there were "touches and gesticulations" and where
the foolish participant was likely soon to be "infested with a Chore-
utical Demon".[4] It was clear of what these Puritan writers were
thinking. What temptation could conceivably have affected those
grave and armoured knights in their seemly saltations? But in
promiscuous dancing it was different. Another element was there
present, and that element was Woman, who, unless carefully brought
into legal and moral subjection, was of all things most likely to be
used by that Infernal Serpent as he had already used her in those
far-off days when

> her rash hand in evil hour
> forth-reaching to the fruit, she plucked, she ate.

Woman was to be watched and guarded against, and the Puritans
were the ones to do it. Even Satan was careful where they were

[1] See John Dod, p. 268; William Ames, p. 214. Cf. the highly pertinent
remarks printed in the admirable collection *A Garden of Spirituall Flowers*
(1687), where (Pt. II, p. 161) nine forerunners to the sin of luxury are listed as
"voluptuous eating, scurrillous talk, a discovered dug, a naked breast, frizled
hair, artificial painting, costly perfumes, a rouling eye, an unchast foot". The
Puritan leaders were simple realists, and this list of things to be avoided shows
clearly that they knew of what they were speaking.

[2] See I. Mather, quoted from his *An Arrow against profane and promiscuous
dancing* (Boston, 1684) by P. G. Miller and T. H. Johnson, p. 411; and cf. L.
Markun, p. 386.

[3] *Op. cit.*, pp. 15, 17. Cf. Solomon Stoddard, who declared that "mixt
Dancings are incentives to lust" (p. 15).

[4] *Op. cit.*

C

concerned, for had he not been taught to dread what might be termed "the new Puritan Hug"? Sometimes the hug was of another kind, even if it were merely in the imagination. Can we not picture the Reverend Seaborn Cotton (1633–86) sitting down to make a few entries in his commonplace book and snatching a hasty glance at his copy of *Witts Recreations*? For amongst the entries in the good man's notebook we find the canons of female beauty as he thought of them —light brown hair, a hazel eye and pure vermilion cheeks, coral lips, slender waist and hips of medium size. Novelty, too, appealed to him, as to most intelligent men then and since, and so we find him copying a passage out of the little book (which doubtless was kept well locked up) in which the desire is expressed that a wife were as an almanack that could be changed every year.[1]

It is when we see the Puritan face to face with the problem of woman that we can see a picture of strong men wrestling with something so intangible and elusive that it seemed impossible ever to obtain a grip firm enough to discover just what it was against which they were struggling. The problem had always been the same. The Fathers of the Christian Church, saints and holy men in all ages and of nearly all faiths, had had the same riddle to solve and had failed utterly to solve it. For here was something that defied analysis; so subtle, so dangerous was it that proof of Satan's power seemed the only clear fact that emerged from mature consideration. One thing was transparently clear. Whatever may have been the origin of this fatal attraction (and to the Puritans it stemmed directly from the Fall), the plain fact remained that man desired woman and that woman desired man, and that God had so arranged things (very queerly, as it must have seemed to many) that through their congress the perpetuation of the human family was achieved.[2] Although woman was necessary for masculine activity—*ex aspectu nascitur amor*—it was through man's action that she gave occasion for sin, for without him she was helpless. However much she desired "equality" and to be able

[1] See Seaborn Cotton's notes, 21 etc.; and cf. *Facetiae...also Wits' Recreations*, vol. ii, p. 37. Many other passages in this pungent collection might well have caught the wandering eye of Mr. Cotton. He would certainly have lingered on the verses "On a Puritan" (vol. ii, p. 136), or the lines deploring "Naked breasts", which, like meat exposed in a shop, "invite flesh-flyes" who might stop to savour those "full spread paps". And then, perhaps with a sigh, he would close the book repeating to himself the line (vol. ii, p. 47), "Were there no women men might live like gods". Cf. E. S. Morgan, who, in his delightful account of the Puritan family, mentions Cotton and his notebook (p. 27).

[2] In this connexion the rule of Benjamin Franklin, that "classic incarnation of Puritan pioneering", as H. W. Schneider calls him (*The Puritan Mind*, London, 1931, p. 256), is instructive. "Rarely use venery," he wrote, "but for health or offspring, never to dulness, weakness, or the injury of your own or another's peace or reputation" (*The Art of Virtue: Writings*, vol. i, p. 328).

to do all that men do and do it as well, the bitter fact had to be faced that, even in order for her to be able to fulfil her supreme biological function, she had to submit herself to man's embrace, whereupon he could leave her and seek another on whom to have his will. It is within this framework of hard, basic reality that lies the core of the struggle between the sexes. Sex antagonism is no modern notion built out of the difficulties and tensions of civilized life. It lies at the heart of the natural process, and compromise only is possible. The aims of the sexes are different and are incompatible. The ways of man are not those of woman and the paths destined for feminine footsteps can never be those trod by men. All attempts to suppress the manifestations of this overwhelming impulse are doomed to failure. Smothered here, it will spring up there; fettered and shackled in one place, it will burst out afresh in another; seemingly utterly repressed, it will emerge transformed, often in the most sinister and unpleasant guises. To the Puritans, however, one fact was clear enough. Whatever might be done, it seemed obvious that this process, natural though it might be, turned men from God, and so contained the seeds of mortal sin. Thus even for man, whose activity had to be aroused if children were desired, the resulting ecstasy was a snare and a supreme spiritual danger; whilst for woman, whose own frenzied delirium was unnecessary for conception, it was a thing of such horror that even to contemplate it made one almost smell in imagination the sulphurous fumes exuding from the maw of hell.[1]

Generally speaking, the domestic code followed by the leading Puritan teachers was simple and direct. Although I am not in full agreement with Haller [2] in maintaining that in it there was nothing ascetic or suspicious where marriage was concerned, it is obvious that the Puritan husband did not deny himself a certain bodily satisfaction, when the number of his children and even of his wives are considered. Marriage often took place in the early twenties, and children followed rapidly, many dying in infancy, and, since birth control was unknown in its modern sense, repeated pregnancies must have seriously sapped the strength of many married women who did not possess the health to withstand the repeated strain. Since human beings were individuals responsible towards God and to each other, the Puritan family and husband–wife relationship was less rigidly

---

[1] It seems to me likely that it is this to which the Arch-Puritan William Gouge (d. 1653) is referring when, in his authoritative treatise on domestic duties, he condemns certain forms of treatment which some give to their wives and which he declares, is "a most shamelesse thing" (p. 416).

[2] W. Haller, p. 120; cf. S. E. Morison, *The Puritan Pronaos*, p. 9.

patriarchal than elsewhere. It is true that the husband was head of the family and that, as Richard Greenham put it, the "wife must be subject to her husband", or, in the words of William Ames, the husband must be "the head of his wife", a position which, according to William Gouge, did not justify him in chastising her.[1]

Marriage to the Puritan was an alliance of two persons joined in love and mutual companionship, help and comfort. It was, as William Ames again so well put it, an arrangement whereby existed a "most sociable and intimate affection between Man and Wife", and anyone who reads the family correspondence in the *Winthrop Papers* cannot fail to be struck by the tokens of esteem, respect and affection in the letters which passed between the two parties.[2] It was thus that in the Puritan family the woman was a responsible individual, an equal partner with her husband before God, and, as the bearer and educator of his children (and in spite of the fact that as a female she was somewhat suspect), began to assume an importance which, as time passed, began to grow and change the general pattern of the family unit. This position of influence and authority grew so rapidly that I do not suppose that there are any competent historians, male or female, who would deny the importance of so striking a factor in the moulding of the American Republic. Opinions may differ as to the relative importance of that influence and as to its results in American civilization. But the fact that women did play, and from the very circumstances of the situation were bound to play, an important rôle, can hardly be questioned, and I do not propose to argue the point here.[3] It is important to remember that the men and women who made their way voluntarily to the New World had certain

---

[1] See Richard Greenham, p. 390; William Ames, p. 156; William Gouge, p. 390. This was some way from the opinion of John Knox, who declared that "woman in her greatest perfection was made to serue and obey man" (p. 13), and still further from the words of Bishop Aylmer in his reply to Knox's pamphlet when he characterized certain hussies as "folish, wanton, flibbergibbes, tatlers, triflers, wauering, witles, without counsell, feable, carles, rashe, proude, deintie, nise, tale bearers, euesdroppers, rumor raisers, euell tonged, worse minded, and in euerye wise doltefied with the dregges of the Deuil's dounge hill" (G. 3 verso). We can hardly see any staid Puritan using such language as this, although the tormented Cotton Mather occasionally did not spare his epithets when he was denouncing certain kinds of "devilish Filthiness" and "damnable Bestialities" (see his *Magnalia Christi Americana*, Second Serm., Bk. VII, 35; appendix, Bk. VI, 38).

[2] See William Ames, p. 156; and cf. Richard Bernard (1568–1641), p. 405.

[3] Cf. H. A. B. Bruce, who deals with this matter in its historical perspective, and for accounts of leading personalities like Martha Washington or Margaret Winthrop see *Women of Colonial and Revolutionary Times*, etc., and cf. M. S. Logan, whose work consists of annotated and classified lists of prominent women. For earlier works of a similar nature see W. W. Fowler, F. E. Willard and L. H. Farmer.

qualities which predisposed them to undertake the adventure. The steady spirit of the pioneer burnt brightly within them. and those who left the Old World on account of persecution did so with their hearts filled with gladness and their minds filled with a determination to carry on their own lives in spite of having to leave their homeland and face unimagined hardships on foreign soil. Moreover, the women who accompanied their men were for the most part as sturdy, enterprising and zealous as their husbands and male relatives, and were fully prepared to face both bearing and raising families whilst their menfolk secured the means to enable them to do so. Others, like those who arrived early in the seventeenth century to work for the Virginia Company, were often probably the wives or female relations of the men who had come to work for the Company as labourers and who had been promised freedom and grants of land after a specified number of years of service. Again, in the case of Georgia—the last of the colonies to be established—the immigrant population was very mixed, and the reasons for the departure from Europe differed, some seeking asylum from religious persecution and others, through the instrumentality of General James Edward Oglethorpe (1696–1785), were enabled to emigrate in spite of many cases of insolvency and resulting imprisonment. As regards New England, the immigrants were inspired mainly by religious and economic motives, and it is here that we can see the beginnings of the Puritan influence which has made so lasting an impression on American life.

As the years went by the population increased and numbers of immigrants of varied stocks began to arrive. By 1763 it numbered about one and a half millions and had become so mixed that possibly one half were of non-English stock. Yet in many respects the women were inspired by the same motives; and their willingness to face the new life indicated an underlying strength of character which cannot be ignored. Many of them had occupied important positions in their own households and had loyally supported their husbands' determination to resist tyranny and emigrate rather than have to endure the miseries of persecution. Thus many of the colonial women were soon engaged in tasks apart altogether from those connected with rearing a family. Except in professions such as Medicine and the Church, their activity was but slightly hampered, and they soon began to deal with administrative, executive and legal matters, while some actually managed businesses, as did Widow Roberts, who was running a coffee-house in Philadelphia towards 1745, or Elizabeth Timothy, who took over the publication of the *South Carolina Gazette* in 1739. Moreover, women living in urban areas whose husbands had become successful were decking themselves out in fashionable attire as early as the middle of the seventeenth century. Indeed, these dresses aroused the ire of the Rev. Nathaniel Ward, who declared that they changed those wearing them into "gant bar-geese" or "ill-shapen-shotten-shellfish". They had only squirrel brains in their heads, he stated, and he went on to speak of the "gut-foundred goosdom, wherewith they are now surcingled and debauched".[1]

Not all of the women, however, were content to remain where they were, for the spirit of the frontier had gripped them as it had gripped their men, and a westward migration became a goal towards which many turned their eyes.

The most important social unit in colonial times was naturally the family, and, as we have said, the woman was the unchallenged head of the home, although her husband was nominally the head of the family. She it was who arranged the work of the house, managed the children, and in urban areas often helped her husband in his business as well. It must be remembered that in those days there was a considerable excess of men and thus the value of women was much enhanced. They were valuable not only as housekeepers but as mothers of large families and companions for lonely men. Indeed, a number of writers have insisted that the reason why the American woman has been placed upon a pedestal and worshipped is largely on account of her value as an object of scarcity which was always in demand. Thus in the charming *Journal* of the Englishman, Nicholas Cresswell, who went to America in 1774, we find it stated that the country was "a paradise on earth" for women because old maids were a rarity.[2] Up to the present day, many foreign observers who have noted the respect shown to women in the United States have accepted this theory that scarcity partly explained the situation. On the other hand, J. J. Ampère, whilst expressing mild astonishment at the treatment accorded to American women, was inclined to attribute it to the general *"rudesse des mœurs"*, since he thought that without it things would have become intolerable.[3] Although there seems little doubt that one, at least, of the factors which, in early days, operated in favour of women was their scarcity, it is a mistake, I think, to maintain that this is the chief reason why they occupy so dominating a position in modern American society. We shall see later that other

---

[1] See T. de la Guard [*i.e.* Nathaniel Ward], pp. 26, 27; and cf. the condemnation of immodest garments and naked necks and breasts in *The Necessity of Reformation*, p. 6.

[2] N. Cresswell, p. 271.

[3] J. J. Ampère, vol. i, pp. 174 ff. Many later writers, such as Rousiers, Feiler and Ferrero, have discussed the same theme.

and deeper-lying causes are operative which, by their very nature, tend towards the same end.

Although the family constituted the most important unit in early days, there were, of course, numbers of unmarried men and women, especially of the former. As we shall see later, the religious influence, which was strong among the New England settlers, continued to have its effect in later years, although the severe control of the private lives of the people was gradually curtailed. Laws were harsh in the early days, but many of them were not unusual at the time, and the attack that has been made on the so-called "Blue-Laws" is not altogether justified. It is true that the Rev. Samuel Andrew Peters (1735–1826), of Connecticut, disliked both republicanism and nonconformity, but the idea that the whole of his famous book was a "mesh of lies" and marred by slanderous statements, as Tuckerman maintains and Byington suggests, is not true. Such laws existed both in Connecticut and in New Haven, as Trumbull has rightly pointed out, and Kendall, whose book of travels was published in 1809 and contains some very acute observations on American life, mentions them without indicating any undue scepticism. Certainly Peters' account contains exaggerations and faulty interpretations, but W. F. Prince has shown that over one half of the laws outlined by Peters did actually exist in New Haven, expressly or in the form of judicial customs under common law, and more than four-fifths are to be found in one or more of the New England colonies. Statements, therefore, such as that made by A. M. Low, that these laws had no existence outside Peters' fertile imagination cannot be sustained, and it is surprising to find Mr. C. M. Webster's account of the *Town Meeting Country* still maintaining that these laws are simply a fabrication on the part of Peters.[1]

Whatever may be the truth regarding the precise legal code on moral offences, there is, I think, little doubt that the authorities frowned severely upon sexual irregularities, which were frequent enough in spite of the attempted social ostracism which some of them

[1] See S. A. Peters; H. T. Tuckerman, p. 329; E. H. Byington, pp. 251–2; J. H. Trumbull; W. F. Prince; A. M. Low, (2) p. 185; C. M. Webster, p. 61. Cf. also the *The Code of 1650 . . . to which is added some extracts from the laws commonly called Blue Laws* (Hartford, 1822); *The Blue Laws of New Haven Colony*, etc. (Hartford, 1838); G. Myers, especially pp. 139–50 and H. W. Lawrence, p. 111. I am not certain how far the oft-told story of Captain Kemble can be regarded as historical. It will be remembered that it was said that the Bostonian Captain Kemble, after returning from a voyage on one Sunday in 1696, kissed his wife at his front door, was seen to do so and reported to the authorities, who had him put in the stocks for two hours on account of what was termed his "lewd and unseemly behavior".

involved. Since indentured servants were often not permitted to contract marriages, illicit affairs were not uncommon, and the attempt to prevent the expression of biological human needs met with the disastrous failure that might have been expected. Since methods of contraception were largely unknown, the number of illegitimate births rose sharply in the middle period of the eighteenth century, and since fornication was thought to be less dangerous to society than adultery, it was regarded with less abhorrence. The practice of bundling, moreover, although probably rarely leading to climax on the part of the girls, could hardly be considered as entirely innocent,[1] although I am of the opinion from a careful consideration of the literature that the evil results attributed to it by some have been exaggerated.[2] Apart from sexual morality being weakened or not by bundling, there is little doubt that the young people of colonial America found love-making difficult to resist and clearly made no effort to conceal their enjoyment of it. Nicholas Cresswell describes some incidents which cannot have been unique. He tells how, one night in August 1776, a fine, blooming Irish girl arrived where he was and immediately took his fancy. Later, as she seemed far from unwilling, "the Flesh overcame the Spirit". Moreover, he actually had an affair with a Mrs. L., a woman who was deeply religious but who, one day after supper, cast amorous glances at him which resulted, as he puts it, in finding that after all she "was made of warm flesh and blood". He had a good deal of admiration for the women that he met and praised their "good shapes", but, like Moreau de St. Méry, Janson and the author of *Men and Manners in America* (Captain Thomas Hamilton), complained of their bad teeth, a fault often attributed to the consumption of too much hot bread and cakes.[3] This partiality for starch does not appear to have affected their figures appreciably, as critics were of the opinion that generally they were, as Hamilton puts it, sadly deficient in "en-bonpoint", while Moreau de St. Méry, although he says that they had

---

[1] Cf. H. B. Parkes, *New England in the Seventeen-thirties*, p. 408; J. T. Adams, *Provincial Society*, p. 160.

[2] The literature relating to bundling is very extensive and cannot be quoted here. H. R. Stiles's book is still useful, and two recent books by A. M. Aurand may be consulted with advantage. In an issue of *The American Weekly* for March 1943 occurred an article on bundling, which was advocated as an ingenious old custom that conveniently combined fuel-saving with courtship and which may become popular again but modernized to meet twentieth-century conditions. Whether the slogan "Fuel giving out? Try Bundling!" was a success or not is uncertain.

[3] See N. Cresswell, p. 271; Moreau de St. Méry, pp. 58, 302; C. W. Janson, p. 444; *Men and Manners in America*, vol. II, p. 34; and for further references see J. L. Mesick, p. 90.

pretty breasts, declared that they began to fade at twenty-three, were old at thirty-five, and decrepit between forty and forty-five, being both nervy and irritable.[1] On the other hand, writing in the first quarter of the nineteenth century, Isaac Candler found the ladies captivating, and he says that nature never produced finer forms than are to be found in America, although the breasts were often insufficiently developed, a feature which was apparently approved, since Moreau de St. Méry stated that some of the girls tried to flatten their breasts, although he did not, unfortunately, give us any details of the process involved.[2] His account of the American woman at the end of the eighteenth century is full of interest in view of her subsequent development and as compared with what other travellers noted in later years. Médéric Louis Élie Moreau de St. Méry (1750–1819) was a French politician and lawyer who was especially interested in the laws relating to the French colonies. At one time he was a bookseller in Philadelphia, whither he had escaped in order to avoid arrest during the Revolution, and his keen, observant mind is noticeable in all that he wrote. He described American women as cold and without passion and thus, knowing little of real love, being inclined towards self-indulgence and wayward phantasies sometimes directed towards persons of the same sex. When they married, he believed that they were usually physically faithful and the interest of the home became paramount, all other things being subordinated to it. He added that in many cases their habits were far from clean, while the unmarried girls, especially in remote rural districts, were not averse to liberties which were not common among the urban population.[3]

Sins of the flesh were often dealt with under the system of Church Meetings then in vogue, and since these misdemeanours were, it seems, far more common than other offences, the records show many cases of fornication, these being often post-nuptial confessions of ante-marital relations. Certainly everything was done to dissuade the young from these practices and to hold out to them the dreadful consequences of their actions. Early in the eighteenth century that industrious neurotic Cotton Mather, or "stone-age Puritan", as Basso calls him in Mainstream (p. 26), had inveighed against all such activities; he had reason to know the power of the body, since, like

[1] Moreau de St. Méry, op. cit., pp. 58, 302.
[2] See A Summary view of America (I. Candler), pp. 67, 69; Moreau de St. Méry, p. 304, and cf. Frances E. Trollope, who stated that according to her observation the breasts of American women were "rarely full or gracefully formed" (p. 244).
[3] Moreau de St. Méry, op. cit., pp. 306, 311, 335, etc.

Swedenborg, he was constantly tormented by lustful visions. To add to his difficulties, he was very popular with young women, who admired his bearing and appreciated his stories and, like so many other Puritans, he was not really a prude, in spite of his almost fanatical fear of bodily desires. His vanity and egotism were abnormal, and there seems some reason for believing that this was possibly a result of the teasing that he had when still quite young and which gradually led to ideas of actual persecution. In denouncing vice he was by no means mealy-mouthed, and his language is interesting when we remember the ban on "indelicate" words and expressions which was to follow a hundred years later. In his sermons he often referred to the serious sins committed among the people, and the Kinsey report on relations with animals would have surprised few at that time, although the punishment for such deeds was exceedingly severe. Mather tells one tale of a man whom everybody believed to be a saintly character until his peculiar predilections were made public. We do not know why this husband and father seemed to prefer the lower creation, but Mather assures us that he had had a cow, two heifers, three sheep and two sows, whilst his wife had actually seen him having relations with a bitch and his son had once caught him "hideously conversing with a *Sow*". As to the Quaker women, Mather was aghast at their behaviour, whatever may have been the motives that inspired them. He stated that two of them had come stark naked into one of the public assemblies, but they were soon dealt with—"Baggages that they were!"—and sent to the whipping-post "for that Peice of Devilism". Then there was the young woman who, he said, could not resist, in spite of having had a number of illegitimate children, one of whom she murdered, and so was taken to her own death. Possibly this poor woman was one of those who were led astray by Samuel May, another of Mather's characters, who used to make a practice of running after the girls and affronting them with "Lewd, Vile and Lascivious Carriages".[1]

It would seem that some of those accused were sometimes not wholly submissive under the penance imposed upon them. For example, Edith Tooker was one day led into church clothed in a white sheet to confess her "foul sin" to those assembled. She caused, however, a terrible scandal when, instead of humbly showing her penitence for the enormity that she had committed, she pro-

---

[1] See Cotton Mather, *Magnalia Christi Americana*, Second serm., Bk. VI, p. 35; App., Bk. VI, pp. 38, 48, 49; Bk. VII, pp. 24, 36, etc. For an appreciation of Mather in relation to the points outlined above see R. and L. Boas, pp. 30, 69, 72, 165, 167; V. L. Parrington, pp. 107–9.

ceeded to lose her temper and thereupon "cut up and mangled the sheet".[1]

From what we know of the women of colonial America, and especially of those in New England up to the end of the eighteenth century, it would seem that they were little different from those of their own class, religion and social standing whom they had left behind in the Old World. Where they differed was, perhaps, rather in their greater independence and, in the upper strata, in their devotion to religious duties and beliefs, which were deeply influenced by the Puritan philosophy and which had a profound effect upon the teaching that was given to the children. Moreover, the effect of the mental ferment generated by the French Revolution could hardly fail to leave its influence on a people who had left Europe to found a freer society elsewhere. How far the *Vindication of the Rights of Women* (1792) was read in colonial America I am not prepared to say,[2] but it is clear that the life of Mary Wollstonecraft was not one of which many would have approved, and that the sentiments expressed in her outspoken book were hardly those which would have appealed to the typical New England housewife. Yet it is here that we can, I think, perceive the germs of those ideas which were later to work such havoc in the lives of American women.

Mary Wollstonecraft (1759–97) was a complex character whose ideas stemmed to a certain extent from her home conditions and especially from the failure of her father, who was a shiftless character with little power of concentration. Her book is remarkably plain spoken and contains material full of sound common sense, such as the section devoted to the sex education of young people. Her principal idea seems to have been to raise the status of woman to one where she could be the helpmate of man in a position of equality, but she was unable to rid herself of the objection which all feminists cherish to what is, after all, a natural process. As she herself says, "The male pursues, the female yields—this is the law of nature; and it does not appear to be suspended or abrogated in favour of woman." These notions are of great importance if we wish to understand their development and results as seen in the life of the American woman and her place in the culture of the United States. For it is this resistance to biological facts that is part of the basis on which the dissatisfaction of women with their lot is founded. Coquetry was anathema to Mary Wollstonecraft. She would have nothing to do with

---

[1] P. A. Bruce, vol. i, pp. 47–8. The case apparently occurred about 1641 in Lower Norfolk, Virginia. The culprit received twenty lashes.

[2] Editions appeared in Philadelphia in 1792 and 1794.

"those contemptible infantine airs that undermine esteem even whilst they excite desire". But while she has to admit that it is not only man who desires woman, but also woman who *wants* to be desired by man *so as to yield*, she declares that such common appetites are brutal only when unchecked by reason, and goes on to say that all the causes of female weakness as well as depravity "branch out of one grand cause—want of chastity in men". From the tyranny of men, she concludes, spring the greater number of female follies.

Mrs. Godwin's radical ideas were coupled with statements which were, to say the least, somewhat unusual. She made caustic references to what women did when alone, how they attended to their more intimate toilet, how they had "nasty customs, which men never fall into", and how the other sex had their own "nasty, indecent tricks", which they learn when "they pig together in the same bedchamber". All these things and many more made Mrs. Godwin's book one to be sought after and avidly read. For, unlike other early feminists in America like Hannah Crocker, the granddaughter of Cotton Mather, Emma Hart Willard (1787-1870) the educated missionary, and Mary Lyon (1797-1849) the founder and principal of Mount Holyoke, who were, apart from their views on higher education, conservative in outlook, Mary Wollstonecraft was a rebel both in thought and in action, a woman who, mentally free, was unable to co-ordinate her intellectual outlook and convictions with her bodily needs. To her the inculcation of principles in which female weakness was stressed was to be strictly avoided; and it was this which caused her to condemn the "mellifluous precepts" of the Scottish Presbyterian James Fordyce who, in his famous *Sermons* (1765) dealt with the duties of young women in what Mary Wollstonecraft thought was an affected style.

As we have said, it was towards the higher education of women that the aspirations of so many of the early feminists were turning. Indeed, it would appear that, although their interest in the training of children was considerable, the development of American education was tardy and, as we shall see later, is still proceeding very slowly in certain rural districts, especially where the coloured population is in the majority.

In the middle of the seventeenth century education in New England was naturally imperfect and somewhat scrappy owing to the social conditions of the time. Young people learnt the practical affairs of life by participating in the numerous group activities of their elders, and book-learning hardly concerned them. What little there was consisted of reading, writing and elementary computation, and reading was mainly encouraged in order that the children might become acquainted with the Bible, catechisms and religious or devotional works like the popular account by James Janeway (1636–74) of the edifying lives and joyful deaths of several children, a manual which so took the fancy of Cotton Mather that he issued a supplement in 1700 with the title *A Token for the Children of New England*.[1] Calling his little readers his "dear lambs", Janeway described the good little dead children and declared that "they are gone to heaven and are singing hallelujahs with the angels". He went on to say that, unlike those to whom he addressed these encouraging remarks, these children "shall never be beat any more", while, on the other hand, the bad ones had gone to the devil and into everlasting burning, in fact into a hell which, as he stated, was worse a thousand times than whipping.[2] Edward Lawrence in his *Parents Groans Over their Wicked Children* (1681) also declared that it was better for the children to be whipped than to be damned, although he added that when the rod was applied it should be used wisely. Similarly, Cotton Mather appears to object to the raving, kicking and scourging that went on both in schools and in families, declaring that he would never give a child a blow except in a case of obstinacy or what he described as some gross enormity.

It was not until towards the middle of the seventeenth century that the education of the children began to be considered a part of social life which had to be more efficiently organized. Thus, in 1644, the General Court in Connecticut ordered a number of townships to appoint an official teacher; and four years later every community

[1] See J. Janeway. Monica Kiefer has compiled an interesting survey of children's books from 1700 to 1835, *q.v.* For a later attempt to compete with Janeway and to bring children to God via the holy death-bed of a companion see the heart-rending account of the death of little Charles in Mrs. Mary M. Sherwood's edifying history of the Fairchild family, p. 165. Cf. Hugh Kingsmill (p. 34), who points out that children in mid-nineteenth century literature died young owing to the supposed connexion between innocence and sexual immaturity.

[2] Although the phrase "love well, whip well" was not unknown in early New England, it does not appear that the practice of corporal punishment ever had the same popularity that it enjoyed in later years, especially after the Mexican War in the 1840s and during the period when the *Illustrated Boston News* regaled its readers with a spicy correspondence which is reminiscent of the famous series of similar letters which were published in *The English Woman's Domestic Magazine* in 1870. Indeed, the American letters were of such a nature that a number of them were actually translated into German by Erna Neumann and published in 1903. The medical writer, George H. Napheys, was fully aware of the effects of flogging, since in his book *The Transmission of Life* (Philadelphia, etc., 1871) he stated that it stimulated precisely what it was intended to check. "How unwise, how reprehensible, therefore, to employ it", he concluded, and he added the usual reference to the experiences of Rousseau (p. 26).

of fifty families was supposed to maintain a school. It must be remembered that in those days education was so closely bound up with religion that a great deal of it could only be classed as religious instruction. Apart from the practical affairs of life, educational instruction was mainly for the purpose of inculcating religious knowledge, and thus the school-teachers continued in the classroom what had already been learnt at the mother's knee. Men and women participated in instructing youth, and the dame school came into being as education progressed, although early in the eighteenth century male teachers were in some parts a majority during the winter months, while the women outnumbered them in the summer. It was gradually, as religion gave way to more material things, that women began so to preponderate in the teaching profession that we find Elizabeth McCracken in her *The Women of America* (1904) (p. 266) saying that the overwhelming majority of those teaching in the United States were women.[1]

It was towards the end of the eighteenth century that men began to see that some plan must be set in motion whereby not only children but also adults received better instruction in the principles of citizenship. Although coeducation was well known in the eighteenth century, private schools for girls were open by 1773, for there was always the feeling that mixing the sexes might tend to lead to habits less desirable than those which were being so laboriously inculcated by the teachers. Moreover, female education was not so thorough as for the other sex. A little religious instruction and the elements of arithmetic were often considered sufficient; and it was possibly this which finally persuaded the authorities to pay greater attention to elementary adult education. Benjamin Rush was fully aware that it was upon women that devolved the principal share in the instruction of young people; and in his plan for the establishment of public schools in Pennsylvania he declared that women must be instructed not only in all ordinary matters but also in those principles of liberty and democratic procedure the understanding of which was necessary in order that they might become patriotic citizens. These opinions concerning the close relations that must exist between a good education and a fuller understanding of the democratic way of life were illustrated by the various plans for a national system of instruction which were urged by writers such as Robert Coram.

How far the employment of women as teachers in the early years

[1] See May H. James, pp. 25, 50, 55; Thomas Woody, vol. i, pp. 505 ff.; and cf. F. E. Chadwick, who summed up the situation in 1914.

was the practice apart from the more developed communities in New England does not concern us here. They were certainly employed among the Quakers to some extent; and it is probable that similar conditions were to be found in other parts, although in the more isolated rural areas education must have been more or less in the hands of women, since it was probably an internal family affair.

If we want to have a clear idea of the nature of the American family and educational system during the early colonial and frontier period, it is important to realize that conditions in New England differed considerably from those elsewhere. People in the Middle States and in the southern regions of the country had their own customs and way of life, and with the coming of immigrants from other than Anglo-Saxon stock came domestic customs and ideas which differed from those of England. Religion also played an immense part in setting the pattern of the life of the family and the control of the children, and there is no doubt that Puritanism, in one sense of the word, not only affected New England but gradually spread far beyond its borders. The conditions of life in the rural areas and the influence of the frontier mentality made the father less and less a power in the home and maternal influences became stronger, while the position of the children, and especially of the daughters, became more and more independent. Marriage was contracted early in life and, although in some areas there was a scarcity of women, unmarried men were not regarded with favour and indeed, in some parts of the country they were looked upon with some suspicion. The wife's place was the home, and her legal position, borrowed as it was from European enactments, was that of inferiority, although the conditions of life were clearly undermining the position of the husband and the ancient patriarchal pattern. The position of dominance that the wife maintained in the home extended not only to the management of the children and the household generally but to a certain amount of control over the husband's purse. In his *Letters from America*, which were translated in 1924, the writer, who seems to have been a German officer and who has described his experiences from 1776 to 1779, declares that the stylish display affected by the women of New England was due to the fact that they insisted on controlling the domestic finances, and he adds that mothers on their death-beds ordered their daughters to retain the mastery of the house and the control over their father's purse-strings. It was thus, he concludes, that "petticoat rule" was spread throughout America (pp. 118–19). Thus the growing power of women arose from a natural process which began to operate very early in the United States and from which the present almost "matriarchal" pattern has developed. Life could not be carried on under conditions of frontier or urban development if women remained merely obedient housewives, nurses and home teachers. Their husbands died, met with accidents or possibly deserted them, in which case divorce sometimes followed, although the arrangements for this differed in the various regions. It was then that the adventurous spirit which had brought them to their new home began to assert itself. They entered business on their own account and, as we have seen, often made a success of their chosen vocation. The fields of supposedly male activity were already being invaded, although signs of discontent among the richer and less energetic women were already beginning to become apparent. With the rise of industrial activity, and the consequent increase of wealth which accompanied it, women began to withdraw slowly from bodily activity and the more strenuous pursuits of domestic life, while their minds were left free to roam the pleasant fields of imagination and the realms of phantasy. This agreeable occupation was nurtured by the growing passion for novels which Jefferson so roundly condemned. The appearance of the satirical romance at the close of the eighteenth century marked an epoch in the life of the American woman, for it is here that we can perceive the seeds of that life of vain and tortured imaginings which is still the lot of so many leisured and idle women in the United States. The popularity of the English novel was very great. It was imported, sold or lent out by such enterprising firms as Caritat in New York, and it paved the way for later American romances which were often constructed around similar themes. The influence of Samuel Richardson's *Pamela: or, Virtue Rewarded*, of which the first part was published in 1740, was very considerable. The steadfast resistance put up by the virtuous maiden to the seductive wiles of her would-be ravisher not only titillated the erotic fancy of those who imagined themselves in her place, but eased their underlying feelings of guilt when they remembered that, after all, virtue was rewarded and vice defeated. Here was a sensual feast in which all the preliminaries to defloration could be enjoyed without the final catastrophe. To women who were already feeling that the commercial pursuits of their husbands were interfering with what, to them, were the more exciting pleasures of the boudoir, such romances came as a balm to carnal titillation. Richardson was popular with women because he understood what went on in some of the more obscure corners of the feminine heart and, whilst bowing to conventional morality, was able to provide his readers with vicarious thrills and the opportunity of enjoying in imagination erotic scenes in which they longed to take an active part. Seduction without the fall was surely a harmless theme for contemplation. Indeed, it not only emphasized the lack of restraint in men and unveiled their villainies, but also stressed the virtue of suffering womanhood, and even gave the chaste maiden an opportunity of reforming the rake and heading him back into the paths of rectitude. The contradiction was solved by a pleasant compromise: virtue was preserved in many cases, although how far the woman's nervy condition was due to the internal conflict we have no means of telling. Perhaps, as Moreau de St. Méry suggested, some of the women, failing to get the satisfaction they craved from the other sex, turned to their own in the hope of allaying somewhat the fires of lust.[1]

With the increasing interest in the sentimental English novel came the attempt to develop the same fictional theme by native writers. It is true that some attempts were made to stem the growing tide of interest, especially where the younger generation was concerned. In *The Young Lady's Parental Monitor* (1790), which was reprinted in Hartford in 1792, a compilation from various authors was presented in which the opinions of these illustrious authorities were quoted with approval. Thus Lady Pennington, the wife of Sir Joseph Pennington, declared that very few novels or romances were worth reading. Much of the material presented was "so much rubbish", and as to the moral portions, they were "like small diamonds, amongst mountains of dirt and trash". As to the desire to learn foreign languages, the Marchioness de Lambert was dubious. Italian was certainly dangerous, for was it not the language of love? On the other hand, the writers held the old-fashioned view that women could hardly be seen in a more ridiculous light than when they appeared to govern their husbands. These matters had to be managed with tact and discretion. When a husband was clearly wrong in his judgement, the way to correct him was not to contradict, but head him off into another more sensible opinion, and do it so discreetly that he would think the new idea was entirely his own.

Among the early American novels the *Power of Sympathy: or, the Triumph of Nature* (Boston, 1789), now usually attributed to William Hill Brown (1765–93), and Susannah Rowson's *Charlotte* (1794) were important, although the author of the former is said to have declared that novel-reading was bad for girls. Here again we have the seduction theme in its various keys, although the thrill is somewhat

---

[1] See Moreau de St. Méry, p. 307. *Pamela* was placed on the Roman Catholic *Index Librorum Prohibitorum* in 1744 and was still there in the 1938 edition (p. 354).

D

lessened by the insistence of the writer on exposing the dangerous consequences of seduction. Similarly, in the famous books by Hannah W. Foster we find gentle hints that foreign publications were somewhat more exciting to the avid reader (foreigners are so perfectly acquainted with the passions!), for in them the authors are able to portray themes of sentimental dalliance in a more convincing manner than are those brought up in the colder English climate. As to the reformation of rakes, opinions differed. James Fordyce had already expressed the opinion that they did not make the best husbands, but their lure was very attractive; for, it was argued, even if they were not converted, the attempts to do so would be accompanied by many an exciting moment which would hardly be experienced with more sedate spouses.

As early as 1802, however, signs of a changing attitude were becoming dimly perceptible. From the daring rake bent upon carrying off the protesting damsel to his lair, there to prey upon her hidden charms, the beau was beginning to be considered a somewhat weak and poor specimen. It is true that the façade of the true, gentle, modest and romantic lover had to be kept up, just as the perfect Ashley had to be presented in *Gone with the Wind*. But the preferences of the ladies were clearly in another direction and the Rhett Butlers of the 1800s were much more popular than the gentle beaux who were likened to syllabub—"all froth and show, white, sweet and harmless". It was not, however, for the ladies to say so, for only females of the lower grades degraded themselves thus. "Ladies" had no such feelings, and thus they were able to rise superior to the other sex, which was clearly much lower in the animal scale. Man was beginning to take the place assigned to him by the American woman, for was it not she who was about to take the moral leadership of the country into her own hands? Freedom for women offered, so it seemed, boundless opportunities for female improvement and advancement, but on the other hand it provided opportunities for libertinism where such was desired. This was the dilemma in which the feminist leaders were always entangled. Jumping from one horn to the other, they became enmeshed in a web between the two, and in this web they are still struggling.

As the years went by and a more discreet approach to dangerous topics became discernible in some quarters, it was noted that elsewhere alarming changes of opinion were to be remarked. Thus Jane West, in her *Letters* (1806), declared that the general view regarding the subject of chastity had suffered "an amazing change" within a few years. At the time she was writing its loss was treated in literature with indifference or even with "playful sarcasm", and she went on to mention as examples of what she was saying such popular plays as *The Stranger* or *John Bull*, where Mary Thornbury was seduced. As to the older women, Jane West was very solicitous to cater for their intellectual entertainment in "the winter of life". Instead of novels it would be better for young women with a view to the future to stock their minds with the facts of "natural history, experimental philosophy, botany, and astronomy", so that these agreeable ideas might solace them in their declining years, when infirmities would seclude them from society and their former dear connexions would have left them desolate.[1]

It would seem that young ladies who wished to obtain solace from more exciting publications had to retire to private spots to get their way. Indeed, they were advised to do so. There is nothing to be afraid of, wrote John Davis (1774–1854), for the governess has gone out and mother is not yet up. Why hesitate? "*Werter* has been under your pillow and *The Monk* has lain in your toilet." Among other writers who commented upon the habit of novel-reading among American girls were the Englishmen Isaac Candler and John Fowler, who, like so many others, noted the ardent pursuit after wealth which characterized so many American men. On the other hand, Branagan, writing in the early years of the nineteenth century, was much more violent and explicit. He declared that "spurious, futile, and pernicious publications" were pouring from the press and that the votaries of seduction were going about like "the voracious shark in the briny deep".[2] Moreover, the fashions of the day were, according to Branagan, simply incitements to lust. Men wore worsted pantaloons which were so tight that they often revealed "spectacles hardly to be commended to the decent eye", whilst many feminine fashions almost forced "the male of ardent passions to acts of violence". Even little girls, far from flattening their breasts, as in

---

[1] Jane West, vol. ii, pp. 310, 316, 424.

[2] Branagan was not the only one who protested against what was being read. Sylvester Graham, in a discussion of sex education published in Boston in 1837, said that parents were quite wrong in thinking that their children were ignorant. Far from it, for these young people "have been clandestinely drinking in the most corrupt and depraving knowledge from mercenary and polluted hands", and he went on to say what results accrued from this sinful knowledge and described the terrible effects of masturbation in both sexes. Similarly, Heman Humphrey, in his famous *Domestic Education* (1840), told parents to strike off "all the cart-loads and ship-loads of plays, novels and romances, which appear openly" and which were opposed to piety, morality and virtue. He expressed himself as sorry that most of Shakespeare's plays had ever been written. Unless carefully expurgated, he was not a fit author for family reading, and even the Bible, according to some parents, had parts not fit for children "on the score of modesty" (pp. 93, 94, 115).

former times, now wore artificial ones, and women, while pretending
to be shocked at the indelicacy of certain words, would not hesitate
to appear in public clothed in such "a lascivious manner, and assuming such wanton attitudes, as to cause the burning blush of shame to
tinge the cheek of the beholder".[1] Similar complaints had been
voiced almost fifty years previously. R. F. Seybolt, in a paper on
Dress Reform in Massachusetts quotes an article which was published
in a Boston journal in June 1755. It was asserted that the current
fashions then in vogue suggested that complete nudity would soon
be achieved, as already "latent Beauties" were being disclosed.
Although the original article probably referred to English fashions,
it seems likely that these were being imitated sufficiently to make the
paper topical in Boston. It may well have been that the more enticing fashions were worn only by young ladies who thought that, as
time was getting on, they had to do something to avoid being left
behind in the marriage race. Young men had to be brought to the
point. Even if

> Eager he drinks her breath, so sweet, so fine;
> Like food on which celestial spirits dine

he must follow it up by the proposal which was so earnestly awaited.
If he failed, then the situation demanded drastic treatment, so perhaps Charles Stearns was right when he said that

> A dress curtailed, and bosom wide displayed
> Denote the misery of a failing maid.

Although attacks on popular literature were not usually so violent
as that delivered by Branagan, the writers fifty years before he wrote
were occasionally concerned at the interest young people had in
what was thought to be improper literature. It is possible that the
immoral books mentioned by Jonathan Edwards about 1744 were
actually *Pamela* and similar works; and it seems likely that the book
which caused him so much concern and worry and which dealt with
such subjects as "women's having children" and which was handed
round by the young men for their amusement, instruction and diversion may have been either *Aristotle's Legacy*, which was issued late in
the seventeenth century, or possibly *Aristotle's Masterpiece*, of which
an edition was published in 1694 and in which "the secrets of generation" were displayed.[2] Pseudo-scientific, medical and even mildly
pornographic literature was naturally occasionally imported and
found ready sale and subsequent distribution. For example, among

---

[1] T. Branagan, *op. cit.*, pp. 13, 31, 33, 169.
[2] Cf. T. H. Johnson, pp. 37 ff.; A. C. McGiffert, Jr., p. 117.

the books sent from London to John Usher, the Boston bookseller, was the famous romance *Venus in the Cloyster*, which was the first English translation of *Vénus dans le Cloître*, which has been attributed, among others, to the Abbé du Prat and the Abbé Barrin.[1]

In spite of the fact that ample evidence exists that female literacy was by no means high in seventeenth-century New England, the basis of what women knew was, at least in the first generation of settlers, clear and not open to doubt. They believed what they had been brought up to believe, and naturally clung tenaciously to those articles of their faith for the defence of which many of them had left their old home. It was, as we have seen, they who controlled the home and instructed the children: it was at their knees that the family learnt the principles of morality and conduct, and thus it was through the ideas of women that the future generation learnt the lessons of life. What was the basis of this teaching and how did it affect the children? As we shall see later, it was clear that, as Wertenbaker has pointed out, the Puritan experiment had failed before the end of the seventeenth century.[2] With the decay of the old beliefs and practices, the dichotomy between faith and works began to be apparent, and what was taught to the children as the basis for sound conduct was not exemplified in the lives of those whom they saw around them. Thus the effect of Puritanism in subsequent generations is not to be judged by reference to the beliefs and deeds of the founders of the Bible Commonwealth, but by principles of moral action which had lost their pristine validity through the disintegration of their spiritual bases. One thing, however, is clear. It is, as P. G. Miller and T. H. Johnson have pointed out, that Puritanism has become one of the continuous factors in the development of American life and thought, and that without an understanding and appreciation of Puritanism there can be no understanding of America.[3] This opinion has been long held in the United States, and I have very little doubt of its essential truth. Yet, through a misunderstanding of the development of the Puritan conscience, many observers (and not all of them foreigners) have failed to perceive that

---

[1] See S. E. Morison, p. 128. In 1716 Benjamin Wadsworth, in a sermon at Boston, fulminated against certain "unchaste practises", by which he probably meant masturbation, but it was not until later that such books as *The Pure Nazarite* and editions of *Onania* began to appear.

[2] T. J. Wertenbaker, *The Puritan Oligarchy*, p. 340.

[3] Cf. P. G. Miller and T. H. Johnson, p. 1, and T. C. Hall, who does not appear to agree that Puritanism, "properly understood" (p. x), had much to do with moulding the American mentality, a view strikingly different from that of Katharine Anthony, who speaks of American society as "incorrigibly Puritan" (p. 321).

what is often called Puritanism has little in common with what the conception once meant in its early simplicity. To say, as the late Nicholas Murray Butler did, in his Copenhagen lectures, that the basic and original Puritanism has contributed so largely towards the formation of American life, is to divert the attention of the student from what has actually happened.

The difficulty which cultured Europeans find in evaluating the civilization of the United States is often due to their being insufficiently equipped with background knowledge and appreciation of complex psychological factors. It is only in the writings of critics like E. A. Mowrer and competent historians of the colonial epoch that we can find a suspicion that the "Puritanism" of the present day lacks elements which were essential characteristics of the Puritanism of the past. As we shall see, the gradual disappearance of certain elements was well known to writers a few years after the beginning of the Puritan experiment, and as the cracks became wider many of those in authority became profoundly disturbed. The early faith was an ingredient in the Puritan conception of life without which many of the remaining ideas were a danger and a curse to men, instead of a blessing. It was as if something had evaporated from a nutritious liquid, so that the character of the food had been so changed that it was now no longer conducive to health but the reverse. Had that "incomparable catechism" *Spiritual Milk for Boston Babes* become a poison?

Before dealing with the changes in New England which were gradually undermining the foundations on which the Puritan theocracy was built, it would be as well to glance briefly at a few further aspects of domestic life in the Puritan home in so far as it affected the daily existence of women and children. It must be remembered that the sincere Puritan was a Calvinist and his views, therefore, of childish depravity were such that the life of young people and the parental training they received were coloured by the prevailing ideas, which, in many respects, could only be described as harsh and gloomy.

We have a good deal of evidence, scattered up and down the literature, concerning the suffering that many children endured owing to the persistence with which they were reminded of their sinful condition, for not only was it believed that they committed many sins in the course of their active life, but also that even before that activity began they were in a state of total depravity. It is true that many of these doleful warnings were forgotten almost as soon as they were uttered. Many amusing stories were told of the naughty children playing during service in the icy meeting-house, where the only heat during winter was often that engendered by the minister in his warnings of hell's flames. The tithing-man used to go round catching the culprits, who were thereupon fined, and might later find themselves ordered to be whipped for their misconduct. It was the thoughts of frying in hell that caused the breakdown of little Betty Sewall, whose experiences we find related in the *Diary* of Samuel Sewall (1652–1730). One day, after dining, the child, for no apparent reason, burst out crying. On inquiry it was learned that she had been reading some of the terrifying sermons, so plentiful at that time, and was fearful that "she should goe to Hell" and that her "sins were not pardon'd".[1] Similarly young Richard Mather was said sometimes to have left his meals in order to offer up lamentations for sin, and doubtless many of the more sensitive children actually suffered acute emotional distress at the thought of what might await them after their death. Michael Wigglesworth's *The Day of Doom*, published in 1662, had an enormous popularity, and the stress it laid on the indifference to the doom of others must have added to a child's need for affection and forgiveness even when it knew it had done wrong.

> One natural Brother beholds another in this astonied fit.
> Yet sorrows not thereat a jot, nor pities him a whit.
> The godly wife conceives no grief, nor can she shed a tear
> For the sad state of her dear Mate, when she his doom doth hear.

For some it was indeed a sad experience to see young people crying and wringing their hands when it was pointed out to them that their "frolicking and dancing" and their "vicious practices of mirth and jollity" were grievous sins, sins which might have to be met with a rain of hell's fiery flakes and pain so great that it might make them bite their very tongues in twain.[2]

As the children grew up it was obvious that many of them would exhibit signs of fear and guilt and that with the onset of puberty their emotional reactions would again find acute expression. Many were, of course, free from these obsessions, but the influence of the Puritan ideals was apparent far beyond the bounds of the ministers'

[1] S. Sewall, Jan. 13, 1696, vol. v, p. 419.
[2] See Peter Thacher (pp. 90, 96, etc.), who was writing of the Middleborough Revival of 1741. He was a learned, serious and solemn person, full of sincerity and even loving-kindness, for on one occasion, when a small child, so shocked at the warnings that he was giving, suddenly fainted and would have fallen, he very kindly "catch'd it in his arms".
The more genial atmosphere of the South is indicated by the popularity of kissing games, which are mentioned by P. V. Fithian, who was the tutor to the Carter children at Nomini Hall, Virginia. See his *Journal and Letters, 1767–1774*, p. 75.

own families and congregations. Courtship was, as we have seen, carried out in a variety of ways, including bundling; and on some occasions it had to be carried on in company, so a hollow whispering tube was said to be used whereby the couple could exchange confidences without being overheard. The process of becoming better acquainted with each other must have been far from easy for many of these young people, since they were often in doubt if the friends that they had were meeting with approval from many censorious eyes. Complaints were often made, and Ann Warder, the English Quaker who married an American, tells in her *Diary* how at a meeting in 1786, probably held in Philadelphia, one Nicholas Waln got up and condemned the practice by young people of mixing in "improper" company, which, he said, was carried on to an abominable extent in some parts of the country.[1] The fact was that the religious fanatics of the time—Puritans, Quakers, or of other denominations— were attempting the impossible, and the figures showed how lamentable was their failure. Sexual irregularities exceeded other offences by a wide margin, and the rate for illegitimacy continued to rise, although how far this was due to increasing population I am not prepared to guess. Drinking also was stated to be on the increase, and other "vices" accompanied it, as might have been expected. With growing prosperity came a forgetfulness of God, and Hell seemed very far away. People began to grow a little tired of the petty restrictions in everyday life and in the more intimate affairs of the heart. Supervision in these matters was of constant occurrence, and in the middle of the seventeenth century the courts were often engaged in hearing cases of meddling and eavesdropping, while censorship of the Press and publication was far from unknown. Some places had what has been rather unkindly described as a "snooping committee", or, in other words, an official tithing-man whose duty it was to report on the misdemeanours of the ten families living nearest to him and over which he was expected to exercise surveillance. Idleness was not a thing to be condoned: it was well known that hands and minds which were not being used in the service of the Lord might well be turned towards the service of Someone else. The Puritans did not come to America to set up a democratic state which would tolerate all shades of opinion. What they wanted (and intended to have if they could) was complete freedom to spread their own ideas and sufficient power to force others to conform or suffer persecution for their errors. Such an idea as freedom of Press and publication was to them merely freedom to spread heresy and

[1] See Anne Warder, p. 53; and cf. G. F. Dow, pp. 224 ff.

dangerous thoughts. To instil the sense of fear and guilt was a necessary means of persuading people to yield and follow the line set for
them. When these means failed, force could and would be applied,
as it was to recalcitrants like Roger Williams and Anne Hutchinson.

It was clear to the leaders of the Puritan theocracy, and indeed to
those who were in authority in the other religious organizations, that
if the various experiments were to flourish and to succeed it must be
through the support of the younger generation. The problem of
moulding the minds of these children was therefore an urgent one,
and the fact that their training and instruction were largely in the
hands of women, especially during the formative years, made the
position of women of very considerable importance. But woman
could not be expected to be totally unaffected by what was happening. The social and economic changes which were everywhere apparent had a profound effect upon her, as they did upon her menfolk,
and the new ideas which were fermenting on all sides had their effect
upon the children through their parents. Thus the early years of the
nineteenth century saw a decided change in the attitude towards the
doctrine of human depravity and the certainty of hell for thousands
of human beings. A more mellow attitude was beginning to creep in,
along with the increase of luxury and additions to good living.
Mothers found it hard to believe that their babes were demons and
that they were bringing them up with the prospect that later the
little darlings would roast and scream in Satan's furnaces. With the
coming of the new century, as Anne Kuhn has pointed out, publications began to appear which cast a doubt upon these harrowing doctrines. Children were being gradually transformed from little devils
into little cherubs, whose supposed innocence and charm were to become the foundations upon which American sentimentality towards
the very young was to be built. The Peek-a-boo era was being conceived.[1] In this reversal of one of the fundamental tenets of Calvinism the mother played a major rôle. In the old South such ideas
were hardly known in the form in which they had been so tenaciously
held in New England. Among many of the other communities also
these notions had never been believed with any real conviction. But
in the East, where Puritanism had held sway, the breakdown in the
structure which had been partly reared upon the doctrine of the
depravity of the human race was serious. The mother became an
important cog in the machine which was undermining the basic

---

[1] See Anne L. Kuhn, p. 18 and *passim*; and cf. the works of B. F. Barrett,
especially *Beauty for Ashes* (1855) and *The New View of Hell*, which was published later.

foundations of the Bible Commonwealth, and her own inclinations were given support in the writings of such teachers as Horace Bushnell (1802–76), who, a master of compromise, showed clearly which way the wind was blowing. The mother became more and more important: not only was it she who, by her influence over the child, was able to mould the future generation, but also from the fact of this influence it was she who had the power to transform at least a part of the social setting, prevent the growth of materialistic ideas and lead souls in the paths of morality, purity and moral excellence. As a mother she was almost divine, but as a mere female she was, it was still thought, without those inclinations which led so surely to perdition. Thus little girls were supposed to be immune to those stirrings which led to lustful passion. The other sex was, unfortunately, in a different position. The demon still apparently lurked within them ready to leap out and show his fangs. American mothers are still worrying over this difficult problem and the consequent danger to their innocent daughters. Thus I read in the *Daily News* of New York for January 28, 1938, that "parents must realize that boys aren't 'poison' ", although the writer is careful to add "though some of them act as though they were".[1]

The importance of the growth of these notions in the development of modern American ideals and customs can hardly be exaggerated. For here we can see the emergence of some of those phenomena operating in American society which present so puzzling a picture to the foreign observer, and which were to become so marked a feature of life in the United States in the twentieth century. The gradually increasing importance of the mother and the supposed innocence of the female child had a profound influence on social custom and behaviour, since to the power exercised by maternal authority was added the myth that women were superior morally to the other sex, and that it was only through an inexplicable arrangement of Nature that they had to submit to what was, after all, something of a degradation. Thus, as we shall see later, women were being divided into two sections, the pure and the impure, and since the children of both sexes were under the influence of the mother, both boys and girls were early trained to conduct themselves in ways which were not only unnatural, but which led directly towards the formation of those neuroses which are so noticeable a feature of the American scene today.

As has been said above, the feeling among many of the leaders of

[1] See G. Bevans; and cf. W. G. Eliot's opinion in his *Letters to Young Women*, 3rd ed., 1854.

the Puritan theocracy that the experiment was failing was not slow to develop. For such a scheme to succeed, even supposing that this were possible, a measure of isolation had to be achieved. Moreover, the religious doctrines and practices upon which the system rested had to be unopposed by rival creeds through the influence of which quite different results on everyday life were to be expected. But isolation was not possible, and many of those who had come to New England itself had done so through economic and not religious motives. To such people the new land was one in which a man could better himself; religion was secondary and the Puritan brand was often actually obnoxious. In the South there was considerable variety of religious belief. Some sections, as in Virginia and South Carolina, were attached to the Church of England, but elsewhere there were to be found groups of Roman Catholics, Presbyterians, Lutherans, Baptists and Methodists. The influence of these groups and the increasing contact through trade was naturally an insuperable barrier to the isolation of the Puritan in New England. A "sad alteration" had been noted by Urian Oakes in 1673,[1] and as the years went by the lamentations became shriller and more piercing. It was beginning to be seen that what was developing was a very serious and distressing dilemma, a dilemma that had to be solved, since it contained elements which, to a Puritan, were deadly. As long as he remained true to his faith and to his ideals there was little danger. He knew that material success was the reward of virtue. Business was not merely a means of making money. It was a sacred calling, and if it were carried out in accordance with God's will and direction it would have the divine blessing.[2] There was nothing to be ashamed of in business. As Niebuhr has pointed out, America was free from those traditions in England, where Puritanism was associated with the middle and industrial classes and where the upper strata were composed of the wealthier landed gentry.[3] It was thus that the commercial community had little to restrain them from seeking to better themselves, and to succeed in so doing was no fault just as long as the methods they employed did not conflict with the moral rules on price and profit to which they were expected to conform by their spiritual leaders. Here, however, was a difficulty. If success in business were due to the undertaking having received the divine blessing,

---

[1] U. Oakes, pp. 27, 57, 60.
[2] See P. G. E. Miller, pp. 471 ff.; and cf. A. W. Griswold, who describes the position of Cotton Mather, Thomas Dwight and Benjamin Franklin and points out how they suggested a code of living which was based partly on the idea that God wanted his followers to be wealthy and lack nothing.
[3] R. Niebuhr, p. 724.

how was it that so many who had no belief whatever in Puritan principles and practice seemed to prosper and grow richer every day? How was it that to buy in the cheapest and sell in the dearest market seemed a way to wealth which, although hardly likely to receive Puritan approbation, nevertheless resulted in a great increase of this world's goods? With the fading of the belief in the dire consequences of their actions in the next world, even Puritan-educated traders were becoming persuaded that success could be achieved here and now without thinking too much about the consequences either on earth or in the next world. Private enterprise without God was being tested and it was being found that it worked. There was the dilemma. The Puritan had to face it, since, in his opinion, prosperity was linked with God. And so we find him fulminating in pulpit after pulpit against the drift away from God. Mammon was winning, and he saw it all around him, just as he saw the flesh warring and winning against the spirit. His dream world seemed on the verge of collapse.

It is impossible to understand the development of modern America if we fail to grasp the significance of the failure of the Puritan experiment. For what was disappearing was not the whole of the Puritan conception of life here and hereafter, but only a portion of it, and it was just this portion which made Puritanism a possible ideal for those whose inclinations lay in that direction. The fact was that God was becoming no longer the supreme good to which all else was subordinate. What was being increasingly emphasized was the importance of those lower goods, and thus all that the Puritans had resisted and thrust away from them began to be practised and enjoyed. What formerly had been done with pleasure and with a joyous feeling of inward satisfaction because it was done in accordance with conscience was now done with a pleasure, perhaps even more acute because it was mingled with feelings of guilt. The spirit had vanished, but the letter remained. The early ideals were still taught and repeated parrot fashion, but they had lost their substance, for the living force had gone out of them. The faith which acted as a sustaining and revivifying agent had withered away. It was as if the kernel of a fresh nut had melted, leaving merely an empty husk, and it was this husk which the women preserved in the education of their children, who were thus brought up to believe in ideals and in a way of life which, when they looked around them, they saw being violated and even scorned. Similar phenomena are to be observed in all societies where religious sanctions are fading but where the education of the young is still carried out in accordance with the old beliefs. But in

Puritanism the two factors of sex and prosperity made the matter one of the greatest importance. As we shall see later in considering the American way of life as it is lived today, the two are so closely interlinked that it is impossible to examine the one without the other. With God as the supreme good, Puritanism might have been lived by some in all its fullness, although it seems to me probable that many of the leading Puritans were not so happy as they pretended. However that may be, Puritanism without God was not food for the soul but poison, and it was from this poison cup that the women had to drink most deeply, and having been poisoned themselves, they passed on the virus to their children and to their pupils. Such was the tragedy of the collapse of the Puritan ideology.

This is not the place to describe in any detail the attempts which were later made by enthusiasts to bring the people back to the old faith and to the old ideas. Such revivals are still going on both in England and in the United States, although in America they present far more bizarre features than are to be seen elsewhere. Such phenomena as were discernible in the Great Awakening of the 1740s, in which the evangelical quickening was largely due to Jonathan Edwards (1703–58), merely indicated that Puritanism in its ascetic aspect was still alive, and that the fear of hell could still be aroused in guilty consciences if the appeal were made in the right way. At the missionary meetings, when conversions were common, the usual manifestations took place, and the excitement which possessed the people sometimes ended in scenes in which the erotic element was noticeable, as might have been expected. The influence of these meetings was usually shortlived. Indeed, many were ashamed of what had occurred. The old fire which had animated the early Puritans for so long was surely dying, and these sudden bursts of new flame seemed to be followed by a blackness and gloom which showed only too clearly the transitory nature of the momentary brilliance. A new body of religious teachers was growing up who, prudish, prissy and hypocritical, preserved what was worst in Puritanism while lacking the sincerity and uprightness of their predecessors. It was these strange products of a perverted faith which were to bring the whole Puritan conception of life into disrepute, caricature the original ideals which had supported noble men and women in their hours of need, and make an indelible stamp upon the American character which can still be seen today not only in New England but elsewhere.[1]

[1] Cf. J. Heron, p. 11.

Although it is true to say, I think, that many of the early Puritans were obsessed with sex and with suspicion of women, these feelings were due, as has already been said, to the fear that any undue attention to them might divert the mind from higher things. But in spite of these views the Puritans were human, and so had to rationalize their actions in certain directions. Thus it has been stated that certain passages of the Bible selected for theological discussion were those which dealt with subjects which had a decided tendency to divert the mind from their divine significance, but the fact that the stories occurred in Holy Writ cast a halo of respectability round tales which, if they had been written elsewhere, might have been cast aside as poisonous and dangerous fiction.[1] It was this obsession which still tormented their faithless descendants. Even though the proper Bostonians may now regard with disapproval the writings and practices of their New England ancestors,[2] they still preserve intact many of the ideas of those who came later and who were far less worthy of respect. Sex obsession is not a monopoly of Hollywood. In short, what the false Puritans did was to perpetuate the traditions and carry forward just those highly objectionable features of early Puritanism which would have made the Puritan leaders as intolerable as they have made their descendants had they not combined with them their unfailing belief in the supremacy of God. It was this tradition which, as E. W. Burgess has pointed out, enforced a taboo upon matters relating to sex, a taboo impossible to maintain and one which, in the nineteenth century, led, as we shall see, to all manner of extravagances and follies.[3] But it did more than this. It profoundly affected the position of woman and man's relation to her, and thus it has had far-reaching effects upon the whole concept and practice of love in the United States. For the problem of woman and the problem of love are two of the most serious questions that the people of the United States have to face. It is true, of course, that there are other highly important problems, such as the economic problem, the problem of the Whites in their relation to the Negroes, and the problems of the relations of the United States with the outside world. Unlikely as it may sound, however, all these questions are linked up with the fundamental disharmony between the sexes, a disharmony distinct from, but still connected with, the sex antagonism in other countries. The position of the American woman and the question

[1] See C. W. Bardsley, p. 71; and cf. L. M. Child, vol. ii, p. 255.
[2] Cf. George Santayana in his *The Genteel Tradition at Bay*, p. 40.
[3] See E. W. Burgess in *The Sex Life of the Unmarried Adult*, ed. by I. S. Wile (London, 1935), p. 120.

of the position of the capitalistic economy in the United States are both problems which are a legacy from the older Puritanism, made even more difficult by the collapse of the former ideology. The ideology is still there and is still active, but its divine component has disappeared, and with it the integral factor which held it together. Without this factor the whole concept becomes to a great extent merely a bundle of superstitions, fears, phantasies and outmoded theories. It is true that many still consider that these terms applied even before the collapse of the Puritan experiment, but it can hardly be denied that the effects of these elements were less harmful to those believing in them when they were enlivened by a fervent faith in the love of God and of His Son, Jesus Christ.

As the nineteenth century progressed we can watch the old ideas still exercising their influence and see how some of them were beginning to assume curious disguises which betrayed little trace of their origin. In this age of transition it was woman who suffered most and who, in an effort to escape and live a fuller life, succeeded only in gaining a world and losing her own soul. For it cannot be repeated too often that, according to Puritan notions, woman and sex were unfortunate necessities and that material prosperity was the reward of virtue and a mark of the divine favour.[1] Both of these beliefs were, I think, fundamentally false, and yet they are still important elements of that ideology which lies at the basis of the American Way of Life. Both the sexual and the economic chaos in the United States stem directly from these ideas, which, in strangely twisted and perverted forms, are handed on from generation to generation through the families and the schools. It was the nineteenth century which saw the gradual emergence of the new American woman from the early days to the days of organized feminist agitation and subsequent power. Her dissatisfaction with her lot can be seen gradually increasing as the dichotomy of the sexes became wider and more pronounced. But through the whole of her numerous activities and troubles a single thread runs from which branch out numerous fibres in all directions. That thread is her love-life, and it is because her love-life is hopelessly awry that the American woman is as she is. She is too often a woman without love, for love in America is not what it is in the rest of the world. Woman is the centre of the moral

---

[1] It was not, of course, only the Puritans who held these views of woman and sex. It has always seemed to me a remarkable thing that so many religious people act as if they believed that the method of propagation presumably favoured by God partakes of the nature of a kind of obscene joke and that, had they been consulted, they would have arranged things very differently.

chaos, the immaturity, the strange fetishes and the even stranger practices which are to be observed everywhere in the United States. Yet it is largely through her that the system which has put her in her present position is perpetuated. How this situation developed and why it continues we shall see in our consideration of the American woman in the nineteenth century.

III

THE NINETEENTH CENTURY

THE story of the American woman in the nineteenth century is the story of her struggle for recognition, of her claim to equality with man and often to superiority over him, and of her gradual isolation and consequently the partial loss of her own femininity. In dealing with so vast a country as the United States it is above all necessary to avoid generalizations. What is true of one group of women is certainly not true of another ; and just as the life and ideas of the wife of the Puritan theocrat differed from those of the indentured servant, so the genteel lady of the nineteenth century differed from the factory girl at Lowell and had few points in common with the Negro mother in her cabin or the wife of some poor white in her southern shack. Yet however great were the differences between the various classes of women in the United States, due for the most part to economic and cultural causes, they all preserved certain elements in common in so far as they were all women and belonged to the female sex. After all, biological human needs remain, whatever may be the economic setting in which they may or may not be expressed; and however much women may resist and resent the forces at work within them, it is perilous to disregard them. Few women have ever tried to resist the promptings of Nature as have the American women, although it must be admitted that their actions have been often dictated by circumstances over which they have had but little control. They are the victims of a peculiar set of conditions which influence not only their own actions and ideas, but those of their menfolk also. It is not they alone who suffer, for the two sexes are mutually dependent upon one another and are complementary. The one cannot exist without the other; and thus the happiness and content of the one sex depend very largely upon the same qualities in the other. It follows, therefore, that if life is ill-adjusted and fundamental biological needs remain unsatisfied, then this condition must inevitably affect the other sex, which must be considered partly responsible and which must, in its turn, suffer varying degrees of deprivation and distress.

It may be said by many that these are commonplaces and hardly worthy of mention, since they are almost self-evident. Yet, as I have

E

already said, how rarely do we find in serious historical and sociological studies any sign of an appreciation of their importance by
the writers of these works. Many of these learned authors write of
the people of the United States as though they were sexless, instead
of being the most sex-obsessed people in the world. To them the
structure of American society and the changes proceeding within it
can be described and discussed without ever mentioning the abnormal psychological condition of so many of the population. In many
of these works the word *woman* hardly occurs in the texts and sometimes never in the indexes, yet it might have been supposed that the
activities, desires and aspirations of one half of the population
would have a considerable influence on operations of the other
half. In reading these works the innocent foreign student would
never suppose that the society therein depicted was one in which
sexual antagonisms and maladjustments are possibly greater than
in any other civilized country, that hundreds of thousands of persons
never seem to grow beyond an adolescent stage and that thousands
of women, having, as one might suppose, attained all that any
woman could wish for, nevertheless remain the most nervous, unhappy and disgruntled women that possibly one might find.[1] Yet
for such a student there would be no real necessity to read works by
foreign authors in order to be assured of the truth of these observations. He could procure the works of such writers as Cohn, Wylie,
Strecker and Mowrer, the novels of authors like Sinclair Lewis,
Erskine Caldwell, John Steinbeck and many lesser-known but
equally valuable source-books, and he would not have to neglect the
exceedingly important mass of psychological material to be found in
the columns for the love-lorn. Even if he came to the conclusion that
the United States was, in the words of Henry Miller, an "air-conditioned nightmare" (and such a conclusion would be, in my opinion,
a wholly unjustified and unwarranted conclusion), he would still
have no idea as to how the people of the United States have become
as they are and what are the means by which they are kept in a
chronic condition of psychological *malaise*. Such understanding
could not be achieved merely by studying the contemporary scene.
Just as the eighteenth century had its roots in the one that preceded it, so the twentieth century arose from the nineteenth, and it is
by studying the men and women of this period that we can best see
how they brought up their children to be the young citizens of today,
and how they themselves could not escape from being influenced by

---

[1] For a recent example of the kind of work to which I refer see *Our Emergent Civilization*, edited by R. N. Anshen (New York, 1947).

ideas and conceptions which found little place in nineteenth-century ideology, although it is true that it was this period which saw far-reaching changes in American life.

For our present purposes it is unnecessary to deal in any detail with the manifold activities of the nineteenth century, although the general picture in so far as women entered into it must be broadly sketched. It was a period of expansion, of ever-increasing means of communication and transport by land and water, of the growth of industrialism and of the emergence of women from the home into active participation in economic, cultural and political life. It was an age of intense activity, ambition and acquisitiveness coupled with a great increase of wealth and gruelling poverty. It was an age of buoyant individualism in the sense that the ordinary American citizen wanted to rise ever higher in the social scale, and to attain his end did not hesitate to enter into harsh and ruthless competition with those around him. Thus developed the policy of devil take the hindmost, and the "private enterprise" of the God-fearing Puritan was transformed into a system of exploitation founded upon a kind of organized selfishness. It paid to be "smart", and as Dickens pointed out, many a swindle and breach of trust was glossed over because those responsible were obviously "smart" men and so were able to hold up their heads with the best.[1] The population, too, was rapidly increasing, mainly on account of increased immigration from Europe, although it must be remembered that there was an immense natural increase between 1800 and 1820, when the population rose from about five and a half million to over nine and a half million and when immigration was slight, the figure for 1820 being but 8,385. In 1820 the total population probably did not exceed ten million, with about 103 males to every 100 females. In 1860 the population had risen to over thirty million, of which just over four million were foreign born and the males being about 105 to every 100 females. At the close of the century the population was estimated at nearly seventy-six million, with only a slight drop in the male surplus. The size of the country and the active mobility of many of the people who were always pushing on to new land made the need for better communications acute, and with the coming of the steam locomotive and the development of canal and river traffic progress was rapid.

One result of the rapid expansion of American life was the growing differences between the urban and rural population. In New England the development of industrial enterprises was remarkable. With new inventions constantly being made, factories and mills soon

[1] Charles Dickens, pp. 322, 373; cf. G. Manigault, p. 132.

sprang up, and the manufactories at Lowell, Massachusetts, became almost a show-place to which visiting foreigners were often taken to see the model conditions said to obtain at these establishments. In the Middle States, where coal was easily mined, iron was also available, and thus the heavier industries were developed, the products coming from the mines and mills being exchanged for the agricultural produce of the rural areas in the Southern States, where slave labour added to the problems of the cultivation of the land and the rise of urban industry. The development of cotton-growing was much accelerated by the invention of the saw gin, and with it slavery became more fully established, since it became very profitable. Prosperity grew as long as the price of cotton held, but once over-production occurred and the land ceased to yield what it had formerly done the price fell, many were ruined and the smaller planters sank into a condition of poverty from which a goodly number never recovered. Distinctions of class became glaring, and they were intensified by the presence of the slaves, some of whom were, apart from their condition of servitude, in a better position than the poor whites.

With the rise of industrialism, especially in New England, great changes were becoming apparent in the condition of women. In the early years of the nineteenth century a large section of the female population was, as it were, still half asleep. As Inez Irwin so well puts it, the female sex in the United States was like a huge submerged continent of which only small portions had become visible above the surface of the ocean.[1] But when factories and mills were erected, labour was required, and since women were paid at a cheaper rate than men, there arose a demand, soon satisfied, for female labour. It has been stated that by 1860 one-third of all the factory workers in New England were women, and in the country taken as a whole about one-eighth were female.

A number of accounts exist of the factories at Lowell and it is noteworthy what emphasis appears to be laid on the condition of the mill-girls and the care taken by the management to preserve their chastity. Thus Michel Chevalier, writing in 1834, stated that 6,000 women were employed in the Lowell works, of whom 5,000 were between 17 and 24 years of age. They consisted, he said, mainly of the daughters of farmers and rural workers from Massachusetts, New Hampshire and Vermont, and their habits and ideas were very different from those that would have been expected in France. He put this down to the influence of a Protestant education and noted as a

[1] I. Irwin, p. 22.

result what he called the "sombre hue" and "air of listlessness" which pervaded the mills.[1]

The girls for the most part were housed in boarding establishments, which were carefully supervised and in which they were locked in at ten o'clock every night; and so effective seemed to be the control over their private lives that one overseer stated, according to H. C. Carey, that he knew of only three cases of "improper connexion or intimacy".[2] In spite of these claims as to the immaculate purity of the Lowell mill-girls, the *Boston Times* and the *Boston Quarterly Review* published critical articles upon the character and condition of the female operatives which were later vigorously answered by E. Bartlett in 1841. How far these charges were justified it is not easy to say. Long hours of work were encouraged, since, as the old Puritans had pointed out, free time led to vice, and moreover it was thought that long hours led to greater production and consequently to more profits, which added a feeling of additional virtue in the minds of the pious factory-owners. Apart from the boarding-houses where many of the Lowell mill-girls were lodged, the slums around the factories were badly overcrowded, cases being reported where forty persons occupied one house of two stories and where sometimes several persons of both sexes shared one bed.

As the years went by more and more women began to enter the lighter industries, and by 1860 there seemed to be few occupations where they had not found some kind of employment. With the increase of population and the rising tide of immigrants, young unmarried women had to earn their own living, and in a world of ruthless competition employers were not too careful as to what happened to their work-people as long as they worked hard and brought in the money. It is true that some voices were raised against the employment of so many young women in tasks which were hardly suited to them and in which little attention was paid to their natural functions and disabilities.[3]

Apart from the women, married and otherwise, who had entered the professions and the industries, there were the others (and they

---

[1] M. Chevalier, Letter XII, pp. 133 ff.

[2] H. C. Carey, pp. 88-9. Cf. Sir Charles Lyell, vol. i, p. 117. It might be of passing interest to note that in 1856 a publisher in New York issued an erotic novel which deals with this very subject. Said to be written by an author concealing himself under the name of "Sparks", the work is entitled *Flora Montgomerie, the Factory Girl: Tale of the Lowell factories. Being a Recital of the Adventures of a Libidinous Millionaire, whose wealth was used as a means of triumphing over virtue.*

[3] For example, Azel Ames (1845-1908), who, in 1875, stressed the importance of the sexual factor in industrial undertakings.

constituted the majority) who were simple housewives, spinsters of moderate means or the more wealthy women of leisure who, like the wives of the richer planters in the South, passed their existence in ease and affluence and remained little affected by the changes going on around them until the Civil War forced them to take an active part in the internecine struggle.[1] Moreover, in the South the position of the white woman was made more difficult by the presence of the Negro female slave. The Negroes were at that time considered to be inferior and to possess all kinds of imaginary and offensive characteristics—as indeed they still are in many places in the United States. Yet the fact remained that the white man found many a coloured woman to be an admirable concubine, for reasons which I shall deal with in a later place. This sexual competition was exceedingly distasteful to the white woman of the South, especially as she herself was, by a tragedy of fate, considered to be without passion and not addicted to those pleasures which made so many of her black rivals such delightful companions to her husband and her sons. This rivalry and the acute dissatisfaction which accompanied it made the white woman of the South a problem not only to herself but to the whole scheme of master–slave relationship, and it continued into modern times, long after slavery had disappeared.

As we have said above, the nineteenth century was a period of frenzied activity in which, apart from a few dissenting voices such as those of the transcendentalists and their followers, the predominating note was success, and success mainly in terms of money. It is true that children were brought up on a diet of sentimental and halfbaked ideas compounded from a mixture of emotional Christianity, success stories in which piety and obedience played their accustomed rôles, and warnings against the wide and wicked world and the fatal effect of strong liquor. How far the admirable moral and social teaching of the *Eclectic Readers* of William Holmes McGuffey (1800–73) influenced the development of the American mind I am not prepared to say, but I suspect that, along with the works of Horatio Alger, they had a considerable effect on many a young person who, when he left school or college, must have had, like George Webber, some difficulty in adjusting the facts of the real world to what he had heard so pompously proclaimed by Hunter Grisewold McCoy and his kind.[2]

[1] See F. Moore's *Women of the War* (1866); M. P. Andrews' *The Women of the South in War Times* (Baltimore, 1920), who gives extracts from a number of memoirs and diaries, including Mrs. J. B. McGuire's *Diary of a Southern Refugee* (New York, 1867).
[2] See Thomas Wolfe, *The Web and the Rock*, p. 191. For the history of the

Whatever may have been the moral lessons drilled into the ears of American schoolchildren regarding the financial gain to be enjoyed from resisting temptation, there was no doubt that the desire to make money and the success in doing so increased as years went by. Opportunity abounded for the man with ideas, initiative and not too much conscience when it came to dealing with other people. By 1865 leisure had come to be looked on as something despicable. It was akin to idleness and, as we know, the Puritan tradition regarded idleness with horror, since it offered Satan the opportunity he craved.[1]

In spite of the wholesome instruction purveyed by Mr. McGuffey regarding strong drink, intemperance was far from unknown in the nineteenth century and seemed to increase as the years went by. William Cobbett, although he found much to praise in the United States, declared that drinking was indulged in far too much,[2] and Harriet Martineau declared that the evil was even found to be prevalent among women of the upper classes. But whatever may have been the facts regarding secret tippling among a few American society ladies, Miss Martineau declared that America was a paradise for women and business for the American woman was the task of being a happy and successful wife and mother. As to the wickedness and depravity of the other sex, Miss Martineau pointed out that men could not be wicked if women were not weak, and if they were bravely pure there would be an end to what she called the "dastardly tyranny of licentiousness".[3] Such opinions must have been welcomed by many who, like Harriet Martineau, believed that ladies merely submitted to the dictates of the curious system of propagation apparently approved by God, while only females were degraded enough to enjoy it.[4] It must be remembered that, as

---

McGuffey Readers see H. Vail, and for an analysis of their contents see H. C. Minnich and R. D. Mosier. Horatio Alger (1834–99), like Cotton Mather, is a fascinating psychological study. Like so many American youths, he was a pronounced neurotic type with sexual obsessions. In Paris he met a singer who seduced him and taught him to dance, but failed to release him from the protracted adolescence from which he never entirely escaped. His upbringing had been of the strictly Puritan kind, and when he turned from Unitarianism to writing, the result was to be expected.

[1] Cf. H. Nickerson, p. 71, and Jacob Abbot's *The Rollo Code of Morals* (1841).
[2] W. Cobbett, p. 201.
[3] H. Martineau, vol. ii, pp. 266, 226, 245, 244.
[4] In Henry C. Wright's outspoken *Marriage and Parentage*, which was in its fifth thousand in 1858, the writer mentions with apparent approval the statement by the English physiologist, William B. Carpenter, *Principles*, etc., p. 625, that in the sex act the "function of the female" is "entirely passive", although he is careful to omit the rest, whereby it is clear that Carpenter means passive

Nathaniel P. Willis said, a lady in American society could do no wrong, for the women of the United States were superior to the men, physically, intellectually and morally. C. J. Furness in his book, *The Genteel Female*, has printed a good deal of useful information on this topic and has included extracts from books on behaviour for young people with instructions on how to conduct themselves, including such discreet advice as to the undesirability of handling the nose, which, "like other organs, augments in size by handling". He refers to those persons who preferred plump to skinny women as those who regarded with favour the "oleaginous charms of female blubber". David L. Cohn in his *Love in America* says with truth that many an American husband still regards his wife as a lady in the same sense that he regards his mother as a lady. It never enters his head, Mr. Cohn adds, that the wife may possibly think that the lady business is being overdone (p. 37). We shall return to this question later, as it is fundamental to an understanding of female unhappiness in the United States.

Although little is known of the lives of the majority of American women in the lower income groups, a good deal of information is available on the ideas and customs of the married and unmarried women in the upper-middle and more wealthy classes. With the increasing absorption of men in commercial and industrial activity, married women tended to become more isolated, since before the rise of the feminist movement the ideals of home and family, as Minnigerode has pointed out (p. 76), were paramount. As prosperity increased, many women needed to spend less time on household tasks and duties and had more leisure in which to develop their own personal interests. However, the social conventions decreed that their sphere was the home, and the increasing dichotomy between the sexes made their home and even their social life increasingly narrow and unsatisfactory. There is no doubt that the separation between the sexes at ordinary social events, which, as we shall see later, is dealt with by numerous modern observers, was noted by travellers in the United States very early in the nineteenth century and was continued up to about 1850 and even later. Thus, E. A. Kendall stated that, in New England, men and women were separated even at tea-parties (Vol. I, p. 327), and Mrs. Basil Hall in her charming letters to her sister of 1827–8 declared (p. 125) that in New York society there

---

as regards generation, since he speaks of sexual feeling being strongly excited and the resulting tumescence. For Wright the woman's "only enjoyment" is the consciousness that she is administering to the happiness of her husband (p. 244). For the cult of the "lady", see D. Wecter, p. 314.

was always a great separation between ladies and gentlemen, a fact also noted by Mrs. Trollope (p. 119) and also by F. Wyse in his *America* (1846), who not only remarked on a pronounced social dichotomy, but also on the high moral tone of the upper-class women as opposed to the very low tone in the lower class (Vol. I, pp. 295, 297). As a comparative view of the differences between English women of the period and their American sisters, the observations of Samuel G. Goodrich ("Peter Parley") are interesting. Goodrich stated that both middle- and upper-class women in England were most accustomed to mix freely in the society of men, since their lives were less secluded and less domestic. Married women, he said, often mingled in matters of business, which in America were left exclusively to men. Moreover, English women were better acquainted with the world,[1] but in matters of "delicacy" were inferior, for topics which in America were considered improper were freely discussed and alluded to in England as legitimate themes of conversation between men and women.

This social dichotomy led many Americans to seek escape into a world of phantasy and romance.[2] In this world many of their own deprivations were exalted into virtues, and the suppressed resentment and hostility towards men who thought dollars more attractive than the charms of their wives found expression in a denial of their own biological needs and associated emotions. The traditional Puritan view of women was still regarded as the guide to conduct, and the distinction between the lady and the female became a convenient rationalization whereby husbands granted to others what might have been bestowed upon their wives. The American husband, as Mrs. Houstoun wrote in 1850, was "merely the medium through which dollars find their way into the milliners' shop in exchange for caps and bonnets" (Vol. I, p. 184). The freedom enjoyed by American women at the period puzzled Mrs. Houstoun considerably, as she was unable to decide whether American men were "so good or so old" that they were not tempted by women, whatever might have been their passion for gold.

The novels and magazines popular among women in the mid-nineteenth century provide clues to their aspirations and a guide to the content of their phantasy life. Most best-sellers were

[1] As Mrs. Lydia Sigourney put it, American females "are happily excused from a part in those political convulsions which leave traces of blood on the tablet of history" (p. 233).

[2] See F. L. Pattee, who (p. 53) states that the New England women in the 1850s were taking to reading novels and to writing romances as a drug and as a method of escapism.

melodramatic romances, such as Emma D. E. N. Southworth's *Ishmael*
and *Self-Raised*, which sold over two million copies each, and Ann
Sophia Stephens' historical novels, one of which, *Malaeska*, was the
first of the famous series of Erastus Beadle's dime novels. The current interest in mesmerism was often centred on the question as to
whether in the mesmeric trance a person might perform actions which
in the normal state would have been morally abhorrent. Thus the
possibility that fornication and adultery might be indulged in without conscious consent had to be considered; and thus the sin which
would have normally accompanied it could be avoided. The theme
as portrayed in literature can be seen in the novel by Timothy S.
Arthur, *Agnes : or, the Possessed : a Revelation of Mesmerism* (1848),
where we read (p. 4) that under the influence "a woman may be made
to believe that any person is her father, or brother, or sister, or husband, and she will act accordingly and afterwards she will have no
recollection of it except such as the operator pleases". In this story
it is obvious that Agnes Wellmore is completely under the power of
that fascinating magnetizer, Florien. Apart from books, magazines
for women began to be increasingly popular, and in New England
twenty such journals had appeared before 1830 and another thirty
were published between that date and 1860. In the 1850s the three
most important magazines were the *Ladies' Magazine* of Boston,
Godey's Lady's Book of Philadelphia and the *Ladies' Companion* of
New York. Of these, the most important was *Godey's Lady's Book*,
which from 1837 was edited by Mrs. Sarah Josepha Hale, who was to
be one of the most important public characters in the advanced
feminine world of the period. It exercised an immense influence on
female thought, acting as a kind of arbiter of taste and fashion and
preparing the way for a greater feminine interest in the outside
world, and consequently for the rise of feminism. Although the
movement for equality and women's rights was to gain momentum
only in later years, the influence of the early transcendentalists
and social reformers was sufficiently great to attract female adherents of ability and some literary skill. Such women as Elizabeth
Peabody (1804–94), Margaret Fuller (1810–50) and Dorothea
Lynde Dix (1802–87) were bound to interest other women less
favoured intellectually; and Miss Peabody's lending library in
Boston became the meeting-place of many who wanted to see
what was new and what French books and magazines were being
imported.

The increasing habit of reading romantic fiction, which was becoming more and more popular, could hardly fail to affect the growing

daughters in the leisured households of New England, and also in
the South. It was, of course, condemned, just as it had been in the
eighteenth century. By far the greater number of novels were "totally improper" and unfit to be "perused by the eye of delicacy",
wrote Charles Butler, who, in his *The American Lady*, had drawn
largely from Thomas Gisborne the Elder who inquired into the
duties of the female sex in the closing years of the previous century.
Just as in the later years of the eighteenth century the seduction
theme predominated, so now romance was full of scenes of love and
passion in which, however, virtue was not forgotten. Young women
imitated the heroines of their novels, and their mental and
physical condition became a subject of concern to many a pious and
virtuous friend of youth. Books of advice and counsel poured from
the press. "A Lady" contributed some *Familiar Letters to Females*
in 1834, while another two years later published *The Young Lady's
Friend*, a very sensible book full of sound advice to the adolescent.
The same year appeared both *A Daughter's own Book, or practical
hints from a Father* and Almira Phelp's *The Female Student*, in which
(p. 69) the author speaks of the evils of tight-lacing, which was then
very common. The following year William Alcott's *The Young Wife*
appeared, and in 1846 Mary S. Gove published a most outspoken
book on female anatomy and physiology. Tight-lacing was described
as "dishonourable and criminal" (p. 25), and the practice of "solitary
vice" among young women was attributed to heredity and "the
structure of society, which forbids the exercise of all their powers"
(p. 244). These diatribes against corsets and masturbation continued for the next thirty years, and were naturally discussed
with fervour by all those who wished above all to preserve the
virginity of girls and the chastity and fidelity of married women.
The whole question, indeed, of the sexual life of the leisured
American women of the nineteenth century was one on which there
were diverse opinions, although the supreme value of virginity was
rarely questioned.

In 1869 Catherine E. Beecher and Harriet Beecher Stowe were
still discussing the evils of tight dresses in their *The American
Woman's Home*, and they joined in the increasing condemnation of
everything masculine, and above all in the attempt to show the
superiority of woman over the mere male. For example, they declared (p. 203) that it was the brother who was to do the hardest
and most disagreeable work. It was for him to face the storms and
perform the most laborious drudgeries. As to the family circle,
it was for him to give his mother and sisters precedence in all the

conveniences and comforts of home life.[1] The authoresses would undoubtedly have approved of the advice given by the Rev. Harvey Newcomb (a guide to both sexes) to boys between the ages of eight and sixteen. Newcomb, perhaps suspecting that the boys might wish to escape from the "laborious drudgeries" in the home, said firmly, "When you feel any inclination to go abroad in search of forbidden pleasure, I advise you to sit down with your sisters and sing 'Home, sweet home'." He also laid down rules of deportment for boys, saying that in a co-educational school they were to "venture no improper liberties" and to "remember that there is One Eye always upon you". He told them that it was a bad habit to puff cigars in the streets, and to "avoid tight dressing as you would a black snake".[2] Mrs. Beecher and Mrs. Stowe were certainly outspoken, for they not only discussed (p. 286) the evils of masturbation, which resulted in "disease, delirium and death", but also dealt in detail with the advantages of the earth-closet.

There seems little doubt that this period produced a great number of works dealing with the evils of masturbation in both sexes. John Cowan, in 1869, advocated continence in his *The Science of a New Life*, and the same year that very remarkable but forgotten American author G. H. Napheys contributed a very sensible account of the *Physical Life of Women*, in which he dealt with masturbation (1891 edition, p. 29), passion and frigidity (p. 75). In 1871 the same author in collaboration with D. G. Brinton wrote a highly interesting account of the laws of health, in which they discussed the varying dictates of fashion and stated that the preference for female curves was at that time so marked that girls used to wear artificial pads and hollow hemispheres made of rubber. In 1873 Abba Goold Woolson wrote an account of women in American society in which, like her predecessors, she declared that the prevailing invalidism of American girls was due to the way they abused their stomachs, and that their pallid, flabby faces were the result of their dislike for fresh air and sunlight. Stressing the premature bloom [3] of the girls of the period,

[1] Writing in 1910, an American lady, Katherine G. Busbey, declared that the American boy was subject to the tyranny of his sisters, and that "an observing Englishman" saw in this fact the beginning of the so-called slavery of the American man to the American woman (see *Home Life in America*, p. 29).

[2] H. Newcomb, *Youth and its duties*, pp. 56, 64, 108, 120.

[3] The rapid fading of American women which was often noticed in the eighteenth century was also observed by travellers in the nineteenth century. For example, R. Weston, who visited America in 1833 with a view to settling there, thought that the young women were pale though not ill-looking, but that the older American women looked "perfectly hideous", whilst the *Gallynipper in Yankeeland*, writing in 1882 of American women after the age of thirty, said that they "go off like rattlesnakes", presumably referring to their bad tempers.

she declared that when young they were envious of boys and the free lives that they led, while at the same time they considered "the whole masculine sex, with one or two exceptions, as fair game for irreverent satire". Indeed, the coming dominance of the American woman was foreshadowed in an interesting article, "The Yankee, No. II", which was part of the series, *American Girls of the Period*, in the London *The Girl of the Period Miscellany* (August 1869, pp. 187–8). "While she sneers at the men as inferior beings", the author declared, "she tries to imitate them in thought, talk and manner", and then went on to say that the American girl was always trying to be a man and yet despising the being that she was endeavouring to rival. It was as though, she wrote, a philosopher should express his dislike of snakes and then pass "most of his time in learning how to writhe and wriggle". The writer continued by saying how much better it would be if American girls could try to be more feminine and womanly, and "if their too sturdy and aggressive independence could be softened by additional touches of gentleness, refinement and sympathy".

Modernism, too, was beginning to affect the American girl. She used to smoke "fiercely against the chimney, exhaling pestiferous odours", while her vocabulary was beginning to include words not to be found in the standard dictionaries. A long lesson at school was called "a tremender": new clothes were a "swelly rig": and if such garments were approved of they were called "splufous". Modern ideas of marriage, moreover, did not appeal to Abba Woolson, who said that in many cases prospective brides might have been labelled with notices such as, "Sold singly to suit purchasers" and "None but wealthy parties need apply".[1] Margaret Fuller herself, who published sections of her *Woman in the Nineteenth Century* in the *Dial*, showed the same tendency to attribute sexual irregularities to man alone, and declared that many women looked upon men as wild beasts, although such a supposition was surely terrifying if they were all alike. Frail was man, indeed, she concluded; but how frail! and how impure! Wholly masculine men and purely feminine women did not exist, and it had to be admitted that the lot of woman was sad, since she was constituted to expect and need a happiness that could not exist on earth.[2]

In 1861 Dio Lewis wrote an account of the American girls of the period, and three years later printed a small volume entitled *Chastity: or, our Secret Sins*. The prevalence of sexual irregularities and undesirable habits in American girls was, I think, instrumental in causing some attention to be paid to educating young people in

<hr />

[1] See A. G. Woolson, pp. 13, 15, 67, 170, 189, 197, 208.
[2] M. Fuller, pp. 15, 116, 150, 151, 159.

matters of sex. In 1874 Dr. E. H. Clarke published a very sensible book on the subject in which he stressed the relations between the sexes and declared that there was no question of either inferiority or superiority, but simply one of difference (p. 13). He spoke of the bad education that girls were accustomed to receive, their constant consumption of pie and doughnuts, their tight corsets, which frequently caused illnesses of various kinds, and finally the perils of ignoring the fact of menstruation, arising out of the mistaken policy of pretending to be boys (p. 48). Dr. Clarke's book met with a prompt response from a number of women who did not care for the home truths there put forward. Mrs. E. B. Duffey immediately replied in her *No Sex in Education*, and the influential Mrs. Julia Ward Howe and others contributed an answer in the same year, announcing that the book was "an intrusion into the sacred domain of womanly privacy" (p. 7), while Caroline H. Dall was said to have stated that the method Dr. Clarke employed was that of "the hand of iron in the glove of silk" (p. 87). The following year the cause of continence was again taken up by A. E. Newton in *The Better Way*, and the whole subject of the physical and moral causes of bad health in American women was discussed by J. E. Reeves. Two years later a further advocate of continence, J. H. Kellogg, published his *Plain Facts about Sexual Life* but it was not until 1883 that Alice B. Stockham contributed her revolutionary volumes on sex behaviour and her theories as to the reasons for sexual intercourse, which were conveniently summarized in her *Tokology* (pp. 151 ff.).

Whatever may have been the truth about the unmarried young women in the leisured classes at various periods of the nineteenth century, there seems little doubt that, up to about 1850, fidelity in married women was the general rule, in spite of the lack of attention of their husbands and the ever-increasing division between the sexes. In his account of the Americans in the 1830s, Francis J. Grund, in stressing the power of the American mother, stated that she was "nurse, tutor, friend and counsellor" of her children, and that, as a Frenchman had said, America was certainly a paradise for husbands because such things as affairs and intrigues were not understood.[1] On the other hand, some twenty years later Bellegarrigue, in a book on American women, declared that virginity was a fiction and that love was suppressed, and told sensational tales about intrigues and secret staircases. How far the attacks on the male sex in general were responsible for an unwillingness to contract marriages it is impossible to say. One of the characters in Timothy Flint's novel

[1] F. J. Grund, *The Americans*, etc., pp. 36, 45.

Francis Berrian (Boston, 1826) ridicules the idea of single blessedness, saying that it is "all stuff", and advising girls to get married to worthy men as soon as possible, since she has experienced more enjoyment in a day after marriage than in a year before (Vol. III, p. 251). This can be compared with the advice given by Rebecca B. H. Davis in the latter years of the nineteenth century. Writing of the "grey cabins of New England", she speaks of the wasted virgins living there and urges them to go where women are wanted and make "a happy home and a happy life for some honest fellow". It must be remembered that Mrs. Davis was a woman who did not hesitate to discuss questions which appeared to the squeamish to be both vulgar and sordid, and her advice to women to marry was doubtless influenced by her opinion, which she herself had expressed before marriage, that the fact was that woman desired man. How far this remark was intended to offset the lack of passion and presumed frigidity in American women I am not prepared to say. There is no doubt that many foreign observers, like J. S. Buckingham, came to the opinion that American women were more frigid and less passionate than Europeans. "I do not think", he wrote, "that they love with the same intensity as the women of Europe", and he considered that instances of passionate attachment were fewer than in any other country in the civilized world. Love, he declared, was purely an affair of judgement, and he noted with astonishment what he called "the frigid indifference" of married couples.[1] This curious relation between American men and women was strangely perplexing to Paul Bourget during a visit to America which he described in his work *Outre-Mer* (1895). American men, he stated, were colder than Englishmen, and as to "that special creation the American woman", he found her inexplicable. One unmarried girl of nineteen actually told him that she would above all things like to be a widow and always thought how nice it would be if her husband were struck dead by lightning as they were coming out of church. With regard to husbands and wives, Bourget considered that their financial relations were very singular. Noting the growing separation between husband and wife, he stated that the husband was rarely to be seen, unless in the form of cheques, an opinion shared by J. F. Muirhead, who, on the other hand, declared that much of Bourget's other criticism was "truly damnatory" and unaccountably false.[2]

[1] J. S. Buckingham, *The Eastern and Western States of America*, vol. i, pp. 477–9.

[2] See P. Bourget, pp. 77, 85, 96; J. F. Muirhead, pp. 49, 58. The latter's appreciation of the American women in Chapter IV does not appear to me to be one which does much credit to the critical acumen of the writer.

Some of the things which Bourget found particularly interesting from the point of view of a Frenchman concerned the question of American prudery. Thus he was unable to understand how it was possible for the people of Boston to refuse to permit the forms of two naked children carved by the American sculptor Augustus Saint-Gaudens to appear on the façade of the public library. Similarly, the story that trousers had actually been put on antique statues at Baltimore and Philadelphia intrigued him mightily; and it was clear that he was unacquainted with the historical basis for this almost pathological fear of nudity. It was not only in the United States that the damaging effect of the nude in art and the unseemly in speech was condemned. In that charming little book *The Virgin's Nosegay* (1744), which was dedicated to Miss Howard, the daughter of Philip Howard, brother to the Duke of Norfolk, the author has a great deal to say about all these matters. Calling chastity "this seraphick virtue" which crowns all others, the author declares that in vain do the "tainted Passions endeavour to disguise the deformity of the hideous Vice" of unchastity. Going on to disclose what leads to this enormity, he declares that curiosity (although less dangerous than reading novels) leads to "intense Examinations of immodest Statues and Pictures, which the Fair Sex should carefully avoid, as such obscene Objects but too generally sully the Imagination". He also gives advice to the young married lady as to how to treat her husband, telling her not to be "eternally hanging" about her husband's neck, sitting on his knee or, more indecently still, putting her hand into his bosom or placing her lip against his cheek. Finally, he actually goes so far as to say that the double standard of morality is useful for preserving families from any spurious mixture, and as to women who spurn their domestic duties, he describes them as "affected Babies, that think it modish to be above troubling their weak Noddles with such homely things as House, Family and Children".[1]

In 1835 Mrs. Lydia Child, the novelist and abolitionist, wrote in her *History of the Condition of Women* (Vol. II, p. 267) that it was true that American ladies were accused of being more prudish than foreigners, and she appeared to argue that there might be an excess even of something that was good. Indeed she declared that when she heard that Horatio Greenough's beautiful little marble cherubs had been condemned because they were undraped, she was reminded

---

[1] See L .... F ......, Esq. In Baltimore in 1809 a book apparently by the same author was published entitled *The Female Friend; or, the duties of Christian Virgins*. This may be a later edition of *The Virgin's Nosegay*, but I have not been able to see a copy.

of what Sir Charles Grandison had said when he asked, "Wottest thou not, my dear, how much *in*delicacy there is in thy delicacy?" [1] Certainly some of the extremes to which prudery went were shocking to many observers. One of the best accounts of what occurred is that furnished by Mrs. Trollope when she visited the nineteenth annual exhibition of the Pennsylvania Academy of Fine Arts. One of the rooms exhibited antique statues, but a screen in front of the door prevented visitors from seeing what was inside. On approaching the door Mrs. Trollope was accosted by the female guardian of the gallery, who, with an air of mystery, said to her that this was just the time for her to go in, as nobody could see her. On asking what that meant, Mrs. Trollope was told that ladies liked to go in alone "when there be no gentlemen watching them". After examining the casts, Mrs. Trollope remarked that there was some reason for the notice just inside and she deprecated the disgusting way the casts had been defaced and marked by visitors. Mrs. Trollope put this behaviour down to the fact that men and women did not enter the gallery together; and she felt that the arrangements for exhibiting the statues furnished as good a specimen of the kind of delicacy on which the Americans pride themselves as could be found.

As early as 1628 Richard Bernard in his *Ruths Recompence* had declared that, when it was necessary to employ certain words, they were to be expressed so as "chaste eares may not be offended", but it was hardly necessary, as J. S. Buckingham hinted, carefully to avoid such expressions as "tail", "hip", "thigh" and "belly", and always to substitute "rock" for "stone", and for "cock" "a certain fowl". The same author noted with astonishment that the men of the South exhibited a strange combination of prudery and licentiousness, thus showing that even over a hundred years ago observers were struck by the ambivalence that is today so marked a feature of the American people.[2] This suggestive prudery regarding the use of certain words

[1] It is said that about the time of the controversy over the chanting cherubs an orang-outan visited Boston in a menagerie. The delicacy of the citizens was such that they would not permit it to be exhibited until it had been suitably arrayed in a pair of drawers (see J. B. McMaster, vol. vi, p. 96). Captain Marryat declared that, in a girls' seminary, he had seen the "limbs" of a piano carefully hidden by frilled pantalettes (see F. Marryat, vol. ii, p. 246).

[2] J. S. Buckingham, *The Slave States of America*, vol. ii, pp. 133–4, 241. In the language of the period, as Mrs. Lydia H. Sigourney (1791–1865), the enormously popular writer of sentimental verse, said, even the body was that "complicated structure and mysterious mechanism of the clay temple" (p. 91). In Longfellow's *Wreck of the Hesperus* the word "bull" caused much trouble, as it was not one which could be uttered with impunity. Viscountess Avonmore tells us in her *Teresina in America* (vol. i, p. 313) that the difficulty was surmounted by substituting the words "gentleman cow" for the offensive term which preserved modesty even though it damaged the poem.

F

was also discussed by Thomas Grattan in 1859. In his account of American women, whose coldness seemed to be "less of manner than of feeling", he stated that their delicacy compelled them to avoid speaking of the legs or breasts of poultry, the words "the dark meat" and "the white meat" being substituted for these offensive terms. He found in many cases that the women had a passion for flirtation, but there seemed little danger, since the men were so absorbed in business and so calculating that there was no cataract over which the willing but neglected victims might be hurried.[1] One of the most interesting commentaries on the prevailing fashion of delicacy was that provided by A. M. Gow in his book *Good Morals and Gentle Manners for Schools and Families* (1873). He condemned the practice whole-heartedly and said that it often manifested an affectation of purity. A woman who talked about "the limbs" of the table and "the bosom" of the chicken was unrefined and exposed herself to well-merited ridicule and contempt. He narrated the story of a young woman who, having been injured in a railway accident, was taken to hospital and asked by the surgeon what was the matter. She replied that one of her limbs was broken, whereupon he asked her which limb it was. " 'I can't tell you, doctor,' she rejoined, 'but it's one of my limbs.' 'One of your limbs,' thundered the doctor, out of patience. 'Which is it—the limb you thread a needle with?' 'No, sir,' she answered with a sigh, 'it's the limb I wear a garter on.' " Having attended to her, the doctor told her never to say the word "limb" to him again in hospital, for if she did she would be passed by; when a woman got as fastidious as that, the sooner she died the better. It can be said, concluded Mr. Gow, that such pretences of refinement as these are disgusting to persons of good taste.[2]

Although, as we have said, the agitation against undraped statues and nude pictures was not confined to the United States, there is no

---

[1] T. C. Grattan, vol. ii, pp. 51 ff., 61; cf. Viscountess Avonmore, vol. i, p. 30. Captain Basil Hall, writing some thirty years earlier, stated that he had never seen anything approaching a flirtation during his travels (vol. iii, p. 150), a statement which, as Frances Trollope noted (p. 297), brought upon him the charge of "moral coarseness"! About thirty years later Varigny observed precisely what Grattan had pointed out, namely that flirtation was less dangerous in the United States than elsewhere, on account of the preoccupation of men with business affairs. He found, as Grund had said some years earlier, that "our business men have no time for cooing" (*Aristocracy in America*, vol. ii, p. 57).

[2] A. M. Gow, p. 199. Cf. the story of the lady's pulse in *Le Facécieux Reveille-Matin* (Nymegue, 1678), pp. 261–2. Little did Gow dream that less than a century later the legs of the American girl would be, to use Rhona Churchill's word, "glamourized", and that a poem would be written about them (see G. G. Currie, p. 325).

doubt that the influence of Puritanism intensified the stifling refinement and pervading gentility of American art and figure-work just
as it hindered the development of lyric poetry in the United States.
What must be remembered is that Puritanism itself was not a movement in which the condemnation of art occupied an important place.
The early Puritans merely pointed out (and surely with some degree
of justification) that nude statues and pictures could hardly fail in
some people to arouse sensations and desires which, if satisfied outside marriage, were sins and which were consequently better
avoided. Such an attitude was akin to that which inspired the
numberless manuals in all countries in which those female fashions
were condemned which led to undue exposure of the neck and bosom,
for, as William A. Alcott said in his *Young Woman's Guide to Excellence*, "Let not the young of the other sex, miseducated as they are,
and the slaves of improper imaginations and feelings, be longer
trifled with in this matter" (p. 275).

With the decay of the true spirit of Puritanism the forms remained, and often became exaggerated, although the spirit which
had formerly animated them was dead. Indeed, feelings of guilt now
sprang mainly from fear of incurring the opprobrium of society
rather than that of the Almighty. It was supposed that a prudish
attitude was one which was in accordance with the views of the
Fathers of the Republic, and thus the upper classes carried on what
they believed to be the American tradition in forms which sharply
distinguished them from the foreign immigrants. This attitude,
moreover, was in a sense forced upon them. The neglect of their
husbands, the lack of opportunity for illicit affairs and the abnormal
emphasis placed upon chastity and virginity were gradually forcing
many American women to adopt a rôle in which their own femininity
was being stifled and the biological urges within them treated as if
they had no existence. While they themselves were denied the
pleasures which secretly they knew they were capable of enjoying,
they realized that by the double standard their menfolk were not
depriving themselves of carnal gratification elsewhere. From this
knowledge arose two factors of profound importance in the history
of feminine development in the United States. Firstly, it was in the
nineteenth century that we can see the beginnings of the theory of
male inferiority and female dominance, not only in the home, but in
society in general, which, as Dickson Wecter points out (p. 293),
women finally dominated completely and occupied a position which
the American man has usually accepted without question. And
secondly, realization of what they were precluded from enjoying

forced them to rationalize their misery by pretending to be immune from passion and desire, while they exhibited their discomfiture and irritation by a domineering and scornful attitude and a rudeness toward men that surprised many foreign observers. For example, A. d'Almbert, in his *Flânerie Parisienne aux Etats-Unis* (1856), said that the women in the United States realized their power to such an extent that they abused it like tyrants who are aware that there is no limit to their despotism. On the other hand, the men showed a boundless patience and a deference to the women that could scarcely be imagined. American husbands, he stated, knew that they were inferior to their wives, and as they secretly confessed it, their attitude was explained. The least sign of any gratitude on the part of a woman towards a man was considered superfluous, a feature which Francis Lieber had noticed twenty years before.[1]

Similarly Alfred Bunn in his book *Old England and New England* declared that if there was one feature more striking than another in the American character, it was the boundless attention that American men paid to women. She is supreme, and they are the mere creatures of her will (Vol. I, p. 84), an opinion voiced twenty years before, when William Faux (p. 416) declared that south of the Delaware woman was "a little divinity, to whom all must bend, give place, and pay idle homage". Bunn noticed the rudeness of women when travelling, and observed one case in which a woman turned a man off his seat and then used both halves of the settee for herself and her baggage. It was women of this kind to whom Anthony Trollope doubtless referred when he spoke of persons who were more odious to him than any other human beings he had met elsewhere. Although generally speaking he found American women charming, he noted that they had "no perception of that return which chivalry demands of them", illustrating his thesis by an account of what he himself observed in street cars.[2] A similar point of view was expressed by Count de Soissons, who was interested to confirm what William Dean Howells had written about the American woman when he had said that it was useless to quarrel with their decisions because there was no appeal from them. Soissons mentioned that in America everything was for the woman. Love played a very small part in her life, for her husband, whom she dominated, was merely a machine for

---

[1] See d'Almbert, pp. 75, 84, 77; F. Lieber, p. 104. It was d'Almbert who caused great annoyance by heading one of his chapters "Les Beaux Arts en Amérique" and leaving succeeding pages (145–6) blank and merely filled with dots.

[2] Anthony Trollope, vol. i, p. 295.

making money. He did not know whom to pity more, the men or the women.[1]

In the above brief remarks it will be noticed how foreign observers of the American scene were at pains to point out the curious separation of the sexes in the upper-income levels as regards their social life. One result of this separation was, as we have seen, the growing tendency of women not only to rely on phantasy rather than on fact when it came to their more intimate lives, but also to develop a social life of their own from which men were largely excluded. Amongst the more wealthy and better-educated women a new form of consciousness was beginning to develop in which two main streams were, I think, discernible. Puritan traditions were still influencing their sexual lives to the extent that virginity and chastity were considered desirable, but in many cases their enforced continence, owing to the attitude of the men, was beginning to be thought of as something desirable and something which, in a sense, made them superior to the other sex, whose animal nature compelled satisfaction with other unfortunate females who became mere victims to their lust.

As we shall see later, these ideas were to lead to opinions so extravagant and so grotesque that it is a little difficult to understand how they were not met with greater ridicule than appears to have been the case. The fact remained, however, that many of the more leisured women were sex-starved, although they knew that their husbands and sons were sometimes finding satisfaction in ways the nature of which no decent woman should know and often with partners taken from the coloured population. This situation led, as we have seen, to an exaggerated but spurious prudery which increased still more the gulf which was widening between them and their husbands. It never seems to have struck these women that the more they emphasized their purity and chastity and denied their sensual natures, the less likely it was that they would appeal to any but the most sophisticated males, and the more probable it was that their husbands would seek others who, at least in appearance,

[1] See S. C. de Soissons, pp. 6, 17, 21, 51, etc. The social superiority of the American woman and the universal deference in which she was held were two of the essential features of American civilization which G. M. Towle mentioned in his important account of American society which he published in London in 1870. Towle was at one time the United States Consul in Bradford in England, and his book, which is a mine of valuable information, was written with a view to providing English readers with reliable matter about the United States; women in America, he wrote, are "never intruders"; they could go anywhere at their own sweet will (see vol. i, pp. 303 ff).

obtained satisfaction and pleasure from fleeting contacts. On the other hand, the men in their frenzied search for wealth had to keep up an appearance of respectability and regard for tradition which engendered within them a sense of guilt and realization of betrayal. The search for dollars became, in a sense, an escape from woman. Their lack of social education and of understanding of cultural values made them feel more and more inferior in social contacts. Social existence was, as Henry James so well put it in *The American Scene* (p. 345), "pounced upon" by the American woman, and he saw that this deep split and chasm between the sexes developed into what he described as "*the* feature of the social scene" (p. 65). James asked whether the American man, having thus allowed woman to dominate the social stage, would ever be able to repair his mistake; and he recorded his opinion, in which I fully concur, that this question is one of the most curious and interesting that America offers to an objective observer. What James failed to see, or possibly what he preferred not to discuss, was the sexual relationships which are so intimately connected with the social life. For not only is many an American woman a woman without love, but she is a woman who, through the operations of a complex concatenation of circumstances, believes herself able to exist happily without it and without that kind of sexual life which is the heritage of every human female in Western civilized society.

The split which James described as existing between the sexes in the United States was not the only one. Although it might perhaps be said that all men were brothers, all women were certainly not sisters, unless we can regard them as divided into the virtuous and the erring. Moreover, it was not that the virtuous merely pitied the erring. They were jealous of them, for was it not a fact that these "unfortunates" were usurpers and, apparently without a twinge of conscience, were enjoying experiences which the virtuous deep down in their hearts would not have been averse from sharing? However that may be (and we shall return later to this matter), prostitution was not unknown in America in early days, and in the middle of the eighteenth century was fully recognized. Thus Gottlieb Mittelberger, in his account of his travels in Pennsylvania in 1750, says that prostitution was not punished in any way; and he notes at the same time that English women in Pennsylvania were held in high esteem, so much so, indeed, that he rather quaintly observed that he would sooner strike three men in England than box the ears of one woman in Pennsylvania! [1]   Forty years later Moreau de St. Méry declared

[1] G. Mittelberger, pp. 82, 87, 88.

that in New York City prostitution was rife, that whole streets were given up to brothels and houses of prostitution, and the most hideous marks of corruption were plainly evident (p. 171). Similarly, La Rochefoucauld-Liancourt, who had some very laudatory things to say about American women, while noticing the pernicious effects on men of the passion for gain, declared that, so far as he was able to observe, prostitution was a well-recognized trade at the end of the eighteenth century.[1]

In the early years of the nineteenth century the accounts of travellers naturally differ according to the opportunities offered to them for observation. Some travellers obviously took a keen interest in the feminine world. For example, John Lambert, who travelled in America in 1806, 1807 and 1808, has a good deal to say about female society in the United States, noting that, at the time that he was in New York, Mrs. Toule and Mme Bouchard were rival leaders of the fashionable world. As to Boston, he declared that prostitutes were so numerous that they numbered one-thirtieth of the total population.[2] On the other hand, Isaac Candler in 1824, while stressing the subject of delicacy and saying that even to mention a shirt was enough to be accused of vulgarity and indelicacy, said that he thought that in America there was less prostitution than in most European countries.[3] His opinion seems to have been shared by James Stuart, who gives an account of vice in New Orleans, Natchez and Louisville without, however, giving sufficient details to enable the reader to arrive at definite conclusions. On the other hand, he does go so far as to say that he never saw any woman of light character on the public streets either by day or by night and, moreover, he noticed no signs of female indecorum in any of the places that he visited.[4]

By the middle of the century prostitution and vice were a general feature of the social scene, and books began to be issued on the one hand of an avowedly fictional character and on the other more or less founded on facts. George Lippard (1822–54), a curious writer who combined the production of florid and sensational fiction with a leaning towards social reform, gained many readers of his exposure of the hidden vice of the City of Brotherly Love. The book, *Dora*

[1] La Rochefoucauld-Liancourt, vol. viii, p. 166.
[2] John Lambert, vol. ii, pp. 196, 120.
[3] I. Candler, pp. 99, 457. It ought perhaps to be pointed out that this delicacy in speech was not confined to genteel society in the United States. It was rife in Victorian England, and at one time, it is said, a true lady was unable to utter the word "constable", but had to use such expressions as "police officer" or simply "policeman".
[4] J. Stuart, vol. ii, pp. 203, 262, 293, 204, 294; cf. H. B. Fearon, p. 171.

Livingstone, was an immense success. Lippard was an acute observer, and he soon perceived in American society the gulf which separated faith from practice, and the sight offended him deeply. Even in the Church and the Law he saw the most brazen hypocrisy, and his disgust seems to have prompted him to portray Philadelphia in what he thought was its true aspect. Lippard was a man of some literary skill and of keen imagination. For the framework of his picture he used every device beloved by the writer of the Gothic novel. Everything will be found in Lippard's work. Horror piles on horror, and even the names of the characters, like Devil-Bug, are sufficient to cause goose-flesh in the susceptible. But even if Lippard was filled with a desire for social justice and a detestation of the conditions which led to poverty and prostitution, he could not resist embellishing his tale with details which were hardly unlikely to arouse emotion in the minds of his readers. Incidents relevant to seduction scenes are embroidered with detailed descriptions of the victim's voluptuous charms, and the interest of his female readers is not forgotten, as in the description of the ecstasy of having the said charms unveiled by a lover, as skilful as he was daring, which he incorporated in his novel *The Monks of Monk-Hall.*

A similar work for New York soon followed,[1] and readers of the daily Press were often invited to buy such ephemeral publications as *The Scorpion*, in which they would find intriguing accounts of beautiful adulteresses, libertine statesmen, lustful widows, amorous doctors and all the other figures beloved of those craving vicarious excitement. For those more interested in supposedly factual reportage rather than in confessed romance, a number of writers contributed their share. J. D. McCabe, Jr., followed Lippard some twenty years later in his *The Secrets of the Great City*, and in the same writer's *New York by Sunlight and Gaslight* (pp. 474 ff.) some details are given of the "lost sisterhood". We learn that there were in 1880 some 600 brothels and ninety assignation houses in New York, together with 487 panel houses (i.e. those used in the prostitution plus robbery racket). We learn something of the abortion business and its famous queen "Madame R[estell]", and in Chapter XLVIII we can read a vivid account of the notorious dance-hall, Harry Hills', at the corner of Houston and Mulberry Streets.

In 1869 G. Ellington described the underworld in his book on the women of New York; whilst three years later a general picture of vice in the great city was presented by Edward Crapsey, who gives an interesting account of the abortionists practising at that time and

[1] *New York: its Upper Ten and Lower Million* (Cincinnati, 1853).

the infallible "French Pills", which were sold for the purpose of pro-
curing miscarriages and were recommended and sold by "Dr.
Mauriceau". A year later another book, which has been attributed to
Gustav Lehning, was published in New York. Entitled *The Dark
Side of New York Life*, it disclosed a horrific picture of the trade in
abortions, dealing not only with Madame Restell at her palace at
52nd Street and Fifth Avenue, but also with the other practitioners
of the art, giving their names, addresses and methods of work.
Another interesting fact outlined by Lehning was the flourishing
trade in obscene literature. From 1850 to 1875 the chief purveyor of
this class of publication was W. Haynes in New York; and the trade
in photographs was carried on by G. Gompert, whilst George Akman
and the firms of Evans and Willis also collaborated. Haynes published several hundred books, and in one case the authorities, during
a raid on a suspected source, discovered a mailing list containing
10,000 prominent names. It was during this period that the great
chaser of smut, Mr. Anthony Comstock, was at his prime. He is an
interesting figure, but would have been more interesting if we could
have discovered what his wife thought about the main interest of his
life. Unfortunately Margaret Comstock was a shy, reserved and
self-effacing person, and if she had her thoughts they are not
recorded.

Comstock himself, like so many other Americans, was profoundly
attached to his mother, and the influence that she had over him was
never obliterated. He was as neurotic as Horatio Alger and even
more simple. His simplicity consisted in never swerving from the
teaching given him in the Puritan household where he was brought
up and in following that teaching to its logical conclusions. In plain
language, Comstock, like so many other neurotic individuals, did not
approve of the Divine plan for the propagation of the species. If he
had been consulted, things would have been very different, but as it
was he had to make the best of what seemed to him to savour of a
joke, and not a very good one at that. He was sincerely convinced
that many souls were lost through the sinister activities of the
peddlers of obscene literature, who were clearly engaged in vile
attempts to ensnare youth. To Anthony Comstock the word "obscene" (which has for so long defied definition) was simple to understand. It was in essence something which excited sensual desire and
thereby led to a wish for gratification. It is true that gratification
depended upon time, place, opportunity and legal sanction, but the
meaning was clear. Such gratification tended to corrupt the lives
of the young, for, according to Comstock and those who thought like

him, relief was only to be sought either when in the arms of Morpheus or when safely tied up in holy matrimony. It was on grounds such as these that Comstock acted, although I do not think he ever went so far as to condemn the Bible, or at least those portions of it which earlier writers had declared quite unfit for family reading. Apart from Scripture, however, Comstock saw "obscenity" everywhere. From the lowest pink-covered booklet to *September Morn* he could see examples of what tended to divert the minds to things forbidden. He did his best, therefore, to suppress them, and he succeeded to a very considerable extent. After all, if we accept his premises and act upon them, our course is clear. The "limbs" of the piano must be covered; preparations for the making of infant clothes must not be shown on the screen,[1] and unclad wax dummies used to display feminine fashions must not be shown in the windows of a department store.[2]

I do not propose here to deal with the vexed question of the nature of obscenity and the prevention of pornographic works from falling into the hands of those not fitted to receive them. Comstock's view can be understood even if it be not accepted. It is an odd commentary upon his work that the United States, in which he spent his life trying to suppress "suggestive" literature and art, should be the land where, today, such material seductively and provocatively presented, is to be found everywhere, from the cheapest pulp magazine to the advertisements of feminine underwear in the costliest fashion journals. It is possible that the American attempt to improve on the Divine plan may have had something to do with it.

Although the sensational literature of the period revealed a good many illicit sexual connexions, there is nothing surprising in the general course of prostitution in the United States in the nineteenth century. With the expanding frontier and the numbers of foreign immigrants, family life was difficult and almost impossible, and what happened during the gold rush in 1849 was bound to happen in any part of the world given the same circumstances. The cribs and sporting joints of the Barbary Coast were typical of such establishments elsewhere and presented few features which could be called unusual or peculiar. It is true that the lawless characteristics of such

[1] See H. Broun, etc. *Nonsenseorship*, p. 7.
[2] Comstock had such figures removed in 1911 (see H. Broun and M. Leech, p. 270), and as late as 1948 the police in Atlanta ordered stores to draw their curtains when the dummies were being dressed in new costumes. The terrible moral risk to those dressing—and still worse undressing—the dummies does not seem to have been considered either by Comstock or the Chief of Police in Atlanta.

times tended to make the brothels centres of corruption and intemperance and, moreover, with the increase of juvenile and above all of poorly paid female labour, the prostitution racket was a paying proposition, which not only put money into the pockets of its promoters but also brought business to towns which tolerated it, thus enriching business men who had no active part in the trade itself. The houses themselves were by no means all of the same character. In the bigger cities they were as large and luxuriously fitted up as those in the great European cities, and that managed by the fabulous Everleigh sisters is not likely easily to be forgotten.[1]

These fantastic ladies are worth more than passing notice, since their activities could hardly have been carried on in any country other than the United States. Ada and Minna "Everleigh", or Lester as it seems their real name may have been, were born near Louisville, Ky. The daughters of a Southern gentleman, they received a good education, and when quite young were said to have married men whom they left soon after, giving the reason that they were cruelly treated. Free to follow their own devices, they joined a stage troupe and looked around to see how they could invest what money they had, which amounted to some thirty thousand dollars. Finally they decided that profits and safety were to be found in the brothel business, and they opened a house in Omaha in 1898. Business, however, slackened, as the sisters' house was exclusive and the charges high, so they decided to go elsewhere, finally deciding on Chicago, where in 1900 they opened the famous Everleigh Club, which was probably the most luxurious and profitable house ever operated in the United States or elsewhere, rivalling even the former great Parisian houses at 12 Rue Chabanais, 13 Rue St. Augustin, 122 Rue de Provence, 6 Rue des Moulins or 10 Rue Papillon. Golden silk curtains discreetly concealed the windows; thick carpets and expensive rugs covered the floors and even the spittoons were said to be of solid gold. On the first floor were a number of private parlours decorated in the tastes of various nations, and in each room perfume was at regular intervals thrown up into the air by a series of ingeniously contrived fountains. Minna Everleigh, covered with jewels, welcomed each client, who was then introduced to the girls, who were in evening dress and were so trained that their manners were perfect and their behaviour decorous. Business was strictly controlled, the girls receiving half of whatever they earned, and the charges for their services plus food and drink were enormous. Although the overheads were very heavy, it is probable

[1] See C. Washburn, *Come into my Parlor* (Chicago, 1936), and Samuel P. Wilson, whose books on Chicago night life ran into numerous editions.

that the net profits were something like 400 dollars a day, each client being expected to pay at least 50 dollars a visit, which, considering the entertainment, could not be termed excessive. The "circuses" were of the ultra-exclusive type and had nothing in common with those given by one of the sisters' neighbours, Black May, which were as extreme as anything to be seen in the old quarter in Marseilles or at Port Said. The Lesters were not at all averse to reformers visiting the house and distributing mission literature. Indeed, they themselves subscribed to these laudable efforts, but the results were negligible. They were too firmly established and had contacted too important a clientele. But they misjudged the extent of the power they wielded. Public attention was being focused on the Levee and the houses therein, and even the reporters (always welcome at the Everleigh Club) had to be careful. In 1911, when one of their more flamboyant advertisements fell into the hands of Mayor Carter Harrison, the blow came. The house was closed, the effects put into store and the Everleigh sisters took a trip to Europe. Returning to Chicago as private citizens, they found the publicity still too great, so they settled in New York, quiet, rich ladies with their memories and, it is said, the gold piano. In September 1948 Minna died in Manhattan, aged eighty, and, as was suitable and proper for a Southern gentlewoman, was taken by Ada to Virginia to be buried.

Just as in California the trade in prostitution was stimulated by the presence of the prospectors and their followers, so in Louisiana the business flourished under the support of the Mississippi river men and the foreign elements in the great port of New Orleans. The truth was that vice flourished in the cities of the United States as it did elsewhere, and the "revelations" of the Kinsey report in 1948 are thus described by G. H. Napheys in 1871. "Sufficient to say," he wrote, "that every unnatural lust recorded in the mordant satires of Juvenal, the cynical epigrams of Martial, or the licentious stories of Petronius, is practised, not in rare or exceptional cases, but deliberately and habitually in the great cities of our country. Did we choose to draw the veil from those abominable scenes with which our professional life has brought us into contact, we could tell of the vice which called vengeance from heaven on Sodom practised notoriously; we could speak of restaurants frequented by men in women's attire, yielding themselves to indescribable lewdness; we could point out literature so inconceivably devilish as to advocate and extol this utter depravity." [1] *Plus ça change, plus la même chose.*

[1] G. H. Napheys, *The Transmission of Life*, p. 29.

The growth of prostitution, stimulated as it was by the American ideas of "private enterprise" and the "liberty of the individual", was regarded by some with increasing dismay, and steps were beginning to be taken to discuss it seriously and suggest remedies and means of prevention. Some of these were a little odd and somewhat revolutionary. Thus a writer (E. N. Jencks) calling himself "Christian Philanthropist" suggested that a plurality of wives might solve the question, as thereby every woman would have to be a wife and therefore could hardly act as a prostitute at the same time. I am not aware what reception his curious volume had at the hands of its feminine readers, although I fancy that a few found it difficult to suppress a smile. G. J. Zeigler had a much more subtle plan. He proposed that sexual intercourse should automatically mean legal marriage, and consequently, if a single woman proved a connexion with a single man, she would at once become his legal wife. This ingenious plan was not, I think, received with much favour by husbands, as they foresaw a continual series of assaults on the fidelity of their wives by persons who did not want to become the husbands of ladies whose attractions had proved for a few moments irresistible.

Attempts to examine the problem on a more rational basis were now and then being made, and some authors, like A. M. Powell, were discussing the question of State regulation as practised in Europe. But little came of their proposals, since the influence of women was beginning to be felt in political circles, and also the magnitude of the profits to be made out of prostitution was too great to be relinquished. Private enterprise on the part of harlots was not encouraged; and the big money was to be made by the prostitution bosses who ran the racket, in which the women were merely employees. We shall see later how, in the twentieth century, prostitution was to become one of the most lucrative of all the mob rackets, once the girls who wished to work on their own had been driven off the streets through the operation of the "morality" drives and vice squads, in which frame-ups were far from unknown. These sudden outbursts of morality led enthusiasts not only to attempt to abolish prostitution by hiding it, but also to condemn the importation of European literature which sullied the minds of pure Americans. Attacks were delivered in 1880 on the "muckraker" Zola, whose book *Nana* was then being read, and it was considered a shame that decent people should take "the foul brood of his incubation" into their homes. Similarly Ouida's account of society women in her novel *Moths* was condemned, and all such examples of "foreign purveyors of infection" were castigated, as for instance by A. F. Fiske in *The North American Review*, in 1880.

As has been said above, the regulation of prostitution in the United States, as in Great Britain, has always been opposed by women in positions of influence and authority. In the United States it would be difficult to imagine that the situation could have been otherwise. It was hardly likely that women who found themselves neglected by their menfolk and forced to live in a state of almost continual frustration and dissatisfaction were prepared to assist in making safe the illicit pleasures of their erring spouses and licentious sons. Indeed, the tendency was the other way. Such immoral practices had their own punishment, the scourge of venereal disease. It is true that the practice of pretending that venereal disease did not exist was widespread in spite of the valiant efforts of some medical men to issue popular expositions of the subject, so that technical ignorance on the part of women merely succeeded in injuring themselves as well as their children. The diseases raged in the United States, and many a married woman dragged out a miserable existence wholly unaware of the cause of her ill-health. But even supposing that regulation had been both possible and successful it could not have been adopted. Anything which made "vice" easier was to be condemned. Women were to be "rescued from these dens of infamy" and placed in homes, there to be trained as domestic drudges on insufficient pay. It is instructive for the student of social affairs to note the emotion and excitement which the proposal to abolish houses of prostitution arouses in its feminine advocates. Although they are fervent adherents to the plan to save women from such a life, they rarely turn their attention to other unpleasant spheres of female activity, let alone to the highly nauseating jobs which some men are called upon to do. It does not raise any excitement in their hearts when they are told that some women have to stand day after day dealing with the intestines of hogs, and that many men are engaged for years of their lives in such surroundings as those of the killing-pens of the great abattoirs or the factories where glues and fertilizers are manufactured. It is clear that other factors are present and that the objections and arguments advanced by these women are in the nature of rationalizations, which conceal the true motives behind their propaganda. It is not very difficult to determine what is the truth behind the façade of virtuous indignation. Apart from those cases where a genuine love of suffering humanity is uppermost, which shows itself in a life of self-sacrifice and altruistic devotion, we find that the majority of fanatical abolitionists are either unmarried or, if married, profoundly unsatisfied and possibly frigid. Knowing nothing of the frigidity of prostitutes, they imagine that many live a life of constant pleasure and stimulation; and that "sin" should thus be enjoyed is intolerable to them. Sex-starved themselves, they envy the supposed sexual satisfaction enjoyed by the prostitute, and the thought that, were prostitution to be abolished, men might also suffer the pangs of unsatisfied sexual hunger is an additional source of satisfaction to them.

It was thus in the nineteenth century and it is the same today, although in modern times the majority of smart women cannot be distinguished in appearance from the expensive harlots of the present century. The position is summed up very neatly by Nina Wilson in Joseph Hergesheimer's novel *The Party Dress*. Her husband is complaining of her appearance and says that she looks like a French whore. To this remark Nina replies by telling him that that is the way women want to look, as he really might have known, and she adds that as unfortunately all women can't be French whores, they do their best to look like them, and the relief to their pent-up feelings is considerable.[1] The same phenomena can be observed in the jealousy with which modern American society women regard others whom they think are in a position to enjoy the favours of men without discovery and therefore without scandal. The WACs during the Second World War were often regarded in this light, especially those who held positions in which they could enter the company of the higher staff. Doubtless this attitude on the part of prominent Washington society women was intensified by the wholesale promiscuity going on in the city, in which it is said that the sitting brass, their secretaries and the wives of serving officers were seemingly engaged.[2]

As we have seen above, the attitude of the nineteenth-century American woman towards prostitution does not seem to have lessened its extent or its importance in the social life of the people. Indeed, it could hardly have been otherwise, since the surplus of men and the fact that so many were immigrants from countries wholly uninfluenced by any Puritan traditions were bound to create a demand, and the fact that the women in industry often received less than a living wage drove many of them into a life which, however unpleasant, was often considered better than drudgery in a factory on starvation pay. It is true that voices were raised against the prevalence of prostitution, but organized feminine resistance had yet to

[1] Joseph Hergesheimer, p. 125. Emile Barbier noticed this in 1893, saying that American girls and young women tried to look like *grues* (*Voyage*, etc., p. 136).

[2] Cf. Elliot Arnold's *Everybody Slept Here* (New York, 1948).

come, and in the meantime feminism was showing signs of renewed life. The independence and business capacity of many of the colonial women indicated that, with the proper stimulus applied at the right time, American women would easily arrive at the position of demanding political and industrial equality and a greater freedom of action after marriage. The influence of Mary Wollstonecraft was already perceptible in the latter years of the eighteenth century and, as we can see from Charles Brockden Brown's *Alcuin* (1798), the fictional Mrs. Carter was advancing radical ideas even in the sphere of family life, such as the desirability of divorce at the wish of either party. But, generally speaking, the bulk of American married women up to the middle of the nineteenth century were brought up to rigid standards of conduct in which the domestic virtues predominated, religion was fostered and chastity was guarded to the extent that to know anything about the vices of the world was tantamount to confessing impurity of thought and possibly also of deed. The home was still sacred, and the clergy were still teaching their flocks that, although woman was head of the home in one sense, she had to remember that she had to submit herself to her master, for was it not written that women should learn in silence? [1] After all, as the Rev. Dr. Gardiner Spring put it, could any earthly restraint or moral power be compared with the wishes of a mother,[2] a point of view even more forcibly expressed in the Philadelphia *Public Ledger and Daily Transcript* for July 20, 1848, when it said that one pretty girl was equal to ten thousand men and a mother was, next to God, all powerful. Women who desired to escape had to join one of the many "reform" movements, which attracted persons of both sexes: they had to be "crusaders" in various campaigns to change the world and arrive at perfection along with others of similar persuasion.

It must not be imagined that all these movements and utopias were supported by mere crack-pots and fanatical enthusiasts. Some, of course, attracted more foolish women than others, but many of them were the signs and symbols of an awakened conscience and showed an earnest desire to improve conditions in all those spheres where social neglect had wreaked the greatest havoc among the innocent and the helpless.[3] The very fact of their existence showed

---

[1] See Marianne Finch, p. 204.   [2] G. Spring, p. 42.

[3] For two admirable accounts of these movements and utopias see Alice F. Tyler and V. L. Parrington, Jr., who, in his *American Dreams*, analyses a great number of novels and other publications in which the authors have dealt with the American Utopia. He rightly stresses the importance of such writers as Edward Bellamy, who, in his *Looking Backward* (1888), drew a picture of a kind of benevolent communism.

that a feeling of unrest and dissatisfaction was abroad, and that men and women even preferred to form separate communities rather than to participate in the social and economic life of which they disapproved and wished to condemn. Not all of the reforming women, however, were willing thus to leave and to build a life apart from their fellows. Many believed that the fight for reform was not to be won by desertion but by strenuous activity, and by the promulgation of the belief that it was on account of the failure of women to assert themselves that so much evil was everywhere apparent. The manmade and man-governed world was clearly not a success: what was wanted was the influence of women, and possibly the drastic control of male power by and through women. The fight of the feminists for equal rights, for education and the advantages accruing from it was beginning, and the struggle was to be made even more bitter in the United States than elsewhere on account of the sex antagonism and the frustration from which so many of the women suffered. Attempts had therefore to be made to show, not only on economic but also on biological grounds that the female was superior to the male, and that therefore her subjection could not be supported upon any grounds except those of brute force and superior physical strength. Such ideas as these were naturally very favourably received by the more advanced women of the United States, many of whom were already convincing themselves that male domination was no longer to be endured and that the subjection of man to woman was only a matter of time.

It would be out of place to indicate here the many volumes which have appeared down the centuries vindicating the female sex against the attacks made upon it. They usually follow an accepted pattern, although some are more eulogistic than others. Such laudatory statements were made as that by Tate (*A Present for the Ladies* (1693), p. 2), which showed from Holy Writ that woman was made *after* man, and was therefore the "consummation of the Works of God". In the early years of the nineteenth century, however, woman, although superior in the home, was not considered superior to man, but inferior to him, and the words of the "Almighty Himself" were invoked to prove it. Later, however, the tone changed. In *Woman and her Needs* (1851) Mrs. Seba Smith, wife of the famous homespun philosopher, summed up the new teaching in bitter and caustic terms. She had noted the lack of interest in social affairs which was exhibited by the men of the period and had put it down to the mental dullness and imbecility of the mere male. One had only, she said, to read but "a tithe of the twaddle" written by men regarding women to see how

G

little the unhappy female was understood, that female who was "undoubtedly the one through which the ultimate goal of the world is to be achieved".[1] Similar views were expressed in the same year by Mrs. Abell, whose *Woman in her Various Relations* indicated which way the wind of feminine emancipation was blowing. "Man's work shall decay and die," Mrs. Abell intoned. "His loftiest and proudest work shall be forgotten, but that of woman is immortal." [2] Not only was the work of woman to be immortal in the United States, but the lady herself was infallible, if we are to believe the opinion of that sprightly dandy and worldly reporter Nathaniel P. Willis, who in his *The Rag-Bag* extolled the American female in terms already quoted.

The finest expression of these views, however, is to be found in the works of the ineffable Mrs. Farnham, that original thinker and physiologist, to whom we are indebted for proof of the superiority of the woman over the man, and who prepared the ground for the later gynæcocentric theories of Lester F. Ward. This astonishing lady was born in 1815 and died in 1864. She was the daughter of Cornelius and Mary Burhans, and when she was only six years old her mother died. For some reason Cornelius, who, if we can believe his daughter's account, was a remarkable man, was unable to keep Eliza at home, and she was sent away to live with her uncle (who drank) and her aunt (who nagged). In 1836 she married T. J. Farnham, bearing him three children, and after a time became interested and immersed in problems of social reform. She showed considerable ability and an abounding energy, becoming a matron in the female section of the great penitentiary of Sing-Sing. Later, she went to California and then studied medicine in New York. In 1859 she became engrossed in the problem of finding accommodation for destitute women, finally organizing the formation of a society for finding them homes in the West. Her husband having meanwhile died, she married again, this time to a Mr. William Fitzpatrick, by whom she had one daughter.

It is not at all clear what was the original spark which set Eliza's imagination aflame. All we know is that towards 1860 she determined to put the world right on the sex question and to prove to all who cared to listen that the superiority of woman over man was a fact which could not be contradicted. In 1864 her book (*Woman and her Era*, 2 vols., New York, 1864) was published and the proof appeared to an incredulous world. "Life is exalted", she wrote, "in proportion to its Organic and Functional Complexity", and since woman's organism was more complex and her "totality of Function"

[1] Elizabeth O. Smith, pp. 80, 84, 102.   [2] L. G. Abell, p. 300.

larger than those of any other being on earth, it followed that the female position in the scale of life was the most exalted, and hence the sovereign one. It was true, Mrs. Farnham had to admit, that woman appeared to have certain weaknesses, although she would never have gone so far as to say, as Elsa Gidlow did in 1937, that Nature had "played rather a horrid trick on the people we call women".[1] Not at all. For her, menstruation proceeded "from a law of order" in the economy of female life which replaced "the licence of mere waste in the masculine". So that was that. But even more surprising things were to come. It seems that Mrs. Farnham had come under the influence of a physiognomist, James W. Redfield, who supplied her with some useful "facts" similar to those held by the ovists whose views still held the field in various quarters. We learn, therefore, that it is the female who had in her ovum the entire living germ of any future offspring. Mere man had nothing to do with it. All he conferred upon the sovereign female creator was "the food which the germ requires to start it into life". His duty was, in short, simply to prepare the female for maternity, a task which must have seemed very odd to Mrs. Farnham, who had to suffer it on at least four occasions.

Having disposed of the pretensions of the man to share in the creation of a new life, Mrs. Farnham proceeded to compare the two sexes, to the great disadvantage of the male. Woman's brain was finer, she wrote, as were all her other tissues: it was, moreover, more complex, as was her general build. Through this fineness arose her higher character, her more delicate grasp, the more penetrative reach of her faculties, her swifter power to seize relations, her more receptive states, which were open to illumination and inspiration, and the more fluent inner life which she enjoyed. As to her body, the same proofs were there. Rudimentary organs were to be found in plants and trees, reptiles, fishes, quadrupeds and in the human male —but not in woman. Look at her breasts, Mrs. Farnham exclaimed. "In the male mammal the apparatus of the lactatory office is hinted at by a rudimentary form." Even her diseases were exclusive to her, and, be it remembered, "exclusiveness in suffering is exclusiveness in power". Apart from these unpleasant topics was the question of actual organs. Counting them up, Mrs. Farnham discovered that woman had two more than man, for no one could call man's rudimentary nipples "organs". But something was wrong. Had Eliza Farnham forgotten something? And was it rather important, and might it upset the list in an embarrassing manner? Not at all. It

[1] E. Gidlow, p. 78.

was not for nothing that Eliza had studied medicine in New York. Woman was also provided with this structure "which is treated in the books as rudimentary". But in the female its purpose was clear. It was for "the wider diffusion of nerves, whose more concentrated presence would scarce consist with the functional economics and health of adjacent parts". Having surmounted that hurdle, Mrs. Farnham proceeded to gallop to the winning-post. Woman, she shouted, "constitutes the highest grade of development of the highest type of living creatures here". For a single woman who exhibited the "depravity of appetite and sense" five hundred men could be found, for it was man who degraded the love relation and woman who elevated it.[1] Men, she went on, revel in bestial sensuality and they dare to speak of "fallen women". "I accept man's language," Eliza exclaimed; "it is a fall for my sex when it descends to meet his at the level of sense", for women abhor sensuality in their own sex, women, who have been shown to possess the most perfect, "complex, varied, refined, beautiful and exquisitely endowed organization, comprising, with its corresponding faculties, the most susceptible, sensitive yet enduring constitution; and also the purest, most aspiring, progressive, loving, spiritual nature of any being that inhabits our earth".

Such was woman according to Eliza Farnham, but even her quotations from Agrippa were hardly likely to persuade the world that she was right. For what she had said was not the reasoned argument of a mature thinker, but the wild and incoherent ravings of a frustrated, jealous and neurotic woman, of an American woman of the middle nineteenth century. She voiced the opinions of many others who found little satisfaction in their attempts to find an outlet for their energies in activities outside the home, and whose education had prevented them from expanding their personalities in those directions proper to the mature woman. They felt themselves cheated and trapped, and thus the fight for equality in the United States was a fight in which sex antagonism played a prominent part. In this connexion Emily Faithfull quotes an amusing skit on the kind of address delivered by an American feminist. "Miss President, feller-wimmin and male trash generally," the speaker began, "I believe sexes were created perfectly equal, with the woman a little more equal than the man. . . . The only decent thing about him was a rib, and that went to make something better."[2]

[1] Could Virginia Leblick have been thinking of Eliza Farnham when she said in 1910 that the lowest prostitute was better than the best of men? (p. 65).
[2] E. Faithfull, 326. The rib was still worrying American feminists in 1948.

Thirty years after Eliza Farnham had explained the reasons for woman's superiority over man, Eliza B. Gamble returned to the same subject, and was even more scientific in her discussion.[1] She mentioned that the fact that the female represented a higher development than the male was proved throughout the various departments of nature. The hair on the male body indicated a later development; and it was notorious that men suffered many disabilities which were not shared by the female sex. More men were colour-blind than women, which caused them to "labor under great and continuous disadvantages". To this defective vision in man was added lack of physical endurance, structural defects and, above all, the presence of those "abnormal appetites which are constantly demanding for their gratification those things which are injurious to his mental and physical constitution" (p. 49). These "abnormal appetites" troubled Eliza Gamble even more than they troubled Eliza Farnham. How were they to be brought under control? By "the cultivation of the higher faculties developed in and transmitted through females", announced Eliza Gamble. So that was settled. Everything, however, was not quite plain sailing, for there was some evidence that educated women—yes, cultured and educated women—occasionally shared those "abnormal appetites" which the two Elizas so roundly condemned men for possessing. For example, there were the Greek hetaerae, who clearly did not object to being both the lovers and friends of men, and from what we know of them actually enjoyed the contacts they invited. Such an idea was abhorrent to Eliza Gamble. It is doubtful, she wrote, if intelligent women of the present age will be brought to believe that "the excesses which are foreign to the female nature, and which belong to ruder and less highly developed structures were practised by these gifted women" (p. 322).

It was thus that Eliza Gamble disposed of facts which, if she had faced them, might have thrown a flood of light into the dark corners of her mind. But, like Mrs. Farnham, she was a slave to the delusions which had been carefully fostered in her from her youth up. Woman was without passion and therefore subject to male brutality.

Ruth Herschberger had some nasty things to say about it in her book *Adam's Rib*. Women, she declared, were not the passive creatures man supposed them to be—no, not even in sexual relations. As a matter of fact, men preferred frigid to ardent women, as the latter gave too much trouble. Such views would hardly have been approved by the two Elizas. American men, however, must be thankful for small mercies. At least one American feminist (Jane Grant) stated in 1943 that she "would not abolish them" even if she could! (p. 684).

[1] E. B. Gamble, *The Evolution of Woman* (New York, 1894).

The ardour of sensual love was something low, bestial and to be condemned, a failing in which women should have no part. It was on
this basis that the American woman of leisure built her world. Little
did she realize the havoc she was creating in her own soul. For by
her attitude was she setting herself apart from life, giving to others
what she was denying to herself, and nourishing within her those
germs of hatred, malice, jealousy and revenge which were to transform her into the unhappy and frustrated creature of modern American life. Lacking maturity herself, she prevented her children from
becoming mature; and we shall see later how what foreign observers
call the "adolescence" of American men directly stems from the
maternal influence. Had the American feminists realized what was
wrong with American society they might have done something to
remedy a situation which was rapidly becoming worse. But they
were slaves to tradition and habits of thought which were handed on
from generation to generation. They failed to see that man's position
in the scheme of things rested upon those "unalterable necessities"
and "fundamental laws of human nature" that Lucy Aiken had
pointed out to them in 1810 in her *Epistles on Women*, when she
urged her fellow women, "instead of aspiring to be inferior men", to
be content with "becoming noble women" (pp. v, vi).[1]

Such advice, however, passed unheeded, and as the years went by,
hatred and scorn of men became more marked. Thomas Beer records
the story of a French governess, Suzanne Beret, who, writing to
her cousin in New York from Cleveland, where she was staying,
declared that the ladies with whom she came into contact loved
to talk adultery to each other, but never seemed to tell of any
amusing love affairs which they had actually experienced. She
found it difficult to accustom herself to the rude way girls treated
men much older than themselves; and the married women treated
their husbands and sons like bad servants, even when others were
present.[2]

Whatever may be said of the sex antagonism fostered by the
American feminists, it can hardly be denied that many of them were
able women. Certainly, as G. V. Seldes has pointed out in his *The
Stammering Century* (p. 279), the success of women reformers in the
United States is remarkable and is only to be understood by reference

---

[1] An editorial in the *New York Times*, entitled "Pants and the Woman",
was still trying to point this out on July 5, 1941. "The happiest societies", the
writer stated, "are those in which women are not afraid to be feminine and
men are not afraid to be masculine." W. Root, writing in 1949, declared that
women had been spared being geniuses, since this was a dangerous abnormality!
Cf. F. K. Frank, p. 279.   [2] T. Beer, p. 29.

to the history of female life in America.[1] For it was not only the
sphere of mental and educational advancement that the feminists
emphasized. They deplored the fashion of female "weakness",
roundly condemning the régime of lemons, vinegar and keeping out
of the sun to preserve a delicate pallor. "A robust development in a
girl is unfashionable," thundered Mrs. Ernestine Rose, a Polish lady,
at the Second National Women's Rights Convention in October 1851.
"A healthy, sound voice is vulgar, a ruddy glow on the cheek is
coarse." Even the sentimental novelists began to venture towards a
little realism, heavily veiled, it is true, and discreetly hidden between the lines. The tears wrung from the fair readers of Maria Jane
McIntosh's *Violet* (1856) were occasionally exchanged for a cardiac
flutter when perusing the erotic and suggestive thrills which were
so carefully sandwiched between layers of religious and conservative
sentiment.[2] Fanatics there were among the feminists, as might have
been expected, and the deadly seriousness of a few was noted by
foreign observers like Mlle Cheminat,[3] who compared the cold way
that they pursued their aims with the methods adopted by her own
compatriots. The famous Grimké sisters (Sarah and Angelina) were
typical of the kind of women of whom Mlle Cheminat was thinking.
Daughters of a slave-owning planter in Carolina, the Grimkés were
soon smitten with reforming zeal. Sarah became a Quaker and decided to discard worldly things, beginning with Scott's works,
which she had just acquired, and proceeding to give to her sister some
undies (those "superfluities of naughtiness") wherewith to stuff a
cushion.[4]

To the alleged personal disadvantages under which American
women suffered were soon added legal disabilities. Although "women's rights" had been discussed for many years and summarized
in a curious book by Mrs. A. J. Graves in 1843, it was much later
that the movement for the removal of legal hardships got into its
stride. Although the influence of Sir William Blackstone, the great
English jurist, was never so strong in the United States as in England, nevertheless his views on the so-called "subjection of women"
had their effect on legal practice and theory, and were followed,
partially at least, by Edward D. Mansfield in his much-quoted book
on the legal rights and duties of woman. Resistance to the common

---

[1] In 1854 that extraordinary woman Sarah Josepha Hale (1788–1879), the
editor of *Godey's Lady's Book*, published a biographical account of some two
thousand notable women, and included every American woman of note prior
to 1850. See S. J. Hale, *Woman's Record*, 2nd. ed. (New York, 1855).
[2] Cf. *St. Elmo* (New York, 1866).   [3] E. Cheminat, p. 6.
[4] See C. H. Birney's *The Grimké Sisters*; and cf. Sarah Grimké's *Letters on the
Equality of the Sexes*.

law theory on the relation between husband and wife was more strenuous in America than in England; and legislation tended to become more favourable towards the woman, although in England many of the more glaring disabilities were swept away by the passing of the Married Women's Property Act of 1882. But in 1860 women in the United States were labouring under very real grievances which were noted by such eminent foreign critics as Auguste Carlier, who observed with some interest the freedom of young women in America before marriage compared with the shocking lack of it afterwards.[1]

Among the exponents of women's rights and supporters of women's emancipation were some who were far more militant and outspoken than women of the stamp of the Grimké sisters. Such, for example, were the fabulous Claflin sisters, whose exploits as the bewitching brokers of New York were equalled only by their pretensions to supernormal powers and medical knowledge. The pages of *Woodhull and Claflin's Weekly* rang with startling discussions of virtue and vice, ignorance and knowledge. Mrs. Grundy was defied to do her worst; woman's duty was to satisfy herself as to the ideals of right, propriety and purity.[2] Indeed, even the crime of seduction was no longer to be a monopoly of the male sex. Woman, declared Tennessee Claflin, was a "magazine of enticement and influence and power" over the conduct of the other sex. The condition into which society has thrust her has compelled her "to make a profession of seduction". She is forced by circumstances to entice, seduce and entrap men for her own ends. Whether such conduct be right or wrong Miss Claflin did not profess to argue. But the fact remained that the great pursuit of many women was the seduction of men.

The effects of this seductive offensive on the part of women were not lost upon Miss Claflin, but she denied that men had any justification for succumbing to it. Just as Margaret Fuller had praised the efficacy of cold baths, so did Tennessee Claflin proclaim the virtues of work and athletic sports, which "will always subdue sensual desire". As to the women themselves, they were so cooped up, petted and spoiled that, in a word, they ceased to be women; and they had been so denaturalized that "not one in four" had any healthy amativeness. Not all the women of the period, however, could be said to have failed in this respect. The spirit of Bohemianism was beginning to stir long before the 1870s, when Paris became the Mecca of every young person who wished to appear advanced, artistic and free loving.

[1] See A. Carlier, pp. 64, 99.   [2] *Op. cit.*, Dec. 23, 1871.

From the 1830s to about 1870 the Queen of New York Bohemian society was Ada Clare (Jane McElheney (1836–74)), who contributed to the pages of various American magazines. In Charlie Pfaff's famous restaurant, north of Bleeker Street on Broadway, the élite of the artistic world would gather to talk art and dramatics and discuss the latest triumphs of Ada Clare's intimate friend, Louis M. Gottschalk. It is true that, on a higher level, where sex was pushed into the background as far as possible, some of the more advanced women worked with the transcendentalists in their endeavour to forget the spirit of the country in which they were living. Elizabeth Peabody and the queenly Margaret Fuller joined with Emerson and Bronson Alcott in proclaiming the new gospel in the pages of *The Dial*, and H. D. Thoreau played at rural seclusion and conversation with the birds. But whatever may be said of the Transcendental Club and its followers, one thing was clear. Although many possessed both optimism and the spirit of individual initiative, they seemed to sense what was happening in the United States, and what they sensed they did not like. The younger people especially, fired with a mystic and missionary zeal, did their best to escape the prevailing spirit of commercialism and wandered hand in hand through the woods seeking peace and refreshment in youthful dreams. But just as those who, while accepting the call of the flesh, failed to combine its delights with the things of the spirit, so the transcendentalists failed to find the peace they craved because they were still enmeshed in the system of religious thought that they had learnt at their mother's knees. The transcendental philosophy of Concord was, in a sense, a kind of moral justification for the essence of American thought. Opposition to authority and the belief in individual self-reliance were linked in their minds with the Divine source; and the unity of all creation with God was the basis of that spirit of optimism and nervous distrust of the kind of sceptical approach to life favoured by such giants of common sense as Montaigne. To Emerson and his followers belief was "natural": to them the world seemed saturated with deity and law; and although at times the glass was dark, a point of light was always discernible which indicated the irresistible stream of truth and goodness. From this point of view, the transcendentalists at Concord remained tied to the beliefs and traditions of their infancy, although these simple notions were dressed afresh and presented as philosophical profundities.

To women especially these ideas were hardly likely to appeal for very long. The ferment in the outside world was too pervasive, even if the strident notes of the Claflin propaganda were at times too shrill. Later discussions of the dangers of the matrimonial bonds were more outspoken than was generally approved even in broad-minded circles, and among those, for example, who read E. H. Heywood's *Cupid's Yokes* (1880) with interest and some distaste. Thus, although the diatribes of the Claflins' paper must have pained and shocked many of its readers, American women outside the equal rights movements lived much as before, although there were already signs of a growing consciousness of change among the younger women. They were paying more attention to their personal appearance, and books of advice on such subjects as make-up, the use of soaps, baths, dyes and the problem of banting (or slimming) were beginning to appear in increasing numbers.[1]

Foreign visitors were less critical than they had been earlier in the century, and some of them were quite enthusiastic over their experiences. Harold Brydges was delighted with the grave learning of the Boston girl who, when dancing, would ask her partner his opinion of the real basis of Schopenhauer's ethics (p. 35). Indeed, he wondered sometimes if American men, engrossed as they were in business pursuits, sufficiently appreciated the "glorious girls of the Republic". Similarly L. P. Blouet, writing under the name of Max O'Rell, was so pleased and charmed with the American woman of the 1890s that he actually stated that, were he to live again, he would like to be born one of them,[2] an opinion hardly shared by Emile Barbier, who found them ignorant and pretentious, incarnations of idleness, and when married, living a life in which a veritable abyss separated them from their husbands.[3]

The whole controversy on equal rights troubled some of the more reflective writers, such as A. Mathews, who, writing as P. Siegvolk, discussed the differences between men and women and what he called the misleading talk about equality generally.[4] But these more moderate views were not regarded with favour or patience. Women were on the warpath, and little now would stop them. Some of the more advanced, like Anna Bowman Dodd, actually pictured a state of society where the family declined and the interest of men in their wives gradually faded away altogether. American women would have entered every sphere of life, and the foreign policy of the Republic would be more easily handled, since foreign statesmen would concede much rather than attempt to negotiate with the

---

[1] See for example Mrs. E. D. Powers' *The Ugly-Girl Papers, or Hints for the Toilet* (New York, 1874).
[2] M. O'Rell, *A Frenchman in America*, p. 103. In his *Rambles in Womanland* (1903) he calls the American woman "an altogether" (p. 75).
[3] E. Barbier, pp. 126, 128, 130.   [4] P. Siegvolk, pp. 74 ff.

female diplomatists of the United States. Again, in 1894 a society for the education and reform of husbands was reported in New York. Formed by Mrs. Jeanette Van Nest, its aims were to reform men either by education or by restraint. Husbands must be dominated by their wives, the members of the society boomed. If they resisted they must be hypnotized or even, if necessary, brought to heel through the use of "medication".[1]

It was perhaps of women like these that Marie Dugard was thinking when she spoke of the great independence of American women in 1896, and of the words in which a Latin might sum them up—"ce ne sont pas des femmes"—but, as she added, ideas and customs differ in different countries and criticisms would be merely puerile.[2] The fact was that foreigners found the American woman an enigma, essentially different from her sister in other countries, as the Italian writer, Dario Papa, put it,[3] and sometimes the behaviour of the younger women puzzled and shocked certain of the visitors from abroad, although it could not be maintained that such conduct was in any way typical or even common. Thus the Marquise de San Carlos de Pédroso, writing in 1890, divided up the American women she observed into the serious and the superficial types. General ignorance was so astonishing, she declared, that it would take "des centaines d'années" in order to dissipate it. But the greatest jolt she experienced was the conduct of some of the young girls, who, outwardly modest and restrained, would give exhibitions before their friends and fellow-boarders of both sexes in which they would disrobe and pose as living statuary.[4] It is possible that these private exhibitions (which, when I lived in New York, had degenerated into "strip poker" parties) were derived from the public displays in the 1840s when Dr. Collyer's *tableaux vivants* caused a good deal of sensation, even though it is probable that those taking part in them were clothed in flesh-coloured tights. It was somewhat later that the burlesque strip-tease shows began to be popular under the able

---

[1] See "Our Sisters across the Sea" (*The Young Woman*, July 1894, vol. ii, p. 360). This passage always reminds me of the opinion of that eminent lady journalist, Jane Grey Swisshelm (1815–84), who, in her *Letters to Country Girls* —a guide to real womanly excellence, according to Mrs. Hale—declared that masculine superiority was a "fever which converted so many men into ruffians". However, she had her cure. What was required was "one week of vigorous treatment", but, she added, it was hard to get the "proper nurses and assistants" (p. 75).

[2] M. Dugard, p. 174. She would probably not have agreed with that veteran feminist Elizabeth Cady Stanton, who, in her remarkable book *The Woman's Bible* (New York, 1895), dealt with the story of our ancestors in the Garden of Eden, and came to the conclusion that, compared with Adam, Eve "appears to great advantage through the entire drama" (p. 25).

[3] D. Papa, p. 12.   [4] San Carlos de Pédroso, pp. 49, 176, 69.

management of the Minsky Brothers. We shall have something to say about this native American art, as it is called, for it is an important feature of the American scene and throws a good deal of light on the effect of sexual traditions and more upon the population. Here it will be sufficient to point out that, even before the rise of the moving-picture industry and the rigid control of prostitution in the interests of the millionaire pimps, these shows were attracting large audiences, especially among those of the foreign-born, whose needs could hardly be even partially satisfied in any other way.

One result of the agitation among advanced American women for so-called "equal rights" was the increased emphasis put upon the necessity for better education. Although in New England the standard of female education was higher than elsewhere, the fact had to be faced that in other parts of the United States it was low, and the chances of higher education somewhat remote. In the ordinary public elementary schools co-education (which from 1833 was beginning to be more and more favoured) was generally the rule, the city schools following the lead given by those in rural areas, where the village children were all educated together. Some of the High Schools, however, were not mixed, the girls being educated separately in institutions which were often founded upon those which had been intended for the boys.

The advantages and disadvantages of co-education have been argued for so long and with so much heat that they need not be recapitulated here. The general and more official view in the United States was that it was more natural and impartial, conferring as it did equal benefits upon both sexes; that through it economy was achieved and duplication of staff avoided; and finally that it had proved beneficial to the minds, morals and habits of the public generally. When it came to the colleges and universities, however, the opposition to co-education was more vocal. It was true that Blount College in Tennessee had been the first to admit women students, and that others, like the University of Michigan, had followed suit as the years went by. But there was a decided tendency to agree to differ, with the result that the great women's colleges were to play an important part in female higher education. Vassar College had been founded in 1861, the objectionable word "female" being later removed from its title, owing perhaps to the campaign against it which was being waged from 1855 onwards by Mrs. Sarah Hale. Smith and Wellesley Colleges were opened in 1875, while Bryn Mawr was only ready for students in 1885. Apart from these colleges, where women attended for the purpose of obtaining a higher

education than could be obtained in the public and smaller girls'
schools, the nineteenth century saw the opening of special schools for
the daughters of the more wealthy classes, and it was in these institutions that the children of society ladies received their training in the
principles of right thinking, poise and general deportment. It is true
that an increasing number of the girls from such schools later went to
college, but the majority did not do so and at once entered the world
of sophistication and fashion in which their mothers moved.

Moreover, what confronts us here is again the curious contradictions that everywhere seem present in the American way of life. The
education at these expensive and select establishments was simple
and direct and stressed the virtues of honesty and simplicity.
Farmington (established 1843) is famous for its inculcation of the
mystic sense of community spirit. At Dobbs Ferry (founded in 1877),
under the majestic supervision of Miss Lily Masters, the girls grew
up under a Puritan tradition handed on in the grand manner, and
still discussed religion seriously and with fervour. On the other
hand, at Brearley (founded 1883), which with Miss Chapin's and
Spence (1892) led smart female education in New York, a good
general education was considered all-sufficient for facing the world
outside, whereas at the two rival establishments, character and
moral rectitude were more openly stressed. The problem of the
"boy-friend", or beau, was always one which haunted the minds of
the authorities at these institutions. Customs differed, as might have
been expected, but the sharpest supervision was exercised, and
when young men were admitted, their activities were closely watched
and unseemly incidents thereby prevented. Indeed, at Miss Hall's
(1898), the boys, when attending the yearly dance, were finally sent
home, while, so report had it, the girls were safely drawn up in a solid
bunch in the middle of the dance-room floor.

Such were the smart schools where the daughters of the affluent
received their training and preparation for life in the nineteenth
century. Filled with romantic illusions and knowing practically
nothing of the realities beyond the narrow circle in which they moved,
they entered a world in which, had they had the eyes to see, they
would have observed that many of the principles which they had
been taught to revere were regarded with an amused, if not cynical
contempt. Some of them must soon have discovered that the sacred
American "Way of Life" was different from the model that had been
presented to them. They saw, for instance, the exaggerated sentimentality about children shown by those who wanted to sell some
new baby-powder or diaper, while at the same time they found that

children of the poor were forced to labour in mines, quarries and canning factories for long hours at starvation wages. They heard the continual pratings about the necessity for law and order, yet it was not difficult to see that what was important was the forms, and not the rule of law. It was the age of the "fixer" and the "shyster". The gangster movement was developing, in which "mobs" were to control whole districts for purposes of gain and preserve their dominion through collusion with the police, the municipal and the legal authorities. Men like Howe and Hummel were heroes to those in trouble. Through the usual methods of fixing, blackmail, sentimental clowning and downright crime these shyster lawyers managed to clear hundreds of guilty persons accused of anything up to murder. It was all part of the "game". It was a well-understood part of the "Way of Life", just as the flagrant evasions of the prohibition laws were paralleled by the equally flagrant black marketeering in 1946. As one American magazine put it, "Who cared about the black market? Not the U.S. people." Everywhere deals were being arranged, sales fixed, bets taken instead of additions to the selling price. It was not that the public were victims. They connived and assisted, for many of them were active black marketeers on their own, though in a much smaller way than the great operators and black-market czars. Law and police procedure in the United States is hardly that which the propagandists for Americanism would have us believe; such salesmen of North American culture are, as one foreign critic put it, either wilfully blind or deliberately crooked.[1]

Such was the world in which the American daughters of leisured parents had to play their parts. Working women were constrained to live a very different life. But almost up to the end of the nineteenth century there was little except the public-school education which served to standardize the general principles of Americanism and the part that women were supposed to play in upholding it. The sanctity of the American home and the sacred character of the American family which was supposed to be the economic, spiritual and moral unit of the nation were qualities which, however useful they were in the social mythology of the United States, were likely to be questioned by reference to the facts. In 1867 divorces numbered some 10,000: in 1929 they numbered more than 200,000. In other words, the rate of divorce increase advanced, as Cahen points out, about five times as fast as the proportion of the married people over a period of sixty-three years.[2]

If we consider the number of cases of desertion, separation and

[1] W. T. Colyer, p. 35.   [2] A. Cahen, p. 21.

marital lack of adjustment which, for one reason or another, did not end in legal divorce, it will be seen that the American woman would hardly be considered highly competent in the one sphere in which she should have been very successful. The reasons for her lack of success and the part played by the American husband in this gloomy state of affairs are many and highly complex. They cannot be dealt with here, and the various theories propounded can be examined in any of the numerous volumes which pour annually from the American publishing houses. Some writers frankly give up the problem, declaring that the increase of divorce must be reckoned simply as one of the costs inherent in what they call "progress". They do not interpret it as a symptom of social disease, for only a few realise that it is intimately associated with changes proceeding in the sexual, social and economic spheres, and to question the desirability of these changes is to question the "American Way", a heresy of which few care to be guilty.

Although the chaos in the sexual life of the United States and its influence on divorce were not so great in the nineteenth century as they were in the twentieth century, there were already signs that the more leisured women were beginning to dominate the scene in ways which would have been hardly possible in the early days. For in the middle of the century the increasing wealth of the captains of finance and industry was beginning to affect the lives of the women who surrounded them. Although the men were too busy making money to regard women as anything more than a passing convenience, the money had to be spent somehow, and the gilded age of florid elegance and ostentatious display slowly grew to maturity. Enormous mansions were erected and estates developed in which lived not only the millionaire and his lady, but also an immense staff of hired help, sometimes numbering over a thousand. The house was stuffed from floor to ceiling with expensive furniture, statuary, pictures and gewgaws imported from all over the world. Here the American woman lived in a world of splendour and suspicion, of rivalry and intrigues. Although Mr. Astor was not often visible, Mrs. Astor, the Queen of the Four Hundred, was in her element, and her parties created sensation after sensation. It was Mrs. Astor who was responsible for the rise of that amazing character Harry Symes Lehr. This man who, in some respects, can be compared with Samuel McAllister as an arbiter of taste and fashion, was, like so many American men, psychologically attached to his mother, and in addition was almost certainly homosexually inclined. He was the kind of person who, to preserve his complexion, wore sun-bonnets when bathing; but in spite of his eccentricities he was sought after everywhere, and was kept by society women, who even managed to get travelling passes for him through the influence of the wives of the railroad tycoons. Although Lehr really disliked women, he used them for his social ambitions, and the story of his marriage to the wealthy Elizabeth Drexel is one of the most extraordinary accounts of an episode in American society ever written.[1] Although Mrs. Astor gradually gained supremacy of the world of fashion, she was not without her rivals, Mamie Fish's "circus" being almost equally famous, and Mrs. Vanderbilt also had a large and distinguished following. When her great house in Fifth Avenue was demolished in 1945, there was talk of a scramble for her bathroom, which, it was said, was going to be taken to Hollywood as a show-piece. But the chance to acquire it was never attained, for when she moved out she took her bathroom with her, a fact not easy to understand unless we realize the enormous importance that plumbing has to many an American, and the great interest that the excretory functions arouse in American life.

We can well imagine the unsatisfied, empty lives of these leaders of American society. Passing from sensation to sensation, they rarely rested; filled with hate and jealousy, their lives were spent in a round of social pleasures and amusements. Yet it is but rarely that we can penetrate behind the mask and see what is going on there. New excitements were eternally sought; and even a rape would not have come amiss now and then. At Caroline Astor's wedding in 1884 General U. S. Grant was present. Although over sixty he still cut a fine figure, and one lady was charmed by him, so much so that she actually inserted a note in her diary to the effect that it would be an ecstasy to be ravished by so distinguished a figure! [2]

It was not every society woman who was able to afford the ostentatious display of the wives of the captains of finance and industry. Less wealthy women had to relieve their boredom in other ways, of which club life and religion were probably the most important. The pioneer of the great American Women's Clubs was the Sorosis, which was organized in 1868 by Mrs. J. C. Croly. Development was rapid, for club life not only formed a diversion for bored women yearning to gossip, but also was a means of passing time once the children were grown-up and had left home. In 1890 the General Federation of Women's Clubs was founded; and at the time of writing the overall membership is said to be about eleven millions.

---

[1] See E. W. Decies, *King Lehr and the Gilded Age.*
[2] See A. Tully (p. 13), to whom I am indebted for some of the information outlined above.

While the wives and daughters of the rich were enjoying the excitements of the gilded age, the poorer people were living as they always had done, although the pace was perhaps quicker than in other countries. America is so vast a land that it is a mistake to suppose that what occurs in one part of the country is in any way typical of the country as a whole. The women of New York society were as different from the mill-girls in the rising factories as the Victorian ladies of Malvern were from the factory workers of Manchester or Birmingham. Moreover, the great influx of foreign workers drawn from the immigrant aliens, who crowded in during 1881-4, contributed to the general confusion of language, religion and custom, and it was generally only the second generation which strove for rapid assimilation. These people had come to the United States in the hope of advancement and success for themselves and their children, and it was natural that they should easily be swayed by the ideas and methods through which success in America could be achieved. The men were quickly absorbed into the skilled and unskilled trades, while the women also entered industry or, if married, kept house for their working husbands. On the farms also, where the tempo was slower, life went on as it had always done in rural areas, although the coming of the agricultural machine made some of American farming more mechanized than in other parts of the world.

Up to 1890 there was little except the school to influence the minds of the younger women and direct them into standardized channels of thought and aspirations. Foreign influence was small except in the upper classes, and even there the culture of France was mainly thought of in relation to fashion, and so there arose the mistaken ideas of the levity and insincerity of the French people which are so prevalent in the United States. But just as the wealthy women enjoyed the reality of riches and adventure, so did the poorer women enjoy them in phantasy. The Queen of the pash novelists was Laura Jean Libbey, who died in 1924.[1] In her novels and articles she poured out the sentimental gush which fascinated its readers and plunged

___

[1] Among the best of Laura Libbey's books are *A Fatal Wooing*; *The Alphabet of Love*; *We Parted at the Altar*; *Willful Gaynell, or the little beauty of the Passaic Mills*; and *Wooden Wives*. She was also a fairly regular contributor to *The New York and Paris Young Ladies' Fashion Bazar*, where she gave advice to those seeking matrimony. "The kind of man who makes home happy," she wrote in October 1891, is the man who loves his wife so well that "he is ever solicitous for her own comfort; who thinks of her welfare before he does his own; who has a love for his mother, his sisters, and the home of his boyhood, and who believes that the church is the stepping stone to God's heart". She also wrote sentimental songs, some of which, like *Lovers Once but Strangers Now*, were very popular, bringing tears to the eyes of him who had once permitted his sweetheart "to drift past him on life's ocean", as a contemporary blurb put it.

H

them into a world of success and happiness in which time was lost, and all that remained was a feeling of expectant longing to learn how the heroine finally succeeded in capturing the elusive millionaire. Book after book poured from the press. Her fifth novel, *He Loved, but was Lured Away*, is typical. It is the tale of Hubert von Gersdorf, Eugène and the fair Isabel. Who could resist the noble Hubert, the smoke of whose cigar "curled like a frame about him from the highly scented Havana which he held daintily poised between the thumb and forefinger of his white, aristocratic hand, on which a diamond of unusual size glowed like a star of flame"? With girls working in factory and office such fiction was as popular as *The Girls' Crystal* and the many similar magazines and serials are with English girls today.

Other methods of escape were, however, open to women who wished to forget, if only for a short time, the drab everyday existence to which many seemed inexorably doomed. The escape into the florid fiction of wealth and sentiment was, at least, a dream which concerned this world; the escape into the illusions offered by religion was one which concerned the next. Ever since the days of the Puritan experiment, religion had played its part in moulding American life. The constant appeals to ethical and moral justification for political acts were but one example of the influence religious ideas and conceptions has on the average American of ordinary intelligence. The absence of any ecclesiastical establishment in the United States tended toward the emergence of many experiments in religion, and thus it can be said that America has more denominations than any other country. Apart from the great religious blocs like the Roman Catholics, the Baptists and the Methodists, there are many lesser bodies and literally scores of "crank" religions and freak beliefs which are largely concentrated in Southern California, where Los Angeles breeds the slickest collection of fakers, quacks and half-baked spoofers to be found anywhere on earth.

In the early years of the nineteenth century it is noteworthy that many of the religious and perfectionist bodies tended to stress the sexual element, and thereby gained converts who might otherwise have stayed away. Such leaders as Tertius Strong and Simon Lovett (to say nothing of John H. Noyes and his Oneida Community) brought women into the field partly through the emphasis on "free" love, and the possibility of enjoying sexual relations without suffering that sense of guilt which is never far from the consciousness of so many Americans. Indeed, I suspect that the persecution suffered by the Mormons, and above all the detestation which so many women professed to have for them, were due to a partly conscious, partly unconscious, jealousy. For in the case of plural marriage not only was polygamy sanctioned as right and moral, but many Mormon wives indicated their satisfaction with the arrangement, a state of affairs not to be tolerated by those who, sex-starved themselves, knew what was right and proper and whose duty it was to chase Satan out of the land. Similarly in the case of the Oneida Community, in which the peculiar sexual ideas of Noyes were carried out by his faithful followers, the fascination that such experiments always have for unsatisfied women was enjoyed, and the feelings of uneasiness were masked by the association of semi-religious ideas with the cruder aspect of physical pleasures.[1]

A later exponent of the peculiar ideas of Noyes and of Chavannes was Miss Ida C. Craddock, a rather pitiful figure, who was pursued to her death by Anthony Comstock. She was a mild-mannered teacher who was interested in the question of sexual education, and was not in the least frightened of the facts of life and generation. She published her ideas on these subjects in such books as *The Wedding Night* and *Right Marital Living*, in the second of which she detailed the strange methods of coitus she championed. Miss Craddock's ideas do not seem to have been fully understood even by herself, for some of her recommendations are very peculiar and must have caused sore bewilderment to the unfortunate readers who tried to follow her instructions. It need hardly be said that the husbands were the ones who had to learn such odd practices.

Miss Craddock's own marital experiences seem to have been limited to the embraces of an angel to whom she apparently believed she was married, yet she was not without some originality in her writings, for she contributed an article on the *Danse du Ventre* to the *New York World* in 1893 which was subsequently re-issued, enlarged and revised in 1897.

As has been pointed out above, women formed a solid basis upon which these cranks built their esoteric cults. The more stable of the female population in the sophisticated urban areas were content, for the most part, with what the Roman Catholics, the Episcopalians or the various Protestant bodies had to offer. But the more dissatisfied, disgruntled and frustrated a woman is the more she will seek relief from her condition, and, as Mabie has pointed out in

---

[1] Cf. J. H. Noyes, *Male Continence* (Oneida, 1872). The practice of *coitus reservatus* is interesting if viewed in the light of female acceptance of a position in which, at least at first sight, she appears to gain, whereas from another angle it is the man who might be supposed to be the principal gainer from the transaction. For the views of an 1857 "muckraker" see Lenderman's *Adventures*, etc. For Chavannes' see his *Vital Force*, etc.

American Ideals, the emotional and sentimental American is ripe for religious experience, or perhaps we ought to call it exploitation.[1] For although the American business man and the American woman executive may appear to be hard-boiled, shrewd and not easily taken in, they are often credulous to almost an abnormal degree when it is a question of religion or of the doctrines of some new faith. Fraud flourishes in the United States as nowhere else for precisely this reason. The fear that so many Americans have of being suckers is partly based upon a realization of the credulity which so easily leads them astray. It is true that the motive behind the credulity is often the desire to get something for nothing or for very little; but it is not always financial advantage that is being sought, and rarely so when it is a question of religion or a new cult. Rather is it in the case of women a desire to become themselves leaders, and thus increase their self-importance, or simply a desire to escape into a world of mystic hocus-pocus, be on friendly terms with Great White Brotherhoods, and generally forget that they are citizens of the greatest materialistic civilization on earth.

Thus an important aspect of religious organizations in the United States is the part that women play in their foundation and management. Moreover, the history of such women often presents similarities which should not be overlooked. For instance, the history of Katherine Tingley, the Purple Mother of Point Loma, can be profitably compared with that of the amazing woman Mary Baker Eddy. Both lived lives of comparative obscurity during their early years; both had three husbands, and both formed their organizations during the later years of the nineteenth century. Although Mrs. Tingley's society was more exotic and colourful than that of Christian Science, it also had its financial side, and both movements succeeded in making plenty of money for those who controlled them. But whereas Christian Science offered little scope for serious competition, the Point Loma Theosophical Community was a centre from which radiated different schools of "New Thought", some clearly run by lunatics and cranks of various kinds, although the majority of these, as for example Krotona, did not begin to function till the twentieth century. What is important to understand is the fact that these bizarre movements and cults attracted women by the thousand and that the sexual element was never very far off. The metaphysical obstetrics of Christian Science, with the emphasis on chastity and virginity, coupled as it was with the theory of malicious animal

---

[1] H. W. Mabie, pp. 327 ff. Cf. Sinclair Lewis's *Elmer Gantry* for a brilliant portrayal of the American revivalist in action.

magnetism and action at a distance, indicated a point of view which, to be attractive to women, could appeal only to those already well advanced on the road to neurosis.

If we look at all closely at the early history of the founder of Christian Science it can hardly be denied that Mary Baker Eddy was herself neurotic. Her hysterical attacks were well known and her comfort at being rocked like a baby during the seizures led, so it was said, to a contraption like a cradle being rigged up for the express purpose of giving her the relief she craved.[1] Sex to Mrs. Eddy was not a thing to be encouraged. Even lawful cohabitation was hardly decent, and if only women could be prevailed upon to live according to the precepts of Christian Science, the propagation of the species could be carried on without the peculiar part that even Mrs. Eliza Farnham had permitted men to exercise. It must have been a severe shock to Mrs. Eddy to find her principles carried out literally when Mrs. Josephine Curtis Woodbury presented the world with a bouncing baby which had grown within her without any external help of any kind. How far Mrs. Woodbury herself was deceived we do not know. But Mrs. Eddy was *not* amused, and the incident created a favourable opportunity to get rid of a possible rival, for Mrs. Eddy could not brook competition, whether it came from virgin mothers like Mrs. Woodbury or from fanatical "daughters" like Mrs. Augusta Stetson, whose views on the dreadful things that are enacted in the marriage state were that they were of the earth and had no place in the life of the enlightened disciple.

Although Christian Science has had adherents in many countries, it could, I think, have been born only in the United States. The combination of acute business acumen with that vague and woolly spirituality that we find in *Science and Health,* together with the neurotic fear of sex and pathetic denials of pain, sickness and death —these and many other features could have arisen only in a culture already showing signs of social and psychological disorder. The figures of Mrs. Eddy, Mrs. Woodbury and Mrs. Stetson were but the better and more successful types of other dissatisfied and energetic

[1] The Americans' partiality for the rocking-chair was, I used to suspect, due to the fact that its motion reminded them of the cradle whither they wished to return, and thus avoid responsibility. Mrs. M. E. J. F. Houston remarked in 1850 how she used to observe young American women in rocking chairs "*doing* nothing, and apparently *thinking* little" (vol. i, p. 70), while F. Lundberg and M. F. Farnham regard the swaying automobile as the rocking-chair's modern successor, "catering for the yearnings of the cradle" (p. 330). In Eliza Leslie's valuable book on etiquette, *The Behaviour Book,* which was published in 1853, rocking in a rocking-chair was said to be discontinued "by genteel people", except when alone, and she added that "rocking is only fit for a nurse putting a baby to sleep".

women who became leaders of cults, famous mediums surrounded by circles of adoring sitters or gifted gospellers and revivalists. The husbands of these ladies were forgotten, for, as the century advanced, the American man was becoming more and more a figure apart, living a separate life and engrossed in pursuits where he earnestly hoped the energy and persistency of women would not impel them to follow him. It is unfortunate that people like Mr. Woodbury and Mr. Stetson did not keep intimate diaries. They would have been amusing reading, but it seems that Mr. Stetson was too busy building ships to worry about the astonishing aberrations of his remarkable wife. After all, she was an American woman, and he was probably proud of her.

It is possible, I think, that one reason why there are so many organizations and cults run by women in the United States is that, in the past, the part that women were allowed to play in religious societies was not prominent enough to satisfy the more ambitious among them. Although the scope offered was wider than in Europe, it was still not wide enough, for the American woman, even in the nineteenth century, was dreaming not of subservience, but of dominance, not of servant, but of master. The American Christian has, generally speaking, little knowledge or appreciation of forms and ceremonies, doctrines and dogmas. He is more interested in practical good works and good fellowship, and much of the religious controversies which convulsed nineteenth-century ecclesiastical life would have little interest and meaning for him. Indeed, the rather complacent and mildly optimistic atmosphere of Protestant American religious bodies, untinged by either violent religious controversy or acute sense of urgency in times of crisis, has led more restless reformers like Niebuhr to look back to earlier conceptions of original sin. But even here the ancient fervour is lacking and the presentation is mildly philosophical rather than a clarion call to action based on a sense of sin and inadequacy before God.

It was natural that the American woman who had been stirred by the fight for equality and even for superiority was not inclined to remain a mere cipher in the established religious bodies apart from the Roman Catholic Church. Scepticism of a muddled kind was often the point from which the road to a new cult began. Many women tried one cult after another and found them wanting, and finally some of the more energetic and resourceful women became leaders of their own organizations. The weaker and less pushing were often content to remain adoring worshippers before their favourite "Mother", or sometimes willing participants in male-run societies in which religion was deeply tinged with overt sexual manifestations which, partially at least, assuaged the longing of these unloved women for satisfaction and the feeling of being wanted.

Almost up to the end of the nineteenth century the ideals of the United States were passed on through the medium of the schools, colleges, universities and by reading books which were either bought, borrowed or read in the public libraries. There was no single medium through which ordinary folk gained an insight into what America stood for and which was able to present a kind of standardized picture on which the lives of the common citizen might be modelled. But in April 1896 occurred an epoch-making event, for in that month were shown moving pictures (the Vitascope) at Koster and Bials' Music Hall at 34th Street and Herald Square, New York City. The modern cinema had been born and was to prove for some years not only the greatest single means of mass education, culture and enlightenment, but also the most effective means ever devised of lowering the public taste and creating romantic illusions and suggestive thrills, while at the same time standardizing a whole series of false values and inane conventions.

At first the moving picture was hardly considered as a serious form of entertainment, let alone as an art. At music halls the "bioscope" used to be shown at the end of a programme when patrons of the theatre were putting on their hats and coats preparatory to going home. When shown apart from other variety numbers, the moving pictures were usually exhibited in small, ill-ventilated and badly lighted halls; and the scenes portrayed were sometimes travel and more often slapstick comedies and adventures in which hairbreadth escapes played a prominent part. Curiously enough, the enormous commercial possibilities of the moving picture were slow of realization. It is true that the first programme presented in New York contained an item entitled *Satanic Gambols*, but that was merely a title devised to draw the custom of the curious. The idea that the moving picture might create a new world of phantasy at a price that even the poor might well afford and be glad to pay was one that only slowly dawned upon those who were later to build a mighty empire with a base of celluloid. Indeed, it was not until the second decade of the twentieth century that the "movies" came into their own. And once they had arrived, nothing could have controlled them except drastic legal action on a wide scale.

As might have been expected, the United States provided a fertile soil for the growth of the moving-picture industry. For here was a vast, heterogeneous population, many of whom lived in poor surroundings but could pay a few cents to be transported to a world of wealth and luxury in which, for a few hours at least, they could forget their own misery and deprivations. Moreover, it was a country where the belief in the almost sacred character of private enterprise made such an invention, once its possibilities had been envisaged, a money-maker on a vast scale. Language was no hindrance to the silent film. The language of the heart was the same everywhere; and thus, through appealing to sentimentality, sensuality and plain crude lust, an instant success was a certainty. For women, above all, the cinema was to prove a godsend. Here, away from household drudgery, they were soon to dream of themselves in luxurious settings where they were wooed and won by beautiful, strong young men who gave them all for which they craved. And while they were being amused, stimulated and sensually aroused they were to learn new standards of conduct and behaviour, which were to lead to a gradual suppression of individual taste and mode of living and to a kind of established code which was accepted by millions of adolescents and even older people. Thus at the turn of the century there began a new and most potent influence over feminine life. In a few years' time fan clubs were to start and millions of girls were to turn their longing eyes to Hollywood, where not only was there the possibility of fame and fortune, but the chance of seeing the dream men of the screen. Was not one of the phantasies of the future American girl to be the undisputed ruler of a vast harem from which she only had to call to see emerging one of the film stars ready and willing to submit to her imperious demands? [1]

It was in an atmosphere of uneasiness, anticipation and hope, tinged with a growing sense of frustration and disappointment, that the American woman faced the coming century. She had gained much in the preceding fifty years, but she had not gained any serenity of spirit. Increase of leisure, due to the rapid development of me-chanical devices for use in the home, had not resulted in any deep-seated additions to her cultural life, although in many cases she did her best to widen her outlook and enlarge the horizon of her interests. But the twentieth century was to bring a series of shattering events to influence the whole framework of American civilization. The stage had been set for a drama of which the ending is not yet in sight. It merely remains for us to ring up the curtain.

[1] Cf. L. Pruette, p. 161.

IV

THE TWENTIETH CENTURY

(1) *Economic and social changes*

WITH the coming of the twentieth century dawned a new era of startling and far-reaching changes in American life. Although transition has always been a marked feature of the American scene, the first half of the new century contained so much that was entirely new and fundamentally important that the transition was rather in the nature of a series of upheavals than of orderly steps along a prearranged course. For example, the increase in population was spectacular. In 1880 the population of New York City was barely 2,000,000: by 1950 it had risen to over 7,892,000. For the same years Chicago had just over 500,000 as opposed to nearly 3,621,000, and Los Angeles 11,000 as opposed to 1,970,000. Immigration reached high peaks in 1907 and 1914 and the resulting flood of new labour was one of the factors responsible for the rising tide of industrial activity, especially in the production of coal and manufactured goods, which began to oust agriculture as primal industries. The means of transport also were rapidly increasing. In 1910 there were not half a million licensed automobiles: by 1952 there were over fifty-three million.

Women began to play an increasing part in industry, commerce and politics. In 1900 there were over 5,000,000 engaged in industry (or 19 per cent. of women in the population), of whom 769,000 were married (5·6 per cent.): in 1913 there were over 2,500,000 (22 per cent.), of whom over 3,000,000 were married (11·7 per cent.), while in 1952 some 18,000,000 were gainfully employed. The increase in the number of professional women was, moreover, noticeable from the beginning of the century, as was also the steady decline among those engaged in domestic and personal services. In politics women were beginning to play a greater part. It is true that in state and local elections women began to vote in 1890, but with the adoption of the Nineteenth Amendment to the Federal Constitution in 1919 the extension of woman's suffrage was achieved, and the patient work of such pioneers as Alice Paul, Carrie C. Catt, Lucy Larcon and Susan B. Anthony was at last brought to fruition.

With the immense industrial expansion came new methods of

production with important effects upon the consumer. The money spent on advertising rose to dizzy heights; and by 1929 it was estimated that the amount had reached the remarkable figure of $15 per head. Along with the fevered attempts to promote the sale of goods produced by private enterprise came the increase of misleading and exaggerated claims, just as in the production of prepared foods and other goods adulteration and even the use of poisonous substances was far from unknown. In spite of the shrill cries of the producers, Congress was forced to take action to protect the consumer from the effects of uncontrolled business, and gradually, through the operation of such salutary measures as the Pure Food and Drug Act (1906) and the Wheeler-Lea Act (1938), the more glaring cases of adulteration were curbed and fraudulent advertising curtailed. In this way the American housewife was, to a small extent, protected from the activities of those whose sole interest was production for profit with little regard for the effects that the goods offered might have upon the health and happiness of the community where they circulated.

The rise in industrial production and the rapidly increasing purchasing power of the population stimulated by high-power advertising created the necessity for mass production on an increasing scale, coupled with a standardization of products which tended more and more to encourage uniformity and discourage individual choice and preference. It was the age of gadgets and labour-saving devices in the home. Women no longer had to spend so much time doing the round of household chores: electrical and other machines began to take over a part of the work, although it was some time before lower-grade workers were able to take advantage of these innovations except through the process of instalment buying, a method not only to become very general but one to lead to serious dislocation and hardship in time of depression. This gradual diminution in the amount of time spent in domestic duties led to a growing desire for better means of recreation and amusement, and thus in turn stimulated the development of the cinema and the radio, which from 1920 onwards spread with amazing rapidity. In 1922 there were perhaps some 400,000 radio sets in use: by 1953 this number had risen to 118,000,000. At first, radio, like the motion-picture, was considered more of a novelty rather than the beginning of a vast enterprise with enormous influence on popular character and ways of thought. As might have been expected, it became a branch of private enterprise in the United States, the programmes being sponsored by commercial firms for the purposes of advertisement. Thus listeners had to endure the musical and other features being interlarded with appeals to buy this or that soap, cereal or what not, just as the popular magazines were so filled with advertisements of soaps, sausages and sanitary towels that it was often quite difficult to discover where an article began and where it ended.[1]

When considering the effect of the motion-picture and the radio on women in the United States we shall see how the producers have constantly to bear in mind the tastes and desires of their feminine and juvenile audiences. For not only in recreation but also in retail buying the women of twentieth-century America played a highly important part. Separate as the sexes were in the nineteenth century, the gulf which divided them was wider still in the twentieth. Women were still dominant in the social sphere and in the home where children are concerned. Teachers were still largely feminine and unmarried, and men still retained a firm but probably weakening hold on business and politics. It was an age when the American Woman was coming into her own at last. She could do all that men could do—almost. It was the age when the American Man was beginning to wonder what it was that had hit him. He saw woman in the ascendancy, and had no idea what was to be done. It was an age when a Methodist divine (Bishop C. Denny) had to comfort his male followers by telling them that, come what might, women at least could not yet "grow a mustache".[2] It was the age when, as an American woman once told me, the American Man was simply a doormat—and liked it!

With the economic and social changes in the United States came a further understanding of the divergence between faith and practice and the manifold contradictions which were so apparent to everyone who chose to look for them. The ideals of the Jacksonian Democrats were beginning to be more fully examined, although it was far from clear how they could be realized without fundamental changes in the whole social and economic structure of American society. But the progress of political democracy accompanied a slower development of social democracy, and with the rise of organized labour the social and economic scene began to take on a wholly new aspect.

Even in business, startling changes were becoming apparent. We begin to see the development of great corporations, combines, trusts and cartels for the control of which the Sherman Act of 1890 had been designed. Immense industrial empires were built up with enormously complex interlocking devices; and these dynasties not only stifled free competition but even interfered with foreign trade

---

[1] Cf. J. F. Steiner, *Americans at Play*, pp. 108 ff., 118 ff.
[2] See H. L. Mencken, *Americana*, 1926, p. 161.

and influenced foreign policy by meddling in the domestic affairs of other nations. These activities tended to concentrate the attention of Americans upon things at home: they did not want to be entangled in foreign commitments, in spite of the efforts of industrialists to secure expanding markets and so to link up American controls with their foreign counterparts. It was thus that the spirit of isolationism in political and world affairs was fostered; and this feeling was intensified by psychological factors which were largely unrecognized by those who were influenced by them. Women also played their part in promoting isolationist activities, and we shall see later how various mothers' organizations were busy with propaganda designed to try to keep the United States out of wars. Their work, however, was largely in vain, for the twentieth century saw America involved in two world wars. In the great financial crash of 1929 the very foundations of American economic life seemed to show signs of disintegration. Women were deeply involved in these slumps, since as guardians of the home and the children they had to secure a steady income in order to preserve their accustomed standards of life.

It was not only, however, the ferment in the world beyond its shores that was affecting the United States. There was a growing ferment within, and the American Woman was at the very core of the conflict. For although, as the century advanced, it seemed that she was attaining all for which she had so long striven, her success nevertheless seemed to bring her no nearer to serenity, tranquillity and the enjoyment of her gains. Instead of calm confidence many a woman exhibited merely restless frustration: many mothers were more often than not maternal tyrants: and the younger girls became stereotyped dolls basing their appearance, manners and dress upon the film stars, the stories of whose artificial lives were transformed through romantic appeal into adventurous tales of wealth, love and passion in which hard reality was cast aside in favour of sensuous phantasy. The American family itself seemed to be breaking up. Marriages were often becoming episodes in a series of trial alliances, although each had to be sanctioned by law to preserve at least an outward semblance of respectability. Young people horrified the older generation by their apparent sexual promiscuity; and, although "chastity" was still officially sponsored and approved in the popular journals, it seemed to be curiously interpreted in some quarters. Two world wars had done little to lessen the tension, and the American Woman was becoming more and more of a problem not only to herself but also to others. Journals carried numerous articles on her, and the question was often asked as to what was "wrong with the American Woman". The more observant foreigners were amazed at what they found and at the way in which so many American men allowed themselves to be dominated and "pushed around" by their female relations and friends. Even the cartoonist reflected the prevailing temper; and the average American man was presented as a figure of fun quite unable to cope with the demands of his wife and mother.[1]

As the century advanced those controlling the motion-pictures began to realize the value of this new means of popular education. That is to say, its *commercial* value. For love was a means of extracting money from rich and poor, educated and uneducated, foreign-born and hundred-per-cent.-American. Here a real generalization was possible. All that was necessary was to realize that what was important was that the human mammal was to be considered as existing only below the navel. What was to be carried out was continuous sexual stimulation and titillation. Beautiful, brown-skinned young men seducing beautiful and voluptuous blondes was something nearly everybody would enjoy and would pay to see. Other business concerns followed the movies. Advertising concentrated upon the appeal produced by "glorifying the American girl", who was portrayed on every possible occasion with her clothes falling off, grinning as if to demonstrate the admirable effects of some new dentifrice. Since the activities of the censor forbade the glorification of her primary charms, male film fans had to content themselves with the secondary sexual characteristics, and gradually the increasing interest in those sections of female anatomy became almost a mania which reached its height during and after the Second World War. Americans became sex-conscious and sex-obsessed to a degree rarely seen in any other civilized communities. At the same time many, as we have already said, exhibited a curious kind of permanent adolescence and immaturity which was reflected in their sexual habits, their amusements and even their language.

Women were the chief sufferers in this world of false values and

[1] On the other hand, possibly less observant and understanding foreigners wrote articles in American magazines in which they attempted to generalize on the American beliefs and habits which they had noticed when conducted from party to party by their hospitable hosts and hostesses. Indeed, we are told by one English visitor that "American women do not dislike men as much as Englishwomen do", although the latter probably "love men more", while not liking them. Moreover, she declares that "the average Englishman" is, in a sense, tied to his mother, behaves like a child and tends to make his relationships with the women he meets replicas of the relationship he bears to his mother. (See R. West in *Harper's Monthly Magazine* in 1925, pp. 449, 727, etc.)

perverted tastes. The traditional ideas of past generations persisted, although practice failed to confirm the living character of the beliefs. In the average medium-sized cities children were still being brought up with the old notions of a Deity who managed the Universe, of the family as something sacred and inviolable, and of sexual relations outside the marriage contract as something immoral and degrading. At the same time the standards which should have been preserved, had these beliefs any basic reality, were gradually weakening, and the publication of the first Kinsey report in 1948 caused a wave of excitement when it was realized how wide was the gulf between faith and practice, between regulations and their observance and between the customs of one stratum of the population and those of another. Yet in spite of the wider range of opportunity afforded to women, and their increasing sexual activity from the time of the first "petting" to the time they married their third or seventh husband, they were neither happy nor contented. They were always seemingly searching for something they could not find. Those with less time on their hands were luckier. Farmers' wives and those belonging to "the underprivileged" had not sufficient leisure to be continually worrying about personal troubles. Negro women were perhaps least of all disturbed by the prevailing *malaise*. The coloured people had never been so deeply affected by the Puritan view of life and the passion for wealth as a symbol of achievement and success. Thus the Negro woman was often without the gnawing conflicts which afflicted her white sister, who, sensing the greater freedom of the coloured woman, was often filled with jealousy and hatred, which added still more fuel to the fire of racial animosity. The Negro problem in the United States is a sexual as well as an economic question and the American Woman is at the very heart of that problem. For just as in the nineteenth century she controlled the early lives of the children, so in the first half of the twentieth she it was who influenced the younger members of the family in their formative years, and, in many cases, her own psychological condition had disastrous effects upon her offspring. What these effects were we shall see in the detailed survey that follows. It is sufficient here to say that in the case of the boys the tendency was towards maternal over-protection and consequent interference with normal development to full adult maturity, and in the girls an encouragement, according to traditional standards, of those romantic illusions which were so attractively portrayed in the motion-pictures and in current popular ideology.

(2) *Infancy, Childhood and Youth*

With the twentieth century came marked changes in the treatment of children and in the social lives of young people generally. Gone were the days when it was the fashion to hold that children possessed "a depraved nature, prone to all evil" and "averse from all good".[1] No longer did parents shudder to think of the tots frizzling in hell and jumping up and down on hot iron plates. These ideas had passed away along with other tenets of Calvinistic teaching, and the tendency was rather to regard children as innocent babes, unspotted lambs in a world where the ravening wolf was never very far off. It is true that these characteristics were assigned almost exclusively to children of the female sex, and the American girl thus started off with a reputation for innate virtue lacking in her unfortunate brother.

This view of childhood, which was not confined to the United States, produced an atmosphere of sickly sentimentality which was intensified by the coming of the motion-pictures and their presentation of American childhood. It was not only the rejection of the old Puritan views that caused this emphasis on the "purity" and "innocence" of childhood to become pronounced during the twentieth century. There was more in it than that. For this view was an almost necessary concomitant of that which postulated the child as the hope of the future, who under proper conditions and in a proper environment would go further and fare better than his parents,[2] and it was also a view which, it was often thought, was supported by the findings of psycho-analysis, which had an immense influence on American thinkers once the work of Freud had become popularized by his American disciples.

There is no necessity here to describe in any detail the methods adopted by American mothers of the upper middle classes in the rearing of their children. Gorer, in the essay cited above, has summed up the general situation with admirable clarity, and has stressed the prevalence of what can only be called "magical" beliefs, which, in the United States, are common not only among parents in relation to their children's nurture, but which are to be found also in many other departments of social life. Such beliefs are, in my opinion, almost directly due to the influence of feminine domination on American culture.

[1] Jabez Burns, p. 256.

[2] G. Gorer (*The American Child*, p. 40) rightly points out that this "basic belief" probably gained original impetus in the second generation among the foreign-born.

In the article above mentioned Gorer has stressed the concept of "being a sissy" [1] as a key concept for any true understanding of the American character. Although I am not entirely in agreement with him as to the importance of the concept, and am of the opinion that he has missed some of the more important elements in it, there is no doubt that it merits more than passing mention in any serious consideration of American childhood. The essential idea behind the concept of "sissy" is one of *dependence* and an inability to "take" what a given situation demands. The term has a much wider significance than it usually has in England, although in England also it may be used in the sense of implying *passivity* in face of an assault which current *mores* declare should be resisted. From these notions springs the desire to be thought "tough" and able to "take it", and to this idea of toughness we find conjoined the concept of babyhood, and Americans talk of "tough babies" when speaking of certain gangsters or violent characters, or even of exceptionally brave and adventurous men. The American parent, and above all the father, dreads the possibility that his child may become a sissy. Although Gorer declares that for a mother to risk turning her child into a sissy is to commit the greatest crime that an American parent can commit, I think it would have been more correct to add that, although such an idea may be currently held, it is, in many cases, not carried out in practice. Indeed, I am inclined to regard the enormous importance of the sissy concept in American life as due to that feminine dominance which is everywhere apparent and of which the nature and effects will be set forth in the succeeding pages. It seems to me likely that the idea stems from an only partly conscious terror on the part of men that maternal domination may so influence the son that he may lack at least some of the masculine characteristics that woman still permits the American male to exercise. Thus the feeling that all such pursuits as art, music or literature are "sissy" is due to the

---

[1] The word "sissy" is almost certainly derived from the ordinary word "sister", and only began to imply something different in the latter years of the nineteenth century. The word is still applied to a sister in the United States (but usually abbreviated to "sis"), and when applied to a male it naturally had a meaning of effeminacy or as if the man were looking or behaving like a sister or a female. In 1890 the word was applied in the United States to dandyfied and effeminate society men, and the word rapidly spread both as a substantive and an adjective. In modern times the term is used in many different senses. Besides being still employed to designate the "kid sister", it is used in reference to a weakling—"one who can't take it", and as an adjective in a variety of ways. Girls sometimes call their tea-time dresses "sissy clothes": a toady is called a "sissy-kisser": and even a drinking straw is occasionally referred to as a "sissy-stick". For homosexuals the term is rarely applied in the United States, there being a whole series of other words to designate these persons, both passive and active.

idea that these things are feminine and do not concern the stronger sex.

At the same time, the American mother, while paying lip service to current beliefs, is not at all anxious to see her sons exhibit too many of the male characteristics, which may remind her of her own deficiencies and thus tend to deflate her assertive personality. Indeed, Menninger, in *Men, Women and Hate*, has recorded one case (p. 165) where a mother actually tried to force the ears of her son back and squeeze his nose in order that he might appear less burly, masculine and negroid. Since, as Josephine Conger-Kaneko pointed out in 1906, the feminine stamp is upon everything American,[1] fathers do their best to prevent their sons from adopting pursuits and interests which are thought to be feminine, for, as Traquair truly said in 1923, it is the women who are really in control of the whole social life of the community. Traquair, however, does not seem to me to have sound ideas on the sissy concept, in spite of his realization that America has a thoroughly feminized society.[2]

If evidence is demanded for the effect of American maternal teaching on children the student has merely to turn to the medical and psychological literature recently published, which goes far to negative the view of the absence of apron-strings sponsored by such writers as Geoffrey Gorer and Margaret Mead. H. Elkin, in his acute discussion of the aggressive and erotic tendencies in army life, published in 1946, goes so far as to say that the profanity and obscenity of the American soldier is the symbolic rejection of the shackles of that matriarchy in which he was forced to spend his early years. He goes on to say that a large proportion of American men have never properly developed beyond the early stages of emotional experience, and that the anxiety and strong reactions they exhibit when required to live by standards expected of mature adults are proof of the kind of upbringing to which they have been subjected.[3] Precisely similar conclusions were arrived at by Dr. E. A. Strecker, who, when considering the reports handed in by such military men as General Elliott D. Cooke on psychoneurosis in the American Army, was of the opinion that lack of maturity was mainly responsible for the failure of the majority of the cases treated, and held that in the

[1] J. Conger-Kaneko, p. 7521.
[2] R. Traquair, pp. 294, 296, etc. It is perhaps interesting to observe that, as might have been expected, many women in the United States have discovered that one result of the fear that men have of being feminized further is that they lack romance, are brusque in their approach and consider even kissing a woman's hand as "sissy". See H. F. Pringle and M. Cookman (*Ladies' Home Journal*, Jan. 1939, pp. 20 ff.).
[3] H. Elkin, pp. 410 ff.
I

"vast majority" the American mother was at fault. How was it, Dr. Strecker asked, that in the South Pacific the favourite song was Brahms' "Lullaby"? And again, how was it that the American mothers sent so many whining and hysterical letters to their serving sons? The fact is that, as Graham Hutton so well puts it, American men, on account of their upbringing, retain "an unparalleled devotion" to their mothers ("Moms"). Their lack of maturity is reflected in what they are called. They are called "boys", often think of themselves as such, behave as such and indeed often continue to be called by this word all their lives.

If these statements and opinions have any substance in them, it seems clear that the American mother in her relation to her sons has not been altogether successful. As regards her daughters the case is somewhat different. Generally speaking, the American girl in her early years is a charming creature. The aim of many parents, as Olive Shapley, who lived in America during the Second World War, soon found out, is to make them "the prettiest and most poised",[1] and one result of this treatment is that they soon become self-conscious and apt to be pert. But they never seem to suffer, like some of their brothers, in being the victims of their mothers' desire to dress them up like dolls or mannikins, as happened during the Second World War, when some American mothers arrayed their sons in miniature uniforms and cooed over them in baby language.

During the early years of the twentieth century American writers and foreign visitors began to pay increasing attention to the American girl. Such writers as Alexander Black and H. C. Christy were sympathetic, the latter going so far as to call her "that incomparable she".[2] It was true that foreign views were apt to be somewhat cynical; and Anne Morgan noted with disapproval the idea said to be prevalent in Germany and France towards 1914 that the American girl was an unsexed and primitive being with an appendage of dollars.[3] This lack of appreciation was inexplicable to Walter L. George, who in his *Hail Columbia!* had much to say on the American woman. Girls, he thought, embodied the national restlessness, and, while admitting that the United States was a woman's country where the cult of gynæcolatry was prevalent, had to agree that the social dichotomy inevitably led to unhappiness and a series of divorces which he aptly styled "legal free love".[4]

With the rise of the motion-picture the desires and wishes of the American girl began to change. Her vitality and desire for happiness

[1] O. Shapley, pp. 582–3.   [2] H. C. Christy, p. 9.   [3] Anne Morgan, p. 3.
[4] W. L. George, pp. 129, 131, 125, 120, 130, 145.

began to be centred upon the kind of life portrayed on the screen. Happiness was to be obtained by being beautiful, rich and well known. To be content meant having a body which men would look at twice, a long sleek car, and one or more long-drawn-out and passionate love affairs. As might have been expected, these phantasies made the girls neither happier nor more contented. The main effect was to standardize their behaviour as it standardized the cut of their hair and the style of their dress. It did not, however, make them more feminine. The American girl, remarked Maurice Dekobra in 1931, is a beautiful little tigress (although without claws) who feeds on orchids (without perfume), gramophone records (without needles) and nocturnal telephone calls (without passion).[1] Another French observer, Christiane Fournier, was even more scathing. Writing a year after Dekobra, she declared that American girls knew nothing whatever about real love. All they wanted were husbands who would both earn a million dollars and also wash the dishes. What was wrong, she insisted, was that in the United States the women had the men completely under their thumbs.

Not all American girls, however, were affected by the movies in the same way. Some were not endowed by Nature with a face or figure which could compete with the idols of the cinema. In some cases this resulted in feelings of inferiority and the usual resulting compensations of unsocial attitudes and a withdrawal from social life. Sometimes this tended towards a desire on the part of some girls to toy with the idea of belonging to the opposite sex, although when a direct question was asked as to whether they would like to be so transformed the answers showed much deviation.[2]

By the end of the first half of the twentieth century the ideals of the average American girl had hardened and her standardized dress and behaviour became the subject of comment and analysis. In the "March of Time" picture *Teen-Age Girls*, which was shown in 1945, a study of American girlhood was attempted which threw a flood of light upon contemporary life and custom in the United States. Here they were presented as a class by themselves, and an important class at that, for were they not consumers on a large scale, who therefore had to be catered for by industry and through advertisement? In the film were portrayed the teen-age girls' interests, the kind of cosmetics they preferred, the clothes they must wear, the baths they lolled in while drinking and reading film magazines, and the boys

[1] M. Dekobra, *Aux cent mille sourires*, p. 126.
[2] See G. Allport, p. 176. Boys seemed less liable to indulge in such phantasies than girls.

they teased by showing their nighties to them as the youngsters cat-called under their windows during the "slumber-parties". The American Father, moreover, was not absent from the picture. He was seen trying to get into the bathroom while his young daughter was fitting a face-mask, or trying to persuade her to stop wise-cracking her friend on the telephone when he particularly wished to get a call through to Chicago. Thus the American girl of the more privileged classes had become a kind of standardized doll, her whole outlook conditioned by the antics of the film actresses on whose lives she attempted to base her own, and whose sordid, adolescent romances seemed to her the height of adventurous glory and excitement. *Teen-Age Girls* was not intended as a caricature, but it was supposed to be a true picture of mid-twentieth-century American girlhood; it was these girls who were to be the future mothers of the American people.[1]

Although the independence of girls as well as of women generally had been a noticeable feature of the American scene all through the nineteenth century and well into the twentieth, the changing sex ratios in the United States indicated an entirely new situation in the future which had to be faced.[2] In spite of losses during the Second World War, the figures showed little change since 1940. At that time there were about 100·7 males to 100 females, and in 1950 the ratio was about 98·1 males to 100 females. One result of this slowly in-creasing female surplus was that the scarcity value of the female would diminish, and with it one reason for the independence of women in relation to men. Scheinfeld, indeed, writing in 1943, stated that the United States was heading towards a condition in which there might exist a permanent surplus of six to eight million nubile women.[3] The situation was again stressed in 1948 by James Bender, the Director of an Institute for Human Relations, who pointed out that the changing sex ratios must have a profound effect upon the marriage relationship. He stated that within fifty years multi-wife marriages might have to be legalized, as some American women were already agitating in favour of polygamy, or that, on the other hand, the fight for men might cause the American female to become so

---

[1] The picture clearly portrayed only the girls of a certain social standard. It must be remembered, however, that even working-class girls are often much better off than is generally supposed in Europe. W. D. Whitney in his *Who are the Americans?* (p. 37) declared that "The poorest working girl" has silk stock-ings and "normally" has her fur coat, but this is clearly an untrue generaliza-tion. Cf. M. Lindsay, *Boycott on Glamour.*

[2] Cf. U.S. Bureau of Census. Estimated future population by age and sex, 1945–80 (Series P-3, Nr. 15. July 1941).

[3] A. Scheinfeld, *Husband Shortage*, pp. 18 ff.

aggressive that 25 per cent. of men might be too scared to get married at all, since even now about one quarter of all American marriages were what he called of the matriarchal type.[1]

Although the changing population figures were hardly likely to affect the behaviour of the teen-agers, it was noticed even during the Second World War that girls were becoming less independent and overbearing in their relations with boys. The girls seemed to be demanding less and adopting a more submissive attitude. Such signs could not fail to be of significance.

Before passing on to consider further aspects of the life of the American girl, a word must be said on the so-called "American Look", which is said in the United States to be unmistakable and to set American damsels apart from those in other countries.[2] The so-called "normal" figure of the average eighteen-year-old American girl was estimated from a sample of about 5,000 and exhibited in 1945 in the American Museum of Natural History in New York. Generally speaking, the figure corresponded broadly with the usually accepted modern American ideal (height, 5 ft. 6 in.: bust, $33\frac{3}{4}$ in.: waist, $26\frac{1}{2}$ in.: hips, 36 in.). These measurements must have been the averages derived from the figures of women possessing the basic types, such as those with small busts and waists and with wide hips, and those with well-developed busts and narrow hips. The tendency seemed to be towards height, with broad shoulders, long legs and slender hips. This form of figure was said to be the first component in the American Look, and those not thus provided by Nature attempted to achieve something of it by choice of suitable clothes and good deportment and carriage. Among the chief components of the "Look" are the appearance of cleanliness, good teeth, confidence, naturalness, good grooming and so-called "glamour". Her *natural* appearance is not quite as natural as at first appears. It is the result of careful artifice and is derived from a generous use of cosmetics, while her air of innocence or "lovely puzzlement", as it has been called, has been assiduously cultivated from a constant study of the Hollywood film idols.

Before passing from this brief account of the appearance of the American girl, a word must be said about the question of "glamour". Glamour in the United States is, it seems, the appearance which is associated with luxury, with rich and elegant living, and with romance. It is closely connected also with sex-appeal and the bodily

[1] See J. Bender, *Crystal Gazing* and his *Man's World or Woman's?* Cf. the "Preview of the Post-war Generation" in *Fortune*, March 1943, pp. 116 etc.

[2] See "What is the American Look?" (*Life* (Intern. Ed.), May 21, 1945, pp. 87 ff.) Cf. J. C. Furnas, *How America Lives*, p. 254.

figure which accompanies it. The type of female body considered charming in the United States, however, varies from time to time, emphasis being placed on different regions according to the mysterious changes of masculine taste. Recently, as we shall see later, a "breast-boom" has been in progress, but seventeen years ago, as Gaudefroy-Demombynes pointed out (p. 168), American men cared nothing whatever for the beauty of the breasts, but much preferred fullness in the hips and graceful lines in the legs.

In its most modern sense glamour first became popular about 1920, when interest in money and sex was becoming acute. Some years later, when glamour became almost a necessity to the successful girl, Miss Ann Sheridan became the queen of the cult or, as the advertisements put it, "The Number One Lady of Allure". She was America's "Oomph Girl", and "Oomph" was, in a sense, Hollywood jargon for glamour. Miss Sheridan became the idol of not only film fans who tried to imitate her, but of many young men who were unable to resist the sex-appeal which she exuded. Indeed, it is said that on one occasion in Los Angeles a student handcuffed himself to the lady in question and promptly swallowed the key, whilst grown men were reported to have started babbling at the mere mention of her name.[1]

Although, as the Chinese writer Helena Kuo has aptly pointed out, there are millions of exceptions, it can hardly be doubted that the glamour female is the national idea of a beautiful and desirable woman. As that late lamented and acute columnist Dorothy Dix said (Baltimore *Sun*, June 11, 1943), all thinking people knew that in the United States the cinema was the chief educational institution, which far exceeded the influence of the Church, the colleges or even the Press. From it the girls took their ideas of manners and morals, clothing and conduct. Hollywood was the heaven to which the teen-ager aspired. The opinions and conventions of the movies dominated young American society, and according to the movies the way to attract men was to be glamorous.

In a later discussion on the meaning of the "date" and of "petting" for the American girl, we shall see how these customs were regarded both by American and foreign observers, above all during the Second World War, when they were imported into Europe along with the American Army. Here it may be of some interest to mention an article by Rhona Churchill in the London *Evening News* of October 19, 1938. Having spent four months in America, she had come to the conclusion that, compared with American women, the English had

---

[1] Cf. T. Strauss, *Farewell to Oomph* (1943), and J. C. Furnas, *op. cit.*, p. 255.

not even begun to learn the art of living. Unlike the Ame_
English did not know how to keep men friends in the
American girls had trained their boy friends to behave as they
them to do, for fifteen minutes or so after leaving the lady, the
would telephone to ask if she had enjoyed the party. Miss Churc
American friend had this custom of telephoning, but despite this, I
do not think he could have been altogether successful with the ladies,
as he had already been married five times. It is true that Miss
Churchill found the conversation at American parties very silly, but
she was apparently told that it was the American men who liked that
kind of patter, and so the American women obliged them. The success which the American girl enjoyed, Miss Churchill stated, was due
to co-education. She had a ten years start over her English cousin.
At an age when the latter was still trying to hide her flushed cheeks
and hot hands, Uncle Sam's little girl, with all the poise of a woman
of thirty, was swinging it in the night clubs with her college-boy beau.

A few years after Rhona Churchill's account of American and
English girls, the American soldier came over to England to see the
girls for himself. One letter, printed in *Time* in 1946, gave the
opinion of an American soldier stationed in England. He noted the
difference stressed by Rhona Churchill but, curiously enough, came
to the conclusion that it would be better if many American girls did
some work and darned a few socks, instead of playing bridge and
sipping cocktails all the afternoon. As to the English belief that
American women were spoiled, he was inclined to agree with it, and
his advice to the American bachelor was to find a wife in England.
Evidently "glamour" was hardly sufficient for this American, who
wanted the more solid and practical virtues.

The education of girls in the United States during the nineteenth
century has already been briefly described. The twentieth century
showed few important changes in the general curriculum. Through
high-powered propaganda American education is usually believed to
be the best in the world, and even though, as Brogan has ventured
to point out, the figures are most impressive, the realities are less so.[1]
One of the more recent works of American education is by Fine,[2] who,
in a long survey of the current situation, pointed out that, whatever
might be the national income, the schools of the United States were
starved of funds. Teachers were so badly paid that many would
really be better off as bar-tenders or garbage-collectors, and as a class
were held of small account in the social scale. For example, he

[1] D. W. Brogan, *U.S.A.*, p. 83.
[2] B. Fine, *Our Children are Cheated* (1947).

stated that in Detroit some teachers started at a salary less than that received by the prison cook or the attendant at an average comfort station. Indeed, it was considerably less than that of the city dog-catcher or the foreman of the squad engaged in the extermination of rats. In supporting his thesis of inadequate education in the United States, Fine maintained that there were at least two million persons who could not read or write and that in the draft registration it was discovered that some 350,000 could not sign their names.[1] There is, of course, great disparity in education in the various zones of the United States. Much naturally depends on the amount of money available and on the money actually spent. In the South, where segregation was insisted upon (which means duplicating many educational facilities), many of the rural and Negro schools were in poor shape, and Fine describes one which was simply an old chicken-shed and where eighty children were supposed to be educated. In discussing the sex of teachers, Fine pointed out what we have already insisted upon in an earlier chapter, namely that the overwhelming majority are women—"unmarried women, sensitive, faithful and feeble", as Santayana calls them.[2] Some of these unfortunate young women have to submit, according to P. H. Odegard, to surprising inquiries and regulations. In the case of a North Carolina schoolteacher test, Odegard stated that before the contract was signed the teacher had to promise not to go out with any young man except when it was necessary to do so to stimulate Sunday School work, not to fall in love or become engaged or to become secretly married.[3]

We have already mentioned some of the effects which may be thought to follow the education of boys by unmarried women, although perhaps it is an exaggeration to say, with John Erskine, that the schools have the best intentions but that what they are actually doing is making girls out of boys.[4]

However, it must, I think, be admitted that one effect is that boys learn to obey women. Indeed, Mrs. Richardson, in her amusing and stimulating *Influence of Men, Incurable* (p. 11), says that, had women not been able to deal with men swiftly, subtly and effectively,

---

[1] In 1947 it was estimated that, of the 106 million persons of fourteen years of age and over, 2·7 per cent. could not read or write.

[2] G. Santayana, *Character and Opinion in the United States*, p. 44.

[3] P. H. Odegard, p. 83. In this acute analysis of the American public mind the author points out various aspects of life in the United States which are not often recognized outside America. For example, he deals with "facts" as reported in different sections of the American Press, and caustically suggests that, were the picture of the United States presented by the films correct, the Statue of Liberty might be thought to be holding up a red light.

[4] J. Erskine, *Influence of Women and its Cure*, p. 70. Cf. C. F. Ulrich's review, "Off with their Heads" (*Sat. Rev. of Lit.*, Feb. 15, 1936, vol. xiii, p. 13).

they would have wrecked civilization. In one of her critical and well-informed columns in the *Washington Post* (August 23, 1943), Mary Haworth declared that she thought that the manners and customs of American men were woman-tailored to a far greater extent than in any other modern society. American men have, she stated, been taught, with a few exceptions, by mothers and nurses in their cradle era, and by women school-teachers in the nursery school, kindergarten and grade-school phase of education. It has thus been possible for the American woman to fashion her ideal man; and his occasional ignorance of the fitness of things (so often deplored by anxious wives seeking guidance in Mary Haworth's mail) must be put down to the failure of women to provide him with an elevating brand of education of the heart and a thorough refinement of feeling. James Truslow Adams, whom Mary Haworth aptly quotes, appeared in his *Searchlight on America* to agree that the American woman had failed to civilize her man, thus leading to complete social dichotomy.[1]

We have not, as far as I am aware, many accounts by European girls of experiences in American schools and vice versa. Since, however, co-education is usual in the United States, a comparison of the experiences of boys in Europe and America may be relevant to the understanding of some aspects of American education. According to American boys, one important difference seems to be that in English schools the boys have an astonishingly slight interest in girls, whereas in America the talk was often mainly about sex and was innocent of serious matters such as politics. Indeed, one boy reported that at St. James's, in Maryland, culture was considered a sign of decadence and devotion to learning the mark of a sissy.

Having completed their schooling, a certain number of American girls proceed to college. Criticism of the effect of college education on the American girl has been centred rather upon its influence as a preparation for life than upon its value as a means of intellectual stimulus. Early in the twentieth century, when co-education was still a matter of controversy, it was thought that mixed colleges might expose the girls not only to the "bacillus of sentimentality" but to even worse things.

For example, the relations between college men and women were often regarded with suspicion, and the German, W. Langewiesche, went so far as to point out that a college girl was always on the look-out for men. The more constant attachment was frowned upon, he

---

[1] J. T. Adams, (2) pp. 197–8. It ought perhaps to be said that it has occurred to Mr. Adams that it may yet be the American man's job to civilize the American woman. I cannot help agreeing with Mary Haworth that this would be a stupendous task.

stated, since the more boy-friends the girl had, the more popular she was.[1] How far these factors were responsible for the future successful marriages of college girls is not easy to estimate. That many college friendships were not wholly platonic seems to be clear from the evidence at our disposal, which we shall discuss later in some detail. A woman, writing in 1938 on *Chastity on the Campus*, declared that the majority of college girls were not virgins, but that it was a mistake to suppose that surrender was accomplished only when drunk, as the pulp magazines often suggested (pp. 176, 180).

In 1942 R. G. Foster and Pauline P. Wilson published a study, *Women after College*, which threw some light on the claim by W. J. Ballinger in 1932 that women's colleges could aptly be called spinster factories. A cross-section of college graduates was taken from the whole country, of which a quarter came from the Middle West. The majority were married and the average age the early thirties, the economic status being relatively high. At the time of the inquiry, 89·0 per cent. had marital problems of some kind, and in the case of these married women the outstanding husband–wife problem was one of struggle for domination.[2]

When discussing the problem of dating and sexual relations in the United States generally, we shall be in a position to see how many American girls emerge into womanhood along a path which is not shared by the majority of Europeans. When entering college, there are sometimes so-called sorority initiations in which candidates have to pass certain tests before they are considered fit to enter into full social life. Some of these tests consist of having to swallow drinks made of noxious ingredients and in having to submit to various kinds of insulting behaviour and even physical chastisement.[3]

(3) *Dating, Petting and Courtship*

We have now to consider one of the most important periods in the life of the American girl: that of adolescence and early womanhood. As we have said above, and as has been repeatedly insisted upon by American authors themselves, the United States is a sex-obsessed country, and one reason why so many American women are unhappy

---

[1] W. Langewiesche, p. 39.   [2] *Op. cit.*, pp. 7, 13, 26, 56, 78.

[3] For a recent account of this see *Time* (Atlantic Overseas Ed.) Dec. 13, 1947, p. 26. And for a foreign view cf. D. Lazard, p. 112. For some amusing instructions for young men when visiting women's colleges see W. Jones, D. Mose and R. O'Riley, *For Men Lonely* (Hanover, N.H., 1947), and for a girl's guide to the college weekend see the same authors' *Weekend* (Boston, 1948). For novels dealing with college life and the sexual life of the students see Percy Marks, and P. Jordan-Smith, and cf. S. K. Winther's *Beyond the Garden Gate*, which deals with the problem of the rural girl and the college boy.

and frustrated is that early in life they fall victims to this obsession, which is directly derived from the American way of life.

As we have seen in the brief survey of Puritan views of love and sex outlined above, women played a dual rôle; and it is this dual rôle, with important variations, which has been carried over into the modern world. To the Puritan, woman was a danger because too many glances in her direction tended to divert the minds of men from the higher goods. The Divine plan for generation was a puzzle, for it surely would have been preferable to have a method that made it less difficult to combine the spiritual aspect of love with romantic or sensual sentiments. Thus woman's importance as a mother and guardian of the domestic hearth was stressed, to the deliberate neglect of her as a lover and a mutual participant in forbidden pleasures. Although the Puritans were not ascetics, romance was not for them. The dangers of romance were well recognized right up to the middle of the nineteenth century. The position was put in a nutshell by the Rev. Daniel Wise, of the Elm Street Parsonage at New Bedford. In his book of counsel for young women he stated that woman's place was in "the peaceful sanctuaries of home" and her paths lay in the "noiseless vales of private life". Romantic, impassioned and immodest ideas were, Wise said, derived "from impure novels and impure fancies". The very suggestion of fading light was to be avoided, since it might bring to the mind possibilities of the most horrid nocturnal activity. "Do not permit your lover to remain in your company later than ten o'clock in the evening," Mr. Wise implored. All this "soft, silly talk about love" must be discarded by sensible young persons.[1]

It is true that such views could not have been readily accepted by many of the Latin immigrants to the United States, and, as Greenbie has pointed out, even the Scotch–Irish attitude to woman stressed her position as companion and mate rather than as housekeeper and lover.[2] But as the years went by the romantic idea became more widely diffused, with the most potent results on American life. As we shall see later, this was due to a considerable extent to the influence of the motion-picture, and the sexual chaos in the 1920s merely added "sex appeal" and all that it implied to the romantic dream. Falling in love was modelled on what the film stars did on the screen. Hollywood's romantic nonsense became a guide to life. One result of this rosy world of phantasy was that, as the French critic Roussy de Sales pointed out in the *Atlantic Monthly* in 1938, love in America

---

[1] Daniel Wise, pp. 197, 208, etc.
[2] M. B. Greenbie, *American Saga*, p. 115.

became a national problem and, like democracy, it did not work.[1]
He showed that there was too much romance in the United States,
that this always tended towards disappointment and disillusionment
and that what was required was a more philosophical attitude.
Although André Maurois believed that Roussy de Sales was inclined
to exaggerate, he also did not fail to indicate the influence of Hollywood's romantic teaching, in which the woman remains to a great
extent a child and unhappy victim of what he calls the American
"chimère Hollywoodienne".[2]

In the preceding pages it has often been said that the social dichotomy between the sexes (concerning which more will be said later)
led to an absorption of men in business, thereby permitting women
to dominate the social scene. This naturally led to a failure by men
to understand the romantic approach which the American woman
so ardently desired. Indeed, in Pringle and Cookman's series of
articles in the *Ladies' Home Journal* it will be seen that the answer to
"What do the women of America think" about men (January 1939,
20 ff.) contained the complaint that men underestimated their
wives' abilities, were not sufficiently romantic, and were generally
more interested in sport and business than in women. This attitude
on the part of men, which is of immense importance in understanding
the culture of the United States, is itself an indication of faulty
psycho-sexual development, and is a manifestation of the emotional
immaturity which is also to be seen in the fascination that the comics
and the fairy-tale movies exercise on grown American male adults.

One fruitful source for understanding the position of women in the
United States and the problems that face them are the question-and-
answer columns in certain American newspapers conducted by such
prominent columnists as the late Dorothy Dix, Mary Haworth,
Beatrice Fairfax and Doris Blake. Dorothy Dix (Mrs. Gilmer) must
have been, as David Cohn maintains, the most widely read woman in
the world. She was said to have sixty million readers and a postbag
of many hundreds of letters a week.[3] Although Miss Dix had to work
within the framework of contemporary American mythology, she
managed to present to the troubled souls who consulted her a mixture of sound advice, wholesome ridicule and sometimes outright
condemnation, which indicated that she was fully sensible of the
basic *malaise* of American civilization. In this respect Mary Haworth
was a close runner-up, dealing as she did with a rather similar stra-

[1] Roussy de Sales, *Love in America*, p. 645.
[2] A. Maurois, *Etats-Unis 39*, pp. 29, 43.
[3] D. Cohn, *Love in America*, p. 142.

tum of the female population, whereas Doris Blake's contributions were shorter and addressed to an audience somewhat lower in the social scale.

By way of illustration it is interesting to note how, in dealing with the question of romance, Miss Dix always managed to show what Maurice Dekobra called her imperturbable good sense. She pointed out how in the United States no amount of education or sophistication or knowledge of what happens to other people prevented women from believing in fairy-tales. They expected to be perpetual brides, trailing their clouds of glory for over forty years, and when this did not happen they could not take it without "squawking to heaven" that marriage was a failure. Men, she said, take marriage as it is, while women yearn for it as it isn't.[1] Or again, a few weeks later she replied to a girl of nineteen who said she was very miserable because her husband did not come up to her idea of the dream husband and the romantic lover whom she thought he would be. Miss Dix said that if she had waited to marry until she were grown-up she would have realized that nobody got a fairy prince for a husband, and it would be far better for her to realize that she was dreaming of some impossible creation built out of her imagination.[2] One more example will suffice. Writing in October 20, 1942, "Brown Eyes", a married woman of twenty-seven, complained of her husband and wanted to contract an alliance with a man of twenty. Miss Dix asked her what was the matter with her brains, as "there isn't one chance in a hundred of her silly dream coming true".[3]

Before dealing in detail with the way in which the romance complex in the United States is built up and sustained and with its effects on the lives of married women, it will be convenient in this place to examine in some detail two phenomena in the relations of young people of both sexes which in the United States are called "dating" and "petting".

The American "dating" system is not well understood outside the United States, and attempts to explain it by Americans who visited England during the Second World War were not successful owing to

---

[1] Baltimore *Sun*, July 3, 1942.   [2] *Op. cit.*, July 21, 1942.

[3] Those of my readers who cannot easily consult the files of American newspapers can find the gist of the philosophy of Dorothy Dix—"the Little Lady of New Orleans"—in *Dorothy Dix—her Book* (New York and London, 1926) and her *How to Win and Hold a Husband* (New York, 1939). Here she maintains that the American husband wishes to be treated as a baby, a demi-god or a good fellow: that the basic principle in treating him is to deal with him as if he were the "littlest baby". Her view is that the majority of American women have no plan of life and no real objective, whilst in the American home—an autocracy run by women—the father has to take a back seat (*op. cit.*, pp. 3, 4, 44, 320, 333). Cf. Faith Baldwin in *America as Americans See It*, p. 91.

their inability both to understand the way that young people conduct themselves in Great Britain and also, I suspect, to assess the
degree of seriousness in the answers given to their questions. Among
those who dealt most extensively with the question of dating from
the American and British points of view was Dr. Margaret Mead, the
American anthropologist, who visited Britain under the joint
auspices of the United States Office of War Information and the
British Ministry of Information. She has contributed her view of the
question in a number of publications, and especially in *Transatlantic*
(June 1944) under the title "What is a Date?". Dr. Mead points out
that in the United States, on account of the system of co-education,
boys and girls meet each other in social life and get accustomed to
each other far more easily than in England, and that part of the
social intercourse of the young consists in what is called *dating*. This
often starts when quite young and continues through life, the word
"date" being applied even to married persons when meeting members
of the opposite sex for certain kinds of social activities. With young
people, however, the date in America is something specific and an
important element in early life.

Both Margaret Mead and Geoffrey Gorer [1] have described the
system of dating, although the former seems to me to have given a
much less adequate account of it in relation to other countries than
has Mr. Gorer, who is better acquainted with British custom and
practice. He links up the practice of dating with the desire of every
American to be successful and thus be worthy of love; and it might
be remembered here that to the Puritan, success was linked with
virtue and was the mark of a man who was loved by God. Dating
is in essence a "highly patterned activity" or group of formal moves
which, although it may be connected with sexual satisfaction of a
kind, is not directly connected with obtaining such pleasure. The
primary object of what can be called a good date is that both parties
may feel that they have been successful in the joint encounter, which
implies up to a point that they have found each other worthy of
"love". One of the most important elements in the date is what is
called the "line".[2] To put it briefly, the line is the method of approach and consists of a combination of light talk, witty wisecracks
and often suggestive insinuations. The girl who is able to meet the

---

[1] G. Gorer, *The Americans* (London, 1948). This book was published in the
United States under the title of *The American People*.
[2] The "line" can be learnt through the appropriate literature. Thus I find
an advertisement in a popular story magazine in which I see that "the Lover's
Companion gives you a 'line' for which they all fall. Impassioned, hot stuff.
. . . The most PEPPY words ever written", etc.

line and successfully parry the talk by appropriate repartee, without putting the boy off on the one hand or surrendering too easily on the other, shows herself an adept in the art of dating and therefore becomes increasingly popular.

Although Gorer is fully aware that the principal aim of the date is not to afford sexual satisfaction on either side, he does, I think, underestimate this aspect, though not to the same extent as does Margaret Mead. When she discussed the relations between the American soldiers and British girls during the Second World War, she seems to have imagined that the line of the American boy had much more serious implications to the English girl than was the case. The art of "picking up" a girl in Great Britain (akin to the "masher" approach in America) contains many elements identical with those in the American date, and it must also be remembered that British girls in wartime, surrounded as they were by foreign soldiers, were behaving in a way which was not always customary with them. American soldiers in their relations with British girls had much more to offer than witty wisecracks. The "Yank hunt" might have surprised Margaret Mead had she realized what the British girl means when she talks of "going serious" or "having a boy". After all, it was not every soldier who had his pockets filled with candy, cigarettes or chewing gum. To suppose, as some Americans do, that many British girls mistook the line for serious courtship is to underestimate the experience of the British maiden. Indeed, it is an American, Ilka Chase, who makes Devon Elliott's lover say that it is amazing how often American girls "mistake attention for intention".[1]

Perhaps where some American commentators go most astray is in their suggestion that when English young people go out together the boy has an "ulterior motive, good or bad". I am not altogether sure what Margaret Mead means by this reiterated expression, but I suggest that she is underestimating the sexual implications in the American date. For anyone at all acquainted with American literature on dating must be aware that the element of "petting" is frequently closely associated with dating. It is true that in her article in *Transatlantic* (p. 57) she says that part of the line is to ask for everything, including total surrender, within the first hour. To these proposals the American girl has to prove her popularity by refusing, thus proving that she can get a date even without giving a single kiss in return for her entertainment. According to Dr. Mead, the boy is usually glad to forgo his kiss, for the girl's refusal shows his perspicacity in choosing a girl who is a really good date. Unfortunately this rosy

[1] I. Chase, *In Bed We Cry*, p. 119.

picture of the American boy's gratification at this intangible reward is hardly supported by the facts. For example, "Tom" consulted Miss Dix on this very point, and his letter was printed in the Baltimore *Sun* of August 31, 1942. Suppose, he says, a boy spends a dollar on taking a girl to the movies and buying her an ice-cream afterwards, what should he expect, "shake hands and go home"? But kisses are a mere beginning to the petting business, and the question of whether to pet or not to pet during a date is one to which we shall turn our attention in a few moments.

Some authorities have actually drawn up twelve commandments by observing which girls may be popular and yet may not need to pet. This is very important to those who object to petting, because it is well known to informed students of American *mores* that there are many boys who will not date a girl at all unless she pets. It is thus particularly valuable to know what assets are essential for a good date if petting be excluded. Thus Mrs. Ruth Yorke, who was a graduate of Wellesley and Teachers College, Columbia, and who has been a dean of girls and a counsellor to them in New England and New York high schools, has printed her prescription of how girls can thus be popular with boys. She starts off by saying that girls should not be self-sufficient, that they should not be unsought, for every girl knows that the way to date is to accept dates and so get started. Girls should be skilful at games and dancing; they should not be affected, dowdily dressed or shy; and they should not be gold-diggers. In other words, they must not belong to the ranks of the "gimme girls", although, as Leaf points out, the boy-friend who will feed you once or twice a week is worth hanging on to.[1] Although Mrs. Yorke says that one of the commandments is that girls must like boys, they must not be boy-chasers; and then she goes on to say that girls must not sell their womanhood for too cheap a price. Petting, she says, is winding up the human dynamo. Complete or even incomplete petting is a waste of power for a momentary kick; the price is too cheap.[2]

It thus appears that the problem of dating, and its implications, is somewhat more obscure and important in the life of the American girl than is generally believed outside the United States. After all, it is not so easy to make dates as is usually imagined. In 1934 a date-booking bureau was started by the students of Brooklyn College for the purpose of bringing young people together, and rules for the art have actually been printed in book form, such as *Dating Do's and Don't's for Girls* (1947) and Elizabeth Eldridge's *Co-ediquette*. The

[1] M. Leaf, *Listen, Little Girls*, etc., p. 193.
[2] Ruth Yorke in the *Boston Sunday Post*, Sept. 12, 1937.

fact that so many manuals of instruction are published indicates that the art of dating is not a simple matter.[1] Indeed, we have only to consult the advice columns to see how difficult some young Americans find the whole business. For whatever Margaret Mead and those who think like her may say, it is a fact that these experienced advisers of youth paint a picture of dating which cannot altogether be squared with the formal, patterned encounters to which allusion has been made above. Thus Dorothy Dix declared in one of her columns that "the great number of girls" are convinced that the only way they can get dates is to let the boys—any boy—"kiss them and maul them". When questioned, she said that "the universal answer" was that "the boys won't take a girl out who won't pet" and that girls were dropped if they became too choosy and particular. Moreover, the boys were often in as great a fix as the girls. "What line of conduct do girls like?" asked one. Did they "crave a little mauling"? He went on to tell Miss Dix that when he tried a little petting the girl refused, but if he did not persist, then she would not date him again, because he was slow. Similarly, if he actively insisted, he lost the date, because then he was too "fast". To these conundrums Miss Dix had a ready answer. She told him that the mystery of how a woman's mind works made the riddle offered by the Sphinx look like a puzzle which any moron could solve without effort. But she followed this wisecrack with a good deal of sound, sane advice. The boys, however, sometimes have their revenge. In an amusing letter, signed "A Wolf", one of them told Miss Dix that they knew well why some girls did not get dates and why some were "wows" and some "drips" or "meatballs". But they weren't telling! To this sally Miss Dix replied that she never heard of anything so heartless, when "thousands and thousands of poor girls" were trying to find out just those very reasons. "The meanies!"

Before passing on to an analysis of petting and its effect on the American girl, a word must be said on the subject of "mashing". There are, I think, two principal meanings to the words "mashing" and "masher" in the United States. In common parlance the ordinary masher is the man who tries to "pick up" women in public places such as museums or picture-houses, or solicits their attention on the street or in the subway by many and devious means. My own first encounter with "mashing" was one day, some years ago, when in New York City. A young woman was walking to the street from the subway lugging a very cumbersome and heavy grip. I offered to

[1] W. von Polenz in his *Das Land der Zukunft* (p. 231) called American flirtation the most puzzling thing in the world.

K

carry it to the street for her, and after a moment's hesitation she allowed me to do so, after giving me a curious and searching look. As it happened, I was on my way to have a chat with one of America's leading sexologists, and I told him why I had been slightly delayed. "Christ!" he said. "You mustn't do things like that! You'll get arrested and taken to the hoosegow [prison] as a masher." It appeared that my offer of assistance might have been mistaken and that I might have joined the "two hundred naughty papas" whom Mrs. Anna Graney and Mrs. Margaret Brennan, sleuths of the New York policewomen, had, from 1915 to 1937, "coaxed to the hoosegow" on account of alleged "mashing" activities.[1]

The attempts to pick up American women are often the subject of complaints in the "love-lorn" columns and occasionally arouse the ire of those replying to them. It is pointed out that American women cannot have it both ways. If they are in reality as independent and self-reliant as they pretend, they cannot demand continual protection by male escorts against casual mashers. Sometimes a really amusing situation develops. In the subway one day a girl was standing against the door of the train when a man near her cautioned her to be careful, as it might be dangerous. She immediately jumped to the conclusion that he was a masher and was trying to get fresh, so she told him sharply to mind his own business. At that moment the door opened and the young woman fell headlong out of the train and on to the platform.[2]

The second meaning of the word "masher" is more euphemistic. It is occasionally used for characters such as exhibitionists and persistent pests who continue their solicitations long after the woman has indicated clearly that she does not desire them. It is men like these who are usually the subject of police interference, which is requested by the woman who has been subject to annoyance.

We must now pass to a consideration of other diversions of American youth. It is here that we shall be able again to see the web of contradictory theory and practice which produces so much of the restless irritation and frustration characteristic of American life.

---

[1] See H. Whitman, in the New York *Daily News*, Aug. 24, 1937. Cf. A. Feiler (p. 250), who says "woe to the man" who goes up to a strange woman in a public street, as it is quite possible that she may report him to the police, a danger insisted upon by Adrien de Meeüs (p. 75). P. A. Vaile, who wrote a violently hostile book in 1909 on the United States, but who makes some shrewd hits and foresaw air-conditioning, has an amusing account of a mashing episode in which a member of the Anti-Mashing Society was involved (see *Ý. America's Peril* (London, 1909), p. 200), with which may be compared the amusing episode narrated by George Rose, *The Great Country*, p. 28.

[2] New York *Daily News*, Aug. 29, 1942. For an admirable discussion of these matters see Mary Haworth's column in the *Washington Post* of Jan. 3, 1943.

Petting is a well-established practice in all civilized societies. It is usually the preliminary to full sexual consummation and, as such, plays an essential and useful rôle in preparing the two persons for mutual satisfaction. In many cases, however, especially among young people who, for various reasons, are unable to proceed to the sex act, it becomes an end in itself, and may range from a kiss or a touch to mutual masturbation.

It must be remembered, as Elsie Clews Parsons has pointed out in *Civilization in the United States* (p. 313), that in the United States sex relations are classified according to whether or not physical consummation has been achieved. As we shall see later, American views on virginity are very peculiar and of great importance when considering the psychology of the American woman. Since full consummation constitutes the only true form of sexual intimacy, it has been assumed by many that petting between young people does not count and little objection can be raised to it. A striking illustration of this point of view is provided by the regulations and arrangements often made in hostels for the accommodation of single girls. For example, in 1942 such a hostel was opened in Washington, D.C., for young unmarried women working in the Civil Service. Styled "Scotts Hotel", the building was well fitted up and had special arrangements to enable the inmates to indulge in the petting that they clearly were expected to want. Off the main lobby there were "beau parlors", and Lovers' Lane was the corridor from which opened small rooms where boy friends might be received. But the privacy was only partial. It was always possible that too much might lead the couple to the nameless and forbidden consummation. So proper decorum was preserved by curtains, which were so cut that they were never completely closed. People could always peep in as they passed down the lane to enter other little cubicles which were given such names as Antony–Cleopatra, Beatrice–Dante, or You and Me. The arrangement reminds one of the so-called tearooms, once to be found in London, in which each table was in just such a cubicle and where tired brokers were entertained by the waitresses while consuming expensive cups of tea. In London such arrangements for petting led to the closing of the rooms, but in the United States the same arrangements for the girls and their boys were considered to preserve morality.

In earlier days people had thought very differently. Petting, as practised by modern American youngsters, would have horrified many Puritans, even if it had been indulged in after marriage: and in the nineteenth century it was often thought that even caresses

within the family were best avoided. With the advance of the twentieth century, however, and the enormous increase of deliberate sexual
stimulation exercised by the motion-pictures and popular romantic
literature, the practice of dating became, as we have seen, more and
more connected with petting. It is true that some writers still de-
luded themselves that boy-and-girl friendships could be established
on the basis of good companionship; but during the roaring twenties
and early thirties, observers of the social scene became anxious as
to where it might all end. Carman Barnes vividly described in her
Schoolgirl (1930) the sexual activity in an American finishing school,
with its petting, necking and Lesbian influences. One of the foreign
visitors, Ferri-Pisani, dealt in detail with the "petting-party" as he
himself had experienced it, and illustrated what Elsie C. Parsons
stated regarding the importance of complete consummation.[1] These
were the days of slimming, and Ferri-Pisani found it not difficult to
believe that the girl who had delivered herself to him for "petting"
was a kind of hybrid from another world. Her flat chest and belly,
coupled with her lightly curved hips and muscular arms and legs,
seemed to him to be neither male nor female, but to belong to "un
troisième sexe, celui de l'Amazone".

As the years went by, literature continued to be published on a
question which was beginning to agitate parents more and more.
Floyd Dell tried to answer the question as to "Why They Pet", and
M. J. Exner examined "The Question of Petting" on behalf of the
American Social Hygiene Association, Inc. Dr. Exner contributed
the orthodox and conservative view to the controversy. Assuming
the current American views on the virtue of virginity and chastity,
Exner maintained that petting implied the cultivation of low tastes,
that it was playing with fire, and above all that it cheapened the girl
who thus indulged herself, since a man would hardly seek a wife
from among those whom he knew were used to petting with other
men. Like Mrs. Yorke in the article quoted above, he maintained
that the price was wrong and that petting was best avoided. On
the other hand, he made no comment upon the constant artificial
sex stimulation to which American youth was subject. Similarly
E. L. Clarke, for the Y.M.C.A., asked if petting was wise or unwise,
while I. M. Hotep tried to console the neglected American girl by
telling her that it was all nonsense that she could be popular only
if she necked and petted, since the less free she was with her body the
more likely she was to get proposals "from fine men".[2]

[1] Ferri-Pisani, *Au pays des Amazones*, pp. 97 ff.
[2] I. M. Hotep, p. 71. The "fine man", that famous character of American

As might be expected, parents were often in difficulties as to how to cope with their daughters. A poor, harassed mother wrote to Dorothy Dix about it in December 1929. Her daughter, she wrote, was "impudent to a colossal degree" and "sassed" her with impunity. What ought she to do? Miss Dix was very sympathetic. Had she a formula for turning the modern girl into a loving, considerate daughter, she replied, she would be working a miracle which would staunch millions of mothers' tears. These girls were too old to be spanked as they deserved. They had no hearts and were completely selfish. Another fictional mother, nearly ten years later,[1] asked plaintively, "What is my daughter doing tonight?"[2] The article was prefaced by a large transparent clock-face indicating 2 a.m., with the erring damsel creeping upstairs silhouetted behind it. Some of the correspondence which had been received by the author of the article supported the fact that American boys of 1938 did not want to have dates with girls who refused to pet. As one said, the girls have to submit to it or be left at home. Moreover, it was a time when petting was not enough. It had never been enough for young people in the lower economic levels, who had little patience with the moral uplift and hypocrisy of American sex teaching.

In the 1930s even the girls in the upper economic strata began to succumb. In some of the girls' colleges it was said that some forty

---

mythology, is often held up to ridicule in the popular cartoons. He is portrayed usually as a person who refuses to be tempted by the glamorous allure of some young lady who decidedly would not object to petting, or his behaviour is held up to scorn and derision. For example, to take but four examples from my files. In the *Washington Post* for Aug. 28, 1943, a cartoon by G. d'Alessio and headed "These Women" was published. It shows two sailors with a girl. She is scantily dressed and has her arm round the neck of one of the men, whilst her over-developed breasts are pressed against him. Both his arms are extended out on either side of him while he exclaims to his companion, "Does she LOVE me? Look—No HANDS!" Here is another distributed by the King Features Syndicate in March of the same year. An airman and a girl are standing by some trees in the moonlight. She is gazing into his face and expanding her full bosom towards him. He is looking at her, eating doughnuts, and saying that this party "is really something", as there are even doughnuts with a jelly filling. Another, distributed by the same syndicate and by the same artist, shows two half-naked girls sitting at a dressing-table. "I was never more insulted in my life," says one. "He said he felt like I was a big sister or an aunt to him!" It is in cartoons like this that certain facts of American life can be ascertained far more accurately than by reading the long-winded and verbose "sociological analyses" which pour from the American presses.

[1] See *Pictorial Review*, Feb. 1938, pp. 15 ff.

[2] The thought of what the men might be doing when they got to Europe must have tormented many a suspicious feminine mind. It was true that they had a shrewd idea, for otherwise how can we explain the presence at one time off New York Harbour of a mysterious vessel, with a long banner stretched along it, on which were printed words containing a solemn warning, JACKIE —BEWARE OF GUINEA HENS.

per cent. of the inmates were no longer physical virgins. What had happened, declared the writer in the *Pictorial Review*, was that the moral code had broken down. The hip flask and the automobile ("the bed on wheels") had helped to do it. On the side roads outside Boston I have seen hundreds of automobiles parked end to end, and in each young people were petting, necking and drinking. They seemed to be enjoying themselves. But the writer in the *Pictorial Review* explained to the erring damsel that there was a far greater pleasure than being petted, or even than actually surrendering to a fiancé with whom marriage was, for the time being, impossible. It was a pleasure which could not be compared with love or "unholy" mating, with the delicious sense of being popular or of acquiring glamour or glory. This ineffable pleasure was simply the "plain down-to-earth *scrubbed* feeling of being chaste" (p. 78). This was the really valuable asset, since it was the only possession that a woman would never have twice.[1]

To many foreigners such an article must appear almost inexplicable. It can be clearly understood only by appreciating the American view of sex in its historical setting. The influence of Puritanism in New England tended, as we have already seen, towards a view of woman which was directly contrary to the facts. Woman was not supposed to have any passions, and if she ever felt any strong stirrings within her, they were things of which to be ashamed and had to be strongly suppressed. These things were unclean: men were lower in the scale of creation, but women had to submit to them, since such was the strange method through which the perpetuation of the race was achieved. Even some modern American experts actually pretend that it is not uncommon to find a girl accepting petting from a boy at a date, not because she in any way enjoys it, but because she uses it merely in exchange for what she can get out of him in the way of popularity or attentions. Such sentiments as these are still the orthodox, standardized attitude to petting as presented by the majority of current writers on the problem of youth. Thus Dr. Ruth Fedder, the Guidance Counsellor of Elkins Park, Pa., became obviously very embarrassed when discussing petting. She clearly knew what the facts were, but was compelled to adopt the orthodox view that petting—climax or not— was not for girls, thus rather weakening what might have been

---

[1] Cf. Mary Hastings Bradley's collection of stories *The Five-minute Girl*. An advertising booklet circulating among women and quoted by T. B. Rice (*Sex, Marriage and the Family* (1946), p. 46) declares that all men are beasts in sex matters and even the married woman must protect herself against her husband's germs!

otherwise one of the best books on the youth of the period (pp. 164–178).[1]

It would be tedious to continue to analyse American publications on petting from 1938 to the present day. The controversy still continues, and is likely to do so as long as psychologists and sociologists in the United States make no attempt to seek adequate explanation of the reason why the youth of the country appear to labour under what can only be called a continuous attack of sex obsession. There is some evidence, however, that heavy petting is becoming less popular with co-eds and students generally. The days of "flaming youth" and the roaring twenties and thirties are over. Moreover, the experiences of the Second World War have led many American men to a fuller realization of the unsatisfactory nature of these adolescent experiments. There is, however, another side to the picture. While many American men were overseas the majority of girls remained at home and many of them took on war jobs of various kinds. With the wartime atmosphere came a renewal of the desire for amorous adventure, sanctified by the "war marriage" or often without it. But, owing largely to the ignorance of elementary biology which is, so Foster and Wilson assert, the lot of the "great majority of college students" (p. 255), many women still feel guilt regarding their petting experiences, and this feeling is intensified by the fact that, in many cases, they are still affected by the parental attitude to sex as a part of life to be feared and dreaded rather than controlled and enjoyed.

It must be remembered, and cannot be too often insisted upon, that petting is an amusement of only a percentage of the population, and not a considerable one at that. Such practices as deep (or French) kissing, and many of the manual titillations practised during petting are considered with pronounced disfavour by the lower economic groups, who, as a rule, prefer the natural and straightforward method of allaying sexual hunger, even though the woman is probably thereby deprived of a good deal of enjoyment which a slower approach might bestow upon her. For, whatever may be said against petting, even by those who regard it as a reprehensible pastime, it can hardly be denied that it can, in many cases, provide some sort of preparation for subsequent thrills which, sanctified by legal permission, can hardly nowadays be considered unlawful except by the most rigid moralists, who have never

---

[1] R. Fedder, *A Girl Grows Up*, pp. 164–78. For an admirable account of pre-marital petting in his sample see Kinsey's *Sexual Behaviour in the Human Female*, pp. 227 ff.

considered female enjoyment and sexual ecstasy as anything but diabolic.

As has been said above, the date in the United States need have nothing to do with formal courtship any more than the "pick up" in England. A date may lead to courtship and often does do so, but a boy or girl may continue to have dates even when courting, although often this may be objected to by one side or the other. We now have briefly to consider courtship in the United States and see how it affects the development of the American Woman.

In all societies courtship varies with the pattern of the prevailing social culture. In primitive societies the rules governing courtship may be simple or complex, but in each case the practise is closely knit with the whole social framework of the community. In such a vast and heterogeneous society as the United States no rigid and general pattern can be said to exist. Among many of the minority groups, for example, the customs and practices brought over from the home countries tend to persist, yet with the second generation the generally accepted American conventions have a powerful influence towards some uniformity. Much naturally depends on the position of women in any given society. In the United States, where the growth of the idea of sex equality has been one of the most important features of the changing social scene, it could be expected that courtship would reflect this tendency to a marked degree. American courtship has never been static: changes in emphasis have at all times been apparent, and with the twentieth century the changes became more marked and (to many observers) more disturbing. The American view of "love" as being all-important in the marriage relation, coupled with those romantic dreams which are nourished and kept alive by the cinema, radio and popular magazines, made American courtship markedly different from that occurring in countries where romance and sentiment play a far less important rôle. The American girl, fed as she is week in and week out by the phantasies of Holly-wood, still dreams of the Prince Charming who will take her away to realms of happiness where life will be one long honeymoon. Since real life is utterly different from that portrayed in the magazine or on the screen, disillusionment sets in: the young wife becomes discontented and miserable, and divorce follows. Thus a procession of divorces can always be justified on the plea that without "love" a marriage is null and void.

As has been said above, there is no general pattern of courtship in the United States. Young people living in the lower-income groups often find it very difficult to arrange matters so that, when they have fallen in love, they can meet the partners of their choice in reasonable privacy and comfort. Some, who cannot afford to join clubs or visit dance-halls, do not always find it easy to meet sufficient numbers of the opposite sex to make a choice of a future mate. The difficulties of American courtship, however, are not only economic or such as could be greatly relieved by suitable introductions or places of meeting. The main obstacle to female success and adjustment in courtship is psychological. Since, in the United States, woman has gained what she believes is almost complete equality with man, the usual female rôle in courtship has to be modified in response to these claims. In other societies man is usually (though not always) the one who woos: woman is pursued and won: she is not the pursuer. This pattern of being pursued and being able to yield to a man equally desired is a source of the keenest enjoyment to a woman, since, when finally overcome, she is able to enjoy the exquisite passivity which is her rôle. Moreover, man is at a disadvantage when pursued, and he is apt to take fright and run away. His idea of courtship is more that of Johnny Beedle as told in the old American story.[1] He does not altogether care for the signs of the times as suggested by the titles of such books as *Get your Man and Hold Him*, *Hold your Man!*, *How to Snare a Male*, or *Win your Man and Keep Him* and *How to Attract Men and Money*.[2] Neither did he much relish the picture painted by Disney's *Bambi*, where the three bold young females soon had the fawn, the rabbit and the skunk all "titterpated". But the fact remained that this was a prevailing tendency, and men had to make the best of it, and run away when the chase became unbearable.[3] Moreover, if he read the magazines intended for feminine consumption, he might not be altogether edified by what he found there regarding the American husband. In 1938 Uhler and Fishback were asking if men were "mice" and saying that they were as timid as amoebae (p. 18). Nine years later Louise Simpson said that a husband was seldom a mouse, but nevertheless could be "trapped"; while in 1942 Popenoe told the readers of the *Ladies' Home Journal* how husbands could be improved "scientifically", and in 1944 a wife revealed the secret of "How I Maneuver my Husband", while the man stated how he liked it!

It is true that in the United States the courting woman, or the

---

[1] See *Traits of American Humour*, vol. i, pp. 66 ff.
[2] See A. Hirst, V. Dengel, J. and E. Bence, and Rosa L. Hill.
[3] The theme of *All Women are Wolves* (Ed. by A. Silver) is that it is the girl who is always out to get the boy and that the chief mission of woman is to pursue the male until capture is effected. The eighteen or more examples in the book are very interesting.

woman who desires to be courted, attempts to make use of all those subtle tricks known to the feminine world everywhere, and her experiences of dating and petting have made her acquainted with what the male wants and how he responds to attractive suggestions. But what makes courtship more difficult for the educated American girl is her incurably romantic approach, with its tendency to divorce love from sex and thus cause disillusionment at the cruder and more practical attitude of men. The frustration and feeling of inadequacy which, in many cases, arose early in life from the very fact of being born a female, is intensified during the courtship phase, in which she often plays a rôle which is unsuited to the feminine being she is, and which not only often wrecks her own happiness when married, but sometimes deprives her of getting a mate altogether.

Before examining the many other aspects of female life in America during the twentieth century a word should be said on the general psychology of the teen-age girl in relation to her environment. Before the rise of the cinema and the influence of two world wars, the American girl, apart from a greater independence and a greater ease in the presence of boys, was very similar to her sisters in England. Her emergence as the jive-jittery bobby-soxer of the nineteen-forties was a gradual one, and was due largely to the influence of the motion-pictures, the sex obsession which everywhere surrounded her, and the numerous experiments in amorous adventure which were an essential part of many of the dates and of all the petting parties. The necessity for sex education was becoming more and more apparent all through the first half of the twentieth century. Although Mary Wollstonecraft had pointed this out in the closing years of the eighteenth century, little was done during the nineteenth century, the age of prudery and purity. It was only when young people began to forgather in private, to take automobile rides and park in dark lanes under the trees, that parents began to wonder what was happening. It soon dawned upon them that, while the less-privileged youngsters were actually making love in many cases, their own children were going nearly as far and perhaps doing themselves more harm in the process. Thus the call for more education became gradually insistent, and books, pamphlets and articles poured from the press urging, protesting, and exposing the evils which supposedly arose from ignorance. The ignorance was certainly massive. It still is, even among adult men and women. Where sex education failed was in the fact that, although it could easily impart the crude bio-logical data, it could do little more, because of the basic idea that alone was permissible in the United States. For purity, virginity

and the joys of the scrubbed feeling which went with chastity w
everywhere proclaimed as ideals. In actual practice, however, the
things were almost openly mocked at. The sordid affairs of Hollywood were front-page news: everywhere the seductive allure of
breast and buttock produced a kind of national tumescence which
was almost infectious. It was like trying to preach virtue in a
brothel. Indeed, simple Americans had earlier actually tried to do
just that in the palatial bawdy house of the Everleigh sisters.

It was thus that in the world of sex and love the same kind of
paradoxes were apparent as in so many other aspects of American
life. Faith and practice clashed, as they did in the economic field, and
just as the trust and the cartel tried to stifle the free enterprise and
rugged individualism of the independent producers, so did the
salacious film and magazine point to the joys of those illicit pleasures
which, according to orthodox American thinking, must hardly be
thought of, let alone experienced. Thus sex education, which, in the
majority of cases, had to conform to current mythology, was not
particularly successful in solving the puzzles offered to American
youth. But the fact that it was becoming less resisted by prudish
parents and educators was encouraging. Certainly, in the early years
of the century nobody could have foreseen that in 1946 Mrs. Hugh
Cabot Jr. would be discussing "puppy love" and "dating do's and
don't's" over the air in Boston in a series sponsored by the Greater
Boston Community Fund.

As has already been suggested, one reason for the general failure of
sex education in the United States is that, as is so often the case, the
basic fundamental facts about sex as it concerns women are either
concealed, passed over as unimportant, or actively resisted. As this
is essential to any clear understanding of the position of the
American woman in the culture of the United States, a word on the
matter may not be altogether out of place.

Of all periods in the life of the child, the early stages are often
thought to be the most important, for it is during this period that
the course of subsequent development is usually laid down. From
the start of life the girl often behaves differently from the boy, yet,
in the aim of "equality" for the sexes, how often—and above all in
the United States—are these differences forgotten, or sometimes
even denied. The ova do not search out the spermatozoa. These
swim in search of them in order to exercise aggression against them
and to penetrate them. The very act of conception implies an act of
male aggression against female passivity. Yet the ovum does not
reject the assault, but welcomes it and enfolds the vigorous visitor.

The very act of love is impossible for the man without tumescence, while in woman it is always possible.

In the life of every child brought up at home the rôle of the mother is all-important, for it is the mother who provides the satisfaction for both hunger and love, and thus the child must inevitably tend to be dependent on her and to lean on her, or in other words its relation to its mother must be anaclitic. The maternal breast must therefore play a leading part in the early life of the child: it is one of the first erotic objects and, an erogenous zone itself, not only attracts the male in later life but craves sensual satisfaction on its own account which it transmits downwards to the primary centres.

In girls the situation is naturally quite different from that in boys. The father tends to regard his daughter with a favour which he does not bestow upon his son. Thus, very early in life, the girl sees that the rival to her father's love is her mother, and a feeling of strain between mother and daughter becomes inevitable. This feeling of antagonism again becomes sensible when the girl begins to attract the attention of men, thus reminding her mother that her own attractiveness is coming to an end. The fond and foolish mother occasionally tries to keep her daughters as well as her sons from growing up, and so from reminding her of the existence of rivalry in which youth would have a decided advantage. This situation is not uncommon in the contemporary American culture. One such example was published in the *New York Journal-American* on April 29, 1943. A young school-girl, holding her school-books behind her, is standing in front of her mother, who is half a head shorter in height. The girl's skirts are well above her knees, and her fully developed breasts look as if they would burst through her thin blouse. She is asking her mother if she can wear long dresses, as, she adds, "I think men are beginning to notice me!"

Apart from these occasions of strain, however, other factors enter into the life of the young girl which are of especial importance in the United States. In this connexion it is relevant to recall Mrs. Eliza Farnham and her attempts to prove the superiority of the woman over the man. It will be remembered that her catalogue of male and female organs indicated a strange forgetfulness on her part (or rather a suppression of knowledge) which was of considerable interest. Now, in the case of some little girls who are brought up in a family of brothers and sisters, it soon becomes apparent to them that they lack something that their brothers possess, and a feeling of inferiority begins to develop. Some try to reconcile themselves to this omission on the part of Nature: others refuse to be complacent and try to behave and act like the boys around them. The girl wishes to be a boy, not because, as she avers, boys have "a better time", but because boys possess what she lacks, and this makes her feel inferior. Later in life the inferiority becomes again oppressive when the woman who claims complete equality with man has to submit to an act in which the very organ she lacks and has always desired plays an aggressive rôle. As Florence says in that brilliant book *Le Roman de Violette* (p. 153), "Je ne veux pas quand je mourrai, qu'un homme ait le droit de dire: Cette femme m'a appartenu," to which the truly feminine Mariette can only reply that, as for herself, "Je sais que je serais très humiliée de mourir vierge".[1] Generally speaking, however, the onset of puberty causes the situation to become easier, and with the recognition of the attraction of her blossoming breasts, the girl buries the earlier feelings, which are then usually consciously forgotten. In a society where women play a predominant part, as in the United States, these defect phantasies, as Viola Klein [2] calls them, are of great significance, for, as every psychologist is aware and as Karen Horney has well expressed it, they "operate as a factor of enormous dynamic power".[3] For not only is there to be found in some women the feeling of inferiority which the lack of something implies, but in addition there arises a desire for revenge on account of their apparent "castration", this revenge sometimes taking the form of symbolic castration of the other sex.[4]

From a consideration of these facts it is clear that the American girl carries within her from her earliest years the seeds of profound neurotic disturbance if the soil be suitable for their unimpeded development. As it happens, the culture of the United States is precisely the kind of medium on which the germs can flourish most luxuriantly. We shall see how much of the discontent, the frustration and the restlessness of so many American women can be traced directly to these phantasies, and that the attainment of "equality" and "independence" has intensified rather than diminished the dissatisfaction with the life they are called upon to live.

Before proceeding with our survey of the later life of the American girl, it will be convenient here to say something about the kind of

---

[1] *Op. cit.*, p. 153. I quote from a reprint of the original edition. The work has been attributed to both Alexandre Dumas père and to Théophile Gautier, but it has been recently suggested that it is by a certain Comtesse de Manoury, a friend of Theodore Hannon. The book is full of psychological material of exceptional interest and value. It has often been reprinted.

[2] V. Klein, *The Feminine Character*, p. 92.   [3] K. Horney, p. 332.

[4] See Emeline P. Hayward, p. 49; and cf. C. Thompson, whose contribution I do not find it very easy to understand, and above all Freud's paper on the psychological consequences of anatomical differences.

evidence we have that the teen-ager's mental stability is hardly that which might be expected from the girlish type of healthy, natural womanhood put over by the propagandists in the American magazines. As has already been noted, the film on the life of the teen-age girls in the "March of Time" series presented what was presumably meant to be a picture of some six million American girls and to illustrate their customs, ways of looking at things and general deportment. Since the number of girls between thirteen and nineteen is over eight million, it can, I think, be plausibly maintained that the picture showed a fairly representative cross-section of the population, although it would seem likely that the sample was weighted in the size of those in the upper and upper middle economic strata. The film, which is American, dealt in an informative manner with the teen-agers of the period (1945) and was greeted in England with amusement, incredulity and even disgust. The London *Times* characterized the girls as "a barbaric little tribe" showing "a terrifying lack of brain and balance", and presenting what could only be described as "a kind of standard, streamlined silliness". Helen Fletcher in *Time & Tide* (October 6, 1945), a London literary weekly, was frankly horrified. Noting that the fawning voice of the announcer declared that these were the American mothers of tomorrow, she realized that the American female teen-ager is "a social phenomenon", or, as she candidly puts it, "a little horror". The young lady must not be different: difference does not make for popularity. Teen-agers try to act alike and think alike, dress alike and make-up alike, with just that little something extra that will attract the particular boy-friend of the moment.

From 1943 to 1945 Sinatra, the successor of Valentino and a heartache for millions of bobby-soxers, ruled as the king of crooners. Francis Albert Sinatra was born about forty years ago, and after trying various jobs, including helping to deliver a New Jersey newspaper, he was engaged as a singer at the Rustic Cabin, a small roadhouse in the same State. There he was spotted by a band leader, and his fame commenced. His effect on young women and some older ones too [1]—was instantaneous and cataclysmic. He was the Prince of Palpitators, the Sultan of Swoons. Girls clawed in screaming mobs to get a sight of him: they dived into snowdrifts to calm their erotic ecstasies: they wrote their names, addresses and telephone numbers in lipstick on posters bearing his adored features. Not that he was particularly handsome. Lean-faced with a mop of unruly

---

[1] Although perhaps John Crain Kunkel or Vic Damone ("Da Moan") were more in their line!

dark hair, he looked to male eyes as if a square meal and a hair-cut were what he most needed. But the girls thought otherwise. When he crooned in his soft, melodious voice they seemed to lose control of themselves and called out to Frankie to take them, as they were all his. Perhaps it was not his appearance (as some thought) but his voice, that "bedroom voice", as one commentator described it. It was irresistible. Once when he went to New York the crowd awaiting his arrival got out of hand: windows caved in, girls were cut and ambulances came clanging up. Those who got into the theatre could not be got out. One sat through fifty-six performances: others stayed so long that they fainted from lack of food and had to be carried out by the ushers. They did not seem to be all the children of the upper middle class. Girls who belonged to the lower economic levels were apparently equally affected. "The Voice"—that voice which was described to me as giving the feeling of "being enclosed in a pair of velvet arms"—touched some hidden spring in the hearts of American teen-agers which defied analysis. Men were hardly able to endure it. When Sinatra appeared at the Hollywood Bowl, where he was greeted with a frenzied, squealing cascade of ecstatic cries, one dour soldier dryly remarked that he hoped they'd remember after it was all over to flush the bowl. Nothing, however, could stop the flood of adulation from the bobby-soxers. They formed fan clubs like the "Slaves of Sinatra" or the "Sighing Society of Swooners"; they tried to follow him from place to place; they sat near his house to see his undergarments hanging out to dry. How could they resist when that melodious soothing and entrancing voice came softly over the foot-lights with such appeals as "Come to me, my melancholy baby"? Frank Sinatra knew his America.

It is not easy to say in a few words precisely what was the cause of Sinatra's vogue, any more than Johnnie Ray's success in England. Perhaps there was more than one cause. It may be that this thin, lean-faced, hungry-looking man touched deeper chords than the one that he reached on the purely erotic level. Whatever it may have been, his success indicates the ease with which the American teen-age girl can be reduced to a state which, even in those who were comparatively slightly affected, bordered on hysteria. It is a valuable commentary on the effect of American education and the success it achieves in turning out well-balanced citizens and future mothers of a great people.

It must be remembered that Sinatra is much more than a crooner appealing to teen-agers. He is a brilliant cinema and T.V. performer. To concentrate merely on his bobby-soxer audience is to lose sight of the very remarkable powers of one of the most notable figures in American show business today.

(4) *Costumes and Perfumes: Breasts and Babies*

To anyone at all acquainted with the life of women the importance of cosmetics, perfumes and fashions need hardly be emphasized. Fashion itself has been dealt with in detail by numerous authors and it would be out of place to recapitulate their findings here. It is, in one sense, as my friend Dr. C. Willett Cunnington so aptly puts it, "a taste shared by a large number of people for a short space of time".[1] Fashion in dress is one means by which women can express themselves, and can not only adapt themselves to that ideal which the men of the period are supposed to favour, but also display to the outside world a kind of index to their position in society. It is true, of course, that practical utility plays a certain rôle in the development and popularity of fashion. Crinolines would hardly be serviceable at the work-bench, and the boyish fashions of the 1920s can hardly be imagined in the eighteenth-century drawing-room, where

> Not ev'n the Ancle could the Lover spy,
> (The Ancle, fatal to the youthful Eye!) [2]

Emphasis, too, had to be considered. At one time attention had to be drawn to the breasts, and when these were thought not to be full enough, bust "improvers", "regulators" and pads were brought into service. Similarly the curve of hip and buttock had to be improved, and the fashionable bustle of the eighties resembled nothing so much as the steatopygian charms of the Hottentots. In men such considerations are no longer very important. In former times emphasis on the genital region was achieved by the employment of the so-called cod-piece, but those were days when the majority of women gloried in their femininity and were not either wanting to be men themselves or trying to pretend that the other sex were not men either.

If it be true that feminine fashions can tell us a good deal of what woman is feeling, thinking and desiring, then a study of female fashion in the United States ought to tell us something of the American woman and the kind of ideals she cherishes from decade to decade. As Jeanne Contini said in 1943, "It is largely true that you can read a woman's character by her hat." How many times, when a woman is worried, distraught or in any way disturbed, can she be heard to say that she must go out and buy a hat. And when she re-

[1] C. W. Cunnington, p. 2.   [2] J. Thurston, *The Toilette* (1730), p. 4.

turns with the object of her desire, how often the hat betrays what her unconscious, and often her conscious, desires and wishes are, and this often without her having the least idea that her hat has betrayed her.

Before passing on to a brief note on some of the more important manifestations of feminine fashion, it may be advisable to say a few words on the search for beauty in the United States. The battle for beauty is long, painful, continuous and expensive. The latter item is important, for beauty is part of a highly organized racket. Many American women fall victims to the beauty business for two main reasons. The first is that it fulfils a deep yearning within them to appear attractive, *chic* and worthy of love; and the second is that they share in common with so many other Americans, male and female, a credulity which, at times, is startling.

The standards of beauty have naturally varied throughout the twentieth century. At the beginning female beauty was hardly considered in terms of cosmetic art, except in that of women connected with the theatre and with professional love. But after the period of the First World War cosmetics and facial treatments began to be much more popular. At first they were confined to the smart set, but later the custom spread, partly on account of the additional allure that paint and powder bestow and partly through the immense influence of the cinema, which portrayed the elaborate make-up of the Hollywood stars. The idea that "make-up" was daring and gave the wearer a feeling of being a little frolicsome, not to say wanton, was an added zest. As time went on the beauty business assumed immense proportions. Charm schools taught ladies how to "vamp" men, how to walk, talk, smile and "how to wrap up every MAN in the room", as one advertisement put it. They sat for hours in beauty parlours: they suffered mud-packs, "facials" of all kinds, perms and artificial eyelashes. They were rubbed, pummelled and kneaded: breasts were made larger or smaller: buttocks were pressed in or made to protrude. Nothing was overlooked and everything was paid for. The beauty parlour became a secondary female club where, beneath their helmets and packs, the women gossiped, talked scandal and discussed men.[1] The body became an object of the greatest interest to its owner and everything was done to make it sleek, daintily perfumed and thereby ready to fulfil its purpose. Even the mysterious essences of the super-sensible world were forced into the service of beauty, since I see that in 1945 was advertised a treatment

---

[1] Cf. Jean De Chant, the hair stylist, who has written an amusing account of the gossip and behaviour of American women in the beauty salons.

which included the use of a cream which claimed to be the only preparation in the world "with a touch of Prana".

The natural odours of the body caused much heartache, and rich profits were sensed by those who believed that they could persuade women that "B.O." was objectionable and should be abolished. Every kind of deodorant was soon on the market, followed by depilatories, as the hair was supposed to hold the odour and diffuse it. Even that was not sufficient for the salesmen of sweet haloes for women. They had to turn their attention elsewhere, and New York daily newspapers began to carry illustrations of beauties who had not attended to these intimate details of their toilet. We are told in one that the love of her husband slowly changed to a frigid strangeness: in another (where the neglected damsel in a provocative negligée has waited to be loved till 3.12 a.m.) that she never guessed why her husband never came; and in another (where she is shown clinging to her bridal photograph) that she was now a wife only in name—a "single wife". Body-odour was clearly a money-maker, not only for those who sold the preparations for combating it, but also for the physicians who had to prescribe remedies for those who had foolishly used them to excess. But the fashion demanded it, and nobody could be considered "well-groomed" who failed to deodorize at least her arm-pits and her mouth. Failure to do so was to court disaster, since by your failure you could ruin the pleasure of one who had to sit next to you at a movie or concert. From women it was but a step to men. It was apparently only through the widespread use of these powerful deodorizers that the members of the human family could approach one another. As one advertisement put it, "Girls use a deodorant: why can't the boys reciprocate?" Apparently "the boys" obediently followed this suggestion, and many others also. By 1947 it was reported that the cosmetics-for-men business was turning over an account worth fifty million dollars a year and was actually selling a paste to conceal the effect of a face apparently or actually in need of a shave. American men clearly liked this new idea of making their faces look like those of women, for they bought (or the women bought for them!) 57,000 jars in the first week.[1]

With the cosmetic business that of perfumery runs hand-in-hand. In American perfumery the influence of France has always been powerful, although within recent years the attempt to create "an American Era" in exclusive scent has been meeting with some success. Modern perfumes in the United States, and above all advertisements through which they are sold, are very revealing of

[1] See H. Rattner, *Cosmetics for Men* (1946).

the purpose in feminine life that they are supposed to serve. Space will permit of only a few examples to illustrate what I mean. Nomenclature varies through suggestion, defence, danger, aggression to the final aim. Thus we find perfumes such as "Innuendo", "Indiscretion", "My Sin", "Shocking" and "Tabu". The last-named has a great reputation. It is said to possess a tempestuous sweetness and to do such important things to her who uses it. One of these things, according to the advertisement, is to cause a musician to clasp his accompanist instead of playing his fiddle, which proves the truth of the assertion that it is almost unaccountable in its maddening hypnotic influence. Other perfumes had even more intriguing names. There were "Heartbeat" and "Risque", "Courage" and "Cobra", "Tigress" and "Black Panther", and finally "Checkmate", "Wild Oat", "Moment Supreme", "Lady in the Dark", and "Unconditional Surrender". What more could women need in the way of scent to capture the elusive and susceptible male? They could vary the perfume to suit the quarry, and when perhaps a little something more was needed to turn the scale between acceptance and flight, there was the fun of having one's garters made of one's own hair—scented, of course—and discussed by the ladies in secret session under the revealing name of "Wolf bait". They were then ready to meet their captures, who had already provided themselves with pyjamas decorated with pictures of wolves sold by the B.V.D. Corporation.

Although the reform of women's dress was attempted in the middle of the nineteenth century by Amelia Jenks Bloomer (1818–94), the only real changes were due to the gradual adoption by women of outdoor activities which precluded the employment of the kind of costume that was habitually used. But before, during and after the First World War there were great changes. We cannot discuss these fully here, but must refer the reader to the many source-books dealing with the period. Women were being employed in industries where voluminous skirts and frilly blouses were dangerous, so these were exchanged for such garments as slacks and clothes better designed to prevent accidents. The age of slimming demanded clothes suited to the prevailing fashion, and young women went about in clothes which had a decidedly masculine appearance. Thus, instead of emphasizing breasts and buttocks, the tendency was to suppress both: "correctors" began to be used and attempts were made to produce "that boyish flat appearance". These methods led to considerable experiments in breast control, and young girls whose bosoms refused to be flattened suffered much misery for not being able to be fashionable. During the craze I was consulted by an anxious Massachusetts mother on the condition of her daughter, who was ashamed to go out or even to be seen in company. I was asked whether such means as tight bandages or even leaden weights might be efficacious. I replied that, not having seen the young lady, I could not say, but doubted the desirability of taking any steps to remedy a situation which, in another era, would have created pride and satisfaction. On seeing the girl it was clear that, fashion being as it was, she was in a difficult position. She had a magnificent figure with breasts which, today, would have been considered her greatest charm. I did my best to assure the mother that her daughter was a splendid specimen of young womanhood, and advised her to take no steps whatever to try to alter what Nature had designed. I hope she took my advice.

I am not aware when the term "brassière" came into common use in the United States. Laver (*Taste and Fashion*, p. 167) states that it was the freeing of the bust that led to the building up of the brassière industry, and Hallgren (p. 412) is of the opinion that the brassière as we know it today came in during 1929, whereas R. C. Holliday thinks that they were worn at the beginning of the century. Apart from the word, however, which was certainly in use in England in 1912 or earlier, the accessory itself was clearly derived from the "dress improvers" which were in use in England about 1890 and which were widely sold. Some of these were made of silvered wire with a band attached behind, and were offered in various sizes from 9s. 3d. to 16s. a dozen. From these, it was only a step to the modern shaped brassière, since in former times the improvers had cunning little pockets in which could be inserted artificial aids towards the ideal of various sizes of breast development. In the United States it would seem that the progress made in the design of these garments may have been more advanced since the review *Corsets and Brassieres* began publication in 1896. However that may be, by the time the boyish figure was no longer fashionable and curves again became apparent, the brassière became an essential feature of feminine wear, and the catalogues of the thirties are filled with designs of every kind.[1]

The return of the ideal of curves and rounded contours naturally led to emphasis being placed upon those parts of the body where such were most noticeable. But when the flat, boyish outline gave way to well-rounded shapes—natural and artificial—few would have

[1] A support for a cow's udder was invented in 1948 and manufactured in Los Angeles. The possibility of reference to the favourite subject was immediately seen. It was promptly styled a "brassière" and the cow was photographed wearing it! (See *Time* (Atlantic Overseas Ed.), Oct. 18, 1948, p. 12.)

foreseen the gradual emergence in the United States of what could only be described as the twin fetishes of breasts and buttocks. Indeed, at one time it would seem that male interest in the breasts, the cleavage between them and their shape and contour, was such as to offer a problem to all students at all interested in the lesser-known aspects of social phenomena. Although it might be thought that here was to be seen the familiar mechanism of displacement upwards, I am inclined to think that the explanation is to be sought elsewhere. Before, however, dealing with any analysis of the fetish itself, a few words describing it will not be out of place.

In the 1850s a well-rounded bosom was not considered elegant or fashionable, since those were the days when a willowy figure was desired and its possession stimulated by lemons, vinegar and keeping out of the sun. Twenty years later the reverse was the case. Girls wore pads of hair or cotton which were fastened over the breasts with straps, but instead of raising the breasts and allowing free development, these contraptions distorted them and pressed the nipples inwards. Those who could afford them, however, were able to buy far better designs. These were hollow hemispheres of vulcanized rubber or wire which fitted over the breasts themselves and gave "a perfect and fascinating outline". Some years later the fashion again demanded less emphasis on chest expansion, and "an unusual womanly development" in a girl, which attracted secret attention, was a thing about which many a mother was disturbed.

After the First World War came, as we have already said, the slimming craze. The "little girl pals", as some called them, had to compete somewhat with the pansies and the elegant whores, so they tried to turn themselves into curious hybrids, and the torso became, in James Laver's graphic words, "a flattened tube" where curves were absent and the young woman could at times wear slacks and excite no attention or ridicule.

Although in 1939 Gaudefroy-Demombynes maintained that the American man preferred a finely formed leg to the curves of a well-developed bosom, there were many signs that a breast boom was well on the way, and by 1942 it was raging, and still shows no signs of abatement. Indeed, the war years seemed to excite the population of the United States to a state of sexual awareness that was unparalleled in the nation's history. Film stars vied with one another as to which could show the most swelling bosom and the most curvaceous haunch. Anne Baxter, Dolores Meran, Esther Williams, Ann Gwynne—all these and many more were photographed for "pin-ups", and in each the bosom was the feature that was most admired.

Advertisements for soap, powders and even books showed the same features. Breasts were everywhere, and brassières became ingenious bags of gadgets for raising them, protruding them and generally emphasizing their existence. False ones were on sale—cheaters, falsies and boob-baits, the men called them—and these were modelled so carefully as almost to defy detection. (In a superb cartoon by Peter Arno in *The New Yorker* of August 16, 1947, p. 35, one of the young ladies has apparently forgotten to insert hers in their proper position.)

The cinema was not slow to cash in on the prevailing mania. The *Sins of Bali* was styled a "brassièreless thing of beauty", for in Bali breasts were bare and, according to one elegant account, resembled chunks of chocolate ice-cream cones.[1] It was true that this picture had other attractions than bare brown bosoms. It was about a savage queen who, with her "wild virgins", conquered the men who came to her island. At least, so the poster said. In Walter Wanger's *Arabian Nights*, with its "100 love thrills", it seemed that Queen Shera's breasts and those of her harem ladies could scarcely be restrained within their filmy coverings, but the same observation could apply to those of Vera Zorini in her sensational Black Magic ballet dance in *Star Spangled Rhythm*. In the *Maid in the Ozarks*— "naughty! spicy! daring!"—a poster showed the young lady on the ground with her legs in the air and her breasts almost bursting through her tiny garment into her boy-friend's face. No wonder the poster called it "bawdy! lusty! unashamed!" In *Rama*, the "dazzling, daring" cannibal girl was depicted with no clothes on at all, but this was to be expected, as in a triple bill at the Studio Theatre in Chicago in December 1942, it was the prelude to another film about the "unashamed nudists" of all nations.

With the passion for the bosom there developed another curious fetish which concerned itself with the cleft between the breasts. Traces of this were to be seen in the posters of films in 1943, such as one of *The Powers Girl*, in which the heroine was depicted lying on the ground with her head towards the observer so that it was possible to look down her dress, this being facilitated by the fact that her legs were raised perpendicularly. Similar suggestions were to be seen in *Silver Queen*, the "siren of the most sinful town in America", and in the burlesque shows and "midnite jamborees" of 1943 some of the girls made a speciality of dresses which emphasized the cleft.

By 1949 the mania seemed at its height. Even though the feminine

[1] See H. Graffis, *A Breast of the Times*, p. 104.

form was never approved if it approached the fat, breasts and buttocks were still emphasized on poster and pin-up to a degree which made the informed observer think that he had forgotten his anatomy. The "Petty Girls", which were the creation of George Petty, were remarkable airbrush productions. Although the girls were of slim physique, the breasts and buttocks were exaggerated to a degree which must have been exceptionally seductive to those making a fetish of such charms. They were known from coast to coast in bar, barn and barracks, and their type, along with others, is brilliantly described by Steinbeck in *The Wayward Bus* (p. 3), where he ponders on what a visitor of another species might think if he cast an eye over these striking, pumped-up and artificial bosoms. Indeed, this remarkable feature of American life was described by Barzun in an amusing article originally published in *Chimera* in 1946. After pointing out the sex obsession in the United States, he stresses the fact that almost every department of life has to be portrayed in connexion with seductive young women making sheep's eyes and nearly always in a state which Mother Nature confers upon them only during the period of lactation.

It was in 1947 that English opinion was aroused and intrigued by the breast fetish when Jane Russell appeared in the film *The Outlaw* at the London Pavilion. Generally speaking, the critics were cool, if not somewhat hostile, as it could hardly be expected that a somewhat largely developed bust (37½ in.) would excite much interest in an adult British audience. In order to stir up publicity it was arranged by a female press agent that the psychological reactions of some members of the audience should be tested, and some British newspaper critics foolishly allowed themselves to be used as material for the stunt. Mr. Dick Richards of the *Sunday Pictorial* was one of those whose reactions on the "emotion meter" were 28 centimetres when Miss Russell appeared in a loose bodice! This was produced as evidence of the "sex-appeal" of the lady in question, which even a hardened British reporter was unable to resist. Alas! the triumph was short-lived. Mr. Richards had to point out that he had registered a higher figure at the sight of a horse! The "boffo terrif", which the curves of Miss Russell hoped to achieve in England, was not so great as had been anticipated, which is what one might have expected. The same reception was accorded to the picture in Bombay. Indeed, it soon had to be withdrawn, I am informed, since people left the theatre, and many of those who remained greeted it with whistles and cat-calls. Doubtless it is not easy for Americans to understand how it is that much of what is for them amusing and attractive is considered silly and offensive by other peoples, and the same thing naturally holds the other way round. Were candour greater, more understanding might perhaps be achieved.

One of the reasons why American women today pander to this curious passion is because they are convinced that they cannot hold a man without it. Thus, to take a sample number of *Modern Romances* (circulation over a million), we find in the issue of January 1946 a number of advertisements for bosom culture; and it is noteworthy that this issue was the first which carried "Bachelor Bill's Postwar Course in Love". For example, on p. 66 we are told that the bust-line is a "key to style" and a firm bust-line is a "basic need". To get it the reader is advised to buy "bra-cups" which will support and elevate the breasts. On p. 80 one is taught how to develop thrilling curves and an alluring bust-line. This will give her who follows the necessary advice a glamorous, glorious personality. This bust-culture in the home can also be achieved by the use of a wonder cream which is absorbed by the breasts, or, if a really new and thrilling "uplift" is required, the reader is advised to write to Hollywood for a cute little Betty-Bra in peach or white which is guaranteed to flatter any woman.

During the war the fetish had remarkable repercussions. The sight of the breasts, seemingly about to escape from the fluffy embrace of bodices or nightgowns, was sufficient to register a high figure on an emotion meter applied to the American man, but when these same glands were beneath a sweater and apparently about to burst the stitches, excitement became almost uncontrollable. Girls who could show the desired curves were much in demand and the sale of sweaters rapidly increased. Miss Dale Belmont—"the Blue Velvet Voice"—got her engagements through her charm and her comely curves, but she became seriously annoyed when she found that her sweatered torso was being used to advertise *The Complete Guide to Bust Culture*, as she thought that the suggestion implied that her curvaceous appearance was due to artifice, and that she had, therefore, deceived the 50,000 soldiers who in the Second World War had received her photograph for a pin-up. The popularity of the sweater was such that competitions were held to show to what extent girls were able to expand their charms beneath the material. Helen Cyriaks, the official Sweater Girl of 1943, was selected from more than 10,000 entrants. In California the same year, Alice Wallace was picked by the Associated Apparel Manufacturers as the State's "sweater girl"; and in 1947, when the bosom fetish was still raging, Hollywood picked glamorous Caren Marsh for a land-girl and chose Marie McDonald for another part in which she was photographed in a pair of extremely tight shorts and sweater which catered for the prevailing taste in both directions. The Sweater Girl became, in truth, a national figure. In 1943, as one newspaper put it, the "War Plant Faces a Major Issue", for the Sikorsky aircraft plant was in trouble. Sweaters were not allowed, on safety grounds, but the girls preferred them and appealed to the War Labor Board Office. The personnel manager knew that the girls wanted to attract the men, but declared that they were in the factory to work and that sweaters were not suitable. In spite of the ban on sweaters, the appearance of what were called the "bubbling cuties" in the war factories caused havoc in many an American home. Dorothy Dix declared in December 1943 that she had received a veritable avalanche of letters from the wives of men working in the factories, complaining that the young ladies had changed their faithful Derbys into philandering Casanovas. Cupid had discarded his bow and arrow in favour of the humble rivet. From a war factory the plant became a matrimonial agency and annexe to the divorce court. The men could not resist the blandishments and the breast and buttock wigglings of the new arrivals. To these complaints even Dorothy Dix could say but little. Men seemed susceptible to the wiles of the glamorous cuties, and they forgot the friend-wives at home and the years of companionship and mutual happiness. It was just one of the casualties of war.

One result of the modern obsession over breasts, belly and buttocks was a fresh slant on the strip-tease business. It was no longer sufficiently attractive slowly to reveal the popular portions of the anatomy. Attention had to be drawn to them more directly; and Miss Sally Keith of Boston showed the way in 1947 in expert fashion. By shaking her breasts and twitching her buttocks she succeeded in manipulating coloured tassels which swung together in different directions, thus going two better than the *danses de ventre* of former days. But it was not only the bare buttocks which were brought into service for these odd wigglings and twitchings. Along with the use of false breasts in the 1940s came gradually to the fore the new American bustle which was popularized in the movie *Coney Island*. This appendage, according to the fashion advertisements, provided a "dramatic silhouette" that was both flattering and pretty, and of which the distinguished effect was made even more striking by a Hollywood designer who so arranged the bustle that the lady was able to illuminate it when she wriggled.

Not all women cared thus to exaggerate their hinder charms.

Janet Lane called it an unpopular (but necessary) "rear excrescence",[1] and Adèle Astaire (then Lady Charles Cavendish) lamented the fact that, in England in 1945, where the "lovely girdles" were scarce, the "posteriors" of ladies visiting that island had "spread quite a lot". The extra weight, however, could sometimes be put to good use in the American art of seeing that men were kept in their place. In 1948 *Time* thought it important enough to tell the world that Adèle Astaire's new coat was made of the skins of male minks and not female, and therefore less fine and delicate. This news was not received well by the owner of the coat, who decided then and there to have it cut up so that the male skins could be turned into a lining, "so's I can sit on it", as she made haste to explain.

With the disappearance of the streamlined figure, the hips, as we have shown above, began to be more and more noticeable and interest in them increased in proportion. Writers went out of their way to tell tales of how bottoms were pinched by Europeans, who should, of course, have known better.[2] Photography was enlisted to feature the fetish in many a seductive pose. "Stars" were chosen as pin-ups and were shown in poses well suited to the prevailing mania: a famous tennis-player was snapped in 1946 at Forest Hills Stadium "taking a tumble" and in a position doubtless pleasing to the fetishists, the same motive being apparently active in the plate illustrating blue, red and green panties and printed in *Life* for August 30, 1948, p. 36.

Before passing on to consider further aspects of feminine apparel it may be useful to comment upon the psychological aspect of the breast and bottom fetishes in the United States. Although from reading the massive treatises on American social life the foreigner would never glean much worthwhile information, he can hardly fail to note the interminable references to these matters in the popular Press, and in any diaries and chatty memoirs that he may be lucky enough to see.

These two parts of the human anatomy are clearly of absorbing interest to the average American, and there must be some reason for this. Indeed, Kinsey (p. 575) declares that interest in the breast among the American men he dealt with seems to have replaced in-

---

[1] J. Lane, p. 68.

[2] See Ilka Chase (p. 34), whose book *Past Imperfect* is full of material for the student of American ways of thought. Thus she says that young Americans want to look like peas in a pod; that the thought of Marion Davies's bedroom with two bathrooms at either end is the kind of thing which haunts a person waking up in the night; that Gary Cooper is the national dream man of the United States; that life minus a man is no life at all; and that adults in America cry all the time (*op. cit.*, pp. 45, 88, 98, 101, 208).

terest in the genitals. As I have said, I doubt whether the shift is due to the well-known phenomenon of displacement upwards, but am inclined to agree with John McPartland when he states in his *Sex in Our Changing World* that this abnormal interest in the breasts is a symptom of the increasing emotional infantilism in the culture of the United States. Of modern authors McPartland is one of the most discerning in emphasizing what is usually ignored, and in his *Footnote on Sex* (1946) he stresses the contradictions in *mores* and ethics, noting sensuality and prudery at the same time (pp. 212 ff.).

Later I shall have occasion to deal with the oft-repeated statement that, to the foreigner, many American men appear to be immature, adolescent in outlook and, in their sexual lives, to remain in a condition which in normal men ceases soon after puberty. We shall see how these features have been observed for many years by writers of various nationalities, and how the evidence that the observation is true is overwhelming. Since the education of Americans is largely in the hands of women, and since the influence of the mother is very strong, it is clear that the clue to this delayed maturity may be found in the treatment which the American male receives in school and at home. Now, one feature of life in the United States that no informed person can deny is the exaggerated devotion to the Mother. We shall see later how that cult operates and what are its results. Here it will be sufficient to point out that a devotion to the Mother, carried to the extent that it is in the United States, cannot fail to influence the unconscious as well as the conscious minds of American men. Many are, in a sense, still tied to their mothers, and although they long to escape, they cannot do so entirely. That they succeed in achieving only a partial freedom from the Mother and from Woman is shown by the social dichotomy everywhere apparent. As Pearl Buck and Muriel Draper have both so truly said, men and women in the United States do not live together, but live "curiously separate lives" in which the man's attempt to escape from woman is shown in his passion for business and the pursuit of the dollar, where he can be free from his mother, his wife and his female children. But although he thinks that by this escape he attains freedom, he is much mistaken. The influence of his early life and education is too strong. He remains tied to Woman by silken bonds, and struggle as he will he cannot escape. He remains therefore in a condition of what observers describe as "adolescence", in which the worship of the Mother and all she symbolizes plays a powerful rôle.

What better symbol of the Mother could be found than "the pure fountain of the maternal bosom", as milk was said to be described by

Heman Humphrey in the nineteenth century? It is therefore not difficult to see why the breasts should be thought of as so attractive, especially when we remember that, apart altogether from their maternal significance, they constitute erogenous zones which have always been admired and commented upon in the love literature of the world. In this connexion also it is interesting to observe how at different times the "fashion" changes, and the less conscious desires and wishes are damped down to make room for more novel and unusual predilections, such as for women resembling men, with flattened breasts and slender hips.

As concerns the buttock fetish the situation is somewhat different, although here again we find a relationship established with events occurring in early life. Anyone conversant with American society will be aware of the immense interest taken by numerous people in constipation, purges, water-closets, bathrooms and plumbing generally. In the late eighteenth century colonial New England had few of the sanitary amenities we enjoy today. Streets were left uncleaned and bathrooms and running water were unknown. Even in the 1830s there were in New York no hot or cold baths in one of the two biggest hotels, while after 1842 the bathroom was not popular, if we can judge from contemporary and other accounts. As late as 1890, when hot and cold water was beginning to be laid on, people were complaining of the unpleasant smells that arose from the pipes. It was only with the increase of wealth, luxury, refinement—and neurosis—that the passion for bathrooms, plumbing and elaborate water-closets began to grow. Moreover, the fear of "germs", which ever haunts Americans, also helped to further the sale of fittings to be used to cleanse the body and assist the processes of elimination, which latter subject seems to plunge so many Americans "into uncontrollable hysterics", and, according to Elmer Rice (*Sex in the Modern Theater*, p. 688), to arouse "gales of laughter" when alluded to in a place of entertainment.[1]

Apart altogether from the utilitarian side of good plumbing, the interest taken in it by Americans is such that there must be other reasons why we find such frequent mention of these matters in their literature. Gorer is apparently of the opinion that this emphasis is to be interpreted as a sign of the belief that these material advan-

---

[1] *The Bedside Esquire*, p. 14. Such jokes in the United States are very curious. Steinbeck in *The Wayward Bus* (p. 153) describes a novelty in the style of a miniature W.C. toilet for measuring drinks; and the sight of one of the sea-lions at San Francisco's Seal Rocks wearing a white toilet seat around its neck caused much mirth, and was thought worthy of being included as "news" in the Atlantic Overseas Edition of *Time* for April 26, 1948, p. 12.

tages are signs of the superior nature of American civilization. Certainly from reading American accounts of the deficiencies in other countries it would seem that American travellers find the lack of this special interest in water-closets abroad very trying. The foreigner also often fails to understand what can be called the American mania for bathrooms, bathrooms so superbly furnished and equipped that Miss Ursula B. Branston, for one, was quite overwhelmed when she visited the United States. In one private house she found the bathroom for the guest-room fitted up so elaborately that even the seat of the toilet had its own little tigerskin jacket! [1]

In 1949 the American public were informed that "it's here", and that a gay new way had been devised by which a sun-bright beauty could be brought into the bathroom. It was an inspiration and was as everlasting as the waves of the ocean and as clean as the sea-breeze. As gay as a mermaid, it was a miracle of miracles, and the public was advised not to hesitate a single minute. Only by using this beautiful device could that "so-right touch of glamour" be brought to the bathroom. It was supplied in varied colours—in rose-orchid, surf-green or coral-peach. It was a pearl at the price, one advertisement actually showing it lying in an oyster-shell. Moreover, it was identified by its own mark, a charming mermaid, half-undressed of course, and carrying a tall hat in one hand. Here indeed was something for which any American would, as the description has it, be thankful *forever*. Here was the last word in bathroom charm, a new kind of seat for the W.C.

During her stay in America, Miss Branston was surprised at the exhibitionism shown by the female students at Duke University, and also by the notice displayed on the walls of the W.C. "Why not flush the John? This means YOU." This desire to preserve the fæces is a well-known phenomenon and is not in any way confined to the United States. It springs from the infant's pleasure in creation, in presenting its first gift to the mother, and in showing its early power to retain and keep to itself something the mother or nurse entreats it to evacuate. The elaborate ceremonials often indulged in by neurotic individuals in the bathroom, and washing compulsions generally, are to be understood only by remembering the unconscious feelings of guilt which often form part of these ambivalent contamination phobias. If the importance of the bathroom and the W.C. as we find it in the United States has any relation to the same importance that is indubitably found in the lives of neurotic individuals, and for the reasons outlined above, then we ought to find in the United States

[1] V. B. Branston, *Let the Band Play "Dixie"*, p. 135.

widespread and chronic constipation. And this is precisely what we do find.

Everywhere are advertisements extolling this or that laxative: one so-called expert advises some "harmless" chemical, while another, like Mr. Albert W. Haberstro, the Master Miracle Mind, preferred a "bio-physical" method. Whole institutions have been opened to deal with the menace of constipation and piles, since it must be remembered that Dr. Béran Wolfe had reminded women that the latter affliction destroyed their sense of humour, while the former clouded their minds.[1] Who can forget the palace of the stately Dr. Bernard in New York, where patients were instructed how to insert rectal cones of different sizes (only $20 for three in velvet-lined case), and to stand on their heads (delicacy assured by wearing the Bernard Bloomers), thus upsetting the internal organs and compelling them to yield and deliver. Interest grew apace and the soldiers of the Second World War were fully indoctrinated with the stercoral ideas "back home", and were prepared to find fault with the upbringing of the uncouth Europeans. So we find such writers as Hamilton Fish Armstrong writing in the sober journal *Foreign Affairs* in 1945 about the thousands of American troops in lands largely innocent of the use of the water-closet, and how naturally the boys longed to get home to taste Mother's pies again. As a matter of fact some of the soldiers seem to have become a little tired of the literature which so often reached them from the folks at home. A letter was printed in *Yank* on June 11, 1944 saying that soldiers did not want to read about water-closets, but the fuss that the reporters and medical officers were always making did little to allow them to forget them, and for the important conferences many preparations had to be made to cater for the American delegations' interests.

As I have already indicated, this abnormal preoccupation with the affairs of the toilet suggests that psychological disturbances of a subtle kind are operating in American society. We have seen how the interest in the breasts can be connected directly with the Mother Cult. Can the interest in the hinder parts be also derived from circumstances similar to those from which the bosom mania stems?

We have already seen how the Puritans regarded sex and, above all, any manifestation of sexual pleasure in women. When the Puritan experiment failed, and much of what was good in Puritanism was forgotten while much that was bad remained, the connexion of sex with sin, and nasty sin at that, was still remembered, and

[1] W. B. Wolfe, *A Woman's Best Years*, p. 5.

caused untold misery and harm. It has been maintained that up to 1905 sex and sin were synonymous, and this was doubtless true in some quarters. But what was more important was the lack of sex-education among young people and (especially among women) the supposition that there was a close connexion between genital and excretory activity.[1] Even in boys genital activity was often regarded as being a mere "evacuation" or "outlet", and a common slang expression in the United States for the term "to copulate" is "to ease nature", thus indicating a close parallel with expressions relating to the excretory functions. The constant warnings and diatribes against masturbation also were often interpreted as a prohibition against "easing nature", and were carried over to the bowel function, thus in many cases causing years of habitual constipation.

The situation in the United States, however, is more complicated than that. Many a child in its early toilet training learns that by withholding its fæces it can cause great annoyance to its mother or nurse: and thus when it is angry and resentful it pays them out by refusing to sit upon its pot. Freud, in one of his papers, dealt with this situation and its results.[2] He pointed out how those "anal-erotic" characters, as he called them, exhibited clearly recognizable traits, among which were an interest in money, in economy and at the same time in latrine wit. Is it by accident that we find all these traits so widely distributed in American life? I think not. The escape *from* woman *to* the dollar can be seen, therefore, as a kind of reversion to an early infantile stage where money symbolizes the fæces which the child collects, creates and occasionally evacuates. The power of the mother, rarely greater than in the United States, can thus be curbed, and one result of this curious revolution is what Mabel Dodge Luhan called "our national weakness: constipation." [3]

We can now get some idea of what may lie beneath the interest that American magazines, films and stage shows exhibit in the display of the hind regions of the human body. The interest is twofold, being partly conscious and partly unconscious, with ample scope for rationalization. It has often puzzled acute observers that the cleft between the breasts appears today to excite even greater interest than the breasts themselves. Joseph Rank, the British film magnate, is reported as having been completely puzzled by this feature when

[1] See *Mental Hygiene*, 1944, pp. 55–63.
[2] *Sammlung kleiner Schriften*, etc., p. 132.
[3] M. D. Luhan, *Intimate Memories*, vol. iii, p. 515. Mrs. Luhan clearly recognized the relation between fæces and money in the United States. As President Eisenhower's physician pointed out, the Americans are bowel conscious.

at Hollywood, and had to point out that in England this division
was not considered "sexy". He failed to understand what lay behind. For it is not difficult to understand what every student of the
comic postcard and the erotic cartoon knows—namely, that the
breasts and the nates have features in common, and that the cleft
between the breasts can be compared with the cleft between the
buttocks. That is why in American slang the buttocks are sometimes
called "the bosom of the parts". Thus here it may be possible to
perceive a displacement downwards and to the back, instead of the
usual mechanism of displacement upwards, as is seen in the common
expression "a pain in the neck". What has possibly happened is that
the mother-image has suffered a kind of distortion in which the nates
have replaced the breasts as a subject of devotion, in which cult, as
we have seen, numerous and complex factors have played a part.

Just as the importance of the breasts in American life showed a
great increase in sales of the more complex form of brassière, so did
the second fetish encourage the use of special forms of panties. Even
in 1935 the girls wore "the briefest little briefs", but by the late
1940s these were literally skin-tight and one style was sold under the
name of skintees. An even more revealing article of feminine underwear were the "Hands off Panties" which adorned shop-fronts in
New York in 1948. These were made of black filmy material and
were practically transparent except for a narrow band of opaque
material. On one side of each of these alluring garments was woven
into the material a large *black* hand. In the autumn of 1947 nightgowns with large black hands woven into the material, to give the
idea that both breasts were being clasped, were shown at a fashion
show, this time in Australia. These nighties were called "Gaspers".

It will not be possible to describe in detail all the clothes worn by
the American woman during the course of the century. The details
can easily be found in the fashion magazines, which provide just
those features which are lacking in earlier times, as anybody consult-
ing such useful books as *The Customs of New England* by J. B. Felt
can see for himself. As fashion changed, and as the century advanced,
it was to be expected that clothes would reflect prevailing ideas and
that, as mass production became more widespread, current ideas on
dress would be adopted by more and more women. Moreover, the
psychology of the wearer was not a thing to be overlooked. A "Black
Panther" perfume, with its suggestive meaning, might go well with
a lady who, like some in 1943, wore fur panties and brassières, for,
as Malvina Lindsay said, a leopard skin over the lady's own skin
would make her feel so feline and dangerous. A year later the idea

had spread, so the charm of the feline touch was observable without disrobing the lady. Leopard-print play clothes were on sale in New York, and those wearing them could thus pretend openly and unashamedly to be what before they kept secret from all but themselves and their more intimate associates.

Again, the bathing-dresses of the early years were soon exchanged for the skimpy garments of recent times, but even these had later to be adapted to the bosom mania and had to be provided with built-in and wired brassières and other contraptions which *Life* described as "a multitude of engineering tricks", and which can be compared with men's idrotobolic hats of the nineteenth century. Indeed, the art of "fitting the feminine form" became more and more difficult, and clothes began to be provided with numerous ingenious gadgets to cater for the popular tastes. Just as the ordinary day clothes and underclothes became more glamorous, so night-attire became more and more alluring. Some nightgowns were openly sold under the name of "Sinners": others were described as "folly ensnared" in translucent lace, which, like black cobweb above, was joined below to a sheer rayon chiffon. Such a garment was, the buyer was assured, a real "rhapsody for the uninhibited" and cost only $7.98.

With regard to hats, the American woman of taste and refinement was supreme. Her hats were, as Mrs. W. D. Humphreys expressed it in 1911, "a never-ending joy", and to those who knew something of the ways fashion can be interpreted they were extremely revealing. Wars, as James Laver and others have pointed out, have always exercised a profound effect on women's clothes, and hats prove no exception to the rule. Indeed, it has been said that as they can be changed in appearance more easily than clothes, they provide a more sensitive gauge to indicate which way social trends are moving. For reasons connected with both the supply of materials and other more subtle causes, hats in wartime and afterwards often assume simple forms, and sometimes these forms are of considerable psychological interest.

I have not the space here to deal with this aspect of female headgear, but from my large file on women's hats will select a single example. During the Second World War, when, at one time, simplification was very noticeable, many hats assumed a very odd shape. Instead of a *cloche* or bowl-shaped hat, in which convexity was the key-note, these hats were concave and looked as if they were modelled on an inverted soup-plate plan. At first these hats were of great simplicity with little decoration, but even in their simplest form I had a strong suspicion what symbolism they suggested.

M

At that time I was engaged on work which necessitated seeing a great number of fashion magazines from Europe and America, and I looked forward to the files placed on my desk in order to trace the development of this form of hat. It seemed to me very probable that it represented a conventionalized form of bird's nest without any eggs in it, and I was anxious to see if its subsequent development proved my suspicion to be correct. As time went on this form of hat underwent a change. Floral decorations appeared round the rim, and finally the hat appeared with a bird sitting on it. Eventually cartoons began to appear, in one of which a live bird actually mistook the hat for a real nest and perched upon it.

I am not aware if any of these hats have been recorded with eggs included among the decorations. I have never seen any, the nearest approach being a perfectly plain inverted "nest" with, in the centre, a black velvet inset of ovoid shape. However that may be, these fertility symbols were very popular. At the same time there began to appear hats bearing conventional models of human genitalia. Some of these were very curious. One model, worn in the United States early in 1943, consisted of a kind of disc sailor foundation on which was perched a remarkable construction in three parts which could have only one interpretation. Others were purely phallic. In some cases the motif was switched to the feminine angle. Hats began to appear with curious double folds of unmistakable design, and others had long open tubes perched upon the top of the foundation pieces. These were called "high, sculptured felts" and were being sold in Chicago in August 1942. Realism, however, went further than these comparatively modest designs. A lady of my acquaintance one day came to see me proudly wearing the new hat that she had just bought. Frankly, I was quite shocked, for perched on the top was a model of male genitalia which might almost have found a place in an anatomical museum. Seeing my look of horrified fascination, she said brusquely, "Well, don't you like it?" I replied that I thought it very realistic and asked her if she had been visiting a medical institution. She looked surprised and, taking it off, gazed at it. Then she uttered a cry of horror. "My God!" she said, "I can never wear it. How could I have bought such a thing without seeing what it was?" She thereupon hurled it across the room and was about to stamp on it when I retrieved it. Calm was restored when I suggested that by an operation the hat could be rendered less obvious. Here was a case in which the lady was completely oblivious of the symbolism of her hat, even though she was a well-known and extremely competent psychologist.

Sometimes, however, the sexual invitations are wholly uncon-
cealed, as when a girl will wear a scarf with "Vive l'amour" inscribed
all over it, or when men's ties have naked ladies as part of their
flamboyant designs. Sometimes the invitation is even more striking
and disguised in the form of a joke. The symbolism in a man's tie
is too well known to need any discussion here, but perhaps my male
readers may recollect the numerous occasions on which they have
seen to its proper arrangement just before entering a room in which
other people are gathered. However that may be, the tie has recently thought fit to remove part of its hidden meaning, and to come
out in the open, as it were. Before me, as I write, lies an advertisement of a fascinating contraption which, I am assured, will make the
"girls go into hysterics". Indeed, this gadget will make a fellow "a
popular guy", whose friends will "remain fascinated". It is called a
"rising tie", and for its movement "up and down" it requires "no
hands, no bulbs". The picture accompanying this clever notion
shows the guy standing between two young ladies, very *décolletées* of
course, and gazing with horrified fascination at the tie which has
risen just in front of them. Behind the central figure is the gloomy
face of a second gentleman whose tie is not thus fitted, and remains
obstinately in place.

Again, as Dr. C. Willett Cunnington reminded me, ladies' dresses
have sometimes drawings of genitals all over them, as he proved by
taking from his collection a photograph of a French model, in which
part of the design consisted of phalli with no attempt whatever to
disguise the fact (see *Vogue*, October 1935), another less obvious *motif*
being featured in an advertisement in the *English Speaking World*
(August 1946). Similar effects can be observed in Maxfield Parrish's
enormously successful decorative picture of the girl in the swing.

Before completing the above brief remarks on woman's dress in
the United States, a word must be said concerning certain fashions
which throw a great deal of light not only upon the rôle women are
called upon to play in American life, but upon American male
psychology in relation to that rôle. Anybody acquainted with the
stereotyped ideal of "glorified" American girlhood cannot fail to
have been struck by the curious doll-like appearance she presents.
Even in the early nineteenth century the famous Timothy Dwight
(1752–1817), who was President of Yale from 1795 till 1817, thought
that education in New England tended not to make the girl pupil
into a woman but into "a doll"; and as the years advanced the worship of the doll-woman grew into a cult of which we have not yet seen
the end. Early in the twentieth century a French observer,

G. Moreau, writing in 1906, found many American women he met "exquisite dolls", who seemed to have learnt their parts and who spoke "like automata". These baby-faced, made-up creatures were called by highly appropriate names in American colloquial speech. For example, they were called babe, baby-bunting, lady-doll, bay-bee, cherub, cutems, dimpled darling, doll-baby, dolly or sweetalums. This desire to look like young teen-age girls was not confined to young women in their twenties. In 1933 Lucie Delarue-Mardrus noted (p. 103) how it often seemed that elderly women got themselves up "exactement comme les filles de quinze ans", and that many of those she met resembled fresh-looking dolls. Precisely the same observation was made in the same year by the Oxford philosopher, L. P. Jacks, who said that he had the feeling when in New York that he was "moving in a world largely peopled with dolls" (*My American Friends*, p. 47). But there was another side to the picture. Not all the middle-aged and elderly women were doll-like and immature.

The doll-like clothes to which the writers refer are indeed very odd, and in many cases it is almost impossible to determine if they are really intended even for teen-agers. Thus I find in my files such examples as the "pinafore Pretty" with its "baby blouse" which was sold in New York in 1944 at about $11. Then there was a garment called "Smarty Pants" at $2.95 which, the advertisement tells us, is cut like "a four-year-old's shorts with a button bib" and "Baby-Doll Panties" advertised in 1951. Finally, we have recently received a photograph of a really remarkable get-up, which apparently consists of merely a small "beruffled bra" and a pair of extremely attenuated shorts which are described as "curt, colourful and curvaceous", the last adjective evidently referring to that portion of the body they scarcely conceal.

This desire of women to appear like babies and dolls can hardly be considered a fact unworthy of analysis, especially as the flood of American magazines into Europe is beginning to cause an appreciation of their alleged charms among the more susceptible of the male population. It is true that protests have been made. A British corporal wrote to the London magazine *Picture Post* on January 20, 1945, asking the editor not to print pictures of pin-up girls, as every magazine the soldiers saw was "daubed with these artificial posing dolls". If pictures of women were wanted, he added, let us have photographs of people with "some resemblance to real women" and not these "vacuous, synthetic creatures, whose brains are as meagre as the things they wear". Indeed, his opinions seem to be shared by the late Mr. Damon Runyon, who can hardly be accused of not knowing the United States. In one of his amusing articles entitled *Dames can be Trained to Act Human*, he says that the best treatment for the doll is to get her away from her mother, from a charge account and from the telephone. It might be possible then, he wrote, to make her act like a human being, for it was clear that the whole fair sex could not all be congenitally giddy, gabby or goofy, and that the reason why some seemed that way was because the conditions in their home environment had been too lax.

It may be thought by some that this attempt by numbers of grown women to appear as dolls or babies was merely a freak of fashion, and presented no other features than the choice of clothes of a somewhat youthful pattern. This is, however, not the case, and at the risk of digressing somewhat from the discussion of women's clothing, I propose saying something about other manifestations of what I call the "baby-cult" in the United States.

As has already been remarked several times, the curious "adolescence" or delayed maturity of many Americans has been noticed by many observers from abroad who have travelled in the United States and has been commented on by numerous perspicacious Americans themselves. But apart from this adolescent attitude to life, the baby-cult is hardly known to foreigners generally, and must be exceedingly mysterious to those who have observed it.

We have already noticed the female teen-agers and their interests. Even in the older groups nearing twenty, some of the observations made by American inquirers are interesting. Thus F. Isabel Davenport, in her study of high-school graduates of about nineteen years of age, found that there was far more interest in the anti-social manifestations of sex and in the more primal expressions than in the questions of love, subsequent marriage and parenthood. Indeed, at the time she wrote (1921–4) she stated that training for motherhood was considered "unclean", and one girl actually asked her if there was "any decent way" of regarding the question of child-bearing.[1] It was just such an attitude towards serious matters that had been so roundly condemned in *The Virgin's Nosegay* in the eighteenth century. Speaking of such young women, the author, "F. . . . L . . . . . ., Esq.", said that there were some "affected Babies, that think it modish to be above troubling their weak Noddles with such homely things as House, Family and Children" (p. 189). However, the cult of appearing babyish in appearance, clothes, speech and behaviour

[1] F. I. Davenport, *Adolescent Interests*, pp. 48, 59, etc., and cf. her *Salvaging of American Girlhood*, pp. 191, 186.

began many years later, O'Higgins and Reede, in their discerning book *The American Mind in Action*, being of the opinion that these child-women first began to attract notice about 1850 and only later became the idols of the typical American (p. 151).

The cult extended rapidly owing to the popularity of such characters in the movies, and by 1936 the "Hey-Ba-Ba-Be-Bop" school was all the rage, again to blossom later in the Mairzy Doats period. In her discussion of American women of the 1937 period, Marjorie D. Kern, after stating that they were the most restless, discontented and neurotic wives in the world, went on to say that Europeans did not care for childishness in women, preferring maturity, and hinted that this adolescence on the part of many American women might be one of the contributory causes why they had to live in a state of "magnificent isolation" and were kept at a distance by their husbands.[1] Similarly, the French critic Georges Duhamel, writing seven years previously, contributed a biting indictment of the American Way of Life from the little that he had seen of it, and spoke of a woman of forty as "délicieusement puérile", concluding that one of the main factors in stultifying the culture of the United States was the cinema and what it portrayed.

By 1939 the cult seemed to be at its height. The cinema excelled itself in fairy-tales, and Shirley Temple and Baby Sandy were box-office favourites. Grown women were beginning to wear the "little girl" or "baby-doll" clothes mentioned above: the radio presented childish games, and cabaret and night-club singers cooed and gurgled baby language. It was the age of the "goo-goo-honey" girls, and, as Erbes pointed out, the average mental age from the point of view of the advertisers was six. Baby suffixes had to be appended to goods for sales purposes. People had to ask for Toesies and Snuggies, for Quickies and Jiffy-Lax. The "talkies" were soon to follow, and doubtless we shall soon have the "smellies".[2]

---

[1] M. D. Kern, *Why American Women Marry Foreigners*, pp. 23–5.

[2] Cf. *Printers' Ink*, Sept., 1929. For an account of these garments see "Kid Clothes" (*Life* (Intern. Ed.) Aug. 2, 1943, p. 67 ff.). Here will be seen a lady of eighteen wearing rompers suitable for a child of ten, and a remarkable picture of young women sprawling on the ground in positions which suggest that the article is not primarily for those interested in fashions.

The article, "'Little Girl' Clothes" in *Life* (1946) should also be consulted. In 1944 the public safety commission at Long Branch, N.J., took action to prevent "200-pound 40-year-old mamas trying to make themselves pin-up girls by walking around in shorts and sarong outfits" (see *Stars and Stripes*, July 14, 1944). Zora Hurston, in her *Dust-tracks on a Road*, tells some revealing stories of the behaviour of adult American women whom she served. One played with dolls and invited herself to tea; another romped like a puppy and conducted herself like an infant. Miss Hurston adds dryly that this lady loved her mother to an excessive degree (p. 124).

In 1943 Rose Franken's *Claudia* was performed. Here is the picture of the American child-wife tied to her mother, who is not only an intimate relation but a symbol reminding her of the life of irresponsibility she never wishes to renounce. Although very different from the theme of Ibsen's *A Doll's House* the essential feature was the same. The young wife, still living in a kind of phantasy world, gradually begins to see that she can no longer preserve that phantasy intact and has, perforce, to face reality. But the world of 1879 as seen in Norway was very different from the world of 1943 in the United States of America. How revealing, therefore, that the child-wife should still be a person to be discussed in the land of feminine freedom and emancipation over sixty years after Nora Helmer slammed the door behind her, and that, like Juliet in Lewis's *Cass Timberlane*, she should still be called "the chronic child-wife", talking baby-talk and running to the "infantile in clothes".

At the end of 1943 a wave of baby-talk spread over the United States, for at that time a new song began to be heard which was first popularized by the Silly Symphonists at the Dixie Hotel in New York. Part of the ditty ran: "Mairzy Doats and Dozy Doats and Liddle-lamzydivey" (Mares eat oats and does eat oats and little lambs eat ivy). In a few weeks "Mairzy" became a best-seller; sales topped the 700,000 mark; contests were based on the "Mairzy" language; letters were sent round written in the "Mairzy" way; baby-talk became a national hit. Comment by more serious American students was singularly revealing. Gertrude Samuels in the *New York Times Magazine* (1944) discussed the new song under the heading of "We enter our Mairzy Doat-age", and pointed out that the song could be heard on some 100,000 juke-boxes from coast to coast. Only a few psychological critics, however, were so bold as to affirm that the song was a hit because it appealed to infantile traits in adult Americans. It was, I think, precisely that, and vividly illustrated a feature of American society which is little understood in the United States and still less in Europe. To return to childhood and baby-talk is to return to security and irresponsibility, to isolationism and a world of peace. The war could be forgotten. By 1944 the "iddly-oozy" words, as *Time* characteristically called them, were still spreading fast, and even those who were making records of the song began to be puzzled. It was, as Bandleader Trace said, "the damnedest thing".

As early as 1940, when the baby-cult was raging, even men were affected by it. They started wearing Peter Pan collars, and bought little "playsuits" which were simply childish rompers. How far this was due to pressure from their womenfolk is uncertain. But four years later a book was written by Monte Sohn which purported to be typical letters written by a small-town socialite to her son at the front. How far these letters were supposed to be a caricature of the kind of letters mothers were writing I do not know, but I suspect that there was far more truth in them than reviewers were willing to admit, as many cartoons of the period suggested the same theme. At all events, these letters to "Pookie Presh" and "my poor little baby-manchild" were interesting to those studying the American baby-cult, as some of the advertisements of the book in the American Press started their notices by asking, "Whom does she remind you of?", clearly suggesting that the lady in question was an American mother.[1]

Women naturally had to suffer the same childish names being applied to them in print. Mrs. W. R. Hearst, Jr., was called by *Time* "pretty, pouty Austine ('Bootsie')", but sometimes protests were made. Margery Wilson in her *The New Etiquette* (p. 411) rather plaintively declared that women really don't have to talk baby-talk or display a wide-eyed innocence they certainly do not possess, and an enraged husband consulted Dorothy Dix in October 1942 as to what he was to do with his wife, who would "talk babyish". Miss Dix was not very helpful, since as a matter of fact she, like so many American women, seemed to imagine that men everywhere liked to be babied as they did in the United States. Indeed, a few days later she told wives that men never entirely grew up and put away childish things, and never outgrew their longing to be mothered. The wise wife, Miss Dix thought, must play up to the little boy in her husband, kiss him when he is good, and spank him when he is naughty. There wasn't a husband, she thought, who did not secretly like his wife to tell him he was the "boofest ting", and said that one only had to look at the gold-diggers with their millionaire sugar-daddies to see that they always treated them as if they were five and not so bright at that. "It's sure-fire tactics," concluded Miss Dix.

(5) *Recreation, Cinema and the Radio*

One of the most striking changes in the social life of urban and rural America since the nineteenth century has been the increase and nature of recreation. As a society becomes industrialized, and

---

[1] Cf. Matt Curzon's cartoon in a Section of *This Week Magazine* for Jan. 16, 1944. A returning American sailor with a long beard confronts his mother, who sprawls almost swooning on a sofa. "Don't you recognize me?" he says, "It's your son—your baby!"

mechanical ingenuity, novel inventions and fresh uses of raw materials become widespread, so does recreation become more popular and a wider choice of leisure become possible. Increasing means of transportation, also, permit rural dwellers to visit the cities, and as the demand for entertainment grows so does the supply of varied forms of such enterprise gradually increase. Moreover, in many cases the field is not left wholly in charge of the private person, and the States themselves take a hand. Urban authorities supply cultural centres which meet a need among the more educated of the population, and, in out-of-door activities, the National Parks and other large-scale enterprises indicate that all forms of recreation are by no means the monopoly of the private and uncontrolled individual.

In the case of women these changes have had a marked effect. For with the great increase in material prosperity came an increase of leisure, since domestic tasks, which previously had to be done by hand, were now taken over by the machine. Thus work in the home was lessened and, with the children at school, many an American housewife found time to turn to other than purely domestic activities. The younger girls too were not unaffected. With the growth of games, swimming and dancing, together with a gradual lessening of parental control and an increasing sense of independence, the younger people began to indulge themselves in forms of recreation which would not have been tolerated in earlier days. The rapid increase in the use of the automobile was, to a certain extent, responsible. Parties of young people became accustomed to leave town and seek amusement in a neighbouring city, or to attend dances at halls away from the city centre or in roadhouses. In the lower strata of the large urban population, pleasure parks of the Coney Island type always attracted their thousands, and the appeal of these forms of amusements was not always confined to the ill-educated or poorer sections. It is recorded in the *Autobiography* of that famous Middle Western newspaperman William Allen White that after he and his family had returned from their European trip they decided to have the real thrill of their journey. They all went to Coney Island and did everything there was to be done, finally adopting as the family motto the sign, "Ain't it Grand to be Bughouse?" (p. 421).

The two forms of amusement, however, that have exercised more influence than any other are, undoubtedly, the moving picture and the radio. For while the moving picture was, until the coming of television, an amusement for which one had to leave home, radio was actually brought into the home, and what it provided could be enjoyed while still going about the ordinary duties of the household.

Before briefly considering the effect of the cinema and radio on the life of American women, a word may be said on the subject of dancing. During the latter half of the nineteenth century the waltz was considered a gay dance, and those taking part would never have dreamed that forty years later young people would be bunny-hugging and turkey-trotting and a few years later to be doing the jitterbug and the big apple. Some of these changes in dancing were undoubtedly influenced by the rise of jazz and Negro rhythm, adapted for modern Western use. Duke Ellington raised jazz to what might have been called a new form of folk-music, but, like so many other novelties in the United States, it was gradually forgotten and became outmoded. The effect of the Negro influence was obvious. No longer was the dance a graceful art in which the movements of the partners synchronized with the music and in which there was little to suggest a sexual rhythm. In the new dances the partners often moved cheek to cheek, and in the stifling night clubs the crowds on the dance-floor were, in many cases, unable to move around, but remained swaying, jigging and pressing one against the other. The dance had become, not a prelude to more private and intimate exercises, but the thing itself in a twisted and perverted form. It had developed into precisely what the Puritans had feared it might do when they forbade it. There is no doubt that many dance-halls cater for clients who are not interested solely in dancing, and thus constitute a danger to young women who are not acquainted with the vice rackets and the means employed to obtain victims. In wartime such resorts had to be specially watched; and many efforts were made to induce soldiers and sailors to patronize the various service centres where the "hostesses" were young women whose history and character were carefully screened before admission.

When the moving picture was first shown in 1896 in New York it was not thought that it would ever have a universal appeal. The pictures were shown to small audiences at cheap halls and were usually of the adventure or slapstick variety with little attempt at dramatic presentation. Indeed, it was only towards 1907 that the film-producing companies had become well organized and began to take advantage of the enormous possibilities for profit that the new invention was beginning to suggest. It took some years before the companies began to realize what actually were these possibilities in the sexual sphere. The early twentieth-century pictures were mainly scenes in which comedy and simple dramatic tales predominated, and in which little of the "glamour" of later productions was discernible. Indeed, as C. A. Lejeune has pointed out, the sexual possibilities of the moving picture were first envisaged in Germany about 1909, and it was about six years later that they were realized in the United States.[1] One of the first signs of the coming deluge was the appearance of Theda Bara (Theodosia Goodman), who was discovered by the Fox Company. This lady must in those days have been a terrifying vamp. She was supposed (for publicity purposes) to have been the daughter of a French artist by his Arabian mistress and her name was an anagram of Death Arab. She received reporters with wild hair and with her body wrapped around in a flimsy shroud and her part in such pictures as *A Fool There Was* made the flesh of the audience creep. Her sinister sex-appeal was a triumphant success. "Oomph" had arrived and was not always to be feared. The appearance of the Vamp marked a step forward in the plans of the industry, and early in the 1920s films began to appear which clearly suggested a drift towards the suggestive, the lascivious and the frankly obscene. This might have been foreseen, since sex was interesting to almost everybody, required no literacy and, if presented in the most telling way, had an enormous and eager audience for ever awaiting fresh thrills. By presenting pictures to suit such a public, success was assured, although care had to be taken to avoid productions so scandalous that they were interfered with on grounds of decency.

Early in 1922 the resentment of some members of the community grew so strong that the industry saw that it must call a halt. Terrified of Federal censorship, it formed the Motion Picture Producers and Distributors of America, Inc., for the purpose of keeping just within those limits beyond which trouble was clearly waiting. After the publicity which had been engineered to advertise the alleged clean-up had subsided, Hollywood took stock of the situation, but the time for drastic control by the Federal authorities had passed, and it was not long before those who realized what was happening again took action. This time the Legion of Decency was organized by the Roman Catholic authorities, and shortly afterwards (in July 1934) a fresh Production Code of Ethics was established ostensibly for controlling objectionable material. How far the success of these bodies has been achieved must be left to the judgment of the individual. But it may be said that the problem of censoring the film on the grounds of alleged indecency is similar to the same problem in the theatre and in literature generally. To some critics, like G. J. Nathan, it seems that censorship is mostly illogical when it comes to the theatre, and the same objection might be raised in the case of

---

[1] C. A. Lejeune, *Sex and the Movies*, p. 76.

the moving picture. On the other hand, it is felt by some that the part that the imagination has to play in the screen robs the pictures of the sensual attraction that is offered by the stage. Actresses in the flesh, it is urged, are in a sense partners in "actes de luxure", whilst on the screen they are idols and what is offered is the unattainable and the impossible.[1] Moreover, it has been pointed out that the standards set by the screen characters are likely to be accepted in many cases even if they be contrary to prevailing *mores*, C. C. Peters giving as an example the fact that, according to his estimate, 76 per cent. of the pictures illustrating love-making present the girl as aggressive as opposed to passive in her behaviour.[2]

In considering the content of the motion pictures it must be remembered that the audience is made up of persons of all ages, and very often, in the case of the more ambitious productions, other countries than the United States have to be considered. Since children visit the cinema in immense numbers, a good deal of attention has been paid to their requirements, although it is not necessary to go into any details here. It may be of some interest, however, to recall the account given by Katherine G. Busbey in her *Home Life in America* of the adoration of the female child in many an American household in 1910. She stated that the "beautiful creed" (p. 74) of American parents included a belief in their daughters' claims to attention, and stated that they desired them to have a theoretical sophistication. They must be treated, it was urged, as if they knew nothing, and writers and dramatists must be compelled to restrict their productions for the sake of the girls, who were to be allowed to go everywhere and see everything. Such a policy may account for the infantile character of so many American amusements.

Apart from the animated cartoons, the main themes of most films are love, sex and crime. Although some studies, such as those made under the Payne Fund, probably exaggerated the effect of these pictures on children, it is true, I think, that in the case of adolescents the harm done by the cinema in the United States is far greater than is generally believed. Although many of the ridiculous scenes of synthetic love put out by Hollywood can only cause small children and educated adults of discernment to laugh derisively, the effect on the adolescent is very different. In the case of the boy the effect is not so lasting as with the girl. The majority of men have jobs to work

---

[1] Cf. Carlos Larronde, *L'érotisme de l'écran*, p. 572.

[2] See C. C. Peters, pp. 97, 84. Among Peters' critics was Mortimer J. Adler (p. 639), who was opposed to the whole of the Payne studies, although I cannot say I am impressed by the presentation of his arguments.

at and businesses to conduct and operate; they usually have not the time to get themselves up like the film characters, and have but a small desire to escape into those forms of glamorous phantasy in which the American woman revels. Thus, as the Lynds pointed out in 1937, adult females often predominate in the audiences at the better theatres, and it is their tastes that the producers have always to bear in mind.[1] The same point has been emphasized by Margaret F. Thorp in her admirable and satirical account of the American moving-picture world. It is, she stated, the ordinary, average American woman who commands the attention of the producer, and the reasons for her love of the movie dream can provide us with a key to much that is difficult for foreigners to understand about the American woman and her needs.

The first point to be noted is that the world of the moving picture is a phantasy world, a world into which one can *escape* from the drab reality of everyday life and can oneself take part in the glamorous scenes that are unfolded. As one advertisement reprinted by the Lynds in *Middletown* pointed out, by going to the movies one can *live* the story, and all the romance lacking in daily life can be found on the screen. Thus if it is only for an afternoon or an evening, you can *escape*. For just as readers of the earlier novelists sought to escape from American actualities in "the flattering mists of sentimental optimism", as H. R. Brown put it in his *The Sentimental Novel in America* (p. 360), so do American women try to escape the "monotonous graceless reality" of everyday life. Of all the phantasies they see, the Disney creations are perhaps the most striking examples. One of the tragedies in the lives of so many American women is that they have never learnt to develop their personalities except in terms of romantic phantasy. This is largely due to the vicious Hollywood propaganda of glamour of which we have already seen the effect in considering the teen-agers. Moreover, with the increase of mechanical household aids and the production of ready-made foods from cans and frozen packets, the American housewife often finds time hanging heavy on her hands, and can be tempted to while away an hour or so in imaginary scenes of luxury and adventure. Cinema husbands are not like the men who daily return worn out from the office, described in *Life* in 1946 as "wrung-out rags".[2] They are very different from the "perpetually tired men" to whom

---

[1] R. S. and H. M. Lynd, *Middletown in Transition*, p. 261.

[2] See Pearl S. Buck, *Of Men and Women*, p. 39; and cf. *Life* (Intern. Ed.), Nov. 11, 1946, p. 12, with which may be compared the passage in J. A. Hübners *Ein Spaziergang*, etc., p. 40.

so many American women are usually married, according to one of Pearl Buck's female informants.

It is thus that the film provides an ideal means of escape for many an American woman, an escape not only from the everyday existence of home life, but an escape from her own personal conflicts and the psychological tensions which continually afflict her. What she wants is glamour, romance and action, sensation, and more and more of it. The American lives on sensation. Every day banner headlines disclose this murder or that rape, this horror or that disaster. All these features can be seen in the movies and the advertisements which proclaim their charms. "Tigers roaring their death-threats! Apes screaming their fear! Terrifying human sacrifices." Such were the words which advertised *Booloo* in 1938, and the woman who was thrilled with these delights was then told the same evening in another charming screen feature *How to Undress*. But, as Margaret Thorp points out, even these thrills lose their savour after a time, in spite of the Hollywood stunts of fake nurses helping fake swooners out of the theatre past the queue, to slip in again at the back door and swoon again at the next performance. More and more horror is wanted, so the time comes when we want to see, as an advertisement had it, "hundreds of people killed in a new and diverting way".

For the purpose of illustrating the kind of material put out in order to satisfy these female cravings for glamour, horror and sensual thrills, I propose choosing a few examples of pictures released during the last few years, noting especially the kind of advertisements printed to draw the public into the theatres showing them.

One of the favourite themes is to show woman not as the civilized and patient American housewife doing her domestic chores and attending her church and club, but as a wild, wild woman who lives a life of barbaric splendour and sexual joys. Thus in *She Devil Island* we find a savage queen ruling a colony of wild virgins who at last are visited by men. In *Duel in the Sun* we have a rip-roaring picture in which the lady (in a low-cut dress, of course) tries to resist the flames which consume her and fails time and time again, only at last to die, thus teaching us that the scrubbed feeling that goes with chastity was really better. Or perhaps the power that women wield is worth it. In *The Moon and Sixpence* the advertisements declare that women were "strange little beasts", for if you treat them like dogs, and beat them till your arm aches, they will still love you, and in the end will get you, and you are then helpless in their hands. "I don't want love," the hero moans, "it interferes with my work" . . . but she says (with her sarong almost falling off), "I know he loves me because he beats me"! As another advertisement said, "Everybody's talking about what Charles Strickland thinks about women". The torture of the half-dressed heroine is sometimes carried to extreme lengths. Paulette Goddard had to suffer it in *The Unconquered*, and the thought of this white-skinned beauty writhing under Indian treatment led many a client to visit the film and see it for himself. A similar piquant situation was revealed in *The Blonde Captive*, where a white woman "goes native", and, clothed in a few flowers, is captured by cave men (whom she prefers to Broadway's wolves) and lives a life of sensual pleasure on the Solomon Islands, where she was found, so we are told, by Dr. Paul Withington of Harvard. Again, what a thrill to think of oneself, clothed only in a short, very short, skirt and a brassière and tied to a tree, whilst advancing towards one is a half-naked young giant with a clasp-knife. Such was the scene depicted in the advertisement of *Tarzan Triumphs* in which Johnny Weissmüller co-operated with Cheta the chimp.[1]

Many critics, like Duhamel, were emphatic in their condemnation of such films. Sir Thomas Beecham, for example, on returning from the United States in 1946, declared that Hollywood was a universal disaster compared with which Hitler, Himmler and Mussolini were trivial. The arts in America, he continued, were a gigantic racket run by unscrupulous men for unhealthy women. These are strong words, and, as might be expected, any criticism of either

---

[1] We shall return later to the Tarzan *motif* when dealing with the American man in his relation to women. It is interesting to observe, however, that the heroic white savage has two faces, as it were, and, as Deutsch points out, he can act both as a seducer and a saviour, or perhaps as a seducer after the saving has been accomplished (see H. Deutsch, vol. i, p. 222). The domination of a woman by a powerful male is naturally a favourite phantasy in the United States, where women so often have to play the rôle of the dominant sex. Many novels harp on this theme, and scenes are in print, as they are on the screen, to show some hairy-chested giant as the wild lover. Cf. Thomas Wolfe's tale *April, Late April*, Brendan Wood's *Sligo*, who was found irresistible by Lydia Wright the sculptress, although it is true that she destroyed him in the end; Morrison Wood's *The Devil is a Lonely Man*, where Anthony Wayne's violence is vividly described; and Ilka Chase's *In Bed we Cry*, where the cosmetic queen, Devon Elliot, suspected that "the beast" in Jasper Doolittle was a "splendid creature". Perhaps also some of the charm of such books as Winsor's *Forever Amber* or Mitchell's *Gone with the Wind* were the insistence on the brutal in love, as where Amber or Scarlett is carried to bed by Rex Morgan or Rhett Butler. Again, such books as *Give him to the Angels*, by Harry Greb, are read with zest by women who are able to live themselves in the tale presented, and even a book like A. B. Guthrie's *The Big Sky* is enjoyed by the more educated women, who see in Boone Caudill the type of wild, hard frontiersman who combines gentleness with violence.

In spite of "chest muffs" (artificial chest hair) being sold to gentlemen for the purposes of adornment, a hairy chest is not the sign of a masculine "he-man", neither do gorillas have hair on their chests. Such details, however, do not bother Hollywood.

Hollywood or its productions is much resented. Indeed, during the last few years literary critics of the films shown by American companies in England have been the cause of attempts on the part of the companies' agents to subdue criticism which has been thought to be unfavourable. The case of Turner *v.* Metro-Goldwyn-Mayer in 1946–7 will be remembered, where Miss Arnot Robertson's film criticisms for the British Broadcasting Corporation were resented; and again in 1947, Mr. Otto Bolls of Twentieth Century-Fox objected to Mr. Paul Holt's review of the film, *The Razor's Edge.*

Perhaps one of the most curious examples of the Hollywood portrayal of the American Way was seen in the picture *The Best Years of Our Lives.* Here we can see one of the basic patterns of life in the United States, a life where the men are childish, nervous and inept, and the women are strong, dignified and wise. The pictures of the sailor who has lost both his hands is especially instructive. For here we have the male who cannot any longer be aggressive. Safe at last, the woman must be the active partner, as the man's passivity is forced upon him.[1]

In the more recent pictures of the post-war years, it was not to be expected that Hollywood would forsake the themes which had so long expanded box-office receipts, namely, sex and violence. Woman had, as always, to be portrayed in her triple rôles, that of the glorified American showgirl, the saintly Mother or the devouring Mom.

Female pulchritude was still displayed in ravishing forms, both wet and dry. Esther Williams succeeded in saving Rome simply by letting Hannibal have a peek (*Jupiter's Darling*); and Jane Russell seemed almost to be usurping Miss Williams's common rôle as the enticing water-nymph by appearing in *Underwater* in the briefest of shorts and other scanties, tempting alike to sharks and to submarine wolves. The irresistible charm, indeed, of the female animal was seen to perfection in *Betrayed*, where Clark Gable, playing the stiff-upper-lipped intelligence officer, found the greatest difficulty in seeing through the charming spy (Lana Turner), whose amorous escapades could hardly fail to arouse fears for the chastity of the Secret Service. The virtue of purity was again finely portrayed in the film *The Seven Year Itch*, where a little cleaning up of the original play was needed to make Tom Ewell's fingers on a certain occasion do some useful work instead of wantoning with Marilyn Monroe,

---

[1] Cf. the film *King's Row*, where a male character is legless. It was Mabel Dodge Luhan who acutely observed (*op. cit.*, vol. iii, p. 228) that women like to have their men sick in bed, as then their patients cannot escape the domination that the female can thus impose upon them.

whose gambols might have been thought capable of seducing St. Anthony.

As Mom, the American parent came in for some rough handling in *The Shrike*; and in the screen version (*Intimate Relations*) of Cocteau's *Les Parents Terribles*, Mama's boy (Russell Enoch) played a part which must have stirred many a chord among the audience.

Violence continued to be portrayed on the screen in various forms. Ernest Borgnini was especially to be noticed for his convincing characterization of villainy (*Violent Saturday*), a rôle for which he first became famous in the screen version of *From Here to Eternity*.

Apart from these major themes, there seemed a tendency to produce more films of a semi-serious or semi-documentary description, both psychology and psychiatry showing here and there a pronounced influence. Many of them dealt with war conditions, as, for example, *The Bridges of Toko-ri*, where the hero loses his life and thus fails to fulfil the "happy-ever-after-with-Grace-Kelly" theme. Finally, there were the frankly reformist films such as *Riot in Cell Block I*, where prison conditions were portrayed as vividly as those in mental hospitals had been in earlier years.

With the rise of the Italian film actresses the American female stars have to face alarming competition, for not only have the Italians more sex appeal than their rivals, but many of them have far more talent. The appearance of Gina Lollobrigida in *Bread, Love and Dreams* was an eye-opener, not only to the American man but to the American girl, who saw that here was a competitor who would be hard to beat. Europe showed it could do all that the Hollywood stars were doing and do it better.

It would hardly be fair to all those who work for and write about Hollywood to maintain that there exists no body of opinion which objects to the tradition of irresponsibility and lust for gain which has so firm a hold over those who hold the power in the motion picture industry. The very existence of the *Hollywood Quarterly* would suffice to dispose of any such assertion. Moreover, the weakness of the censors is sometimes shown in reverse. Minney in his *Hollywood by Starlight* (p. 152) said that in certain States the local authorities refused to permit any picture to be shown in which a man, woman and bed appeared together, even in a shop! Such proximity might, like cradles, suggest thoughts best forgotten. These are, of course, mere details in the immense ballyhoo which permeates the city of celluloid. But they may be straws in a wind which one day may reach tornado force.

As we have seen, the cinema as a form of feminine amusement had

N

a profound effect upon the general pattern of women's lives, both physical and mental. The coming of the radio was going to add its effect to that pattern, although the fact that it would be enjoyed without leaving home made it an essentially different form of relaxation from the motion picture.

From the female point of view, the radio is a mixed blessing. In the evening it may often happen that members of the family want to listen to different programmes, and certainly they would hardly care to tune the receiver to what the advertising concerns have kindly provided for the women of America during the day-time hours. For during this time certain of the radio networks broadcast a programme which is said to be listened to by eighty million women every month.[1] The nature of these broadcasts has to be heard to be believed. Whenever I arrive in my hotel in the United States I turn on the radio, hoping that one of these so-called "soap-operas" may be in progress. Sponsored as they have been by certain soap interests (hence the name), this deluge of sentimental folly is of profound psychological interest and importance. For this is what the radio thinks millions of American Women want, and *in fact* millions do listen to the activities and sayings of a troop of moronic characters, sobbing, drooling, sniggering and sometimes reeking in gore mixed with gush, until even the most hardened investigator has to turn the radio knob to silence. Here we find, as Philip Wylie has pointed out, "mother-love" of the lowest kind, for those who listen can hardly fail to be stamped with the matriarchal brand. For in the mixture of what has been described as the "furious retchings" and "inane stupidities" of these daytime serials can be detected certain broad outlines of what might almost be called policy. Although clearly defined moral codes are blurred and distorted, yet what remains must not shock the listener into rejection of the tale. And in the core of the story is generally a woman's problem placed before women: poor, suffering, tenderhearted women, from whose beautiful eyes stream tears—salty tears, buckets and buckets of them. Here, in these poignant dramatic scenes, the women of America can learn how good and long-suffering they are, how self-sacrificing and self-effacing—how superior, in fact, to the mere man who always creates the troubles, and who is weak, miserable and generally inept.

The soap-operas are triumphs of American sob-dramas. As wish-dreams fulfilling the needs of millions of frustrated American women they are masterpieces. Beneath their imbecilities lies something that

[1] See *Radio Research*, 1942–3, pp. 3 ff.; E. Hawes, *Anything but Love*, p. 5, and cf. R. Palter's *Radio's Attraction for Housewives*.

women want, something with which they can live and escape the drab uniformity of life at home. The characters become alive and vital to them. Their hearts leap when little Annie is almost killed, and they are full of pity when someone else has a sore throat. Remedies are sent to the studios to soothe the inflamed tonsils. Tit-bits are dispatched if a character states that he or she likes a lollipop. These dramas of the air assume the pattern of straight news. Phantasy becomes reality. Moreover, the troubles in the drama, unlike so many of those in real life, are resolved. Money is not so important, as the serials are listened to mainly by women in the middle-income groups. And since they are often written by women —American women—it is natural that man should be put in the place reserved for him by the dominant sex in the United States.

I am unable to agree entirely with those who denounce the soap-operas and maintain that they do much harm to those who listen to them. Indeed, the same charges are often made against the comics and here, also, I am inclined to disagree. For those who do not know the United States and have no true idea of what the American Way of Life consists, it is easy to condemn and ridicule these pathetic attempts to amuse millions of people who imagine that their civilization is a model of human culture. To the starry-eyed innocents who believe these things the mental diet has to be presented in accordance with that belief. Just as long as private persons are permitted to control the minds and ideals of the American people for the sake of gain, so long will the population remain in great part an immature, adolescent-minded and ignorant mass. The aims of the radio executives who run the score or so of soap-operas is not the public welfare. It is to sell products and make money, and to do both it is necessary to give what millions of frustrated and discontented American women want. The soothing syrup is like balm. It does nothing to cure the disease, for that stems from the American Way of Life itself. To question that Way is to deviate from the line, and to do that is heresy.

With the coming of television a new and potent form of mass media invaded the American home. Everything known to the advertising industry was put into operation in order to persuade the people to invest in television sets. It was no longer a luxury for the rich: it was a necessity for all. In 1951, so it was said, some 300,000 sets were going into service every month; and the time was fast approaching when almost three families out of every ten would have one installed. By the end of 1953 it was estimated that over 27 million sets were in use.

The initial impact of this invention was startling. The American Press was full of articles, scares and warnings of calamity. *Fortune* asked who was afraid, and educators replied that they were and gave the reasons. The President of Boston University declared that if the programmes continued on their present level the people were destined to become a nation of morons. Commissions sat, debated and reported. The Federal Communications Commission stated in 1950 that only 3 per cent. of the commercial programmes were educational in type, while a large percentage of those designed for children were based on crime and violence. Indeed, the effect on children was the most widely discussed aspect of the problem. Horror plays became a popular feature for those craving sensation, and children gazed with a terrified fascination at scenes of murder, stabbings and shootings, interspersed with the less violent adventures of Hopalong Cassidy.

The effect on many women was greater than on men. Household tasks were neglected in order to watch the screen, and the time spent previously in going to the movies or listening to the radio was reduced. Time spent in reading or visiting friends was also curtailed and the evenings were spent in darkened rooms, thus causing tension and domestic strife. Many men did not care to watch the kind of programmes devised for women and children, and thus in the smaller homes they had to retire from the living-room and sit upstairs or in the kitchen, for it can hardly be imagined that, in many cases, they would dare to flout the wishes of their wives and families.

It seems, therefore, quite possible that TV will widen still further the gulf between men and women in the United States, and this in the one direction where some contact was previously made—that is to say, in the home. Moreover, the American man had a new terror to face if he left home to find some relief from the cavortings of the television stars. He was warned by one American magazine with a four million circulation that he must be "good", for television was watching him, and his wife might easily spot him supping with a blonde when he was caught by TV's roving eye. Whether television was in reality "mama's friend or foe", as B. Bradbury in *Good Housekeeping* put it, was indeed a moot point. But it was clear that some of the programmes for women in the beauty line were of considerable appeal. Who but an icicle, for instance, could have resisted the virile Mr. Buster Crabbe in his Figure Fashioning show, when, in the flimsiest of flimsy garments, which left but little to the imagination, he taught the ecstatic viewers how the figure should be preserved, modified or improved? Features of this sort could hardly fail to attract the average female television fan who, in the darkened privacy of the parlour, could give herself up to enjoyment less easy to attain in the more public atmosphere of the picture-theatre.

There are, of course, many women in the United States who deplore the soap-operas and condemn the kind of lessons they teach. Many of these women belong to the women's clubs which have already been mentioned when dealing with the nineteenth century. These clubs are run by women who are certainly the best-informed and the most intelligent in the United States. The majority of the most prominent business and professional women belong to them, and although some may laugh at their activities and interests in current events and international problems, the women themselves are doing their best to escape from the atmosphere of the nursery which the great movie and radio executives try to compel them to breathe. What these women lack is the mental and educational background by which they could better understand what it is that they discuss with so much vigour and earnestness. But when all is said and done, the American women's clubs are not, as many foreigners believe, organizations run by snobs for social prestige, although doubtless social position and birth play a part in their make-up. They are very real attempts on the part of women to take their place in an informed public life, and their influence on policy is not to be overlooked.

It is unnecessary here to discuss many other aspects of feminine leisure in the United States. In the theatre great activity has been shown, especially in such urban centres as New York and Chicago, but the competition of the movies, the radio and even the intimate form of vaudeville is severe, and the drama as acted on the stage cannot be said to play any very important part in the lives of average city women. Similarly, reading and card-playing, although practised to a certain extent, cannot be said to enter seriously into the life of the ordinary young woman, who is more interested in the movies and outdoor sports. Reading in America is largely centred on the great magazines, although possibly there has been an increase of serious reading among women during the last twenty years.

Before closing this section perhaps a word should be said on the way that American women of leisure and even business women patronize the thousands of religious and psychological quacks who do a roaring trade in the United States. So many American women are discontented, frustrated and unhappy that they fall ready victims to the rascals who promise relief in return for fees. Lee R. Steiner has recently written a fascinating account of this army of scoundrels, fakers and frauds, and in her descriptions has included the part played by the beauty business in teaching "poise" and self-adjustment. Similarly, Carey McWilliams in *Southern California Country*, has written a brilliant account of the fake religions and occult sects with their thousands of dupes, drawn to a certain extent from retired people who have nothing to do, no real purpose in life, and no cultural background from which they can draw sustenance to enrich the remaining years of their existence. The millions of dollars drawn from the American people by these parasites cannot be estimated. What is important to understand is that the great majority of them are able to ply their trade because the United States is full of thousands of discontented and unhappy people, who, to seek relief from their conflict, will go to anyone who promises succour. The education that they have received has done little to inculcate a spirit of inquiry and cautious thought. The credulity that can be observed in the dim parlours of the New York occultists, healers and soothsayers and in the temples of the Southern Californian fakers is almost incredible and I doubt if anything like it can be seen anywhere else in the world.

V

SEX AND THE AMERICAN WOMAN

ALTHOUGH the United States is almost, if not quite, the most sex-obsessed country in the world,[1] in no department of life is the American pastime of make-believe carried on more gamely. When something is unpleasant, disturbing and liable to cause trouble, a common mode of action is to look the other way or to pretend that it does not exist. We see this happening everywhere in the United States, for were it not so the gulf between faith and practice might become too obvious and too glaring. The unpleasant is pushed away out of sight; or, if that be impossible, it is glossed over or explained away.

In matters of sex it is natural that these traits should be especially noticeable. American standards of morality are derived mainly from New England and are heavily tinged with supposed Puritan traditions, which have been handed down and disseminated through the schools. It will be remembered that the virtues of chastity and virginity were stressed, and also that the notion that woman herself had pleasure in the sexual relation was not one which could be easily held unless it referred to "abandoned females" or "brazen strumpets".

As the years advanced we saw how these ideas were developed and how, side by side with the so-called emancipation of women, arose the quaint idea that women were superior to men, one reason being that women were not swayed and controlled by these ignoble passions which afflicted the opposite sex. The substance of these views was not unique to the United States, but was shared by many in England and throughout the Anglo-Saxon world generally. But it was in America that they were coupled with ideas of female dominance and the cult of the Mother, to which was added the belief in the innocence of the child that arose from a late rejection of the belief in hell and its relation to infant sin and damnation.

With the twentieth century and the rise of modern industrialism,

[1] Cf. the views of such critics as J. L. Segall, where he says that America is "sex mad" (p. 7); Bradford Smith, who asked if there was ever a more sex-conscious people (p. 48), and even the not very observant Robert Waithman, who said that American women gave the impression of a "consistent preoccupation with the question of being desired" (p. 131).

the First World War, the roaring twenties, psycho-analysis and the knowledge of contraception, it was soon seen that chastity and virginity in girls and young women were beginning to be forgotten. By the late 1930s the position became critical and articles began to appear in which the case for chastity was taken up in plain language. Of these articles I shall select two, firstly because they appeared in *The Reader's Digest*, with its immense circulation, and were reprinted in pamphlet form, and secondly because the authors must be considered to have been thought representative of the best-informed opinion in the United States in 1937.

In her article, "The Case for Chastity", Mrs. Margaret C. Banning did her best to explain to young women how to be chaste. To be unchaste, she stated, is to court moral and psychological breakdown. On the other hand, she declared that normal young people of both sexes do not want unchastity. What they wanted was fidelity and marriage. Premarital chastity and early marriage was Mrs. Banning's receipt; and at the same time she was realistic enough to understand the dangers of petting. But what we do not find in Mrs. Banning's paper is *one single word* on the wholesale sexual propaganda and invitations to lewdness put out by those who control and distribute the material that finds its way on to the movie screen, into the magazines and into the advertisements. Young people are to be allowed to be put into an almost permanent condition of tumescence, but they must not yield. For were it proposed to control the activities of these salesmen of sex, the sacred rights of the individual would be threatened.

The same year appeared a remarkable letter from Mr. Donald C. Peattie entitled "A Way to Chastity". To Mr. Peattie, "missteps" in love lead to shuddering revulsions, hardening of the arteries of the spirit and a relentless coarsening of the soul. None of these horrors seem to happen if the "misstep" downwards is made a step upwards by the sacred ceremony of marriage. After a misstep it is possible, Mr. Peattie stated, to climb up again and scrape oneself clean. After a few marriages, however, this does not appear to be necessary. Mr. Peattie clearly believes in magic, and, like Mrs. Banning, had not one word to say about the sexual stimulation with which American youth was continually bombarded. Another point, however, is even more puzzling. Mrs. Banning (p. 8) stated that we could not ignore a man's preference for a virgin for a wife, so that a girl gambles away her later chances of lifelong married happiness if she sacrifices her chastity. It is odd that none of these disasters occurs if the chastity is sacrificed after the magic words are said. Mrs. Banning

THE NURSERY (1899)
See pages 75–76 ; 208 (note 1)

"I may be bad, but I am not the worst man in the world."
"Then I won't accept you. I'll wait until he proposes."

LIKE OTHER GIRLS
See page 191 (note)

"Between me an' you, Uncle Jasper, don't you get awful tired of doin' what
you're told? Don't be scared to answer. I won't give you away to Aunt Jane."

UNCLE JASPER

See page 208 (note 1)

THE OVERWORKED AMERICAN FATHER (1897)
See page 210

THE AMBITIOUS MOTHER (1902)
See page 237 (note 2)

does not tell us what happens to widows and how it is that so many widows and divorced women marry again. In these cases it does not seem that the man's preference for virginity is satisfied, and, moreover, the fact that they have lived possibly for years with a man does not seem to affect their desirability in the eyes of others. Moreover, the fact that so many American girls failed to accept the advice of Mrs. Banning, Mr. Peattie and their followers, seems to show that they are not like the nymphs of which F. W. H. Myers sang, "on whose foreheads sit proudly a glad virginity".

The attempts made during the thirties to frighten or persuade the young people of the United States into being chaste were, of course, doomed to failure. Since, however, sex-education was still very poor, the results of their experiments were even more disastrous than the most fearful critics had foreseen. The widespread psychological damage was itself something to be reckoned with. Since the young people in the upper middle classes had been brought up on the kind of traditional morality taught by Mrs. Banning, a sense of guilt was bound to develop as a result of their sexual activity and loss of chastity. For not only had many girls been told that dire results would accrue from the loss of their virginity, but also in some cases it had been urged upon them that the sexual relation was completely unnecessary either to health or to well-being. Since the social atmosphere of the United States is, as I have said, not particularly conducive to purity of thought or deed, many young women, terrified by the warnings of the purity publicists, sought refuge in masturbation, which, as we have seen, seems often to have been practised in previous times.[1]

How far the lower-income levels were affected by the kind of moral uplift put out by the popular magazines is not easy to say without careful inquiry conducted on scientific lines. But from what we know, it seems improbable that the poorer women were likely to accept this kind of teaching, especially when they must have known the frequency of disease and the constant scandals affecting the upper levels of American café society. Moreover, as has been shown by

[1] The literature on masturbation in the female in the United States is very extensive, and some of it, e.g. the works of R. L. Dickinson, rather peculiar and, it seems to me, needing confirmation. I shall neither summarize nor discuss it here, but merely refer the reader to his works and to those with his colleagues, Lura Beam and H. H. Pierson; see also P. S. Achilles, p. 35, who apparently harbours the same doubts as the present writer regarding Dickinson's interpretations; and for a less sober account see *inter alia* M. Chideckel. How far the constipation, so prevalent in the United States, leads to the practice I do not know, although Kelly suggests (p. 292) that it may be a contributory cause, and appears to agree with Dickinson that the habit may be detected from certain physical signs (pp. 293-5).

Kinsey and others, the youth of the lower-income levels have little use for the mental and physical titillations without consummation as practised by college youth, regarding such behaviour as silly and even despicable.

Something must be said regarding female frigidity in the United States, although our knowledge of this subject in any society is very meagre, and we have only case-notes by various inquirers and information from women themselves, which is often unreliable and difficult to assess. Moreover, the term is itself vague and unsatisfactory, and its meaning ranges from the alleged complete absence of all physical, sexual sensation of pleasure to mere absence of the orgasm.

In 1842 J. S. Buckingham came to the conclusion that the women he met were "more frigid" than those of Europe, and since then nearly every kind of opinion has been expressed. H. L. Mencken, for example, had little belief in the alleged frigidity of American women, differing in this from Thomas Wolfe who, in his *You Can't Go Home Again* (p. 39), speaks of some American women as lacking the "living curves" of body and spirit, and, indeed, as showing themselves deficient in love, tenderness, lust or even in any feminine fullness of the earth whatever.[1] In the South, where, as we shall see later, the dominance of the male is accepted in theory, although often, as elsewhere in the United States, not in practice, the presence of frigidity in women has been noted, although our information on the matter is practically non-existent, and no valid opinions can be offered on either the white or the coloured women.

Whatever may be the facts regarding female frigidity in the United States, the reasons for the condition are not likely to differ basically from those operating in England. Apart from the more complex mechanisms, which sometimes centre on a conflict between contradictory tendencies due to a persistence of early trends, it seems probable that many cases are due to a series of comparatively simple inhibitions mainly of the anxiety type, which depend upon bad sexual upbringing and early education. Indeed, before the First World War it might be expected that many of these cases would occur in the United States, where prudery and the coupling of sex

---

[1] These harsh judgments can be compared with one said to emanate from A. Moore, the American artist. The American woman, he stated, was a fraud and an abomination: she was aloof and emanated ice. "Who Wanted Her?" (see London *Evening Standard*, Jan. 19, 1949). It was a Swiss dentist, Dr. P. H. Lugeon, visiting California, who, in commenting upon the American habit of refrigeration, declared that even the young ladies were refrigerated! (*Time* (Atlantic Overseas Ed.), Sept. 6, 1948, p. 15).

with sin were especially liable to influence any demonstration of sexual passion by women. Women were often regarded as without feeling, which in itself was thought to be a sign of virtue, whereas any inclination towards physical love was apt to be construed as the mark of a "bad" woman. In this connexion Thurman B. Rice is discerning when he stated that the tragedy of the American way of life as regards marriage was to try to make girls mountain peaks of cold and snowy virtue, whereas no such ideal was presented in the case of the sons.[1] It is here that some American writers grasp the key to much that is perplexing in life around them. For, as we have seen earlier, it is precisely these fantastic "ideals", derived from a degenerate Puritanism, that are always in sharp conflict with the real world, and thus not only generate conflict leading to neurosis, but, even if they are lived up to by the unfortunate women who believe in them, can only result in unhappy, frustrated lives both inside and outside the marriage relation.

It is very curious to see how these ideals of feminine "purity" and icy aloofness are disregarded under the cold light of reason. In the United States it is a more or less understood thing that if two normal human beings of the opposite sex spend the night in proximity and unchaperoned, they are bound to make love. Such a belief is, as critics have pointed out, very difficult to prove on the movies, but there it is, and the foreigner travelling in America will note indications of it on every side. The floor clerks on the various hotel floors have vigilant eyes lest a male or female guest smuggle a friend into a bedroom; and many are the stories told of the results of disobeying the rules, some of which are to be found in other countries besides the United States.[2]

Before dealing with the American woman in the marriage state, a few words must be said on the American man, especially as regards his relation to and attitude towards the American woman. The man's world is that of finance, industry, business and politics. He is the provider and support of home and family, even though the Great Depression forced many men into inactivity, and the position of seeing their wives take jobs while they were idle or on relief work.

In the United States the world of business (with a few notable exceptions) is closed to women except in the lower levels. The golden age of finance, so graphically described by F. L. Allen in his *The Lords of Creation*, was not a world in which women shared

---

[1] T. B. Rice, *op. cit.*, p. 85.
[2] For an instructive view of such regulations and how they are carried out see Mary Haworth's *Mail* in the *Washington Post*, Oct. 14, 1942.

except in the acceptance of the results of that amazing era. It was a period in which American business was supreme in the lives of hundreds of men, and was an activity in which women were excluded from nearly all the higher manipulative positions. Thus it may be said that in general it was the men who made the money and the women who spent it, the Beards estimating in 1933 that women bought seven-tenths of all manufactured commodities.[1]

In any consideration of the nature of American business and the drive behind it, the cult of the self-made man must never be forgotten. It is a vital element in the American conscience, and one which has to be understood in its historical and cultural background. For success, as we have seen, was akin to virtue, and the virtuous man was loved by God and favoured by Him. Hence, wealth was much more than money: it was a symbol of success and the sign of being loved, besides being a symbol of other things deeply buried in the unconscious, but none the less potent for all that. To be self-made meant to be able to do business freely without let or hindrance. Authority and control became inimical to the exercise of the unrestrained drive towards what was, after all, a form of self-expression in economic terms. "Free enterprise" became a kind of religion, an essential and all-important part of the American credo.

It is this desire to make money and be a success that is at the bottom of much of the corruption and scandal in the United States. The vast black-market operations in Europe after the war were closely connected with the American Army of Occupation, in the ranks of which there were naturally some who were not averse from such a magnificent opportunity of making money, as the fantastic revelations of the manipulations of the printed invasion currency in relation to the Russian marks and dollars clearly revealed. In business, industry, finance and politics the American man is supreme. Although woman is slowly invading these strongholds, her progress is very slow, and not likely to succeed to any great extent. In the past the pace was too fast. Few women could have taken the place of the great political "bosses"—those petty dictators of whole districts, whose word was law, and who always had a crowd of sycophants crawling at their feet to do their bidding, follow the line and share in the "gravy". Women could hardly compete with the violence of these men, or in controlling the private armies and goonsquads which flourished under private enterprise. What influence they had was directed rather from the boudoir than from the office, and even there what power they had was modified by the presence of

[1] C. A. and M. R. Beard, p. 753.

secretarial "cuties" and "girl friends" who entered into competition with them.

As we have already indicated, the apparent lack of maturity and the adolescent way of looking at things is so common in the United States that it could hardly have been expected that those in business and politics would exhibit anything very different. Politics, therefore, besides being a business, is also a "game", a point of view admirably illustrated in the recently published *Jim Farley's Story* by James Farley himself. We can see here how members of both political parties play the game in Washington and act in a manner which indicates that their actions are often divorced from any realistic approach to the problems with which they are pretending to deal.

It has been said by some writers that harm is likely to be done by too great an emphasis being placed upon the view held by a number of observers that America is "incurably juvenile" and also "recessively childish",[1] and in this I am inclined to agree, although at the same time the facts of the situation are such that they deserve some analysis. There must be some meaning in the observations of so many writers over so long a period, even though propagandists for the American Way of Life are anxious to hush the matter up or explain it away on the ground that America is a "young" country.

Strictly speaking, *adolescence* is the period of life in which a transition is apparent between childhood and what is termed "maturity". Its implications are both social and physiological: an adult behaves in an adolescent manner if his conduct can with fairness be compared with that to be observed at the time that the physiological changes are proceeding.

American men at varied economic levels often conduct themselves in a way which can justly be compared with the behaviour of adolescents. G. T. Mayes, writing in the *New York Times Magazine* in 1946, stated that many American men had one-track minds which all the evidence suggested were being operated by "not-too-sensitive adolescents" who had only been recently initiated into the facts of life. As S. Bent pointed out in 1927, the constant preoccupation with sex which the American popular Press exhibits is in itself a sign of an adolescent mentality in its readers;[2] and we have only to

---

[1] See R. J. Cruikshank, *The Future of Anglo-American Relations*, p. 520; F. Frost, *The American Impression*, and Juvenal's *An Englishman in New York*, p. 51.

[2] S. Bent, p. 22. Canon Barnard I. Bell has actually spoken of the century of the perpetually adolescent man, and Mr. John M. Loughran was reported in 1944 as having told a meeting that most American adults are no more grown

remember the Conventions of the American Legion to see how this childishness can be seen in all its perfection. At the 1947 Convention water-filled paper bags were thrown about; women were squirted with water-pistols and were made to jump by the application of battery-operated "jump-boxes". Many of these men, squealing and cavorting in public, were middle-aged and responsible citizens, who had "loosened up" for the occasion and shown the world what was just beneath the surface of their staid, everyday appearance. A man drunk is often more revealing than a man sober, and nowhere more so than in the United States. After all, the American hero, Horatio Alger, was, as we have already seen, a man who might almost be thought to have suffered from arrested development. He used, it is said, to play with building-bricks like a child, run after fire-engines in the streets, and beat the big drum with the best.

If we have to seek further evidence of the childish tastes of millions of Americans, we have only to turn to the comics, those fantastic strip tales of phantasy and adventure which are read with such avidity and which are, unfortunately, becoming popular in other parts of the world influenced by the "American Way". These strips first began as a kind of coloured supplementary section for the enjoyment of children, but soon became so popular that it was clear that adults as well as young people found them amusing. In the comic strip the character is all-important, since the reader has to identify himself with the character and live with him, either in a world similar to that in which he moves or, more often, in another world of thrills, excitement and adventure. The plot is usually simple and direct and the setting strictly "scientific". Here is a child's world set with every conceivable gadget, probable and improbable. The simple faces the complex, but the complex is never subtle or intangible; it is always of the earth or beyond the earth. Just as many motion-pictures regard the spectator as of small account above the navel, and the commercial soap-operas cater for an audience of sentimental morons, so do the comics provide mental fodder suitable for children, although often supplemented with just sufficient spice to be of service to the millions of American men who crave some escape from the drab uniformity of their lives. They are

---

up than school-children. Similarly, Herbert Agar, dealing with "democracy's greatest crisis", asked the American people if they could pass the test, as he added, "we shall be tempted" to behave like children, and said a decision would have to be made as to whether the coming months would show Americans conducting themselves as adults or as "brats". Cf. the paper by the Spanish critic, Madariaga, "Americans are Boys", in *Harper's Magazine* in 1928 and N. F. Joffe's study of the same subject in *Complex*, 1951, pp. 28–33.

indications of the character of the population of the United States, and they all point to the same lesson. As John Mason Brown is reported to have said in a debate in 1948, the comics are despicable trash, and he added that as a people the Americans "must grow up".[1] Similarly, H. Elkin stressed the fact that, since everything "impractical", like literature, music and art, was considered "sissy" in the United States, "a very large proportion" of American men never attained the stage beyond childhood in their emotional experiences, and thus began to crack immediately they were confronted with situations which demanded the approach of a mature adult.[2]

It is, as we have seen, not only foreign observers who have remarked upon the curiously delayed maturity of so many adult male Americans. Indeed, the strongest condemnation is to be found in the pages of the serious American periodical Press. In a female-dominated country like the United States the man must always be trying to escape from the bands—swaddling bands—which are constantly throttling him. Yet, since his early years have been controlled by woman, he finds complete escape impossible. Only in athletics and business does it seem that the women cannot often follow him; and even in the latter occupation he is often surrounded by painted "cuties" ogling him and titillating him. It is true that some American women entered business like Mildred Horton and Dorothy Shaver, and, like Vivien Kellems (who waged a ceaseless war against Government regulations or taxation) and Ruth Kerr (who combined business with religion), succeed in a department of life in which men thought themselves safe from competition. Even in politics the women are beginning to infiltrate actively in what was thought to be man's domain. Marion K. Sanders, in an article in *Harper's Magazine* for August 1955 stresses this very point and says that the "ardent amateurs" of today will be the "Great Battle Axes" of the future. The men will, however, still be useful, since when their wives are extolling the glories of the Democrats or the G.O.P. their husbands will be working at home as the "warmers-up of stew". In baseball, Paul Gallico maintained, was one excellent escape. Here his "boss-inhibited psyche" might be freed; and he

---

[1] It sometimes happens that people outside the United States are able to make their wishes known when these infantile comics are published in their papers. This has happened in the case of the London *Sunday Pictorial*, which began to print a strip about an idiotic American creation, the "Shmoo", which was all the rage in the United States and pictures of which were actually dropped on the heads of unhappy Berliners. Readers of the London paper protested against the "daft, dopey, benighted, sloppy" stuff, and the proprietors withdrew the strip with apologies.

[2] H. Elkin, *op. cit.*, pp. 410 ff.

went on to explain that the "average American" was a down-trodden and henpecked creature, existing within the framework of a strict and rigid matriarchal system. He is always being told what to do and how to do it, and so it is that when he can escape the women he loves it.[1]

At home, however, it is otherwise. As S. H. Holbrook has said in the *American Mercury* (1937) the dominant woman has no need to put a ring through his nose. "Menfolks are not menfolks any more," lamented Lois H. Baylis (p. 501) in the correspondence which followed Mr. Holbrook's article.

Even in athletics accusations of childishness followed the American man. It is true he asked for it, even if it were in jest. "Babe" Ruth, the baseball player, was a household word for years, and the doings of the "Bambino" were more important than the activities of the President. The American athlete, Eliot Spalding stated bluntly, is an "incurable cry-baby", and the big-time performer never seemed to have grown out of the cradle.[2] Thus it would appear that even in the female-free world of athletic contests, the American man is still a victim to that form of delayed maturity imposed upon him through the influence of the American woman.

It is true that there are some compensations for this attitude to life on the part of the American man. One result is that in the United States we have a nation of gadgeteers, a nation where in-genious contrivances and improved devices invented by others are to be found as nowhere else. The American knows how things work and can be made to work: he has the youthful passion for contraptions of every kind. That observant American reporter, Eric Sevareid, puts the situation in a nutshell when he speaks of men with the mentality of "simple children" and the hands of wizards.

It is amusing to read the comments in the American Press during

---

[1] See Paul Gallico, *The American Goes to the Game*, pp. 29 ff. Perhaps here it is relevant to recall the two delicious drawings by Charles Dana Gibson, repro-duced from Gibson's *Americans* and *Gibson's New Cartoons* in F. Downey's *Portrait of an Era*, pp. 191 and 353. In the first the nursery age is portrayed with Junior on the ground being driven by his sister, who holds the reins. She has a proud and queenly look, while his expression of downcast submission is marked. In the second, which appeared in the old *Life*, a small girl, with a look of amused contempt, is asking her Uncle Jasper if he is not getting "awful tired" of doing what he is told. "Don't be scared", she adds, since she promises not to tell on him and inform Aunt Jane. A delightful cartoon of the "Over-worked American Father" being led by two strapping young women is in-cluded in Gibson's *Sketches and Cartoons* (1898).

[2] E. Spalding, p. 65. For the Americans' views on foreign women see E. Laytha, *Doughboys and Diggers*, p. 60. Cf. V. Dallaire's *American Woman? Not for this G.I.*, and J. P. Dolch's comments on the same theme.

the Second World War on what was going to happen to the returning soldier. Every aspect of his "troubles" and necessary "readjustment" was discussed.[1] Thus in the *Courier-Journal* of Louisville, Ky., I find an article on January 17, 1943 by Harry Shaw on what to do with Johnny when he comes marching home again. It is written for the benefit of the American female reader, and it assures her that all is well. "Don't let them kid you, girls," the writer says. Johnny and Willie will be very useful. The returning soldier will be a "first-class kitchen help". He will peel the spuds, shred the cabbage, wash up and clean the room in case the lady wants to go to a show after dinner. Yes, Johnny will make a fine "little helper" after the war is over, and "don't let him tell you any different".[2]

From the above brief review of what various authorities have said about the condition of many American men with regard to women, it is clear that the picture is hardly that of male domination even as head of the family, and we shall see later how the American Father is regarded as compared with the American Mother. The two sides of the American man's character were well described by George Cabot Lodge (1873–1909) in one of his letters to Langdon Mitchell in 1904. The American man was an anomaly, he wrote: and then he went on to compare his efficiency in the practical affairs of life with his sentimental idiocy. As regards women, Lodge bluntly stated that man had been dethroned and a woman ruled in his stead, while as a husband he was "inept and drivelling" in everything but making money. With reference to the upper-class American women

---

[1] See H. Kitching for his sex worries, and cf. the amusing sketch, *Mom, I'm Home*, by S. Hoff, and an account of what he found there in Bill Mauldin's *Back Home*.

[2] Comment is superfluous. In the *Washington Post* (Aug. 8, 1943) a cartoon by Gregory d'Alessio was printed showing the husband preparing the meal for his wife, who worked in a munitions factory. She has brought four female co-workers to dinner, and her husband says that she might have called him earlier to tell him so! For a pathetic letter addressed to Dorothy Dix by an American man who declares he is but a servant in his own home, being expected to cook the dinner, clean the house and do the laundry, see the Baltimore *Sun* (Jan. 4, 1943). The writer declares that he is a foreman on a construction gang and is told he handles men very well. But, he confesses, "my wife handles me better"! How different must this wife be from that great American, Abigail Adams, who, although at times she deplored the supposed "tyranny of men", wrote (Letter to Mrs. Shaw, June 5, 1809, p. 402) that woman was a help-meet for man and the woman who failed in those duties did not answer the end of her creation. In 1943 a man sued for divorce in Stamford, Conn., and stated that he received only ten cents out of his $50 wage-packet that he handed to his wife. She only allowed him to sit down at meal-times! An interesting commentary on how Negroes regard the domination of white American women is found in the character-study of Almina Small by E. F. Frazier (*Negro Youth at the Crossways*, p. 256). She declared that she hoped that her future husband would not be a person whom you can order what to do and then he would run off and do it!

O

Lodge was even blunter. They lead discontented, sterile and stunted lives, he declared, and these comprise what he called the "most real Americans". Nearly forty years later Dr. M. F. Farnham, writing in *Coronet*, stated that the American husband, far from being the once dominant male, was now a "sad imitation". More often than not, she declared, he was a cringing and timid person, henpecked and even afraid to say what he wanted. She mentioned cases of men who were not allowed to walk on the living-room rug except when visitors were present, who could only smoke cigars in the privacy of the bedroom, or, "believe it or not", an instance of one husband who was only allowed to go out alone to play bowls with his friends once every three months. Finally, she suggested that it might be as well if "our women" quietly retreated from a few of their indefensible positions while they can still do so gracefully.[1]

It has been a puzzle for many years how long the American man is going to tolerate his position, though there is little doubt that in thousands of cases he has no idea that any other life is possible, so used to it has he become. Indeed, Gerhard Venzmer in his *New York ohne Schmincke* hazards the joking assumption that some mysterious hormones act upon him in a way which favours his subjection. In a review of his book, published in a Hamburg journal, Dr. Nettebaum asserted that men can be seen in the United States kneeling before women putting on their overshoes, and that it is not unknown for a husband to have his ears boxed by his wife in a public place.[2]

It might be thought by some that things have changed in the last few years, or, as Bernard Valery seems to have thought, that there existed a kind of conspiracy against the fair sex. But if we can judge from the notes contributed by Mr. John Fischer, of *Harper's Magazine*, in the issue of August 1955, the situation does not seem to have altered very much. Indeed, he declares that "never in history has any country contained such a high proportion of cowed and eunuchoid males", for it is in the United States that the Ideal Male "dedicates his life to the pampering of women".

Before passing on to a consideration of the sexual life of the American man in his relation to woman, a word may be said on the American Father—"Poor old Pop"—who is almost a national figure

---

[1] It is instructive in this connexion to observe how Paul Wooton, the doyen of Washington correspondents, was unable to resist the temptation of referring to the position of the American husband when welcoming Princess (now Queen) Elizabeth in November 1951. "Different from many American husbands," he said, Prince Philip is "master of the house."

[2] See *Our Petticoat Government*, etc. Cf. the cover of *Vogue* (Sept. 15, 1946), which shows the meek man kneeling before the woman, who is standing on a chair.

of jest. Although the father of a family is often on the friendliest
terms with his children, paternity is not what it is in other parts
of the world, and this is what would be expected from what we know
of the pattern of American society. It is true that some writers deny
that Father is the underdog. For example, in speaking of the Middle
West, Graham Hutton explains the remark of the American who
said that the only two depressed classes were Negroes and white
husbands by saying that the henpecked husband, although a Midwest figure of fun and a feature of the comic strip, is almost as rare
as the English dandy complete with his monocle. In view of the
facts, however, I am not inclined to accept such statements, since
the success of such plays as *Life with Father* (Lindsay & Crouse) and
comic strips such as *Bringing up Father* and *Blondie* shows quite
clearly that the characters are representative of many an American
household. However, I would not go so far as P. A. Vaile, who declared, in 1909, that the American Father was "under the female
whip", or, as the woman author, quoted by Elizabeth Hawes,[1] who
declared that it was idle to pretend that Father was head of the house,
and that were he to think so the female members of the household
would merely laugh. The cartoons of "Father" with his flower, the
dandelion ("the more it's stepped on the better it grows"), are
sufficient to indicate the kind of place the American Father is supposed to take in the society of the United States.

It would not be relevant here to discuss the thesis advanced by
Geoffrey Gorer in his *The American People* that, in the immigrant
society of the United States, the father has been "rejected", since he
stands for the old world and the old customs which the younger
generation have to forget in order to absorb the "American Way"
and attain full assimilation. However, when he asserts that England
is the "image" of the father and that the ambivalence of the attitude
towards that country implies that indifference can never arise, I am
inclined to disagree with him, although this is not the place to discuss the reasons for my own attitude. Nevertheless, I think he is
right in drawing attention to this form of psychological rejection,
and I have little doubt that his general thesis can be maintained up
to a certain point.

I now propose to refer, as delicately as I can, to some extraordinary
features in men's clothing in the United States and to suggest in
what direction an explanation is to be sought.

We have seen above that, from the early days of American extreme
feminism, attempts have been made to pretend that women were "as

[1] *Anything but Love*, p. 20.

good" as men and could do all that men did. It will be remembered how Eliza Farnham conveniently forgot her anatomy in her analysis of man and woman, and how, as Viola Klein and Karen Horney have both pointed out, castration phantasies now and then play some part in the development of the American girl, and how occasionally there arises a desire for revenge followed by a symbolic castration of the opposite sex.

Now, it has often been asserted that women dictate the purchase of a good deal of male clothing in the United States, and thus it is possible that the obedient American man is inclined to accede to the wishes of his womenfolk more easily than would be the case elsewhere, especially if the favoured garments are exhibited and described in an attractive manner.

Towards 1936-8 there began to appear on the American market a variety of odd articles of male attire, and at the same time sports clothes were shown on male models in which the gentlemen had an exceedingly "sissyfied" appearance.[1] At the same time a number of undergarments were being exhibited, and were we not aware of the American sexual obsession, we might think that some of these were hardly suitable for public display, let alone for illustration in magazines. These curious contraptions, which went by the name of "Paris Gards", "Bracers", "Support U's", "Y-Fronts" and "Gantner Wikies", were all designed in order, apparently, to disguise the fact that the wearer was masculine and to pretend that he was feminine. There were odd snap-pouches and "concealed no-gap" flies; and in one advertisement the device was so drawn that not only was all trace of the objectionable bulge obliterated, but the tight binder was so designed that the rôle of the wearer was reversed. He had been turned into a fake woman.[2] Having attended to the necessary adjustments beneath the outer clothing, the trousers themselves had then to be adapted. Photographs of the front portions were published showing "unsightly gaps" and a lady was depicted climb-

[1] Cf. *Esquire*, May 1938, p. 135. Nearly ten years later even some male dogs had to be "sissified" by their female owners. *Time* (Atlantic Overseas Ed., Dec. 15, 1947) featured Mrs. John Jacob Astor's Wow-Wow wearing a sapphire necklace and diamond rings on each paw.

[2] For an excellent example of the effect produced by these trunks fitted with their "built-in supporters" see that featured in *Life* (May 21, 1945), p. 20. A kind of symbolic castration has been achieved, just as the threat of actual castration is often used to deter children from undesirable habits. Indeed, one American mother declared that all she had to say was "scissors" to have immediate effect (see *Frustration and Aggression*, p. 58). The same threat to sexual delinquents was made at the Denver Women's Club, when Mrs. Gano Sentner said that the proposition was to start people thinking. It must have done so, since her phone hardly stopped ringing, the response being 100 to 1 in favour of the idea.

ing into the seat of a car, her eyes fixed on this portion of her escort's clothing. But everything was O.K. He was safe. He was wearing the new zip talon trouser fastener which automatically *locks* (advertisement's italics) at the top. Nothing could open "by accident". "Offensive gaps" could no longer appear.

How far interpretation of these customs throws light upon the prevalence of homosexual activity in the United States I am not prepared to discuss here. Certainly Kinsey's findings would suggest that contacts and experiences of this kind are commoner than has been supposed, and a number of recent novels are concerned with this subject.[1]

Before passing on to consider the American woman in her relation to marriage, the family and industry, a few words on the feminine ideals favoured by the average American young man may be of interest.

During the war a good deal of attention has been paid to the "pin-up girl". These illustrations, often of film stars and actresses, were printed inside some magazines and on the covers of others, and were then cut out, and adorned the quarters of the soldiers overseas and at home. Such papers as *Yank*, the *Army Times* and *Esquire* vied with each other to produce the most alluring, provocative and captivating types. Europe and the East were flooded with large photographs of half-dressed and undressed American cuties flaunting their charms in a way which made many of the folks back home in America blush for shame.

Although there is no doubt that the pin-ups were much appreciated by the American soldiers, who often taunted the British for not possessing a similar gallery of pulchritude, or what passed for such, a number of serving soldiers and their relations at home wrote protesting against the appearance of these designs. Thus three soldiers wrote to *Yank* in April 1944, saying that they doubted if some of the pin-ups were what was wanted, and declaring that when they sent one of the issues home an apology accompanied it. Again, in June of the same year *Yank* printed a letter from a soldier asking for a change from the cuties—"which begin to look like so much horsemeat"—and suggesting pastoral scenes of rural America or a sunset over Golden Gate Bridge. Perhaps one of the most pathetic letters on the subject of pin-ups was that printed in the issue of *Yank* for July 2, 1944, in which three British Army girls (A.T.S.) wrote to the Editor asking him to give them a treat for one week by printing a "picture of a Pin-up Boy".

[1] See A. Towne, *Homosexuality in American Culture.*

The American pin-up craze is of importance for our present purposes merely for the effect it has upon ideals of womanhood in the
United States. For, as we have seen, the twin female ideals in
America are in sharp contrast. On the one side we have the good,
pure woman of phantasy who is often identified with the maternal
image, and with whom therefore any sexual relation is regarded as
incestuous,[1] and on the other the "female", who in a sense is supposed
to have fallen from grace, succumbed to passion and thus is open to
sexual advances. The pin-ups are, to all intents and purposes, the
photographs of women who have allowed themselves to be exhibited
for gain, with the aim of stimulating sexual activity in those who
contemplate them. If the pin-up is not a kind of pornographic art,
then there is no such thing, unless pornographic art be defined as
limited to the representation of sexual activity itself.

What is so curious at first sight is that, in a female-dominated
country like the United States, there should be this flood of semi-
pornographic literature and art, which, it might be supposed, would
be offensive to many women, especially to those whose social and
economic standing makes them leading members of the community.
How far such women are aware of the facts is not easy to say. During
the inquiry into the mailing privileges of *Esquire* in 1943, Mrs.
Harvey W. Wiley, Chairman of the Legislative Committee of the
General Federation of Women's Clubs, and representing 2,500,000
women, was called to testify to the worth or otherwise of some of
Varga's pin-ups; and it was disclosed that she had never seen any of
these designs till just before being called to the stand. When she did
see them, however, she did not like them. The importance of the
pin-ups can easily be exaggerated. Such pictures are naturally
popular with men in both Europe and America; and it is to be expected that a sex-obsessed country like the United States would produce more and better examples of this kind of "art" than any other
country, although the pictures of Raphael Kirchner (1876–1917)
were very similar to those of Varga, and in many respects superior
in the delicacy of their technique.

We have now to pass to an examination of the American woman
in her direct relation with the American man. It will only be possible
to give indications of some of these relations, since any form of
generalization is clearly out of the question, so vast is the country and

---

[1] A term used among the lower classes in the United States for such a relation with the mother is the most intense term of opprobrium in the vocabulary
of American abuse. See Justinian, *pseud.*, *Americana Sexualis*, p. 29, and cf.
the Dozens game among lower-class Negroes.

so heterogeneous the population. Perhaps one way of obtaining an idea of marital satisfaction is to examine the divorce figures. In 1952 the preliminary estimate was about 392,000 as against the peak year of 1946 (610,000), and the previous rate seems to have advanced steadily ever since the time of the first statistical report which covered the period from 1867 to 1886. No good purpose would be served here in describing and analysing the position of woman in the United States as regards divorce. It has often been believed that failure and unhappiness in marital relations were largely confined to the higher economic levels and that the working classes were not so plagued. The evidence, however, according to E. W. Burgess and L. S. Cottrell (*Predicting success or failure in marriage* (1939)), seems not to support this assumption, although how far the data are reliable I am not prepared to say. The one fact that is important at the moment to bear in mind is that divorce in the United States is widely diffused among all classes of the population, and that this indicates a degree of dissatisfaction which is also to be found in other countries and may be part of the price that we have to pay for what is often called "progress".

In the United States, where "unhallowed" love is frowned upon, it is interesting to observe how many prominent personalities seem to be engaged in a perpetual exchange of partners, the changing relationship being considered almost a game like musical chairs. It is true that café and film society leads the way in these intrigues, but little appears to be done to prevent the news of some fresh adventure among the smart set from being banner headlines in the popular Press. Divorce goes on and on in spite of E. Bergler's plea that "divorce won't help" and his insistence that it is for the woman to manage her husband, that "four-flushing" baby dressed up in adult clothing who has never psychologically outgrown the nursery and who is called *man*.[1]

It is clear that frequent divorces, however useful they may be to those seeking relief, are a source of steady income to the legal advisers of the parties concerned. Since, through migratory divorce, it is possible to obtain separation more easily in one State than another, a lively competition exists, and what is called the "divorce mill" has thousands of customers, the unhappiness of some individuals being used in the market for the profit of others. As is well known, Jews and Roman Catholics are at one in regarding divorce with pronounced disfavour and in every way seeking to prevent, avoid or limit it. A similar trend is to be observed in

[1] E. Bergler, *Divorce Won't Help*, p. 189.

Episcopalian circles in the United States. Yet their combined efforts, together with the support given to them by educators and writers of popular manuals of advice and guidance, appear to do little to stem the tide. The fact is that the root of much of the sexual chaos in America is to be found in the belief that "private enterprise" is sacrosanct, so that the poisonous rubbish put out by Hollywood, the pulps and the salesmen of "culture" cannot be controlled. As long as profits can be made by "selling sex", so long will men and women seek to gain them, just as they are doing in the vice and dope rackets. It is the American woman who is the chief sufferer from this exploitation of sex for gain, and in considering marriage in the United States we shall see how her failure in adjustment may be traced back to sources arising in the Puritan experiment in New England. As we have seen, great stress is laid in the United States on the *legal form* of marriage for without such sanction what is often thought of as "the wrongest thing in the world" becomes "holy and right".[1]

However, not every foreign observer was in agreement over the failure of American marriage, even though this was strongly suggested by the divorce statistics. In 1908 Monsignor Vay, Apostolic Pronotary, although he saw that men recognized the superiority of women in cultural and social affairs, yet came to the conclusion that in the home woman was supreme, and that in every respect woman was man's mate and married couples were "regular partners".

It was following the First World War, when young people seemed to be preparing for marriage in ways which would have horrified their grandparents, that attempts began to be made to evaluate the position, status and results of marriage generally in statistical terms. As in so many of these surveys, the data were insufficient to provide any generalized picture, and often the sample used was not a true random sample from a thoroughly mixed population. Thus in 1929 appeared G. V. Hamilton's *A Research in Marriage*, which was based on 200 cases of married persons resident in New York City of varying economic levels. Some of the replies from women, however, were interesting, if true, and it is probable from what we know of the facts that these answers approximated to the truth. It must be remembered that the answers were written down and not answered verbally according to the quick-fire technique now sometimes employed. Thus of 100 women, over 66 per cent. confessed to fear, disgust and shock at their first sexual contact, although a test designed to ascertain if, by pressing a button, the person could find himself or

[1] R. S. and H. M. Lynd, *Middletown*, p. 112.

herself not married to his or her present partner, gave a result of only fourteen who would actually press that button. This would suggest that, if true, the absence of sexual satisfaction on the part of the women was not sufficient to determine the complete failure of a marriage. This is in agreement with other findings, such as those by L. M. Terman (*Psychological Factors in Marital Happiness*), who, in a sample taken from middle- and upper-class Californians, found that the sex factor was not by itself a major one in determining marital success or failure.

Whatever may be the importance of female orgasm as a feature of success in marriage, there is little doubt that a woman's lack of the supreme pleasure has a damaging effect upon the development of her personality. What percentage of women who indulge in sexual relations attain complete orgasm it is impossible to say. Some authors, like G. C. Cooke, writing of American women, have stated that every third woman fails to attain it. I have known numbers of women who say that they do not know if they have had it, while similarly I have known men declare that they do not know whether the women with whom they have consorted have experienced orgasm or not. Thousands of men, unfortunately, do not care, and many women also have a feeling that a total abandonment to ecstasy is "unladylike". In these cases the absence of full orgasm seems to me to be a reasonable assumption, since, as a woman told Lundberg and Farnham (p. 85), her first orgasm was like going over the falls of Niagara in a barrel, and in those cases where women state that their "orgasms" lasted over a minute, I suspect that what is referred to is one of the mounting waves of sensation and not the final explosion.

Our knowledge of orgasm in women is very meagre and I have little faith in much of the material collected by some of the writers of "surveys" and statistical "analyses". For a woman who has never experienced an orgasm it is impossible to reply yes or no to an inquiry whether she has had one, as she does not know what it is. A mounting crescendo of pleasure is not orgasm. Orgasm is a final release of tension in which the sensation is so exquisite that control is lost (see Kinsey's admirable discussion in his second report (pp. 627 ff.)). As one of my correspondents put it when describing such a climax, "I shall scream; I can't help it, I must yell," and then later she adds, "What a fearful racket I made. . . . It was the most frantic and exquisite sensation that I got; I felt beside myself; it simply drives me crazy. . . ."

I have stressed the part played by the orgasm in female sex life because I believe it to be of importance in the case of the American woman. Indeed, I am of the opinion that the unsatisfactory nature of love as understood in the United States is largely responsible for the frustration, dissatisfaction and neurosis which are everywhere apparent. The American woman knows that she is denied what she rightly believes is her due, yet she does not know how to obtain it, and more often than not her man does not know how to give it her. In other words, she has failed to develop a perfect femininity, and thus tries to compensate herself through means which only lead to further disappointment, frustration and nervous hate. As we proceed, we shall see how these develop, and how woman's need is not met by the men who should fulfil it.

The publication of the early surveys on marriage was one indication of the growing awareness of changing *mores* after the First World War. The "vast juvenile intrigue" mentioned by F. Scott Fitzgerald in his *This Side of Paradise* was merely part of a scene where sexual adventure was becoming as true and as well known as that portrayed in Warner Fabian's *Week-End Girl*, or in the dozens of similar novels of the 1930s.

In 1937 Alan Devoe, in the *American Mercury*, commented upon the growing spate of advertisements of semi-pornographic books in the United States. There were a number of translations of foreign works and adaptations from books dealing with the sexual life of people abroad.

Moreover the growing knowledge of birth-control was also becoming a factor in encouraging some young women to indulge themselves without fear of the consequences. In 1929 the report of Katharine B. Davis on factors in the sex life of over 2,000 women showed that only 78 out of 1,000 women disapproved of any form of contraceptive, whereas over 80 per cent. stated that, in their opinion, a woman was not justified in having any sexual relations before marriage, a view which must be related to the important place that consummation plays in American thought regarding virginity. Davis's sample has been criticized by some, as, for example, by F. M. Strakosch, on the grounds that it was taken from only selected social groups, but, assuming this to be true, I see little reason to question the general conclusions as regards the class to which her figures refer, although Kinsey's findings (pp. 409–45) should be carefully considered in this respect. Methods of contraception had been known in the United States since the first quarter of the nineteenth century and probably before that, but the National Birth Control League was not founded till 1917, and it was not till six years later that the New York Birth Control Clinical Research Bureau was opened under the auspices of

Mrs. Margaret Sanger and her colleagues, to be followed by others in different parts of the United States.

One result of the growing awareness among women of what they considered to be further steps in sexual freedom was an increasing discussion of what is called the "double standard". The reasons given for its acceptance as laid down (p. 155) in *The Virgin's Nosegay* (1744) were beginning to weaken with the coming of birth control, and by 1931 it was actually stated that it had already gone in the West and Middle West,[1] although this was clearly an exaggeration, since, as James West pointed out (*Plainville*, p. 194) in 1945, the double standard was still accepted in the smaller towns of central United States at the time of his investigation.[2] The "double standard", moreover, was supported by some writers in an effort to curb growing irregularities among women, and an article by a wife entitled "I Believe in the Double Standard" was printed in *The American Mercury* in 1937. Here it was bluntly and somewhat crudely stated that the average man was not "chemically conditioned" to monogamy, lashed as he was by "billions of boisterous spermatozoa", which statement, although perhaps a little weak physiologically, had something to commend it. A vigorous correspondence followed, critics seething with rage, being afflicted with "nausea", and reminding the original writer that "after all this *is* the United States". One woman complained that her second husband still clung to her apron-strings; whilst a male correspondent expressed disgust at the tacit acceptance by the American man of female dominance, a feature of life in the United States which he completely failed to understand. Indeed, he went so far as to suggest that wives in America would be better if soundly spanked every morning at nine o'clock, apparently not having heard of the Club of Spanked Wives, which was only open to those who had actually been spanked by their irate (or amorous) spouses! In the issue of November 1937 the author of the article replied to her correspondents. Noting the "tumult and shouting" her article had caused, she dryly remarked that all the "rabid ravings" had proceeded from women, which is, we might add, exactly what might have been expected.[3]

[1] See *Woman's Coming of Age*, p. 215.
[2] The factual picture of "Plainville" as portrayed by James West may profitably be compared with the *Small Town* of Granville Hicks and the horrific picture of *The People from Heaven* painted by John Sanford, in which the gulf separating faith from practice is shown wide open with all the appropriate settings in vivid and at times nauseating realism.
[3] Cf. another note by a woman in the *American Mercury* for July 1938. Entitled "Virgins for Husbands", the writer stated it as her opinion that it

A year later the question was discussed in Pringle and Cookman's series of articles in the *Ladies' Home Journal* (Nov. 1938, 22 ff.) and it often finds a place in the columnists' advice articles, "An Old Washingtonian" writing to Mary Haworth in the *Washington Post* on September 9, 1943, defending the single standard, and declaring that some men were "lower than tom cats" in their social attitudes.

Whatever may have been said by the supporters and opposers of the double standard, there was little doubt what the facts were. The increasing interest of women in the question was not so much that they demanded a single standard for men, but a double standard for both sexes. With what V. F. Calverton called "the bankruptcy of marriage", came the sudden realization that it seemed somewhat odd that, in choosing a husband or wife, no preliminary life together was permitted before legal sanction was obtained. From such reflections as these came the growing interest in "trial" marriages, and the immense interest in Lindsey and Evans' *The Companionate Marriage* (1928) clearly indicated which way the wind was blowing. It is true that valiant attempts were made to point out the difficulties in such unions, the secrecy and subterfuges which hindered any really satisfactory experiment. But in spite of the numerous papers on the technique of marital adjustment, the tendency among the more advanced women was towards a realization that there was something very wrong with the American marriage, and that, in spite of easy divorce, the experts had not really begun to deal with the fundamentals of the problem.

As the years went by, and in spite of the flood of books and guidance pamphlets, marriage in the United States remained a problem which disturbed every serious thinker in the country, whatever were his religious views or social theories. Yet it was often forgotten how many happy homes were to be found in the United States, in which the parents were suitably matched, and in which the younger generation was hardly influenced by the tide of discontent which was surging around it. The increase of knowledge about the sexual life had affected women for the worse rather than for the better. For the more she knew, the more she suspected that she was being cheated. Reality seemed so different from what she had anticipated, for she had not learnt (and had little opportunity of learning properly) that, in the words of an acute writer, Alison Hawgood, sex for

---

was very dubious whether virginity was a desirable asset in a young husband, an opinion which could not have been palatable to many readers. See also "Little Boys make Lousy Husbands" by L. Galton, *Better Homes and Gardens*, 1950.

women, "is like caviare, an acquired taste".[1] Many women knew little of the art of love as described by Marcel Barrière in his *Essai sur le Donjuanisme Contemporain* (p. 129). The art of love, he says, consists in initiating women into sensual pleasure, in revealing to them its poetry and secret mysteries, and in transporting them into that region, still so obscure from the physiological point of view, where tremblings, faintness and spasms and even apparent death are mingled in a symphony which only gradually approaches the final paroxysm. The man's pleasure is forgotten; what is important is only the pleasure that he bestows, so that his partner can say it was to him that she owes her deepest bliss.

It is interesting to observe how the American female *before* marriage has to play the part of the romantic doll, and how *after* marriage, when the dreams of youth have been shattered and Prince Charming is seen without the halo, she adopts the rôle of the dominating Mother ("Mom"), ruling not only her children but her husband also.

How far such a dominating position is desired or enjoyed is far from clear. It is obvious that, in many cases, the adoption of such a rôle is compensatory and is, in a sense, forced upon the woman. Through it she attempts to become apparently independent and not in any way "inferior" to the man, whom she secretly despises for his spineless acceptance of the position allotted to him in the United States. Now and then revealing incidents find their way into print in which the feelings aroused by this position find vent in outbursts of resentment. Minney (*op. cit.*, pp. 198 ff.) tells of how a girl addicted to excessive smoking was reproved by the man with whom she was sitting. In cooing tones he begged her to desist, told her of what the doctor had said, etc. Sickened by this display, a man at the same table took the cigarette from the woman, stubbed it out and declared that she was not to smoke any more. Her escort was thunderstruck, and rose from his chair protesting angrily. But his lady friend gave him a sharp order to behave himself and asked him to tell her why the man should not have acted as he had done if he wanted to!

Similarly, a case printed in "The Worry Clinic" in the *New York Post* of January 15, 1943, referred to a young woman, aged twenty-two, engaged to the type of "fine man" so idealized in the United States. She declared that sometimes he irritated her so much that she could scream. "Some day I may scratch his eyes out, so there!" ended her complaints. Further analysis showed what was wrong.

[1] A. Hawgood, *A Family is Fun*, p. 85.

Her irritation stemmed from the fact that her "fine man" was, as the psychologist put it, one of "these long-suffering doormats", and the girl herself finally declared that she only wished that her fiancé would give her a sound spanking. Summing up the situation, the psychologist declared that the more men submit to "such petticoat rule", the more irritated and angry the women become. He summed up one of the basic reasons for the frustration and unhappiness that so many American women experience. Yet it is not often that American women complain and confess their true feelings, and doubtless they often accept their position and even glory in it.[1]

One way out of the American wife's dilemma is to have more than one husband to fulfil her demands in various directions. This solution was amusingly put forward in 1925 by Alexander Black, and the relevant sections condensed in *The Reader's Digest* for February 1946. One husband would look after her material needs, another would act as handy-man about the house, and the third would attend to her during the night, and when not active would have to be a "noiseless sleeper", so as not to disturb her ladyship.

The question of the skill or otherwise of American men in the practice and art of love is a common topic in the United States, and is also widely debated among foreigners when no Americans are present. As I have said, I am of the opinion that the lack of full sexual satisfaction is at the core of the discontent manifested by so many American women, and as it has therefore its repercussions in every department of life, it will be necessary at this stage to examine this matter as objectively as possible.

From what we have already seen of the relationship of man to woman in the United States it ought to be clear that, at first sight, the sexual approach would seem to be a risky experiment on both sides. The man, for his part, has to contend with a complex of ideas and ideals which are fundamentally hostile to satisfactory relations. Tied to the maternal image, adolescent in behaviour and

[1] See Emily Hahn, who stated that Englishwomen and American men "know their place", that a "female minority" rules the States, and that American "boys" are scared to death of not loving their mothers (London *Evening Standard*, March 16, 1948, p. 6). Cf. the article, "America's Pampered Husbands" by that disillusioned feminist, E. M. Stern, where she says that the task of "re-educating men" to their new rôle in the home will not be easy! As Mrs. M. A. Hamilton said, on Feb. 21, 1949, when broadcasting on American women in the United States, "Mother knows best" for "Mom rules the home". She even stated that in that "woman's Paradise" men wear overshoes because women insist, for the United States is ruled by women and they know it and "everybody knows it". J. C. Ohessex's estimate of the status of the American husband is questioned by Cazamian, *L'autre Amérique* (1931), who (p. 240) found him perfectly obedient.

outlook, and with a picture of woman completely out of focus, many an American man finds that full and satisfactory relations are impossible. Full virility is not lacking: where he fails is in not using his powers so as to obtain not only the maximum satisfaction for himself, but also that for his partner, without which no full realization of the joys of the mutual embrace is in any way possible. As in so many of the really important affairs of life, the art of making love is not easy. It is, indeed, one of the most difficult arts to practise, and it is one in which the average American is lost. The early training he receives is inimical to any true appreciation of love's thrills: guilt and shame cloud the pleasure that might be his; and the attitude of dominance and superiority adopted by the American woman is fatal to her own enjoyment.

It must not be imagined that these deficiencies are found only in the United States. They are all too common elsewhere, though arising, perhaps, from other causes. However, in America it is mainly among those persons living in the upper-income levels where failure is often most noticeable, and it is these classes who possess and enjoy all those material advantages which are so useful and desirable for successful contact. Clearly part at least of the difficulty is psychological, and the reader who has had the patience to follow me thus far will not be at a loss to see where the trouble lies.

After David L. Cohn's devastating exposure of *Love in America* (1943) it might be thought that there was little more to be said. For in this work the author has pointed out most of the factors that put the American man as a lover "out of sight", to use the words of M. F. Ponsonby, who adds the caustic remark that American love-making "stands supreme among the erotic efforts of the nations". Odette Keun was even more biting. She found the American man the most insensitive mate imaginable, his meek acquiescence in female ideas both undignified and positively stupid, whilst in courtship he could only be described as "awful". She declared that he had no notion of the subtleties of love-making, and his vocabulary was what might have been expected from an automaton. Indeed, had she been asked the question recently put to readers of *The Reader's Digest*, "Are Yanks lousy lovers?", she would have emphatically answered "Yes"! [1]

---

[1] *Are Yanks Lousy Lovers?* (1945). T. Sugrue, writing in 1948, stated that, socially speaking, the modern fashionable American husband was merely his wife's "eunuch" (p. 17), and the accounts of love scenes in modern American fiction are positively painful to read. For example, see the story of the love of Wenny (a great hysterical dolt) and Nan in Dos Passos' *Streets of Night* (pp. 120 ff.).

We have already seen that some of the complaints made by women are that their husbands are absorbed in business, are perpetually tired and are therefore unable to spare the time or take the trouble for the more intimate affairs of the boudoir. Bedroom customs and habits in the United States, as one might have expected, have received some kind of statistical analysis. For example, the John B. Pierce Foundation of Manhattan issued such a survey in 1944 in which 131 supposedly typical families were investigated, ranging from incomes of $2,000 to $3,000 per year. In 87 per cent. of the cases the double bed was still in use, although 42 per cent. of the wives showed preference for twin beds. 20 per cent. of the women neither dressed nor undressed in their husband's presence, and as James West (*op. cit.*, p. 179) pointed out, in some of the smaller American communities some married people never see one another undressed at any time. Activity when in bed was carefully inquired into. Of the husbands, 22 per cent. read, 12 per cent. talk, 7 per cent. listen to the radio, 3 per cent. pray, 2 per cent. smoke, 2 per cent. eat and 50 per cent. do nothing. Comparable figures for the women were 29 per cent. read, 11 per cent. talk, 8 per cent. listen to the radio, 5 per cent. pray, 2 per cent. smoke, 2 per cent. eat and 40 per cent. do nothing.[1]

Apart from these "scientific" surveys of the activities of Americans in bedrooms, we have the less detailed opinions of various writers, the evidence as seen in advertisements and the evidence of the cartoon. For example, in the *Saturday Evening Post* in 1942, Ogden Nash contributed an inset declaring that the "trouble with women is men", for the husband was merely a man, Mr. Nash proclaimed, who was snoring like an overloaded omnibus two minutes after his head was upon the pillow. In the same year Americans were able to enjoy pictures of the husband doing this, since John Falter designed two charming scenes in order to advertise the *Beautyrest* Mattress. In one the man is fast asleep in his double bed. His wife kneels on the bed and gazes at him before herself getting in. In the other, twin beds are used. The husband, his mouth wide open, is sleeping. The wife, half sitting up in bed before turning out the light, casts a look of resigned pity at her husband. But ought she not to be pleased at the result of her husband's sleep? He will make more propeller blades and drive more rivets tomorrow, so the advertisement assures us.

[1] See "Family Survey" (*Business Week Magazine*, April 1, 1944, pp. 28 ff.). For amusing commentaries see *The New Yorker*, May 20, 1944, pp. 20 ff.; S. J. Perelman's *Keep it Crisp*, p. 111, and cf. R. Y. Hopton and A. Balliol's *Bed Manners* (1934) and *Better Bed Manners* (1936), of which the former is founded on H. Powel's "Bed Manners" (*Vogue*, Dec. 1, 1933).

The American cartoon is frequently valuable as a pointer towards the more intimate social relations between the sexes. A subject very commonly portrayed is the spineless male being bullied, cajoled or persuaded to wake up and realize what a woman wants. Thus the "reading in bed" found in the Pierce report was amusingly satirized in one of the drawings by Dos Mismos in the *Saturday Review of Literature* (August 7, 1943). A married couple are in their double bed. The man is trying to read: his wife, sitting up, looks at him with disgust and irritation. "Go ahead", she says, "read, educate yourself", adding that perhaps in the morning he'll be worth talking to.[1]

It might be imagined from what we know of the sexual life of the United States as revealed by such limited studies as the Kinsey reports and other similar attempts at analysis, that the dissatisfaction and frustration of women could hardly be due to any lack of actual sexual relations, and that therefore the whole theory that the common discontent among American women is due mainly to sexual causes must fall to the ground. Such opinions (which I have often heard expressed) disclose a complete inability to grasp fundamental features in female psychology. It must be remembered that the standardized attitude of American husbands is indifference towards women, and that American men in general are peculiarly indifferent to the psychology of woman. This is due mainly to the man's faulty upbringing, to his sexual ineptitude and to the common belief that such things as literature, art and love poetry are "sissy". Women do not desire to be used as "outlets", in order that selfish men may "ease nature". They want to be loved, awakened, brought to a state of extreme excitation, and then to be possessed fully and completely. They can attain perfect satisfaction only if their trust in their partners is such that complete abandonment can be achieved. They do not even object to roughness, if the preliminary courtship is so technically skilful that extreme eroticism is aroused. And it is this technique which is lacking in many an American man.

---

[1] Cf. *Peter Arno's Circus*, nr. 38. A fantastic picture of the "best man . . . never a groom" was put out in 1944 by the WOR radio station. Even the girls smirked at "Eustace". For four years he had been waiting for leap-year day. "Will any woman ask him" or must he sit at home pressing his wedding pants? Eustace is portrayed as a tailor's dummy, the legs missing and the trousers cut off just below the knee. Similar highly revealing scenes are depicted in cartoons in E. Simms Campbell's *Cuties in Arms* and *More Cuties in Arms*.

Many stories are current in the United States relating to the behaviour of the frigid woman when caressed by her husband. It is said that some read the stock-market reports, others remain completely passive, while in one case a wife is said to have demanded a fee every time. Such tales always remind me of the similar story in Sterne's *Tristram Shandy*, when mother asked father whether he had forgotten to wind up the clock (p. 3).

P

Moreover, were he to possess the technique of a Casanova and the virility of a sexual athlete, his work would be in vain were he to attempt to court many an American woman. For if the American man's courtship is a "wash-out", to use Odette Keun's words, an American woman's bed-manners are a disaster. This truth came to the British author, R. W. Thompson, when he was in New York. There he saw these superb American women with their "lovely limbs", their "beautiful legs", with that amazing background of "breasts, buttocks and bellies" on the bookstalls, on the boards and even on the bedposts. Here they were, perfectly turned out, ready made and patterned, *but* "not for love".[1] For he saw clearly that he was in the motherland of dominant women who were making idols of themselves and demanding tribute. Such women were to be worshipped at a distance. Could it even be imagined that, to use Thomas Wolfe's phrase, they would ever be obedient to bed or whip?[2] Such a thought was impossible.

Yet might it not be possible to learn what the pampered American woman wanted from indirect sources? Her "baby" rôle was scarcely one which could inspire respect in any adult man; whilst in her later attitude of female dominance she inspired merely fear and aversion, except from those few who longed to conquer her and force her to submit. Is it possible, in short, to discover any evidence that the adult American woman in the middle and upper economic levels secretly harbours a longing to escape from the position in which she finds herself, to come down from her pedestal, where man, that "bifurcated radish in trousers", as M. Struthers Burt called him,[3] has placed her. Does she wish to take her true place, no longer symbolized as a long cake of ice, as in the ritual of the Key-Ice fraternity[4] at Tuscaloosa, Alabama, but as a warm-hearted, warm-blooded human being, the very fibres of whose being crave for that love and that happy companionship that spring from the relation of the sexes when uninhibited by neurotic fears and feelings of guilty shame?

This may be woman's ideal, but how to attain it in the United States is a problem which still awaits solution. It might be an

---

[1] R. W. Thompson, *Black Caribbean*, pp. 50–1.

[2] T. Wolfe, *You Can't Go Home Again*, p. 39.

[3] M. S. Burt, *Our Feminized United States*, p. 268. This curious article maintained that no women were treated so badly mentally and spiritually as in the United States, and that the country was run exclusively by and for men. Nevertheless he recognised that the Rochesters and the Rhett Butlers represented the "gentle rapist" so dear to the female imagination (see pp. 268, 266 269).

[4] See C. L. Carmer, *Stars Fell on Alabama*, pp. 14, 15. The block of ice is carried in on a cart with attending acolytes. The leader then gives the toast to "Woman", as pure and chaste as sparkling water and as cold as gleaming ice.

American axiom, as Varigny averred in 1889, that in the United States woman was queen: she might be "unique", or, as F. Roz expressed it in 1927, "un objet précieux et rare, infiniment recherché", she might be "envied" in England and "revered" on the Continent, as the Nearings maintained in 1912; she might, as Mrs. M. A. Hamilton expressed it when broadcasting from England in 1949 be "the Eighth Wonder of the World", but could she be *happy* when her men never seemed to grow up, and now and then she had to recognize the fact, and, like the woman quoted by the Nearings, had to call her beaux "her kindergarten"? [1]

It was rarely that she lost her patience with the men who failed her. To do so would be undignified, and also it would show that she was at least partially dependent upon men for her own satisfaction. Occasionally, however, it was too much. One day the Baltimore *Post* carried a story of an incident where three girls offered a man a lift in their automobile. Driving to a quiet spot, they stopped, proposed a "petting party", but found the guest unable or unwilling to gratify them. Stung with contempt and fury, they seized him, stuck pins into him, and left him in such a condition that he had to be removed to the nearest hospital.[2]

When the situation in which the American woman found herself was calmly examined, it frankly seemed hopeless. For not only was her sexual life awry partly through the fault of her man, but her own attitude also made love seem impossible to achieve. The very position of dominance she adopted at a mature age as effectively held off adult men as did the "baby-girl" rôle that she had previously adopted. Many persons of both sexes seemed conditioned from their youth up to an adulthood in which normal, human love relations were rendered so difficult as to be nearly impossible. And from this perpetual conflict arose a good measure of the frustration, unhappiness and neurotic discontents with which so many thousands of American women are burdened. It is true that seductions were far from unknown. But, as Emily Hahn has put it in *Seductio ad absurdum*, seduction was really the art of persuading a person to do what

---

[1] *Woman and Social Progress*, p. 363.
[2] See *Americana, 1926*, p. 87; and cf. the *American Mercury* (March 1926). Another case has recently been reported. Margery Wilson, in her revealing book, *The Woman You Want to Be*, stated that women should not be doormats (p. 234) and that men never grow up emotionally, which, she thought, was one of their most "charming and exasperating attributes" (p. 249). On the other hand, she asked herself the question why women should please and placate the annoying creatures. Her answer was clear and concise. "Because", she wrote, "both women and men get more out of that arrangement than from any other" (p. 238). Cf. the same author's *How to Live Beyond your Means*.

he or she really wanted to do all the time. The question was, did the American woman want anything *done* to her? Did her position as the dominant sex permit any act of aggression, without some kind of psychological conflict ensuing? Certainly, aggression *with* her consent was difficult. But what about it *without* her consent?

This question always brings to my mind an incident in a theatre I once attended. During one of the scenes in the play, a number of women were together and about to be interviewed by a mysterious man. Much whispering went on in the waiting-room, and then one said in a high-pitched voice, "Do you think he'll rape us all? How wonderful!" The house broke into applause, and women all round me were clapping and stamping, their eyes bright with anticipation.

In 1953 the United States Government crime reports show 17,900 cases of rape. How far these were genuine cases of rape with violence on unwilling and resisting victims I do not know, and it does not concern us here.[1] What is now of interest to consider is whether or no some American women cherish phantasies of rape, or perhaps it would be better to say of violent love-making, thus relieving themselves of the pretence of dominance, and enjoying what otherwise they would have resisted as being incompatible with their ideas of superiority and moral virtue.

One source of information for matters of this kind is the modern American novel, in which contemporary culture is reflected and occasionally analysed. Among the mass of available material it is not easy to make a selection, and I shall merely mention one or two of the more interesting stories. As might have been expected, the twenties provided a good deal of realistic fiction, and we have already noticed some of the examples when dealing with "flaming youth". In Ring Lardner we see a master-hand sketching the convulsions of a social order in decay, where many of the women characters seem devoid of any true femininity and remain merely gold-diggers and money-spenders. Both Dos Passos and J. T. Farrell paint certain aspects of the American cultural pattern and their women of the urban cities are often markedly different from the more refined circles painted by Hergesheimer or Sinclair Lewis. It is in novels like Edith M. Hull's *The Sheik* (Boston, 1921) that we can see

[1] Cf. J. A. and R. Goldberg, in *Girls of City Streets* for an analysis of 1,400 cases of alleged rape. Some time ago the Louisville *Times* decided to print the names of women who complained of rape in cases where the defendant was found not guilty. It was apparently found necessary to do this as a protection for men against the designs of frustrated and sex-starved women. In 1943 a girl of seventeen complained that she had been raped by twelve men during a cinema performance at the Bronx Opera House, where some time previously a woman had stated that she had been raped twenty-five times!

the change in approach towards the cruder aspects of love, and
Diana's struggles and joys in the arms of her Arab must have thrilled
many a heart, especially as it all came right in the end! Again, in
A. Rand's *The Fountainhead*, the account of the rape by Howard
Roark, with his mop of hair the colour of "ripe orange rind" (pp.
230 ff.), was particularly vivid, especially when we consider the
constant visits to the quarry by the victim to gloat over her possible
conqueror, a man whom she loathed although the very thought of
being broken by him "left her weak with pleasure" (p. 218).

This desire for the more elemental thrills is well illustrated in
Louis Bromfield's *Mrs. Parkington*. This delightful sketch of an
American lady, gracefully growing old and full of kindly wisdom, is
ushered in by an account of her strict early childhood and her early
marriage to the buoyant and energetic Gus. Frightened of what to
her might have been a terrifying experience, she was treated by her
young husband "not as a wife but as a mistress", and for this she
"was grateful to him always" (p. 65). Indeed, it seems to be the
lesson of the book that Mrs. Parkington's charm and worldly grace
were largely due to the successful adjustment of her marriage,
in which her old Puritan standards and fears were obliterated
under the handling of one to whom women "would always be
mistresses".[1]

Perhaps one of the most illuminating sources for the study of the
effect of rape on the imagination of many American women is the
record of the trial of the film actor Errol Flynn in 1942. In October
of that year film-struck Betty Hansen complained that, at a party
to which she had been invited, she was raped by Errol Flynn, protesting but not struggling "very hard". At the same time the actor
was accused of another rape, this time of a singer and dancer. The
trial was a sensation. The girls described in detail how they were
undressed and then submitted to Flynn's advances. The second
accuser was aged sixteen or seventeen, and since the age of consent
in California was eighteen, intimacy meant rape in law. In the
course of the trial it was disclosed that this young lady had been
living—platonically—with an aviation film adviser, and that her
mother was aware of it. She must have been a gay companion. On
one occasion, it was stated in court, after a round of night-clubs, she
and her friend visited a mortuary, played hide-and-seek round the

---

[1] Mr. Bromfield's sketch of the financier Amory is extremely competent. He
is portrayed at fifty as having the mind of a child, but without the curiosity or
enthusiasm common to youth (p. 145); and the author declares that to explain
these features in adult Americans there must be "some deep-seated colossal
fault" at the base of the whole social structure.

corpses, lifted the shrouds, and finally she laid her head beside the body of an elderly man.

As the trial proceeded the court become more and more crowded, women being the majority of those craving admittance. The film star's brightness seemed to wax even greater; and one girl hitch-hiked all the way from Newark to Los Angeles to get his autograph. She was photographed gazing into the idol's face as he signed her book. On February 6, 1944, Errol Flynn was acquitted by the jury of nine women and three men. Two of the men objected, but the women insisted. I knew they would, stated one of the damsels of whose rape Flynn was now declared not guilty (*Courier-Journal*, Feb. 7, 1943).

During the trials a few attempts were made to sound female film-goers on their attitude to the accused star. In the "Inquiring Foto-grapher's" column of the New York *Daily News*, Esther Maki declared that she believed the girls were not at fault; Barbara Soulatis said that in such cases "it was always the woman's fault unless she was hit on the head"; Jean Sussman declared that it was not Flynn's fault; and Phyllis Turner thought that the women were merely using the incidents as a stepping-stone to the movies. Of the two men whose replies were printed, one said that Flynn had done nothing more than any other man would have done in the circumstances; and the other regarded it as a female "hold-up", and thought Flynn a real man to go to court instead of paying up.

It is, I think, this suspicion among American women that their treatment as "wives" is depriving them of something which they would receive were they "mistresses" that is partly responsible for the great interest taken in Latin types of men, and incidentally may have a bearing on their attitudes towards Negroes. Indeed, I have a suspicion that the persistent "misunderstanding" between the United States and the South American Republics is partly due to the fact that the former country is dominated by women, while the latter states are very definitely countries in which male dominance is customary. As Mrs. Paxton found when she lived in Bogotá, Colombian girls were taught that their husbands were in a superior position, whilst in the United States they were taught "well, something very different from that" (*Penthouse in Bogotá* (p. 101)).

For our present purpose it will be sufficient to touch merely upon one more aspect of culture contact. Students of the sexual life have long been aware of the supposed success of Latin lovers in the case of women of Anglo-Saxon stock. The enormous success of Rudolf Valentino, Ramon Novarro and others indicated a general leaning towards the dark, sultry type of man, who promised greater thrills

SEX AND THE AMERICAN WOMAN

in the boudoir than the harassed business man or the half-drunk playboy of American café society. How exciting, how enticing was Maurice Chevalier in *The Big Pond*, who, as a Venetian guide, so easily captivated the susceptible daughter of a chewing-gum magnate; or a similar hero, this time in Naples, who thrilled British film audiences with *The City of Song*. It was even better when such enchanters appeared in person, for when Miguelito Valdés appeared in New York, it proved quite costly to remove the lipstick which women had implanted upon the idol's photographs in the lobby. What else was it but a weakness of knee and fluttering of heart that led Pearl Lusk to shoot Mr. Rocco with a gun disguised as a camera in 1947? Is it too much to suggest, as Bergen Evans has done, that what we have here is simply an ascription of libidinousness to these swarthy gentlemen which is, in a sense, a wish-projection on the part of sex-starved and inhibited white women?[1]

I am well aware that such an interpretation will be indignantly rejected, and that many women like Helen B. Norden will declare that "Latins are lousy lovers".[2] Miss Norden prefers Americans, and she is entitled to her own opinion, for it would appear that she made extensive inquiries among Cubans, whose wives are apparently longing to be embraced by American tough babies. I do not know if Miss Norden really exists—she is credited with a book (1942) entitled *The Hussy's Handbook*—or is merely an amusing creation designed by *The Bedside Esquire* to while away an idle hour. Anyway, she added that what the Cubans were after was American money. Perhaps it was they who did not find the American ladies attractive, and I fancy that in that they might find others to agree with them. I can hardly imagine a Cuban standing at a bar, asking his friend to "have another" and adding that, after all, his wife could only live his life once! (See *Esquire*, June 1943, p. 62.)

The attraction that Latin men indubitably exercise over white women, and especially white American women, leads directly to the question as to how far white American women are attracted by Negro men. In dealing with this matter one fact is clear. There can be no possible doubt that the belief, true or false, exists in the United States, that Negro *men* find white *women* attractive. I have already dealt with the whole question in my *Racial Pride and Prejudice* (pp. 68 ff., 229 ff.), to which, therefore, I must refer the interested reader. Suffice to say that, as Margaret Halsey has recently pointed out, the

---

[1] B. Evans, *A Natural History of Nonsense*, p. 224.
[2] See *The Bedside Esquire*, pp. 12 ff. Mrs. E. Stern wrote a book in 1934 called *Men are Clumsy Lovers*, which is very revealing.

belief regarding the partiality of Negro men for white women is accompanied by the belief that, were white women allowed to know Negro men better, they would find them attractive.[1] I have no doubt whatever that this is true, and that one of the main reasons for the violent colour prejudice in the South is due to the fact that the white women are sexually unsatisfied and jealous of the attention that coloured women get from white men, while white men are often jealous of coloured men, since the former labour under the common delusion that people of dark skin colour are more virile, sexually competent and capable of sustained activity than persons of lighter pigmentation.

These beliefs permeate the South and have created great trouble, misery and psychological tension. Before the civil war, Southern society, always very different from that of the East, was partly centred upon the position, charm and desirability of women, but the presence of the Negro embittered relations, since the white woman had to be represented as the antithesis of her coloured sister. Young men consorted with black women as a matter of course, and indeed it is said that a Southern jest tells of how men in the South do not know till they marry that they can embrace a white woman. Thus the white woman of the South was supposed to have no desires and no passion. She was a block of ice, a white goddess, pure as the snow and as cold, and any approach was, in a sense, a violation of an ideal, almost sacrilegious. Under these conditions is it strange that the white American woman of the South is full of resentment, frustration and a sense of lack of fulfilment and purpose? As I wrote a few years ago in my *Racial Pride and Prejudice* :

"It was natural that the South, dominated as it was by a master class in which burned a fanatical Protestant zeal, should exhibit this dilemma in its most acute form. But not only on the Negro question was the South divided. It was not that the Southerner was a hypocrite and a conscious deceiver. Far from it. According to his lights he was sincere, honest and well-meaning. The dilemma that confronted him in his relations with the Negro was intensified by the dilemma which harassed his whole attitude to life in general. It was as if the luminous haze of the Southern atmosphere had entered his mind and rendered everything vague, blurred and indistinct. His was a mind divided against itself: it was almost that he lived in two worlds. In many respects he was, as we say today, almost schizophrenic. The very conditions under which he lived made such tendencies almost unavoidable. His religious inheritance of rigid Pro-

[1] M. Halsey, *Color Blind*, p. 101.

testant dogmatism was supposed to blend, not only with a frontier mentality, but with all the temptations of life in a country where the sun by day and the moon by night seemed almost to be deliberately calculated to bring about his downfall. Life on the plantations was a continual test; and it was a test to which flesh and blood, least of all Southern flesh and blood, could hardly submit and come out unscathed. Colour prejudice and arguments about Ham were forgotten when the moon rose and hung like a great Chinese lantern over the cotton fields. The Negro woman was not only complaisant; she was free from that ever-present sense of guilt and sin which still permeates all American society. Thus she offered a contrast to the white woman of the South, who was thereupon raised on a pinnacle and presented to the world as the perfect example of ice-cold chastity, purity and innocence. The result of this gynæcolatry was (and is still) catastrophic. For the terrible frustration which the Southern woman suffered was turned outward and became aggressive, and her aggression was directed quite simply and naturally against those whom she believed were partly responsible. It is thus that we find that the whole question of colour prejudice in the South revolves around the sexual question. The ever-present thought of rapes; the eternal question as to whether one wants one's daughter to marry a Negro; the marked sadistic elements in certain lynchings; the growing jealousies and rivalries which are beginning to spring up—all these to the student in abnormal psychology are unmistakable pointers towards what J. W. Johnson has called 'the core of the heart of the American race problem'."

If there is any lesson to be drawn from the few observations outlined above, it is that the love-life of many an American woman is imperfect, and that its failure is directly due to the results of American teaching and ideology regarding both men and women. Moreover, the increasing "emancipation" of women has done nothing to ease the situation, but rather tends to exacerbate it. A vicious circle is created, and there seems no easy way of breaking it. Woman becomes the victim of a series of factors which are woven tightly into the American way of life itself. The Puritan notions of female virtue still remain; and the Puritan regard for the value of individual effort and initiative permits the exploitation of millions by a few who are wholly free from any regard for public welfare, but who think only in terms of financial gain. Nothing is exempt from the activities of these gentlemen. Maternity can be made to pay just as well as the health of children. Fear is almost as lucrative as sex. Before me is an advertisement which appeared in a New York paper in 1944. A young woman is portrayed clasping her handkerchief and looking soulful. Above are two words which, according to the caption, are "most dreaded" by women. They are *cancer* and *childbirth*. It is a curious combination, but that would not deter those who see that fear of the one, of the other or of both, can be turned into money, just as the fear of "germs" makes so many Americans ridiculous when they travel abroad, and at the same time fills the pockets of the manufacturers of the various bug, fly and germ exterminators that are advertised and sold in huge quantities.

The American mother in her earlier years has so difficult a part to play that it is surprising that she is as successful as she so often is. For during the first years of marriage many young wives have to discard most of the romantic nonsense of their teens, discover that their husbands want mothering and not loving in an adult sense, and at the same time have to deal with the multifarious duties of running a home. Childbirth in the United States is often regarded among the upper classes as a major operation or worse; and this idea is encouraged in the numerous articles devoted to the subject. Popular books pour yearly from the press to instruct mothers in the mysteries of parturition and baby management, and many women are victims to the prevailing mania for "schedules" and "rules for feeding" which are put out by the various "experts" in child management.

In the successful marriages the family tends to become the kernel round which the life of the unit is constructed. Husband and wife may be mutually compatible and the love-life of both satisfactory and well-adjusted. But, as we have seen, marriage in the United States tends to break; and, indeed, the situation has reached a stage in which there is what Raymond Recouly in his *L'Amérique Pauvre* called "une polygamie véritable" (p. 344), although in the United States the women succeed one another, instead of co-existing. The search for satisfaction is, of course, bound to fail. In the United States female tranquillity is an impossibility. The failure to find the mate she needs is finally accepted, and the domination which was partly the cause of the failure becomes a kind of compensatory device whereby her own self-respect may be maintained. The American Mother becomes "Mom", and takes her place in the curious matriarchal set-up of American society, where she reigns supreme and even excites the admiration of some foreigners who, like Orsini Ratto (p. 156), declared that the American gynæcocracy produced some fine women who were always interesting, whatever else they were.

During the Second World War foreigners had the opportunity of noting the anxiety shown by American soldiers to observe "Mother's Day". Some wrote to the Press complaining that in England they "don't even know what Mother's Day is"; and when Lady Cavendish (Adèle Astaire) returned to the United States in 1945 from a visit to Britain she explained that "over there" it was a man's world, and that they did not adore their mothers as they did in America. The same discovery was made by Mrs. L. S. Florence, an American married to an Englishman. Writing in the *Leader* for October 27, 1945, she called Britain that "unfeminine land", and she mentioned with pleasure seeing in England a long line of American "boys" (*i.e.* soldiers) lining up to order flowers "for their mums". Women in England have been "subtly suppressed for generations", Mrs. Florence averred, and there is little doubt she agreed with Lady Cavendish about Britain being a man's world. An illustration of Mrs. Florence's article was very revealing. An American girl's bedroom is shown with the young lady making her bed. On the walls are eleven "pin-ups". No, not of boy-friends or actors, says the caption, but of famous pin-up *girls*. Indeed, it was an all-woman room, and possibly the caption suggests the "forerunner of an all-woman world". Mrs. Eliza Farnham must be smiling!

In the correspondence following Mrs. Florence's article a number of letters indicated that the writers were wholly unconvinced of the beauties of female life in the United States. Indeed, one writer said that the article should have been headed "America—Land where Women are Rapidly Ceasing to Be So", and, considering the illustration described above, he had, I think, some justification for his opinion.

The other side of the question is revealed with a startling clarity in the advice columns in the American Press. For the purpose of illustration, I propose picking out a few specimens from my files of these questions and answers, selecting the examples from a short period. For instance, in the *Washington Post*, Mary Haworth is constantly having to deal with the question of maternal dominance and the adolescent attitude of the married man. On December 20, 1942 she was advising a divorced wife who married one of a mother's five spoilt sons. He proved to be impossible, two of the others died of alcoholism and another committed suicide. Two days later another wife told how her husband wanted to go back to his mother, and not live with his wife, as he was the "perfect mama's boy". In March the following year another wife wrote complaining about her husband, so she was told that it was clear that he was "a mama's boy" who almost fainted at the thought of being loosed from her apron-strings. His wife had to realize that he was "hamstrung and hag-tied by maternally implanted" fears which paralysed him. Two months later, another husband was being described as being a child who wanted marriage to be a "mother-and-boy relationship", and not a union of two adults.

Dorothy Dix's column told the same story. In 1942 two sisters (aged twenty-eight and twenty-three) and their brother (twenty-six) wrote asking advice on how to escape "their mother's tyranny". They were not allowed to invite their friends to their home (which they had to pay for), or to ride in the automobile (which they had bought). They declared that they suffered a tongue-lashing whenever they went out in the evening. They were desperate, and signed themselves "Three Miserable Children". The same year a young woman wrote asking advice on how to deal with mothers who try to prevent their sons from having anything to do with her. She described the maternal barrage of insinuation and abuse, and then remarked that "of course . . . Sonny crawls back safely to Mamma and I lose out". In October of the same year Miss Dix had a whole article on the dominating woman. When a man marries, she said, this kind of woman believes he belongs to her "just as much as though he were a slave she had bought in the market-place". As to the children, every symptom of initiative is ruthlessly crushed. "They must always hold on to Mother's hand and be guided by her." They are left in perpetual babyhood even after they have grown up. The divorce courts are filled with their complaints that they aren't pampered "as Mother did". Men have their wardrobes, their stomachs, their eyes, their tastes and their thoughts taken over by women.

In 1943 a bewildered wife wrote to Miss Dix asking what was to be done with her mother, who, young, well and strong, insisted on living with her and being supported by her, and at the same time tried to persuade her to leave her husband and child and live with her elsewhere. Finally, in 1943 Miss Dix said in plain words that "thousands upon thousands" of American mothers were wrecking homes because they could not bear the thought of their children's independence. This was what was called "mother love", Miss Dix dryly remarked, but it would be better for the children if it were hate.

During the Second World War the American Press was filled with comments, some humorous, some not so humorous, on the power of the American Mother. It was, for example, reported in 1943 that Mrs. Roosevelt had chided some of them for opposing the establishment of an International Police Force, because it would keep their

sons away from home for longer periods; and a year later it was noted
that mothers had been asked officially by the American military
authorities to tell their sons to keep their overcoats buttoned,
although whether this was a joke or not I have not been able to
ascertain. Again, *The New Yorker* was full of sly hits and digs at the
American Mom, her dominance and the way she regarded her
soldier son and the wife he occasionally brought home from the wars.
It told the tale (August 28, 1943, p. 17) of the young recruit and his
mother who were challenged by the military policeman for the
soldier's pass. To this request the mother replied that it was all
right, as "he's with me". Then there was the story (December 4,
1943, p. 26) of the soldier and sailor telling how their mothers knew
they smoked. "My mother knows," said one. "So does mine," the
other replied; "I *told* her." Certainly, as *The New Yorker* put it (on
April 29, 1944, p. 15), "veneration of Mother" is part of the foundation of the American mind.[1]

The influence of the American Mother on her daughters also, has
often been made the subject of fictional treatment, and judging
from the recent novels on the matter, interest is increasing. Ruth P.
O'Malley's *Mrs. Cassatt's Children* was a vivid account of strong
maternal authority; while in *Mrs. Heaton's Daughter*, Dorsha Hayes
drew a striking picture of the relationship between mother and
daughter and the shifting passions of hate and love. Similarly,
James Ronald, in his *The Angry Woman*, dealt with the problem of
feminine antipathies and the struggle between mother and daughter
regarding the latter's marriage.[2]

It was not until during the Second World War that the growing
power and influence of the American Mother began to disturb
Americans, who saw the evils ensuing from the exercise of her power
over husband and children. The storm broke with a sensational
attack by Mr. Philip Wylie in his *Generation of Vipers* (1942). In a

[1] In 1946 the draft soldier was actually called "Mamma's Boy" by *Time*;
and in 1948 the same journal said that the new regulations regarding recruits
indicated that they were to be considered as if each had "a militant Mom
poised and ready to holler"! Cf. G. Jessel's amusing conversations entitled
Hello, Momma (Cleveland and New York, 1946).

[2] An interesting commentary on the mother–daughter relationship in the
United States is given by Randolph Ray, the well-known Rector of "The
Little Church around the Corner". He tells how one poor girl at her marriage
said, "It is not my wedding: it is my mother's"; and how at another the bride's
mother kept them all waiting an hour because her hat had not arrived (see R.
Ray, *Marriage is a Serious Business*, p. 84). In another case the mother of the
groom sobbed loudly throughout the service (p. 56), and Mr. Ray stated that,
judging from his experience, these "cannibalistic mothers" played an enormous
part in the United States in preventing and marring the marriages of their
unfortunate children.

long and violently worded indictment of the culture of the United States, Mr. Wylie denounced the American "mom" as a rusting, raging, brass-breasted Baal whose very urine was so acid that it would etch glass. She was a "middle-aged puffin", a "woman in pants", an "American Pope". This "megaloid momworship", Mr. Wylie contended, had got completely out of hand. A bride at every funeral, she became a corpse at every wedding. The men of America, he declared, were being raped by the women, "not sexually, unfortunately", but morally. Moms looked after the serving men in the clubs, and tried to persuade them that they were mom-sick and would like to hold mom's hand instead of taking Betty into the shrubs. Even the automobile was dragged into the web of Mr. Wylie's diatribes. This "sheet-iron womb" was used, he averred, to transport the "floating fœtuses" into a place where they could be safe from prying parental eyes. Even accidents might, he suggested, be due to an unconscious desire for revenge on the all-seeing mom.

The more serious, though equally devastating attack delivered by Dr. A. E. Strecker in 1946 has already been mentioned. The advertisements of this book were sensational. One tabulated forty questions for every woman to answer, for "you don't have to be a woman to be a mom". A key as to how a "mom" would reply is provided at the bottom of the page. Moreover, Strecker enlarged the meaning and scope of "momism". He said that for many years he had seen the writing ("mom's handwriting") upon the wall. She was clearly failing to rear her children emotionally, for the majority of the soldiers who failed did so because they were immature (p. 21). It was true that the mother–child relationship was not an easy one to solve, but no nation was in greater danger of failing to solve it than the United States, for in America momism was the result of a social system which was clearly veering towards a pronounced matriarchal pattern.

Strecker saw clearly some of the reasons for this mother-cult, but he has not seen fit to put it in its historical setting, even if he is aware of it. For example, he maintains that momism is partly due to the fact that American women are striving to avenge themselves for the frustration and disappointments of their own sex lives. Thus they tend to reject all that sex stands for, and with it the masculine image, which is associated with "brutal lust", and the picture of ruthless violators seeming to entrap, seduce and ruin the delicate, innocent and virginal females. It is, he says, a part of "our way of life", for everywhere is mom glorified and extolled. In about 80 per cent. of the alcoholic cases that he had himself investigated he found that the basic cause was the presence of momism in the life of the patient. Finally, he summed up his conclusions in a pregnant sentence (p. 212). Mom, he maintained, was not entirely to blame for this deplorable situation. It was true that she might be the catalyst, but other ingredients were also present. Perhaps, he added, part of the blame is to be found in the very nature of American culture and way of life.

Although, as I have said, Dr. Strecker has not attempted to link up his observations with historical antecedents, those of my readers who have read the preceding pages will, I hope, understand the importance of his remarks, and note how they can be fitted in to the argument which has been proceeding. For, however evil "mom" may be, and however injurious her influence in American life, she herself is a victim, and is to be pitied far more than blamed. Indeed, it seems to me that, considering the immense handicaps under which American women have to conduct their lives, many of them succeed to a greater extent than would at first seem possible in gaining a tolerable adjustment and partial tranquillity. The same may be said of many of the American men, and it is in these facts that may be perceived the greatness of the American people, their energy, buoyancy of spirit and general capability.

There is little doubt that what impelled writers like Wylie and Strecker to give vent to their feelings was the serious condition of things during the war. With so many men away, America's "wayward wives", as they were called, became a major problem; and another fact which disturbed American women at home was that so many soldiers were marrying foreign women in preference to waiting till they got home to marry their own. Indeed, some of the jilted girls formed themselves into a "Brush-off Club", the rooms of which were decorated with the photographs (full-face, profile and numbered) of the men who were responsible for getting a new member elected. Many men, hearing of the Club, wrote offering their services to the jilted ones.

In 1944 it was said that several thousand American soldiers in Australia had already married, and the effect of the war on the sexual life was painted in lurid terms which did little to comfort American wives and sweethearts, who were not all like those who were badgering the columnists to tell them how they could push their husbands into the Army.

From what we know of the marriage relation in the United States, it is clear that the instability is rooted deeply in the psychological condition of the two parties. The search for satisfaction is not the same in the two sexes, although basic features are shared by both.

The technique of love-making is so little understood in the United States that many women have no knowledge of the pleasures which could be theirs. Thus, although intellectually some realize they are being cheated, it is the failure of their marriage to be the romantic adventure of their adolescent dreams that actually causes the most sorrow and resentment. Men, on the other hand, finding their wives unresponsive, and little realizing that the blame is also on them and not solely on their wives, seek satisfaction elsewhere and, as we shall see later, find a poor substitute in prostitution and similar "outlets". In the smaller communities infidelities are soon known and are much frowned upon, whereas in the greater urban areas secrecy is more easy to attain. In these rural areas it is perhaps true, as the author of *America and the Americans from a French Point of View* said in 1897, that much of the immorality is "rather mental than physical" (p. 70), a thought confirmed by such books as Sherwood Anderson's *Winesburg, Ohio*, where dark forces are shown to be seething beneath a surface which seems to show merely occasional ripples. In spite of the moral literature stressing the thousand little shabbinesses and the humiliating subterfuges which are part and parcel of the affair, the rich and affluent classes undoubtedly contract numerous alliances, and their doings are well described not only in fictional form but in actual biographical memoirs.

The advice columns, also, are constantly concerned with the problems sent in by worried wives on the subject of their erring husbands. Indeed, one wrote to Mary Haworth on December 23, 1945, telling her that her husband was a skirt-chaser, and that he told her that the only men who were not were those dominated by their wives. To this young lady Miss Haworth replied sharply. Her husband, she told her, had a character which looked and smelt like Limburger cheese, and her own station was simply that of a "harem favourite". Now she knew. Sometimes the advice is subtle and indicates a change in the American conventional attitude to legalized union. In March 1943 a rich and worried widow wrote to Dorothy Dix. She had been married twice, having divorced her first husband and outlived her second. Now a man eleven years her junior wanted to marry her, but he had no savings and no home. Ought she to marry him? Miss Dix, in reply, asked her why she wanted to chance another marriage. Rich widows should be suspicious of poor young men who woo them. They could have a good time without that. *A companion could be hired more cheaply.* (Author's italics.)

In this brief consideration of American marriage and its failure, the facts can all be discovered in American publications. Some

Europeans reading Mr. Sinclair Lewis's brilliant novel of husbands and wives, *Cass Timberlane*, must feel they have been transported to another world, and in this they are right. When Perry Claywheel wondered if there was any country except the United States in which men were continuously frightened of their own wives (p. 299), he was asking a question which is basic to any understanding of the culture of America; and the sexual starvation which made Bernice ask Dr. Drover if there were brothels for women to get men (p. 297) [1] is symptomatic of the psychological tension which fills so many of the women of America.

[1] For an account of a visit to such an establishment by an American woman who wished to inflict upon the inmates the same indignities that were inflicted on women by men, see Maryse Choisy's *Un Mois chez des Filles* (pp. 210 ff.). The same account appears in A. Esterhazy's *Das lasterhafte Weib*, and on p. 36 of vol. iv of A. Kind's *Die Weiberherrschaft*. For an inside account of one of these houses see the valuable material in Y. Forestier's *Messieurs à louer* (Paris, 1937).

Q

VI

SEX AS A PROFESSION

IN the preceding section we have discussed the more intimate relationships between the sexes, both in marriage and in the casual affair. It must be remembered that it is only within recent times that the numbers of men and women in the United States are beginning to approximate, and that in earlier days there were considerably more men than women. The vast influx of foreign workers, moreover, tended to create a pool of single men whose sexual needs, if they were to be satisfied at all, had to be catered for through prostitution or other means. In many cases prostitution in the lower income groups was not considerable, and thus gratification was in many cases not easy except through casual contacts and through phantasy. In the latter case there is, I think, little doubt that so-called "strip tease" played an important part, and that Gorer is quite right in his book [1] on the subject when he points out that one of the main aims of the burlesque show combined with strip tease is to provoke solitary pleasure.

The burlesque shows which at one time flourished from coast to coast consisted mainly of comedy turns in which the strip-tease act was merely an interlude. The act consists essentially of the gradual disrobing by the performer, the climax being reached when, having removed everything except perhaps a small cache-sexe or minute frontal triangle, she turns her back on the audience, removes the cache-sexe and then sidles to the side of the stage, where, wrapping herself in the folds of the curtain, she acknowledges the applause. In the majority of cases the burlesque theatres were patronized only by men, and it is noteworthy, as Gorer pointed out, that it was only the younger men who came in groups, whilst the older men seemed to come singly. From the psychological point of view, strip tease provided lonely bachelors with an actual setting for their dreams in which their unfulfilled longings might be to some extent realized. In some of these entertainments, especially in the smaller houses, the "tease" is intensified by having the dances take place in separate rooms, more money being demanded the more clothes are taken off.

In the ordinary burlesque performance the whole act had been a

[1] *Hot Strip Tease*, p. 51.

unit in the show, and thus it was easy, when civic authorities began to disapprove, to incorporate strip tease into the general setting of a revue or musical. In 1942 the Roman Catholic Archbishop, Francis J. Spellman, when speaking before the Police Department Anchor Club in New York, denounced the revival of burlesque and strip-tease shows in the city, and maintained that New York was becoming like Sodom and Gomorrah. Rallied by the Archbishop's speech, the supporters of stage decency induced the authorities to take action, and a first step was made by summoning the producer and managers of an entertainment called "Wine, Women and Song" then operating on Broadway. The prosecution created a sensation, as the strip-tease artists themselves were called to give evidence, and described in detail not only what they wore and what they took off, but various movements, "bumps" and wrigglings that accompanied their act.

In spite of sporadic attempts to suppress strip tease, popular interest was hardly likely to allow the practice to disappear. Georgia Sothern, the "grand old lady of undress", seemed to be in trouble with the authorities in 1948; and a student magazine, *Pell Mell* of Louisiana State University, was banned the same year for dedicating one of its numbers to a strip teaser operating in New Orleans. Although strip tease is by no means peculiar to the United States, its popularity there and the variety of its forms are of interest, if it be considered as a form of passive enjoyment, in which further action is not permitted and thus has not to be preceded by any form of "loosening up".

It must be remembered that the position of the American woman makes her an object, not only of desire but also of veneration, and since sex and sin are so closely allied, the sexual side of the man–woman relationship has something sacrilegious about it. Direct contact, therefore, has to be preceded by artificial stimulants, of which alcohol is the most useful. I have always been amazed at the quantities of alcohol that American men consume preparatory to love-making, since they apparently have no idea that sobriety in a supremely difficult art provides a better background for both parties. Indeed, Gorer has actually gone so far as to say in *Hot Strip Tease* (p. 63) that there were many Americans in New York who had never made love sober during the whole course of their lives. Can it be that prior consumption of alcohol is essential because the conflict within the American male mind necessitates this form of breaking down his inhibitions, and that without alcohol he thinks that his potency might not be sufficient or his courage adequate? If this be so, strip tease as a phantasy must inevitably be popular. It is difficult or impossible for many an American man to have a normal spontaneous relation with a woman who has an attitude of cold dominance or of a goddess requiring worship. Sexual satisfaction, therefore, has to be attained either in phantasy or with women to whom sex is a profession and who do not fall within the class of "good" women to which belong the mother, the sister and the wife.

The connexion between sex and drink is especially interesting when we consider the problem of Prohibition. Americans are often filled with reforming zeal, and the subjects of prostitution, gambling and drink have always been to the forefront when "cleaning-up" campaigns have been in progress. The very fact that all these pursuits apparently gave pleasure to the participants was an added inducement to suppress them, and there is little doubt that, apart from the ulterior motives, the prohibition movement was due to an idea that drink was sin and led to even worse things. Just as efforts were made to control and suppress drinking, so similar attempts have been made to suppress and hinder the practice of prostitution. The history of female prostitution in the United States is a long one and cannot be dealt with here. Frontier conditions and the influx of immigrant groups from countries where moral views and conditions differed much from those in their new home, caused many new problems to arise, and in the great centres of expanding industry the brothel business was naturally a success, so great was the demand.

With the early years of the twentieth century came a change, partly induced by the growing freedom of women, feminist ideals and a more active participation by women in public affairs. The "red-light" districts were regarded with aversion and, although any form of State control had been resisted since the 1870s, it was seen that some form of control was overdue. Accordingly, in 1902, an inquiry was instituted in New York, and the results published in the famous Committee of Fifteen's Report in 1912.[1] Other investigations followed, and the principal result was the disappearance of the segregated, or red-light, areas and a complete change in the manner of conducting the business of prostitution. Before the commencement of the 1914–18 war much had been done to study the problem and various inquiries instituted, since the Bureau of Social Hygiene had been founded in 1911 and surveys in connexion with the project had begun to appear. Women were often to the forefront of these attempts at inquiry and clarification; and Helen M. Wilson's paper at the eleventh Congress of the International Abolitionist Federation

---

[1] See *The Social Evil*, etc. (1912).

in 1913 did much to stimulate interest in the economic factor, which, it was thought by some, was largely instrumental in furthering the spread of prostitution.

The growing tendency in the United States to try to suppress prostitution was what might have been expected, and anyone acquainted with American conditions and ways of thought could have foreseen the subsequent development. For, by driving the practice underground and substituting clandestine resorts for known "red-lights", the girls were no longer able to resist the protection offered by the pimps, although this was difficult enough before the attack on their trade became more sustained.

The years between the two wars showed the greatest changes in public and social morality as it concerned prostitution. In spite of the supposed disappearance of the prostitute from the streets, where she was thought to offer an offensive spectacle to the moral eye, it was not difficult to discover that she had not gone very far, and that her little trip was closely connected with America's two most striking characteristics, namely the tendency towards moral uplift and the desire for profits. For, if girls were permitted to ply for hire in the public streets and engage in a very private enterprise, they would be getting away with all the profits, and that was not to be thought of. Clearly, then, those who urged the "cleaning up" of the streets *and* had a finger in the brothel pie would be doing themselves a double benefit, since they would gain esteem for their "moral" outlook and at the same time obtain a percentage of the profits that the girls earned in the various houses and joints to which they were assigned. Prostitution had become big business and the turnover was enormous, since in the days of prohibition the gangsters had often combined drink with prostitution and knew the trade thoroughly.

It would not serve any useful purpose to pursue the later history of prostitution in any detail. The American prostitute is not markedly different from her sister in other lands; and I fancy that the girls in the former house of the Everleigh sisters in Chicago were as apt at their job as those of the old Chabanais in Paris or at the even better house in the Rue St. Augustin. No understanding of prostitution (and above all of prostitutes) can ever be achieved by reading official reports of inquiries and sociological treatises. To know prostitution one must know prostitutes, talk to madams, and sit with pimps as they count their takings.

In default of practical experience with the parties themselves, a substitute can be found in the novel, diary or memoir. In the United States a number of such sources exist, and are of very considerable interest. Since David Graham Phillips' *Susan Lenox* (1917) and W. L. George's *A Bed of Roses* (1919) there have been a number of studies, some of which contain valuable information. The author (O.W.) of *No Bed of Roses* and *God Have Mercy on Me!* which were compiled by Marjorie E. Smith, has given us a vivid and fascinating picture of the life of an American kept woman, and these works can be compared with Wallace Smith's admirable account of prostitution in Chicago in *Bessie Cotter*. The London edition of the latter book had to be withdrawn on the charge of "indecency", as, in the same year, did Sheila Cousins' *To Beg I am Ashamed*, which is one of the most interesting surveys of the psychology of the prostitute that I know, and has since been published without complaint.

Apart from these fictional treatments of the problem, much valuable information may be gained from a study of the documents and reports of the trials of two of the great vice czars of the American prostitution racket. Here is to be found the mechanism of the vice business laid bare. We see lines of girls, madams and pimps enter the witness-stand and testify as to how the call-houses are operated, how the clients are served and at what price, and what the girls get out of it when all the rake-offs are collected. Convenient summaries of these trials have been published; that of Nick Montana in Michael Stern's *The White Ticket* (1936) and that of Salvatore Lucania ("Lucky Luciano") in Hickman Powell's *Ninety Times Guilty*, which is a vivid account of the great clean-up of prostitution in New York City under Thomas E. Dewey. Similarly, a short account of the vice-squad framing racket will be found in *What's the Matter with New York?* by N. Thomas and P. Blanshard.

With the coming of the Second World War and the setting up of military camps and the movement of large bodies of troops, the problem of professional and amateur prostitution in the United States again assumed a major importance, not so much on account of the morals involved, but rather from the point of view of venereal disease. It was made a Federal offence to engage in or in any way to abet prostitution within a "reasonable distance" of military and naval camps. The word "promiscuity" is variously defined in the United States. One explanation of the word was given by the San Francisco City Clinic in 1945, according to *Time*. In this case a single woman who had sexual relations with more than one man or even with the same man more than twice in six months was said to be "promiscuous". Police drives seemed merely to lessen the appearance of the evil for a time or to drive it underground. Mere children were found soliciting in the streets; and in 1942 it was proposed that the New York parks be closed to children in the evenings, since girls were to be found in them at 4 and 5 a.m. It had already proved necessary to impose a curfew on Boston Common, where remarkable scenes had been reported. A year later the country was startled by the revelations concerning the vice activities in Washington, and the cases of Carmen Beach Martin and the Hopkins Institute shed light on the growing importance of the more select resorts for high-class prostitution. Even the theatre was invaded, for in *Manhattan Nocturne*, by Roy Walling, Ann Stevens made a considerable success of her part as Terry Holmer, a call-girl in a small house, who acts as a paid co-respondent and apparently suffers from amnesia, which, when broken, is utilised for telling her story.

In January 1944, when the drives were at their height, it was stated by Federal Security Administrator, Paul McNutt, that red-light districts had been eliminated in 662 American cities. Prostitution was well on the way to becoming illegal, although the Gallup Poll late the previous year showed a conflict of opinion, and a marked tendency to return to a consideration of regulation to combat prostitution. In this Poll, it was asked whether, in order to control venereal disease around Army camps, regular medical examination and quarantine for those found infected was desired, or whether police drives should be carried out "to get rid of all prostitutes". To these two questions 55 per cent. approved the first (61 per cent. men and 49 per cent. women); and 45 per cent. approved the second (39 per cent. men and 51 per cent. women). Meanwhile the drives continued, as any open form of regulation was not likely to succeed. In New Orleans, besides 100 known brothels, many call-houses were known to exist, and taxi-men were closely concerned with the business, since, on taking a client to a house, they were allowed 40 per cent. of what that client spent. In the drive 2,000 women were rounded up, of whom 80 per cent. had venereal disease; some of them had been entertaining up to fifty clients in one night.

Although the question of venereal disease was of great importance to women, the whole problem was prevented from being adequately discussed on account of the prudery and shame which accompanied it. The idea that these "social" diseases were punishments for sin was widespread in the English-speaking world, and it was only gradually that people began to wake up to the stern reality of the facts. Upton Sinclair's novel *Sylvia's Marriage*, which was first published in 1914, created some consternation, but in the United States the public were not fully aware till about 1937, in spite of the mass of valuable material which had been issued since 1923 in the

United States Public Health Service's admirable *Venereal Disease Information.*

In consultation with various high medical authorities, Dr. Thomas Parran, Surgeon-General of the Public Health Services, opened the campaign in 1937 with his *Shadow on the Land: Syphilis*, a work which caused a sensation and was quickly followed by a book by S. W. Becker with the alarming title *Ten Million Americans Have It*. Parran disclosed the fact that there were six million cases of syphilis in the country; that every year 60,000 babies were born with congenital syphilis, and that half of all the infections had been acquired innocently.

Public propaganda soon got under way, and the ease with which taboos may be swept away when necessity arises is shown by what occurred. The anti-syphilis campaign was sponsored by a number of women's organizations, such as the Association of Women in Public Health, the General Federation of Women's Clubs, the National Board of the Y.W.C.A., the National League of Women Voters and others. Posters suggesting blood tests in order to "safeguard Baby's Right to be Born Healthy" appeared on many an outdoor billboard, and the Press and radio co-operated in an all-out fight against the scourge. Guidance for the coming battle had been sought abroad. In 1935 a group of New York physicians had gone to Scandinavia to examine the situation; and it was soon seen that, prudery being non-existent, the disease was treated on a national basis. The decline in the figures was startling, but the hope that this might be due to the moral behaviour of the population was soon shattered, since, as Parran points out (p. 99), the totals for gonorrhœa still showed a high level by reason of the difficulty then experienced in making the disease non-infectious.

Certainly the problem in 1943 was serious. Even in some of the great industrial plants, the civilian rates equalled if not exceeded the Army figures, which were said to show an increase since 1941 of something like 400 per cent. It was pointed out that, in 1939, New York State had twenty-six times as many cases of syphilis as Denmark, Norway and Sweden combined, the population of which approximated to the same figures (12,588,000 in the census of 1930); these figures are not, however, comparable in view of the nature of the population. On the other hand, the new treatment of venereal disease gave rise to much hope, in spite of the fact that human carelessness was well exemplified in the continuing difficulty of dealing with gonorrhœa, and the apparent failure to persuade men of the Armed Forces to use the millions of prophylactics which were issued.

The drive against venereal disease did as much to break down prudery as did the former interest in psycho-analysis to release the morbid sexual interests which were so apparent before the First World War. Women were no longer the sheltered beings who were prevented from knowing the vital facts which directly affected not only their own health but that of their children, both born and un-born. Proposals to demand certificates of health from prospective husbands and wives were accepted, and today such examinations and blood-tests are fairly common throughout the United States. From the darkness of ignorance and shame the whole subject of venereal infection had been brought out into the light and, apart from official reports, popular expositions and propaganda leaflets, made its way into light literature and, following Sinclair's admittedly didactic *Sylvia's Marriage*, was now and then material for romantic, if not sensational, fiction.

In the years following the Second World War, progress in the control of venereal disease became noteworthy. For example, in the incidence of gonorrhœa, and taking the 1951 figures, there was a fall of 32·5 per cent. from the 1947 peak year. This must be partly due to the control measures instituted by the United States, of which the discovery of cases and tracing contacts are perhaps the most important. Mass serum testing has been used on a considerable scale in the search for cases, and the employment of novel forms of propaganda has not been neglected. Similarly in the case of syphilis, there has been a fall from the United States 1943 peak of 64·8 per cent.

Much of the terror which venereal disease used to inspire has been greatly weakened by modern methods of treatment and the more natural and open approach to the problem which has now become general. Although the sulphonamides proved disappointing, peni-cillin has lived up to its reputation, and with the introduction of diamine penicillin further progress seems likely. In any event, the secret suffering portrayed in *Sylvia's Marriage* is (or ought to be) a thing of the past. The American woman will certainly gain much from the intensive campaign which has been carried out during the last few years.

VII

FINAL REMARKS AND CONCLUSIONS

IN the preceding pages an attempt has been made to sketch very briefly some of the principal factors which have influenced the sexual life of certain American women since the Puritan experiment in New England. I have tried to avoid generalizations, and when the words "American Woman" are used, no suggestion is to be entertained that I mean *every* American woman, foreign- or native-born, white or coloured. *Every* American woman does not succumb to the mass persuasion put out by the radio, the cinema, the Press and the advertisers. But many do so, and it is they who attempt to base their lives, ideas and behaviour on the models displayed by these powerful organs of mass propaganda. It is with these women and their female relatives that I have been mainly concerned. In other words, the American women whose lives and ideas I have been trying to analyse in relation to the society in which they function, are precisely those to whom American writers refer when they use the words "American women" in dealing with the females of the country in which they live.

When the Gallup Poll of August 1947 found that the "average American man" thought that women in the United States were petted and kissed too much prior to marriage, I had some doubts as to the accuracy of the statement. Perhaps it might be true of the "average" man of certain social strata. But in a country as large and complex as the United States I am dubious as to the validity of any statements about "average" men or women.

Whatever may be the group, however, to which Americans refer when they speak of "American Women", there is little doubt that it is not a small one. Were it insignificant, it is unlikely that American critical writers would have paid so much attention to it, and, moreover, stressed the discontent, frustration and unhappiness found in connexion with it. As Barbara Heggie said in the special United States issue of the London journal, *Picture Post*, in 1940, American periodicals since 1930 never seem to have stopped discussing why the modern American woman was so discontented and unhappy. Summing up the reasons, she declared that one was that in the past the American woman was fighting *for* her man, and that now she was fighting *against* him. As to their glamour, she added that many a French grandmother of sixty had more, since, although Americans may succeed in "getting ahead", they lose their femininity in doing so. In 1946 Dr. Margaret Mead added her quota to the critical deluge. In an article in *Fortune* entitled "What Women Want", she maintained that more than 25 per cent. of American women were disturbed about their lot as women, although I am not aware what evidence she has for her chosen figure. She declared that women should be educated to act as full individuals, and not merely as persons whose sex ordained that they should be mainly child-bearers, and she added that the general trend in the United States was to minimize biological limitations to human activity. Finally, Dr. Mead concluded that men should be brought into the home and made to undertake a greater part than hitherto in sharing the life of the home and the rearing of the children.

If this be what American women want, then they can hardly expect anything else than what they get. To maintain, as Margaret Mead does, that when women "can act by choice rather than by necessity" (p. 172) they will be content, is to engage in that favourite feminine pastime of crying for the moon. Indeed, it is precisely to the minimization of the biological factor in female life that we can ascribe so much of the growing lack of satisfaction among the women of so many lands, and above all of the United States. As Arthur Stringer said in his article in the *North American Review* in 1939, entitled "Why Women Make no Sense", the body of the woman is made expressly for allure, for love and "for certain implacable biological purposes" (p. 297). To neglect such facts is merely to indulge in wilful blindness.

The present situation as regards the American woman was admirably summed up by the American writer, Leland Stowe, in an article, "What's Wrong with our Women", printed in *Esquire* in 1948. He began by comparing the French view of what was desirable in women with that favoured in the United States, and almost repeated what had already been written in the same journal eleven years previously in an anonymous article on "They Order it Better in France". He bluntly declared that American women were spoiled, self-centred, exceptionally aggressive, unhappy, dissatisfied, very expensive in their tastes; they were becoming less and less interested in men, husbands, home and family and were restless and bored. Indeed, he catalogued most of the features we have seen commented on repeatedly by other observers throughout the twentieth century, and which have become especially applicable to the richer and more leisured women, who have never been able to obtain a sufficiently broad intellectual background to fulfil their mental and spiritual needs.[1]

These passages indicate quite clearly that the writers are of the opinion that all is not well with what they call "the American woman", and they suggest those factors in herself and her environment that they would like to see improved. But, as far as I have been able to ascertain, few, if any, of these writers have shown how it is that, in a country where woman is apparently almost supreme in so many different fields, she should be so dissatisfied and conduct herself in a way which seems continually to evoke a chorus of criticism. For it must be remembered that not all of the critics that we have quoted belong to those who contribute volumes of what has been termed social protest. Literature of this kind, it is true, is common in the United States, and C. C. Regier has collected a useful list of the more extreme examples in his *The Era of the Muckrakers* (1932). But much of what we have seen has been taken from what Mrs. Mary A. Hamilton has called the "shelves of books and sheaves of articles" which are almost annually devoted to showing how "lamentably ignorant and non-adult" the citizens of the United States can be.[2] Foreigners merely notice what the more discerning Americans themselves are pointing out. Writing in 1923, A. Holitscher in his *Amerika heute und morgen* (America: Today and Tomorrow), wrote (p. 386) of the bottomless ignorance of the Americans whom he met. Serious discussion he found to be impossible; and he stated that he had heard fantastic views expressed

---

[1] Cf. Clare Boothe's picture in *The Women* (1937); the satirical comments on the grumbling American housewives of the war period—e.g. M. Lindsay's "At the Wailing Wall" (*Washington Post*, Nov. 5, 1942); and for a foreign note "Pity these Poor Rich Women" by William Brown in the London *Reynolds News*. The rudeness of American women in their own country was noted both in the nineteenth and twentieth centuries. To take but three examples. Eliza Leslie in her *The Behaviour Book* (1853) noted it with disapproval (p. 89), and in 1890 O. F. Adams wrote a paper entitled "The Mannerless Sex", which was replied to by A. Croffut the same year in the same journal. Over fifty years later Paul Gallico, in *Women have no Manners*, declared that "the average American woman took the jelly-roll" for unadulterated boorishness and complete lack of human consideration (p. 13), features which were being constantly demonstrated at sales where the crowd of pushing females could only be compared to sour-faced vixens. Finally, he concluded with a really pathetic appeal to the women of America. You are, he wrote, the unchallenged rulers of the United States. For the sake of sweet and gentle living, help to make it a tolerable place in which to live. In 1950 Mrs. Hedden hit out in the *American Scholar*. "There's nothing wrong with women," she declared, "the trouble is with the Woman Critic . . .", an attitude supported by Cathleen Schurr in *Coronet* for Sept. 1951.

[2] Mary A. Hamilton, *The Place of the United States of America in World Affairs*, p. 20.

on the history of art, literature and the customs of foreign peoples. In 1944, twenty-one years later, Mr. H. Cantril, the Director of Public Opinion Research at Princeton University, declared that of 90 million adults in the United States, at least 54 million had not heard or read about the Atlantic Charter, and that 27 million did not know that the Japanese had taken the Philippines.

Perhaps the late Mr. H. G. Wells was entirely wrong when he described the United States in his *'42 to '44* in one place as the "great problem child of humanity", and in another as "a vast illiterate thoughtless instability" (pp. 83, 89). As to the sacred "American Way of Life", it was, so Wells averred, "a mere empty phrase" (p. 84). Yet in the past this was far from being the case. The American Dream, at which today so many are apt to become sentimental, was once a living reality giving promise of a glorious future. *The Sentiments of an American Woman*, printed in an eighteenth-century broadside preserved in the collections of the Historical Society of Pennsylvania and reprinted in 1894, proves what faith inspired the writer when at last the "odious yoke" of the British had been cast off for ever. The Jefferson dream of equal opportunity for all, coupled with the ideals of individual freedom, was the dream not only of Americans, but of thousands in the whole English-speaking world. The ideals are still there, but they are obscured and made difficult of realization through the very structure of that society in which they were meant to operate and to be brought to fruition.

Ill-informed critics are often apt to complain that they do not find the old European culture in the United States, and to this I can only echo J. A. Spender's reply when he said that of course it is not to be found, since what was developing was what promised to be a "new thing". It is precisely this "new thing" which the informed critic is sometimes apt to regard not altogether favourably, although it must be remembered that what has emerged in the United States is hardly the kind of culture that Crèvecoeur expected his New Man to create.

On the other hand, it must always be realized that ideals are the goals of the hopes and aspirations on which political and social institutions are reared. Criticism of imperfect institutions can in no wise be transferred to ideals, as if the two were the same thing. The fact that the United States has fallen so far short of the ideals that animated the Founders is no reason why condemnation should be pronounced upon the ideals themselves. It is the American dream of freedom and opportunity, if dream it must ever be, that unites the English-speaking world in invisible bonds of fundamental unity and understanding. The American problem is, in part, the question how far the lack of control inherent in the ideal of freedom does not of itself produce a situation where paradoxes and contradictions are endemic, thus leading to those psychological tensions which bring so much frustration, guilt and misery in their train.

It is clear that, considering the predominant position women occupy in American public-school education (the female teaching staff in 1951 numbering some 729,000 out of a total of over 944,000), the responsibility of inculcating these ideas into the minds of future citizens must be considerable; and it is to be noted, as Margaret Mead has pointed out, that the American emphasis on making citizens in one generation must make the position of women teachers more important than in countries like England, where no such problem presents itself.

Moreover, there is little doubt that most women teachers try to do their duty to the best of their ability and under grave disadvantages. But the whole situation as regards mental influences is against them. Their efforts are, to a certain extent, nullified by that ambivalent attitude to the ideals of life which we have seen operating in American society ever since the decline of the Puritan experiment in New England. The comics, the radio and the cinema are the powerful factors which influence the young. The "mass persuasion", which Robert Merton so well described in his account of the psychological suggestions put into motion for selling war bonds, is ceaselessly at play, not only in the life of commerce and advertising, but in the life of the mind and of the spirit. As Merton shows, the employment of the "mother-image", as illustrated in the appeal of Kate Smith, is used so as to maintain the maximum emotional drive, while at the same time an attempt is made to touch feelings of guilty conflict (with the promise of forgiveness and redemption), so that even the unwilling donor may be forced to give, and thereby to ease his own feelings of tension and lack of tranquillity.

A study of social trends shows that the gulf which separates the sexes in the United States with regard to their social and intellectual lives opened so early that it has become an American characteristic. The building of the vast new structure demanded so much practical activity that men simply did not have the time to attend to anything more than the work on hand. Thus, as is described in the preceding pages, woman stepped down from her pedestal to attend to social affairs when she was not dealing with the house and the education of the children. Since all women did not want to marry or did not have the opportunity to do so, other openings had to be found for them. But whatever course of action they chose to take, or had forced upon them, they were still, in a sense, the guardians of social intercourse, and thus the feminization of American culture was inevitable. Indeed, James Truslow Adams, in his interesting study of *The American*, has gone so far as to say (pp. 329–30) that the feeling of guilt aroused in the man for his neglect of the woman has been partially assuaged by the fact that the woman, in turning away from the man, has managed to find fresh fields for her own life and interests apart from the home and domestic duties.[1]

What the American is capable of producing, when the obstructionist tactics of selfish groups are overcome, can be seen in such magnificent achievements as the T.V.A. (Tennessee Valley Authority) and other projects. Yet, with every fresh proposal the same wall of difficulties has to be surmounted, the same old arguments countered, and the same old fallacies exposed and refuted. But progress is being made; and in the United States progress is sometimes spectacular. Once informed opinion realizes the inner meaning and origin of the tension and frustration that afflicts society, then and then only will a beginning be made to end a state of affairs which makes the United States an enigma to so many.

At the very core of that puzzle stands the American woman, and it is only by understanding her relation to the industrial framework of American civilization that a true realization of the basic factors operating in American society can be achieved. For with the freedom of the American woman from the mesh in which she is vainly struggling, will come the liberation of the American man from the invisible influences which retard his growth and stunt his mental development. We have not far to look to see what the American people are capable of achieving. In many of the more material and useful activities of the human race they stand supreme. It may have been merely an accident of history that their development has been along lines which have led them to their present condition. But, if I have interpreted that development at all correctly, it would seem that the general trend was inevitable. With Puritanism gone sour, and the age of private enterprise leading to unparalleled periods of prosperity and slumps in which Mammon stifled the things of the mind and of the spirit, the position of woman became intolerable. "Equal rights" and the ideals of feminism contributed but little to

[1] As early as 1862 I. J. Benjamin stated that America worships two idols (*betet zwei Abgötter*), Mammon and the female sex, and that these two deities were always at war with each other (*leben miteinander in beständiger Fehde*). See I. J. Benjamin's *Drei Jahre in Amerika: 1859–62*, Th. I, pp. 63–4.

the essentials for which she craved. With feminism triumphant she lost her femininity, and with her femininity her peace of mind.

It is thus that we can see how the American woman is a victim to the old ideas, which were so firmly planted by the Puritan theocracy, and which, once God had been dethroned from His supreme position, have borne such bitter and poisonous fruit. The American enigma can only be solved by understanding whence all the contradictions and paradoxes arise. Once the general picture is seen as a whole, then all the odd-shaped and jagged pieces of the jigsaw puzzle can be made to fit into the whole. The riddle is solved.

Before closing, it may perhaps be thought that an apology is needed for what might seem the impertinence of a foreigner in analysing another society in the way attempted in the preceding pages. I doubt, however, if such an apology is either desirable or necessary. As Sir Winston Churchill said in one of his secret session speeches (p. 81), it would be foolish not "to try to understand what is passing in the minds of other peoples" and what are "those secret springs of action to which they respond". After all, the Americans are not averse from criticizing the British, and I, for one, am sincerely grateful for their analyses. Such books as Grant Allen's *The British Barbarians* (1895), Margaret Halsey's *With Malice towards Some* (1938), J. F. Muehl's *American Sahib* (1946), Edmund Wilson's *Europe without Baedeker* (1948) or Dorothy J. Ward's *English Enigma* (1948) ought to be of great interest to the people of Britain, as was G. J. Renier's *The English, are they Human?* (1931) or similar works on the character of the British people. As H. C. Owen said in 1929, America is surely now big enough to take the rough with the smooth, and to be told how the culture of the United States is viewed in certain quarters. Yet the reviews that I have seen of such works as those by Geoffrey Gorer and Robert Payne still indicate an attitude of extreme sensitivity, and a tendency to deny that the authors know anything of the matters on which they write. Yet, as I have said, American authors do not hesitate to contribute books of criticism about the customs of other countries, and some of these volumes can hardly be called objective, like W. L. White's *Report on the Russians* or the less happily named *In Anger and Pity* by Robert Magidoff. Nevertheless, such works are to be welcomed, since it is always desirable to see ourselves as others see us.

The English-speaking world is linked by bonds which can hardly be broken by candid criticism of the varying cultures which make up this powerful combination of peoples. These links, intangible though many of them be, stem from fundamental ways of looking at life and the belief in the freedom of the human spirit to climb upwards and onwards so long as its progress does not hinder and impede the same path in other people.

The main difference between the two great blocs of English-speaking peoples is, I am convinced, the position of women in the two societies. In the one case we have a culture through the development of which feminine influence has become dominant, and through this dominance a kind of infantilism and immaturity is spread among considerable portions of the population. In the other, as among the great Latin peoples, feminine influence is pronounced, but woman has never attempted to usurp the position accepted by man, and thus bring him under her undisputed sway. Such an empire brings neither happiness nor peace of mind to her who rules it and nothing but neurotic restlessness to him who submits. This is one key to the American enigma, and through an understanding of the American woman's place and sexual activities in the industrial society of the United States, the paradoxes and contradictions in American life may become resolved.

SHORT TITLE LIST OF AUTHORITIES QUOTED

Note.—The following list is not a bibliography. It comprises only the books and articles in periodicals which are quoted in the text, and refers to the editions which I have found it most convenient to consult. In many cases, therefore, London imprints will be found where, of an American work, an edition published in the United Kingdom was available. For the sake of brevity both definite and indefinite articles are frequently omitted, especially before the titles of periodicals and newspapers.

ABBOTT, JACOB.   *The Rollo Code of Morals.* Boston, 1841.
ABELL, L. G.   *Woman in her Various Relations.* New York, 1851.
ACHILLES, P. S.   "The Effectiveness of Certain Social Hygiene Literature." (*American Social Hygiene Association Publs.*, 1923.)
ADAMS, ABIGAIL.   *Letters.* 4th ed., Boston, 1848.
ADAMS, B. P.   *You Americans.* New York, 1939.
ADAMS, HENRY B.   (1) *The Life of George Cabot Lodge.* Boston, New York, 1911.
                        (2) *The Education of Henry Adams.* London, 1919.
ADAMS, JAMES   (1) *Provincial Society, 1690–1763.* New York, 1927.
  TRUSLOW.   (2) *A Searchlight on America.* London, 1930.
                        (3) *The American: the Making of a New Man.* New York, 1943.
ADAMS, O. F.   "The Mannerless Sex." (*North Amer. Review*, Sept. 1890, CLI, 379–81.)
ADLER, MORTIMER J.   *Art and Prudence.* New York, 1937.
AGAR, HERBERT.   "Will You Pass This Test?" (*This Week Magazine*, Feb. 20, 1944, 2.)
AGRIPPA, H. C.   *H. C. Agrippae de nobilitate & praecellentia foeminei sexus.* . . . Coloniae, 1532.
AIKEN, LUCY.   *Epistles on Women, Exemplifying their Character and Condition.* London, 1810.
ALCOTT, WILLIAM.   *The Young Wife.* Boston, 1837.
                        The Young Woman's Guide to Excellence. 10th ed. Boston, 1846.
ALLEN, F. L.   *The Lords of Creation.* London, 1935.
ALLEN, GRANT.   *The British Barbarians.* New York, London, 1895.
ALLPORT, G. W.   *Personality: a Psychological Interpretation.* London, 1938.
ALMBERT, A. D'.   *Flânerie parisienne aux Etats-Unis.* Paris, 1856.
America and the Americans from a French Point of View. London, 1897.
America as Americans See It. Ed. by F. J. Ringel. New York, 1932.
American Gynecology.
American Journal of Sociology.
American Magazine.
American Medicine.
American Mercury.
American Scholar.
American Thought. New York, 1947.

Amerika beim Erziehen: eine Sammlung Briefe von Anhängern der körperlichen Züchtigung als Strafmittel für jung und alt. Uberz. aus der "Illustrated Boston News" von E. Neumann. Leipzig, Dresden, 1903.

AMES, WILLIAM.   *Conscience with the Power and Cases Thereof.* [London], 1639.

AMPÈRE, J. J.   *Promenade en Amérique.* Paris, 1855.

ANDERSON, SHERWOOD.   *Winesburg, Ohio.* London, 1922.

ANDREWS, MATTHEW P.   *The Women of the South in War Times.* Baltimore, 1920.

Annual Reports of the American Historical Assoc.

ANTHONY, KATHARINE.   "The Family." In *Civilization in the United States.* London, 1922.

Archives of Psychology.

"Are Yanks Lousy Lovers?" (*Reader's Digest,* Dec. 1945, XLVII, 10.)

ARISTOTLE.   *Aristotle's Masterpiece: or, the Secrets of Generation Displayed.* London, 1694.
                Aristotle's Legacy. [London, 1699?]

ARMSTRONG, HAMILTON FISH.   "Last Time." (*Foreign Affairs,* April 1945, XXIII, 349 ff.)

Army Times.

ARNO, PETER.   *Peter Arno's Circus.* London, 1933.
                  Peter Arno's For Members Only. London, 1936.
                  Peter Arno's Cartoon Review. London, 1942.

ARNOLD, ELLIOTT.   *Everybody Slept Here.* New York, 1948.

ARTHUR, T. S.   *Agnes: or, The Possessed.* Philadelphia, 1848.

Atlantic Monthly.

AURAND, A. M.   *Little-known Facts about Bundling in the New World.* Harrisburg, 1939.
                   Slants on the Origin of Bundling in the Old World. Harrisburg, 1939.

AVONMORE, MARIE T. Y., VISCOUNTESS.   *Teresina in America.* London, 1875.

AYLMER, JOHN.   *An Harborowe for faithfull and trewe subjects. . . .* At Strasborowe, 1559.

BALDWIN, FAITH.   *Week-end Marriage.* New York, 1932.
                     Self-made Woman. London, 1933.
                     Men are Such Fools. London, 1937.

BALLINGER, W. J.   "Spinster Factories." (*Century and Forum,* 1932, LXXXVII, 301–5.)

BANNING, MARGARET C.   "The Case for Chastity." (*Reader's Digest,* Aug. 1937, XXXI, 1–10.)

BARBIER, EMILE.   *Voyage au pays des dollars.* Paris, 1893.

BARDSLEY, C. W.   *Curiosities of Puritan Nomenclature.* London, 1880.

BARNES, CARMAN D.   *Schoolgirl.* London, 1930.

BARRETT, B. F.   *Beauty for Ashes.* New York, 1855.

BARRIÈRE, MARCEL.   *Essai sur le Donjuanisme Contemporain.* Paris, 1932.

BARTLETT, E. A.   *Vindication of the Character and Condition of the Females Employed in the Lowell Mills. . . .* Lowell, 1841.

BARZUN, J.   "Social Criticism. Myths for Materialists." In *American Thought, 1947.* (New York, 1947), pp. 459–68.

BASSO, H.   *Mainstream.* New York, 1943.

BEARD, CHARLES A. and MARY R.   *The Rise of American Civilization.* New ed. New York, 1933.

BECKER, S. W.   *Ten Million Americans Have It.* Philadelphia, etc., 1937.

Bedside (The) Esquire. Sydney, London, 1940.

BEECHER, CATHERINE E., *The American Woman's Home*. New York, 1869.
and STOWE, HARRIET
E. B.

BEER, THOMAS.   *The Mauve Decade*. New York, 1926.

BELL, BERNARD I.   "We are Indicted for Immaturity." (*New York
                         Times Mag.*, July 20, 1947, 8 ff.)

BELLAMY, EDWARD.   *Looking Backward*. Boston, 1888.

BELLEGARRIGUE, A.   *Les Femmes d'Amérique*. Paris, 1853.

BENCE, JEAN and   *Win Your Man and Keep Him*. Chicago, 1948.
EUGENE.

BENDER, JAMES F.   "Man's World or Woman's?" (*New York Times
                         Mag.*, Aug. 10, 1947, p. 14.)
                         "Crystal Gazing." (*Science Illustrated*, June 1948.)

BENJAMIN, I. J.   *Drei Jahre in Amerika, 1859–62*. Hannover, 1862.

BENT, S.   *Ballyhoo*. New York, 1927.

BENTZON, T. (i.e. MME   "Condition de la Femme aux Etats Unis." (*Revue de
BLANC).   Deux Mondes*, 1894, CXXIV, 138 ff.; CXXV,
                         94 ff., 872 ff.; CXXVI, 574 ff.; 1895, CXXVIII,
                         802 ff.; CXXX, 560 ff.)

BERGLER, E.   *Divorce Won't Help*. New York, London, 1948.

BERNARD, RICHARD.   *Ruths Recompence*. London, 1628.

Better Homes and Gardens.

BEVANS, GLADYS.   "Parents and Children." (*Daily News* (New York),
                         Jan. 28, 1938.)

BIRNEY, C. H.   *The Grimké Sisters*. Boston, 1885.

BLACK, ALEXANDER.   *American husbands and Other Alternatives*. Indiana-
                         polis, 1925.
                         Modern Daughters. London, 1899.
                         "A Woman Needs Three Husbands." (*Reader's
                         Digest*. (Brit. ed.), Feb. 1946, 15–16.)

BLACKSTONE, SIR   *Commentaries on the Laws of England*. London,
WILLIAM.   1765–69.

BLANCH, LESLEY.   "Pin-Up Boys." (*Leader* (London), Sept. 29, 1945.)

                         Blue (The) Laws of New Haven Colony. Hartford,
                         1838.

BOAS, R. and L.   *Cotton Mather*. New York, London, 1928.

BOOTHE, C.   *The Women*. New York, 1937.

Boston Sunday Post.

BOURGET, PAUL.   *Outre-Mer*. London, 1895.

BRADBURY, B.   "Is Television Mama's Friend or Foe?" (*Good
                         Housekeeping*, Nov. 1950, 131 ff.)

BRADLEY, MARY H.   *The Five-Minute Girl*. New York, London, 1936.

BRANAGAN, T.   *The Excellency of the Female Character Vindicated*.
                         Philadelphia, 1808.

BRANSTON, URSULA B.   *Let the Band Play "Dixie"*. London, 1940.

BRINTON, D. G., and   *The Laws of Health in Relation to the Human Form*.
NAPHEYS, G. M.   Springfield, Mass., 1871.

BRISTED, C. A.   *The Upper Ten Thousand*. New York, 1852.

BROGAN, D. W.   *U.S.A.* Oxford, 1941.

BROMFIELD, LOUIS.   *Mrs. Parkington*. London, 1944.

BROUN, H., and others.   *Nonsenseorship*. New York, London, 1922.

BROUN, H., and   *Anthony Comstock: Roundsman of the Lord*. London,
LEECH, M.   1928.

BROWN, CHARLES B.   *Alcuin; a Dialogue*. New York, 1798.

BROWN, HERBERT R.   *The Sentimental Novel in America, 1789–1860*. Dur-
                         ham, N.C., 1940.

BROWN, WILLIAM.   "Pity These Poor Rich Women." (*Reynolds News*
                         (London), March 5, 1944, 6.)

BRUCE, H. A. B.   *Woman in the Making of America*. New ed., Boston,
                         1928.

BRUCE, P. A.   *Institutional History of Virginia in the Seventeenth Century.* New York, 1910.
BRYCE, JAMES.   *The American Commonwealth.* New York, 1888.
BRYDGES, HAROLD.   *Uncle Sam at Home.* London, 1888.
BUCK, PEARL S.   "America's Medieval Women." (*Harper's Mag.* 1938. CLXXVII, 225 ff.)
                              Of Men and Women. London, 1942.
BUCKINGHAM, J. S.   *The Eastern and Western States of America.* London, Paris, 1842.
                              The Slave States of America. London, Paris, 1842.
BUNN, ALFRED.   *Old England and New England.* London, 1853.
BURGESS, E. W.   See WILE, I. S. *The Sex Life of the Unmarried Adult.* London, 1935.
BURGESS, E. W., and   *Predicting Success or Failure in Marriage.* New
  COTTRELL, L. S.   York, 1939.
BURNS, JABEZ.   *The Mothers of the Wise and Good.* London, 1846.
BURT, M. S.   "Our Feminized United States." (*Forum and Century*, May 1937, XCVII, 266–71.)
BUSBEY, KATHERINE G.   *Home Life in America.* London, 1910.
BUSHNELL, H.   *Christian Nurture.* New York, 1887.
Business Week Magazine.
BUTLER, CHARLES.   *The American Lady.* Philadelphia, 1849.
BYINGTON, E. H.   *The Puritan in England and New England.* London, 1896.

CAHEN, A.   *Statistical Analysis of American Divorce.* New York, 1932.
CALEF, R.   *More Wonders of the Invisible World.* London, 1700.
CALL, ANNIE PAYSON.   *Power through Repose.* Boston, 1891.
CALVERTON, V. F.   *The Bankruptcy of Marriage.* London, 1929.
CAMPBELL, E. S.   *Cuties in Arms.* Philadelphia, 1942.
                              More Cuties in Arms. Philadelphia, 1943.
CAMPBELL, JOHN D.   *Everyday Psychiatry.* Philadelphia, etc., 1945.
CANDLER, ISAAC.   See *Summary (A) View of America*, etc.
CANTRIL, H.   "What We Don't Know is Likely to Hurt Us." (*New York Times Mag.*, May 14, 1944, 9 ff.)
CAREY, H. C.   *Essay on the Rate of Wages.* Philadelphia, 1835.
CARLIER, AUGUSTE.   *Le Mariage aux Etats-Unis.* Paris, 1860.
CARMER, C. L.   *Stars Fell on Alabama.* New York, 1934.
CARPENTER, W. B.   *Principles of Human Physiology.* London, 1842.
CAZAMIAN, M. L.   *L'autre Amérique.* Paris, 1931.
Century.
Century and Forum.
CHADWICK, F. E.   "The Woman Peril in American Education." (*Educational Review*, 1914, XLVII, 109–19.)
CHASE, ILKA.   *Past Imperfect.* New York, 1942.
                              In Bed We Cry. London, 1945.
"Chastity on the Campus." By a Co-Ed. (*Amer. Mercury*, June 1938, XLIV, 175–80.)
CHAVANNES, ALBERT.   *Vital Force and Magnetic Exchange.* Knoxville, Tenn., 1888.
                              The Future Commonwealth. New York, 1892.
                              In Brighter Climes or Life in Socioland. Knoxville, Tenn., 1897.
                              Lizzie Melton, a Self-reliant Girl. Knoxville, Tenn., 1900.
CHEMINAT, E.   *Quelques Observations sur l'Américaine des Etats-Unis.* Paris, 1873.
CHESSEX, J. C.   "Morale et Science aux Etats-Unis." (*Revue Bleue*, 5 juillet 1930, LXVIII, 389–92.)

CHEVALIER, MICHEL.   *Society, Manners and Politics in the United States.*
                         Boston, 1839.

(Chicago) Daily Tribune.
Chicago Medical Examiner.
CHIDECKEL, M.   *Female Sex Perversion.* New York, 1935.
CHILD, LYDIA MARIA.   *History of the Condition of Women.* London, 1835.
Chimera.
CHOISY, MARYSE.   *Un Mois chez des Filles.* Paris, 1928.
Christian Century.
Christian History.
Christian Philanthropist. *The History and Philosophy of Marriage, or Mono-
                         gamy and Polygamy Compared.* Boston, 1869. (This work has been attributed
                         to E. N. Jencks.)
CHRISTY, H. C.   *The American Girl.* New York, 1906.
CHURCHILL, RHONA.   "The Country to be a Girl In." (*Evening News* (Lon-
                         don), Oct. 19, 1938.)
CHURCHILL, SIR   *Secret Session Speeches.* London, 1946.
  WINSTON S.
CIARLANTINI, F.   *Roma–Nuova York e ritorno. Tragedie dell' ameri-
                         canismo.* Milano, 1934.
Civilization in the United States. Ed. by H. E. Stearns. London, 1922.
CLARKE, E. H.   *Sex in Education; or a Fair Chance for Girls.* Boston,
                         1874.
CLARKE, E. L.   *Petting: Wise or Otherwise?* New York, 1938.
COBBETT, WILLIAM.   *A Year's Residence in the United States of America.*
                         3rd ed. London, 1822.
COCHRAN, T. C., and   *The Age of Enterprise.* New York, 1943.
  MILLER, W.
*Code (The) of 1650 . . . to which is Added some Extracts from the Laws Commonly
  Called Blue Laws.* Hartford, Conn., 1822.
COHN, DAVID L.   *Love in America.* New York, 1943.
Collier's.
COLYER, W. T.   *Americanism: a World Menace.* London, 1922.
Complex.
COMSTOCK, ANTHONY.   *Frauds Exposed.* New York, 1880.
                         Traps for the Young. New York, 1883.
CONGER-KANEKO,   "Effeminization of the United States." (*The World's
  JOSEPHINE.   Work*, 1906, XII, 7521–24.)
Congressional Record.
CONTINI, JEANNE.   "Head Start on 1943." (*Washington Post*, Jan. 17,
                         1943.)
COOKE, G. C.   "Sexual Inadequacy." (*North Carolina Med. Journ.*,
                         1940, I, 657–61.)
CORAM, ROBERT.   *Political Inquiries.* Wilmington, 1781.
Coronet.
COTTON, JOHN.   *Spiritual Milk for Boston Babes in either England.*
                         Cambridge, Mass., 1656.
Courier-Journal (Louisville, Ky.).
COUSINS, SHEILA.   *To Beg I am Ashamed.* London, 1935.
COWAN, JOHN.   *The Science of a New Life.* New York, 1869.
CRADDOCK, IDA C.   *The Danse du Ventre.* Philadelphia, 1897.
                         Right Marital Living. Chicago, 1899.
                         The Wedding Night. Denver, 1900.
CRAPSEY, EDWARD.   *The Nether Side of New York, or the Vice, Crime, and
                         Poverty of the Great Metropolis.* New York, 1872.
CRESSWELL, NICHOLAS.   *The Journal of Nicholas Cresswell, 1774–77.* New
                         York, 1924.
CRÈVECOEUR, M. G. J. DE. *Letters from an American Farmer.* London, 1908.
                         Sketches of Eighteenth-century America. New York,
                         1949.

CRUIKSHANK, R. J.   "The Future of Anglo-American Relations." (*The English-Speaking World*, Aug.–Sept. 1946, XXVIII, 516–24.)

CUNNINGTON, C. W.   *Feminine Attitudes in the Nineteenth Century.* London, Toronto, 1935.

CURRIE, G. G.   *Woman in Her Infinite Variety.* London, 1925.

Daily News. (New York.)

Daily Telegraph. (London.)

DALLAIRE, VICTOR.   " American Woman? Not for This G.I.; He Says Her European Sister is Much Nicer." (*New York Times Mag.*, March 10, 1946, 15 ff.)

Dark (The) Side of New York Life and its Criminal Classes from Fifth Avenue down to the Five Points. New York, 1873.

Dating Do's and Don't's for Girls. New York, 1947.

Daughter's (A) Own Book, or Practical Hints from a Father to His Daughter. Philadelphia, 1836.

DAVENPORT, F. I.   "Adolescent Interests: a Study of the Sexual Interests and Knowledge of Young Women." (*Archives of Psychology*, 1923, No. 66.)
    Salvaging of American Girlhood. New York, 1924.

DAVIS, JOHN.   *The Wanderings of William.* Philadelphia, 1801.

DAVIS, K. B.   *Factors in the Sex Life of Twenty-two Hundred Women.* New York, 1929.

DAVIS, REBECCA B. H.   "In the Grey Cabins of New England." (*Century*, Feb. 1895, XLIX, N.S., XXVII, 620–3.)

DE CHANT, JEAN.   *I'm Letting My Hair Down.* New York, 1946.

DECIES, ELIZABETH W.   *King Lehr and the Gilded Age.* London, 1935.

DEKOBRA, MAURICE.   *Aux Cent Mille Sourires.* Paris, 1931.

DELARUE-MARDRUS,   *L'Amérique chez Elle.* Paris, 1933.

DELL, FLOYD.   "Why They Pet." (*Parents' Magazine*, Oct. 1931.)

DENGEL, VERONICA.   *Hold Your Man!* New York, 1945.

DEUTSCH, H.   *Psychology of Women.* New York, 1944–5.

DEVOE, ALAN.   "Any Sex Today?" (*Amer. Mercury*, June 1937, XLI, 175–8.)

Dial.

DICKENS, CHARLES.   *American Notes.* London, Glasgow, 1906. (First published in 1842.)

DICKINSON, G. L.   *A Modern Symposium.* London, 1905.

DICKINSON, R. L.   "Hypertrophies of the Labia Minora and their Significance." (*Amer. Gyn.*, Sept. 1902, I, 225–54.)
    "Urethral Labia or Urethral Hymen." (*American Medicine*, Jan. 27, 1904, VII. 347–9.)

DICKINSON, R. L., and BEAM, L.   *A Thousand Marriages.* London, 1932.
    The Single Woman. London, 1934.

DICKINSON, R. L., and PIERSON, H. H.   "The Average Sex Life of American Women." (*Jour. of the Amer. Med. Assn.*, Oct. 10, 1925, LXXXV, 1113 ff.)

DINGWALL, E. J.   *Racial Pride and Prejudice.* London, 1946.

DIX, DOROTHY.   Advice Column in the Baltimore *Sun*.
    Dorothy Dix—Her Book. New York, London, 1926.
    How to Win and Hold a Husband. New York, 1939.

DOD, JOHN A.   *Plaine and Familiar Exposition of the Ten Commandments.* 18th ed., London, 1632.

DODD, ANNA B.   *The Republic of the Future.* New York, 1887.

DOLCH, J. P.   "American Girls are Swell, but . . ." (*Amer. Mag.*, Jan. 1946, CXLI, 45 ff.)

DOLSON, HILDEGARDE.   *The Husband Who Ran Away.* New York, 1948.

DOS PASSOS, J.   *Streets of Night.* London, 1924.

Dow, George F.   *Everyday Life in the Massachusetts Bay Colony.* Boston, 1935.
Downey, F.   *Portrait of an Era.* New York, London, 1936.
Draper, Muriel.   *In America as Americans See It*, p. 101.
Dreiser, T.   *Hey, Rub-a-Dub-Dub!* London, 1931.
Duffey, Mrs. E. B.   *No Sex in Education.* Philadelphia, 1874.
Duhamel, G.   *Scènes de la vie future.* Paris, 1939,
Dumond, D. L.   *America in Our Time: 1896–1946.* New York, 1947.
Dwight, Timothy.   *Travels in New England and New York.* London, 1823.

Educational Review.
Edwards, Jonathan.   *Some Thoughts Concerning the Present Revival in New England.* (In *Works*, VI. London, 1817.)
Eldridge, Elizabeth.   *Co-ediquette.* New York, 1936.
Eliot, William G.   *Lectures to Young Women.* 3rd ed. Boston, New York, 1854.
Elkin, H.   "Aggressive and Erotic Tendencies in Army Life." (*Amer. Jour. of Sociol.*, March 1946, LI, 408–13.)
Ellington, G.   *The Women of New York, or the Underworld of the Great City.* New York, 1869.
English-speaking World.
Ernst, M. L.   *The First Freedom.* New York, 1946.
Erskine, John.   *Influence of Women and its Cure.* Indianapolis, New York, 1936.
Esquire.
Eszterhazy, A.   *Das Lasterhafte Weib.* Wien, 1930.
Evans, Bergen.   *A Natural History of Nonsense.* London, 1947.
Evening News. (London.)
Evening Standard. (London.)
Exner, M. J.   *The Question of Petting.* New York, 1933.

Fabian, Warner.   *Week-end Girl.* London, 1932.
Facécieux (Le) Reveille-Matin des Esprits Mélancholiques. Nymegue, 1678.
Facetiae . . . also Wits' Recreations. London, 1817.
Fair, James R.   *Give Him to the Angels.* New York, 1946.
Faithfull, Emily.   *Three Visits to America.* Edinburgh, 1884.
Familiar Letters to Females. By a Lady. Boston, 1834.
Farley, James.   *Jim Farley's Story.* New York, 1948.
Farmer, L. H.   *What America Owes to Women.* Ed. by L. H. Farmer. Buffalo, 1893.
Farnham, Eliza W.   *Woman and Her Era.* New York, 1864.
    The Ideal Attained. 2nd ed., London, 1870.
Farnham, M. F.   "Who Wears the Pants in *Your* Family?" (*Coronet*, March 1948, XXIII, 10–14.)
Faux, William.   *Memorable Days in America.* London, 1823.
Fearon, H. B.   *Sketches of America.* 3rd ed., London, 1819.
Fedder, Ruth.   *A Girl Grows Up.* New York, London, 1939. (New ed., 1948.)
Feiler, A.   *America Seen Through German Eyes.* New York, 1928.
Felt, J. B.   *The Customs of New England.* Boston, 1853.
Ferrero, L.   *Amérique, Miroir Grossissant de l'Europe.* Paris, 1939.
Ferri-Pisani.   *Au Pays des Amazones. L'Amour en Amérique.* Paris, 1927.
Finch, M.   *An Englishwoman's Experiences in America.* London, 1853.
Fine, B.   *Our Children are Cheated.* New York, 1947.

[FISCHER, J.] "The Loving Care of Determined Women." (*Harper's Mag.*, Aug. 1955, CCXI, 20 ff.)

FISHER, ANNE B. *Live with a Man and Love It!* London, 1937.

FISKE, A. K. "Profligacy in Fiction." (*North Amer. Rev.*, 1880, CXXXI, 79–88.)

FITHIAN, P. V. *Journal and Letters, 1767–74.* Princeton, 1900.

FITZGERALD, F. S. *This Side of Paradise.* London, 1921.

FLINT, TIMOTHY. *Francis Berrian.* Boston, 1826.

FLORENCE, LELLA S. "Britain—Unfeminine Land." (*Leader*, Oct. 27, 1945, 9 ff.)

FORDYCE, JAMES. *Sermons to Young Women.* London, 1765.

Foreign Affairs.

FORESTIER, Y. *Messieurs à Louer.* Paris, 1937.

Fortune.

Forum.

FOSDICK, RAYMOND. *Crime in America and the Police.* New York, 1920.

FOSTER, HANNAH. *The Coquette.* Boston, 1797.
The Boarding School. Boston, 1798.

FOSTER, R. G., and WILSON, P. P. *Women after College.* New York, 1942.

FOURNIER, CHRISTIANE. In the *Daily Telegraph* (London), March 21, 1932.

FOWLER, JOHN. *Journal of a Tour in the State of New York in the Year 1830.* London, 1831.

FOWLER, W. W. *Woman on the American Frontier.* Hartford, 1877.

FRANK, F. K. "Bisexual American Woman." (*Amer. Mercury*, March 1950, LXX, 279–83.)

FRANKEN, ROSE D. *Claudia.* New York, 1941.

FRANKLIN, BENJAMIN. *The Writings.* New York, 1905–7.

FRAZIER, E. F. *Negro Youth at the Crossways.* Washington, D.C., 1940.

FREUD, SIGMUND. *Sammlung kleiner Schriften zur Neurosenlehre.* 2, Folge. Wien, 1909.

FROST, F. "The American Impression." (*English Speaking World.* Oct.–Nov. 1947, XXIX, 720 ff.)

Frustration and Aggression. By J. Dollard (and others). London, 1944.

FULLER, MARGARET. *Woman in the Nineteenth Century.* New ed., Boston, 1874.

FURNAS, J. C. *How America Lives.* London, 1943.

FURNESS, C. J. *The Genteel Female.* New York, 1931.

GALLICO, P. "The American Goes to the Game." (*Transatlantic*, Sept. 1943, 28 ff.)
"Women Have No Manners." (*Collier's*, Jan. 19, 1946, CXVII, 13 ff.)

Gallynipper (The) in Yankeeland. By Himself. London, 1882.

GALTON, L. "Little Boys Make Lousy Husbands . . ." (*Better Homes and Gardens*, March 1950, LXXXVI, 131–3.)

GAMBLE, ELIZA B. *The Evolution of Woman.* New York, 1894.

GARDNER, G. E. "A Factor in the Sex Education of Children." (*Mental Hygiene*, 1944, XXVIII, 55–63.)

GAUDEFROY-DEMOMBYNES, JEAN. *La Femme aux Etats-Unis.* Paris, 1939.

GEORGE, W. L. *A Bed of Roses.* New York, 1919.

GEORGE, WALTER L. *Hail Columbia!* London, 1923.

GIDLOW, ELSA. "Will Women Enslave Men?" (*Forum and Century*, Feb. 1937, XCVII, 78–83.)

Girl (The) of the Period Miscellany.

GISBORNE, THOMAS.   *An Enquiry into the Duties of the Female Sex.* London, 1797.

Godey's Lady's Book.

GOLDBERG, J. A. and ROSAMOND.   *Girls of the City Streets.* New York, 1935.

Good Housekeeping.

GOODRICH, S. G.   *A Pictorial Geography of the World.* 9th ed., Boston, 1841.

GORE, CATHERINE G. F.   *Mrs. Armytage, or Female Domination.* London, 1836.

GORER, G. S.   *Hot Strip Tease and Other Notes on American Culture.* London, 1937.
"The American Child." (*Pilot Papers*, June 1947, II, 37–54.)
The Americans. London, 1948. (The American edition of this work was entitled *The American People.*)

GOUGE, WILLIAM.   *Of Domesticall Duties: Eight Treatises.* London, 1622.

GOVE, MARY S.   *Lectures to Women on Anatomy and Physiology.* New York, 1846.

GOW, A. M.   *Good Morals and Gentle Manners for Schools and Families.* Cincinnati, New York, 1873.

GRAFFIS, H.   "A Breast of the Times." (*The Bedside Esquire*, Sydney, London, 1940, 103 ff.)

GRAHAM, S.   *A Lecture to Young Men on Chastity.* Boston, 1837.

GRANT, JANE.   "Confession of a Feminist." (*Amer. Mercury*, Dec. 1943, LVII, 684–91.)

GRATTAN, T. C.   *Civilized America.* London, 1859.

GRAVES, MRS. A. J.   *Woman in America.* New York, 1843.

GREB, HARRY. *See* FAIR, JAMES R.

GREENBIE, M. B.   *American Saga.* New York, 1939.

GREENHAM, RICHARD.   *The Works of the Reverend and Faithfull Servant of Iesus Christ, M. R. Greenham.* 4th ed., London, 1695.

GRIMKÉ, SARAH M.   *Letters on the Equality of the Sexes and the Condition of Woman.* Boston, 1838.

GRISWOLD, A. W.   *Three Puritans on Prosperity.* Boston, 1934.

GRUND, F. J. (ed. by).   *Aristocracy in America.* London, 1839.
The Americans in their Moral, Social and Political Relations. London, 1837.

GUARD, T. DE LA [i.e. NATHANIEL WARD].   *The Simple Cobler of Aggavvam in America.* London, 1647. (Quotations from the Boston 1843 edition.)

GUNTHER, J.   *Inside U.S.A.* New York, 1947.

HAHN, EMILY.   *Seductio ad Absurdum.* New York, 1930.
"Pampered Husbands—Beware!" (*Evening Standard*, March 16, 1948.)

HALE, SARAH J. B.   *Woman's Record.* 2nd ed., New York, 1855.

HALL, BASIL.   *Travels in North America in the Years 1827 and 1828.* Edinburgh, 1829.

HALL, MRS. BASIL M.   *The Aristocratic Journey.* New York, 1931.

HALL, T. C.   *The Religious Background of American Culture.* Boston, 1930.

HALLER, WILLIAM.   *The Rise of Puritanism.* New York, 1938.

HALLGREN, M.   *Landscape of Freedom: the Story of American Liberty and Bigotry.* New York, 1941.

HALSEY, MARGARET.   *With Malice towards Some.* New York, 1938.
Color Blind. New York, 1946.

HAMILTON, G. V.   *A Research in Marriage.* New York, 1929.

HAMILTON, MARY A.   *The Place of the United States of America in World Affairs*. Nottingham, 1947.

HAMP, P.   *Perdu dans le Gratte-ciel*. 6th ed., Paris, 1938.

Harper's (Monthly) Magazine.

HAWES, ELIZABETH.   *Why Women Cry: or Wenches with Wrenches*. New York, 1943.

   Anything but Love: a Complete Digest of the Rules for Feminine Behavior from Birth to Death. New York, Toronto, 1948.

HAWGOOD, ALISON.   *A Family is Fun*. London, 1948.

HAWORTH, MARY.   " *Mary Haworth's Mail*." *Washington Post*.

HAYES, DORSHA.   *Mrs. Heaton's Daughter*. Chicago, 1943.

HAYWARD, E. P.   "Types of Female Castration Reaction." (*Psychoanalytical Quarterly*, 1943, XII, 45–66.)

HEDDEN, W. T.   "People in Skirts." (*The Amer. Scholar*, Winter 1950, XIX, No. I, 93 ff.)

HEGGIE, BARBARA.   "The Women." (*Picture Post*, Special Number, June 1940, 106–111.)

HERGESHEIMER, J.   *Cytherea*. New York, 1922.

   The Party Dress. London, 1930.

HERON, J.   *A Short History of Puritanism*. Edinburgh, 1908.

HERSCHBERGER, RUTH.   *Adam's Rib*. New York, 1948.

HEYWOOD, E. H.   *Cupid's Yokes: or the Binding Forces of Conjugal Life*. Princeton, 1880.

HICKS, GRANVILLE.   *Small Town*. New York, 1946.

HIGGINSON, T. W.   *Woman and Her Wishes*. Boston, 1853.

   Common Sense about Women. Boston, 1882.

   Women and Men. New York, 1888.

HILL, ROSA L.   *How to Attract Men and Money*. Meriden, Conn., 1940.

HILLIS, MARJORIE.   *Orchids on Your Budget*. London, 1938.

HIRST, ANNE.   *Get Your Man and Hold Him*. New York, 1931.

HOFF, S.   *Mom, I'm Home!* New York, 1945.

HOLBROOK, S. H.   "The Vanishing American Male." (*Amer. Mercury*, March 1937, XL, 270–9.)

HOLITSCHER, A.   *Amerika Heute und Morgen*. Berlin, 1923.

HOLLIDAY, R. C.   *Unmentionables. From Fig-leaves to Scanties*. New York, 1933.

Hollywood Quarterly.

HOPTON, R. Y., and   *Bed Manners*. New York, London, 1934.

BALLIOL, A.   *Better Bed Manners*. New York, London, 1936.

HORNEY, K.   "The Flight from Womanhood: the Masculinity Complex in Women." (*Intern. Jour. of Psychoanalysis*, Oct. 1926, VII, 324–39.)

HOTEP, I. M.   *Love and Happiness*. London, 1938.

House Beautiful.

HOUSTOUN, M. C. J. F.   *Hesperos*. London, 1850.

"How I Maneuver My Husband, by a Wife; How I Like to be Maneuvered, by a Husband." (*Better Homes and Gardens*, Sept. 1946, XXV, 174–5.)

HOWARD, SIDNEY C.   *The Silver Cord*. New York, 1927.

"How to Snare a Male."   *Ladies' Home Journal*, June 1950, LXVII, 56 ff.

HOWE, JULIA W.   *Sex and Education*. Cambridge, Mass., 1874.

HÜBNER, J. A. FR. VON   *Ein Spaziergang um die Welt*. Leipzig, 1885.

HULL, EDITH M.   *The Sheik*. Boston, 1921.

HUMPHREY, HEMAN.   *Domestic Education*. Amherst, 1840.

HURSTON, Z. N.   *Dust Tracks on a Road*. London, 1944.

HUTTON, GRAHAM.   *Midwest at Noon*. London, 1946.

HUTTON, O. C., and   *Conquerors' Peace*. New York, 1947.

ROONEY, A. A.

Hygeia.

"I Believe in the Double Standard." By a Wife. (*Amer. Mercury*, April 1937, XL, 421–6, and later issues.)

Illustrated Boston News.

Index Librorum Prohibitorum. Romae, 1938.

International Journal of Psychoanalysis.

IRWIN, INEZ.   *Angels and Amazons.* New York, 1933.

JACKS, L. P.   *My American Friends.* London, 1933.
JAMES, HENRY.   *The American Scene.* London, 1907.
JAMES, MAY H.   *The Educational History of Old Lyme, Connecticut, 1635–1935.* New Haven, 1939.
JANEWAY, JAMES.   *A Token for Children.* London, 1763.
JANSON, C. W.   *The Stranger in America.* London, 1807.
JESSEL, GEORGE.   *Hello, Momma.* Cleveland, New York, 1946.
JOFFE, N. F.   "The Prolongation of Adolescence in America." (*Complex*, 1951, No. 4, pp. 28–33.)
JOHNSON, T. H.   "Jonathan Edwards and the 'Young Folks' Bible." (*New England Quarterly*, Jan. 1932, V, 37–54.)
JONES, W., MOSE, D., *For Men Lonely.* Hanover, N.H., 1947.
  and O'RILEY, R.   *Weekend: A Girl's Guide to the College Weekend.* Boston, 1948.
JORDAN-SMITH, P.   *Cables of Cobweb.* London, 1923.

Journal of the American Medical Association.

JUSTINIAN.   *Americana Sexualis.* Chicago, 1939.
JUVENAL.   *An Englishman in New York,* 1911.

KELLOGG, J. H.   *Plain Facts about Sexual Life.* Battle Creek, Mich., 1877.
KELLY, H. A.   *Medical Gynecology.* New York, London, 1909.
KENDALL, E. A.   *Travels through the Northern Parts of the United States in the Years 1807 and 1808.* New York, 1809.
KENNEDY, R. C.   "The Conqueror." (*Christian Century*, April 17, 1946, LXIII, 495–7.)
KERN, MARJORIE D.   "Why American Women Marry Foreigners." (*Forum and Century*, Jan. 1937, XCVII, 23–7.)
KEUN, ODETTE.   *I Think Aloud in America.* London, 1939.
KIEFER, MONICA.   *American Children Through Their Books, 1700–1835.* Philadelphia, 1948.
KIND, ALFRED.   *Die Weiberherrschaft von heute.* (Bd. IV d. *Die Weiberherrschaft in der Geschichte der Menscheit*). Wien, Leipzig, 1931.
KINGSMILL, H.   *After Puritanism, 1850–1900.* London, 1929.
KINSEY, A. C., etc.   *Sexual Behavior in the Human Male.* Philadelphia, 1948.
                      Sexual Behavior in the Human Female. Philadelphia, 1953.
KITCHING, H.   *Sex Problems of the Returned Veteran.* New York, 1946.
KLEIN, VIOLA.   *The Feminine Character.* London, 1946.
KNOX, JOHN.   *The First Blast of the Trumpet against the Monstrous Regiment of Women.* [Geneva,] 1558.
KUHN, A. L.   *The Mother's Role in Childhood Education: New England Concepts, 1830–60.* New Haven, 1947.
KUO, HELENA.   "American Women are Different." (*Amer. Mercury*, June 1942, LIV, 728 ff.)

L .... F ......, ESQ. *The Virgin's Nosegay, or, the Duties of Christian Virgins.* London, 1744.

Ladies' Home Journal.

LAMBERT, JOHN.   *Travels through Lower Canada and the United States of North America.* London, 1810.

LANE, JANET.   *Your Carriage, Madam.* 2nd ed., New York, London, 1947.

LANGEWIESCHE, WOLFGANG.   *Das amerikanische Abenteuer.* Stuttgart, 1933.

LA ROCHEFOUCAULD-LIANCOURT, F. A. F., DUC DE.   *Voyage dans les Etats-Unis, 1795, 1796, et 1797.* Paris, an VII [i.e. 1799].

LARRONDE, CARLOS.   "L'Erotisme de l'Ecran." (*Mercure de France,* 15 déc. 1932, CCXL, 570–7.)

LAVER, JAMES.   *Taste and Fashion.* London, 1937.

LAWRENCE, EDWARD.   *Parents Groans over their Wicked Children.* London, 1681.

LAWRENCE, HENRY W.   *The Not-quite Puritans.* Boston, 1928.

LAYTHA, EDGAR.   "Doughboys and Diggers." (*Sat. Evening Post,* June 6, 1942, CCXIV, 22 ff.)

LAZARD, DIDIER.   *Contrastes Américains.* Paris, 1940.

Leader. (London.)

LEAF, M.   *Listen, Little Girl, Before You Come to New York.* New York, 1938.

LEBLICK, V.   *The New Era. Woman's Era; or Transformation from Barbaric to Humane Civilization.* [New York?, 1910.]

LEEN, NINA.   "The American Man; his Appearance and His Habits Examined by Photographer N. Leen." (*Life,* Intern. Ed., Sept. 1946, 16, XXI. U.S. Ed., Aug. 26, 1946, XXI, 87–91. Correspondence on, *Ib.* in later issue.)

LEJEUNE, C. A.   "Sex and the Movies." (*World Review,* Aug. 1940, 75–9.)

LENDERMAN.   *Lenderman's Adventures among the Spiritualists, and Free-lovers.* Cincinnati, 1857.

LESLIE, ELIZA.   *The Behaviour Book: A Manual for Ladies.* Philadelphia, 1853.

Letters from America, 1776–9. Tr. by R. W. Pettengill. Boston, New York, 1924.

LEWIS, DIO.   *Our Girls.* New York, 1871.

     Chastity: or, Our Secret Sins. [New York?] 1874.

LEWIS, SINCLAIR.   *Babbitt.* London, 1922.

     Elmer Gantry. London, 1927.

     Bethel Merriday. London, 1940.

     Cass Timberlane. London, 1946.

     Kingsblood Royal. New York, 1948.

LEWISOHN, LUDWIG.   *Expression in America.* London, 1932.

LIBBEY, LAURA JEAN.   *A Fatal Wooing.* New York, 1883.

     Willful Gaynell, or, the Little Beauty of the Passaic Mills. New York, 1890.

     Lovers Once but Strangers Now. New York, 1890.

     He Loved, but Was Lured Away. New York, 1891.

     "The Kind of Man Who Makes Home Happy." (*The New York and Paris Young Ladies' Fashion Bazar,* Oct. 1891.)

     We Parted at the Altar. New York, 1892.

     The Alphabet of Love. London, 1896.

     Wooden Wives. Is it a Story of Philandering Husbands? New York, 1923.

LIEBER, FRANCIS.   *The Stranger in America.* London, 1835.

LIEBMAN, J. L.   *Peace of Mind.* New York, 1946.

Life. (Chicago.)

LINDSAY, H., and   *Clarence Day's Life with Father Made into a Play.*
  CROUSE, R.   New York, 1942.
LINDSAY, MALVINA.   "Boycott on Glamour." (*Washington Post*, Dec. 2,
                          1943.)
LINDSEY, B. B., and   *The Companionate Marriage.* New York, 1928.
  EVANS, W.
LIPPARD, GEORGE.   *The Quaker City: or, the Monks of Monk-Hall.*
                          Philadelphia, 1844.
                          Dora Livingstone, the Adulteress, or the Quaker City.
                          London, 1848.
                          New York: its Upper Ten and Lower Million. Cin-
                          cinnati, 1853.
Listener. (London.)
Literary Digest.
LODGE, GEORGE CABOT.   *See* ADAMS, HENRY B. (1)
LOGAN, M. S.,   *The Part Taken by Women in American History.*
  MRS. J. A.   Wilmington, Del., 1912.
LONGFELLOW, H. W.   *Poetical Works.* London, 1868–9.
LOW, A. M.   (1)   *America at Home.* London, 1908.
                    (2)   *The American People.* London, 1909.
LUHAN, MABEL D.   *Intimate Memories.* London, New York, 1933–7.
LUNDBERG, F., and   *Modern Woman: the Lost Sex.* New York, 1947.
  FARNHAM, M. F.
LYELL, SIR CHARLES.   *Travels in North America.* London, 1845.
LYND, R. S. and H. M.   *Middletown.* London, 1929.
                          Middletown in Transition. New York, 1937.

MABIE, H. W.   *American Ideals, Character and Life.* New York,
                          1913.
MCCABE, J. D., JR.   *The Secrets of the Great City.* Philadelphia, etc.,
                          1868.
                          New York by Sunlight and Gaslight. Philadelphia,
                          1882.
MCCRACKEN, ELIZABETH.   *The Women of America.* New York, 1904.
MCGUFFEY, WILLIAM H.   *The Eclectic (Readers).* Cincinnati, 1838, etc.
MCGIFFERT, A. C., JR.   *Jonathan Edwards.* New York, 1932.
MCGUIRE, JUDITH E.   *Diary of a Southern Refugee.* By a Lady of Virginia
                          [i.e. Mrs. J. B. McGuire]. New York, 1867.
MCINTOSH, MARIA J.   *Violet: or, the Cross and the Crown.* New York,
                          1856.
MACMASTER, JOHN B.   *History of the People of the United States from
                          the Revolution to the Civil War.* London, 1883–
                          1913.
MCPARTLAND, JOHN.   "Footnote on Sex." (*Harper's Mag.*, March 1946,
                          CXCII, 212–14.)
                          Sex in our Changing World. London, 1948.
MCWILLIAMS, CAREY.   *Southern California Country.* New York, 1946.
MADARIAGA, S. DE.   "Americans are Boys." (*Harper's Mag.*, 1928,
                          CLVII, pp. 239–45.)
MAGIDOFF, ROBERT.   *In Anger and Pity.* New York, 1949.
MANIGAULT, G.   *The United States Unmasked.* London, 1879.
MANSFIELD, EDWARD D.   *The Legal Rights, Liabilities and Duties of Women.*
                          Salem, 1845.
MARKS, PERCY.   *The Plastic Age.* London, 1924.
MARKUN, LEO.   *Mrs. Grundy.* New York, London, 1930.
MARRYAT, FREDERICK.   *A Diary in America.* London, 1839.
                          —— *Part Second.* London, 1839.
MARTINEAU, HARRIET.   *Society in America.* New York, 1837.
Massachusetts Historical Society. Collections.

MATHER, COTTON.   *Ornaments for the Daughters of Zion.* Boston, 1692.
A Token for the Children of New England. Boston, 1700.
Magnalia Christi Americana. London, 1702.

MATHER, INCREASE.   *An Arrow against Profane and Promiscuous Dancing.* Boston, 1684.
An Essay for the Recording of Illustrious Providences, especially in New England. Boston, 1684.

MAULDIN, BILL.   *Back Home.* New York, 1947.

MAUROIS, ANDRÉ.   *Etats-Unis 39.* Paris, 1939.

MAYES, G. T.   "The American Male is O.K., but..." (*New York Times Mag.*, May 12, 1946, 18 ff.)

MEAD, MARGARET.   "What is a Date?" (*Transatlantic*, 1944, 54 ff.)
"What Women Want." (*Fortune*, Dec. 1946, XXXIV, 172 ff.)

MEEÜS, ADRIEN DE.   *Amusante Amérique.* Paris, 1938.

Man and Manners in America. By the author of *Cyril Thornton*, etc. [i.e. Thomas Hamilton.] Edinburgh, London, 1833.

MENCKEN, H. L.   *Americana, 1926.* London, 1926.

MENNINGER, KARL A.   "Men, Women and Hate." (*Atlantic Mthly.*, Feb. 1939, CLXIII, 158–68.)

Mental Hygiene. (New York.)

Mercure de France.

MERTON, ROBERT.   *Mass Persuasion.* New York, 1946.

MESICK, JANE L.   *The English Traveller in America, 1785–1835.* New York, 1922.

MILL, HUMPHREY.   *A Night's Search.* London, 1640–6.

MILLER, HENRY.   *The Air-conditioned Nightmare.* London, 1947.

MILLER, P. G. E.   *The New England Mind.* New York, 1939.

MILLER, P. G. E., and JOHNSON, T. H.   *The Puritans.* New York, etc., 1938.

MINNEY, R. J.   *Hollywood by Starlight.* London, 1935.

MINNICH, H. C.   *William Holmes McGuffey and His Readers.* New York, etc., 1936.

MINNIGERODE, MEADE.   *The Fabulous Forties, 1840–50.* New York, London, 1924.

MITCHELL, MARGARET.   *Gone with the Wind.* New York, 1936.

MITTELBERGER, G.   *Gottlieb Mittelberger's Journey to Pennsylvania.* Philadelphia, 1898.

Modern Romances.

MOORE, FRANK.   *Women of the War.* Hartford, Conn., 1866.

MOREAU, G.   *L'envers des Etats-Unis.* Paris, 1906.

MOREAU DE ST. MÉRY, M. L. E.   *Voyage aux Etats-Unis de l'Amérique, 1793–98.* New Haven, 1913.

MORGAN, ANNE.   *The American Girl.* New York, 1915.

MORGAN, EDMUND S.   *The Puritan Family.* Boston, 1944.

MORISON, S. E.   *The Puritan Pronaos.* New York, 1936.

MOSIER, R. D.   *Making the American Mind.* New York, 1947.

MOWRER, E. A.   *This American World.* London, 1928.

MUEHL, J. F.   *American Sahib.* New York, 1946.

MUIRHEAD, J. F.   *The Land of Contrasts.* London, New York, 1900.

MYERS, F. W. H.   *The Renewal of Youth and Other Poems.* London, 1882.

MYERS, G.   *Ye Olden Blue Laws.* New York, 1921.

NAPHEYS, G. H.   *The Physical Life of Woman: Advice to the Maiden, Wife and Mother.* Philadelphia, etc., 1871.
The Transmission of Life. 10th ed., Philadelphia, etc., 1871.
See BRINTON, D. G.

NASH, OGDEN.   "The Trouble with Women is Men." (*Saturday Evening Post*, Nov. 21, 1942, p. 108.)

Nation. (New York.)

NEARING, S. and   *Woman and Social Progress.* New York, 1912.
N. W. S.

Necessity (The) of Reformation with the Expedients Subservient thereunto, Asserted . . . Agreed . . . in the Synod at Boston in New England, Sept. 10, 1679. Boston, 1679.

NEVINS, ALLAN.   *John D. Rockefeller.* New York, 1941.

New England Quarterly.

New York and Paris Young Ladies' Fashion Bazar.

New York Journal and American.

New York Post.

New York Times.

New York Times Book Review.

New York Times Magazine.

New Yorker.

NEWCOMB, HARVEY.   *The Young Lady's Guide to the Harmonious Development of Christian Character.* 5th ed., Boston, 1843.
Youth and its Duties. London, Edinburgh, 1873.

NEWTON, A. E.   *The Better Way.* New York, 1875.

NICHOLS, FAN.   *Possess Me Not.* New York, 1946.

NICKERSON, H.   *The American Rich.* Garden City, N.Y., 1930.

NIEBUHR, R.   "Puritanism and Prosperity." (*Atlantic Mthly*, June 1926, CXXXVII, 721–5.)

NORDEN, HELEN.   *The Hussy's Handbook; including Latins are Lousy Lovers, and Others.* New York, 1942.

North American Review.

North Carolina Medical Journal.

NOYES, J. H.   *Male Continence.* Oneida, 1872.

OAKES, URIAN.   *New England Pleaded With, and Pressed to Consider the Things Which Concern Her Peace.* Cambridge, Mass., 1673.

ODEGARD, PETER H.   *The American Public Mind.* New York, 1930.

O'HIGGINS, H., and   *The American Mind in Action.* New York, London,
REEDE, E. H.   1924.

O'MALLEY, RUTH.   *Mrs. Cassatt's Children.* New York, 1943.

Onania. 10th ed., Boston (repr.), 1724.   (Other eds. in 1726 and 1742.)

O'RELL, MAX.   *A Frenchman in America.* Bristol, London, 1891.
Rambles in Womanland. London, 1903.

ORSINI RATTO, M.   *Gli Stati Uniti di Domani.* Milano, 1930.

OUIDA, *pseud.*   *Moths.* London, 1880.

Our Emergent Civilization. Planned and edited by Ruth N. Anshen. New York, 1947.

"Our Petticoat Government through German Eyes." (*Literary Digest*, June 27, 1931, CIX, 15.)

"Our Sisters Across the Sea." (*Young Woman*, July 1894, II, 360.)

OWEN, H. COLLINSON.   *The American Illusion.* London, 1929.

PALTER, RUTH.   "Radio's Attraction for Housewives." (*Hollywood Quarterly*, 1948, III, 248–57.)

PAPA, D.   *La Donna in America.* Milano, 1894.

Parents' Magazine.

PARKES, HENRY B.   "New England in the Seventeen-thirties." (*New England Quarterly*, 1930, III, 397–419.)

PARRAN, THOMAS.   *Shadow on the Land: Syphilis.* New York, 1937.

PARRINGTON, V. L.   *The Colonial Mind.* New York, 1927.

PARRINGTON, V. L., JR.   *American Dreams: a Study of American Utopias.* Providence, R.I., 1947.

Partisan Review. (London ed.)
PATTEE, F. L.   *The Feminine Fifties.* New York, London, 1940.
PAXTON, VIRGINIA.   *Penthouse in Bogotá.* London, 1944.
PAYNE, ROBERT.   *Report on America.* New York, 1949.
PEATTIE, D. C.   "A Way to Chastity." (*Reader's Digest,* Dec. 1937,
                           XXXI, 30–3.)
Pell-Mell.
Pennsylvania Magazine of History and Biography.
PERELMAN, S. J.   *Keep It Crisp.* New York, 1946.
PERRY, R. B.   *Puritanism and Democracy.* New York, 1944.
                       The American Cast of Mind. Radio talk for the
                       British Broadcasting Corporation, Dec. 8, 1947.
PETERS, C. C.   *Motion Pictures and Standards of Morality.* New
                       York, 1933.
PETERS, S. A.   *A General History of Connecticut. By a Gentleman of
                       the Province* [i.e. S. A. Peters]. London, 1781.
PHELPS, ALMIRA H. L.   *The Female Student; or Lectures to Young Ladies on
                       Female Education.* New York, 1836.
PHILLIPS, DAVID G.   *Susan Lenox: her Rise and Fall.* New York, 1917.
PHILLIPS, MARGARET E. *The Education of the Emotions through Sentimental
                       Development.* London, 1937.
Pictorial Review.
Picture Post. (London.)
Pilot Papers. (London.)
PLUTARCH.   *Opera.* Paris, 1841–55.
POLENZ, W. VON.   *Das Land der Zukunft.* Berlin, 1903.
PONSONBY, M. V.   *The Preposterous Yankee.* London, 1903.
POPENOE, PAUL B.   "Improve your Husband Scientifically." (*Ladies'
                       Home Journal,* Dec. 1942, LIX, 27.)
Popular Science Monthly.
POWEL, HARFORD.   "Bed Manners." (*Vogue,* Dec. 1, 1933.)
POWELL, A. M.   *State Regulation of Vice.* New York, 1878.
POWELL, HICKMAN.   *Ninety Times Guilty.* London, 1939.
Power (The) of Sympathy; or, the Triumph of Nature. Boston, 1789.
POWERS, MRS. S. D.   *The Ugly-Girl Papers; or, Hints for the Toilet.* New
                       York, 1874.
"Preview of the Post-war Generation." (*Fortune,* March 1943, XXVII, 116 ff.)
PRINCE, W. F.   "An Examination of Peters's 'Blue Laws'." (*Ann.
                       Rept. Amer. Hist. Assn.,* 1898 (Washington, 1899),
                       97–138.)
PRINGLE, H. F.   "What the Men of America Think about Women."
                       (*Ladies' Home Journal,* April 1939, LVI, 14 ff.)
Printers' Ink.
Productivity Team Report, Steel Founding. London, 1949.
PRUETTE, L.   *Women and Leisure.* New York, 1924.
"Psychiatric (The) Toll of Warfare." (*Fortune,* Dec. 1943, XXVIII, 141 ff.)
Psychiatry.
Psychoanalytic Quarterly.
Pure (The) Nazarite. Boston, 1723.

Radio Research, 1942–43. Ed. by G. P. F. Lazarsfeld [and] F. N. Stanton. New
     York, 1944.
RAND, A.   *The Fountainhead.* London, 1947.
RATTNER, H.   "Cosmetics for Men." (*Hygeia,* Oct. 1946, XXIV,
                       744–5.)
RAY, RANDOLPH.   *Marriage is a Serious Business.* London, 1944.
Reader's Digest.
RECOULY, RAYMOND.   *L'Amérique pauvre.* Paris, 1933.
REDFIELD, JAMES W.   *Outlines of a New System of Physiognomy.* New
                       York, 1849.

REDFIELD, JAMES W.   *The Twelve Qualities of Mind.* New York, 1850.
REEVES, J. E.   *The Physical and Moral Causes of Bad Health in American Women.* Wheeling, W. Va., 1875.
REGIER, C. C.   *The Era of the Muckrakers.* Chapel Hill, 1932.
RENIER, G. J.   *The English, are They Human?* London, 1931.
Revue Bleue.
Revue de Deux Mondes.
Reynolds News. (London.)
RICE, ELMER.   "Sex in the Modern Theater." (*Harper's Mag.*, May, 1932, CLXIV, 665 ff.)
RICE, THURMAN, B.   *Sex, Marriage, and the Family.* Philadelphia, New York, 1946.
RICHARDSON, MRS. E. R.   *Influence of Men, Incurable.* Indianapolis, New York, 1936.
RICHARDSON, SAMUEL.   *Pamela.* London, 1741, 1742.
RITA, *pseud.*   *America—through English Eyes.* London, 1911.
ROMAINS, JULES.   *Salsette Discovers America.* London, 1942.
Roman (Le) de Violette: oeuvre posthume d'une Célébrité Masquée. Lisbonne, 1870.
RONALD, JAMES.   *The Angry Woman.* Philadelphia, 1948.
ROOT, W.   "Women are Intellectually Inferior." (*Amer. Mercury*, Oct. 1949, LXIX, pp. 407–14.)
ROSE, GEORGE.   *The Great Country.* London, 1868.
ROUSIERS, P. DE   *La Vie Américaine.* Paris, 1899.
ROUSSY DE SALES,   "Love in America." (*Atlantic Monthly*, May 1938,
   R. DE.   CLXI, 645–51.)
    "What Makes an American?" (*Atlantic Monthly*, March 1939, CLXIII, 295–304.)
ROWSON, SUSANNAH.   *Charlotte. A Tale of Truth.* Philadelphia, 1794.
ROZ, F.   *Les Etats-Unis d'Amérique.* Paris, 1927.
RUNYON, DAMON.   "Dames can be Trained to Act Human." (*Courier-Journal* (Louisville, Ky.), May 29, 1943.)
RUSH, BENJAMIN.   *A Plan for the Establishment of Public Schools and the Diffusion of Knowledge in Pennsylvania.* Philadelphia, 1786.
    Thoughts upon Female Education. Philadelphia, 1798.

SAMUELS, GERTRUDE.   "We Enter our Mairzy Doat-age." (*New York Times Magazine*, Feb. 20, 1944.)
SAN CARLOS DE PÉDROSO,   *Les Américains chez eux.* 2 éd., Paris, 1890.
   LA MARQUISE DE.
SANDERS, M. K.   "Women in Politics." (*Harper's Magazine*, Aug. 1955, CCXI, 56–64.)
SANFORD, JOHN.   *The People from Heaven.* New York, 1943.
SANTAYANA, GEORGE.   *Character and Opinion in the United States.* London, 1920.
    The Genteel Tradition at Bay. London, 1931.
Saturday Evening Post.
Saturday Review of Literature.
SCHEINFELD, A.   "Husband Shortage" (*Collier's*, June 26, 1943, CXI, 18 ff.)
SCHNEIDER, H. W.   *The Puritan Mind.* London, 1931.
SCHURR, C.   "Don't Blame Women for *Everything!*" (*Coronet*, Sept. 1951, XXX, 28–31.)
Scorpion.
Scribner's Magazine.
SEGALL, J. L.   *Sex Life in America.* New York, 1934.
SELDES, G. V.   *The Stammering Century.* New York, 1928.

"Sentiments (The) of an American Woman." (*Pennsylvania Mag. of Hist. & Biog.*, 1894, XVIII, 361–6.)

SEVAREID, E.   *Not so Wild a Dream.* New York, 1946.

SEWALL, S.   *Diary . . . 1674–1729.* (Mass. Hist. Soc. Colls., V–VII.) Boston, 1878–82.

SEYBOLT, R. E.   "Dress Reform in Massachusetts." (*New England Quarterly*, April 1930.)

SHAPLEY, OLIVE.   "Children in America." (*Listener*, May 2, 1946, 582–3.)

SHERWOOD, M. M.   *The History of the Fairchild Family.* London, 1889.

SIEGFRIED, A.   *Les Etats-Unis d'Aujourd'hui.* 5 éd., Paris, 1928.

SIEGVOLK, P.   *Ruminations; the Ideal American Lady and Other Essays.* New York, London, 1893.

SIGOURNEY, LYDIA H.   *Letters to Young Ladies.* London, 1841.

SILVER, ABNER. (Ed.).   *All Women are Wolves.* New York, 1945.

SIMPSON, LOUISE M.   "Husband is Seldom a Mouse, but he can be Trapped." (*House Beautiful*, May 1947, LXXXIX, 206.)

SINCLAIR, UPTON.   *Sylvia's Marriage.* Philadelphia, Chicago, 1914.

SMITH, BRADFORD.   *American Quest.* New York, 1938.

SMITH, ELIZABETH O.   *Woman and Her Needs.* New York, 1851.

SMITH, WALLACE.   *Bessie Cotter.* London, 1935.

Social (The) Evil, with Special Reference to Conditions Existing in the City of New York. . . . A Report Prepared (1902) under the Direction of the Committee of Fifteen. New York, London, 1912.

SOHN, MONTE.   *Your Loving Mother.* New York, 1943.

SOISSONS, S. C. DE, COUNT.   *A Parisian in America.* Boston, 1896.

SOUTHWORTH, E. D. E. N.   *Ishmael; or, In the Depths.* Philadelphia, 1872.
                        Self-Raised: or, From the Depths. Philadelphia, 1876.

SPALDING, E.   "America's Cry-baby Athletes." (*Amer. Mercury*, Sept. 1937, XLII, 65–75.)

SPARKS.   *Flora Montgomerie, the Factory Girl; Tale of the Lowell Factories. Being a Recital of the Adventures of a Libidinous Millionaire, whose wealth was used as a means of triumphing over virtue.* New York, 1856.

SPENDER, J. A.   *The America of To-day.* London, 1928.

SPRING, GARDINER.   *The First Woman.* New York, 1852.

STANTON, ELIZABETH C.   *The Woman's Bible.* New York, 1895.

Stars and Stripes.

STEAD, CHRISTINA.   *Letty Fox; Her Luck.* New York, 1946.

STEARNS, CHARLES.   *The Ladies' Philosophy of Love.* Leominster, Mass., 1797.

STEINBECK, J.   *The Wayward Bus.* London, 1947.

STEINER, J. F.   *Americans at Play.* New York, London, 1933.

STEINER, LEE R.   *Where Do People Take Their Troubles?* Boston, 1945.

STEPHENS, ANN S.   *Malaeska, the Indian Wife of the White Hunter.* London, 1861.

STERN, EDITH M.   *Men are Clumsy Lovers.* New York, 1934.
                        "America's Pampered Husbands." (*Nation*, July 10, 1943, CLVII, 40–2.)

STERN, MICHAEL.   *The White Ticket.* New York, 1936.

STERNE, LAURENCE.   *The Life and Opinions of Tristram Shandy.* London, 1914.

STILES, H. R.   *Bundling; its Origin, Progress and Decline in America.* Albany, 1869.

STOCKHAM, ALICE B.   *Tokology.* Revd. ed., Chicago, 1889.

STODDARD, SOLOMON.   *An Answer to Some Cases of Conscience Respecting the Country.* Boston, 1722.

STOUFFER, S. A., etc.   *The American Soldier.* Princeton, 1949.

STOWE, LELAND.   "What's Wrong with Our Women?" (*Esquire*, Sept. 1948, 31 ff.)

STRAKOSCH, F. M.   *Factors in the Sex Life of 700 Psychopathic Women.* Utica, 1934.

STRAUSS, THEODORE.   "Farewell to Oomph." (*New York Times*, Oct. 10, 1943.)

STRECKER, E. A.   "What's Wrong with American Mothers?" (*Sat. Evening Post*, Oct. 26, 1946, CCXIX, 14 ff.)
Their Mothers' Sons. Philadelphia, 1946.

STRINGER, ARTHUR.   "Why Women Make No Sense." (*North Amer. Rev.*, 1939; CCXLVII, 36–311.)

STUART, J.   *Three Years in North America.* 2nd ed., Edinburgh, 1833.

SUGRUE, T.   *Stranger in the Earth.* New York, 1948.

Summary (A) View of America. . . . By an Englishman [i.e. Isaac Candler]. London, 1824.

Sun. (Baltimore.)

SWISSHELM, JANE G.   *Letters to Country Girls.* New York, 1853.

TATE, NAHUM.   *A Present for the Ladies.* London, 1693.

TERMAN, L. M.   *Psychological Factors in Marital Happiness.* New York, London, 1938.

THACHER, P.   "Account of the Revival of Religion at Middleborough East-Precinct." (*Christian History*, 1745, II, 90.)

"They Order It Better in France." (*Esquire*, Sept. 1937, 36 ff.)

This Week Magazine.

THOMAS, N., and   *What's the Matter with New York?* New York, 1932.
BLANSHARD, P.

THOMPSON, C.   "Penis Envy in Women." (*Psychiatry*, 1943, VI, 123–5.)

THOMPSON, R. W.   *Black Caribbean.* London, 1946.

THOREAU, H. D.   *Walden.* Boston, 1854.

THORP, MARGARET F.   *America at the Movies.* London, 1946.

THURSTON, JOSEPH.   *The Toilette.* London, 1730.

Time.

Time & Tide.

TOCQUEVILLE, A. DE.   *De la Democratie en Amérique.* 4. éd., Paris, 1837.
Democracy in America. Cambridge, Mass., 1863.

TOWLE, G. M.   *American Society.* London, 1870.

TOWNE, A.   "Homosexuality in American Culture." (*Amer. Mercury*, Aug. 1951, LXXIII, pp. 3–9, cf. *ib.*, LXXIV, pp. 22–7.)

Traits of American Humour, by Native Authors. London, 1852.

Transatlantic. (London.)

TRAQUAIR, RAMSAY.   "Women and Civilization." (*Atlantic Monthly*, Sept. 1923, CXXXII, 289–96.)

TROLLOPE, ANTHONY.   *North America.* London, 1862.

TROLLOPE, FRANCES E.   *Domestic Manners of the Americans.* 5th ed. London, 1839.

TRUMBULL, J. H.   *The True Blue Laws of Connecticut and New Haven, and the False Blue Laws Invented by Samuel Peters.* Hartford, 1876.

TUCKERMAN, H. T.   *America and her Commentators.* New York, 1864.

TULLY, ANDREW.   *The Era of Elegance.* New York, 1947.

"T.V.—Who's Afraid?"   *Fortune*, July 1950, XLII, 55–8.)

TYLER, ALICE F.   *Freedom's Ferment: Phases of American Social History to 1860.* Minneapolis, 1944.

UHLER, A., and FISH-
BACK, MARGARET.   "Are Men Mice?" (*Forum*, July 1938, C, 17–21.)

ULRICH, M. S.   "Off with Their Heads." (*Sat. Rev. of Lit.*, Feb. 15, 1936, XIII, 13.)

U.S. BUREAU OF
CENSUS.   *Estimated Future Population, by Age and Sex, 1945–80.* (Series P-3, Nr. 15, July 1941.)

UZZELL, T. N., and
LEROY, V. E.   "Decline of the Male." (*Scribner's Mag.*, Dec. 1936, C, 19–25.)

VAIL, HENRY.   *A History of the McGuffey Readers.* Cleveland, 1910.
VAILE, P. A.   *Y., America's Peril.* London, 1909.
VALERY, B.   "What is RIGHT with American Women." (*Coronet*, Sept. 1952, XXXII, 60–3.)
VARIGNY, C. DE.   "The American Woman." (*Popular Science Monthly*, 1893, XLIII, 383 ff. Adapted from *La Femme aux Etats-Unis* in the *Revue de deux Mondes*, 15 mars, 1889, XCII, 350 ff.)
    La Femme aux Etats-Unis. Paris, 1893.
VAY, A., COUNT.   *Inner Life of the United States.* London, 1908.
Veneral Disease Information. Washington, D.C., 1923, etc.
Vénus dans le Cloître. (Paris, 1862?.)
Venus in the Cloyster. (London, 1683.)
VENZMER, G.   *New York ohne Schminke.* 6 bis 8 Aufl., Hamburg, 1930.
VIDAL, GORE.   *The Season of Comfort.* New York, 1948.
"Virgins for Husbands." (*Amer. Mercury*, July, 1938, XLIV, 366–8.)
Vogue.

W., O.   *No Bed of Roses.* New York, 1930.
    God Have Mercy on Me! New York, 1931.
WADSWORTH, BENJAMIN.   *Unchast Practices Procure Divine Judgments. A Sermon in Boston, July 29, 1716.* Boston, 1716.
WAITHMAN, R.   *Report on America.* London, 1940.
WARD, DOROTHY J.   *English Enigma.* London, 1948.
WARD, LESTER F.   *Pure Sociology.* New York, 1903.
WARDER, ANN.   "Extracts from the Diary of Mrs. A. Warder." (*Penn. Mag. of Hist. and Biog.*, 1893, XVII, 444–61; 1894, XVIII, 51–63.)
WARSHOW, R.   "The Anatomy of Falsehood." (*Partisan Rev.* (Brit. ed.), May–June, 1947, XIV, 305–9.)
WASHBURN, C.   *Come Into My Parlor.* Chicago, 1936.
Washington Post.
WEBSTER, CLARENCE M.   *Town Meeting Country.* New York, 1945.
WECTER, DIXON.   *The Saga of American Society. A Record of Social Aspiration, 1607–1937.* London, 1937.
WELLS, H. G.   *'42 to '44.* London, 1944.
WERTENBAKER, T. J.   *The Puritan Oligarchy.* New York, 1947.
WEST, JAMES.   *Plainville, U.S.A.* New York, 1945.
WEST, JANE.   *Letters to a Young Lady.* New York, 1806.
WEST, REBECCA.   "These American Men." (*Harper's Monthly Mag.*, 1925, CLI, 448–56.)
    "These American Women." (*Ib.*, 722–30.)
WESTON, R.   *A Visit to the United States and Canada in 1833.* Edinburgh, Glasgow, 1836.
WHIPPLE, T. K.   *Spokesmen.* New York, 1928.
WHITBREAD, J., and
CADDEN, V.   *The Intelligent Man's Guide to Women.* New York, 1951.

WHITE, WILLIAM ALLEN.   *The Autobiography of William Allen White.* New York, 1946.
WHITE, W. L.   *Report on the Russians.* London, 1945.
WHITMAN, H.   "She Jails Mashers, Adores Bob Taylor." (*Daily News* (New York), Aug. 24, 1937.)
WHITNEY, W. D.   *Who are the Americans?* London, 1941.
WIGGLESWORTH, M.   *The Day of Doom.* New York, 1929.
WILE, I. S. (ed. by). *The Sex Life of the Unmarried Adult.* London, 1935.
WILLARD, F. E., and   *American Women: Fifteen Hundred Biographies with over Fourteen Hundred Portraits.* New York, etc., 1877.
  others (Editors).
WILLIS, N. P.   *The Rag-Bag: a Collection of Ephemera.* New York, 1855.
WILSON, AUGUSTA J. E. *St. Elmo.* New York, 1866.
WILSON, EDMUND.   *Europe without Baedeker.* London, 1948.
WILSON, HELEN M.   *On Some Causes of Prostitution, with Special Reference to Economic Conditions.* London, 1916.
WILSON, MARGERY.   *The Woman You Want To Be.* Philadelphia, New York, 1792–1942.
                      How to Live Beyond Your Means. Philadelphia, New York, 1945.
                      The New Etiquette. Philadelphia, New York, 1947
WILSON, SAMUEL P.   *Chicago by Gaslight.* [Chicago, c. 1895?]
                      Chicago and its Cess-pools of Infamy. [Chicago, c. 1910?]
WINTHER, S. K.   *Beyond the Garden Gate.* New York, 1946.
Winthrop Papers. Boston, 1929, etc.
WISE, DANIEL.   *The Young Lady's Counsellor.* New York, 1851. (Quotations from the edition of Otley, 1863.)
Witts Recreations. London, 1640.
WOLFE, THOMAS.   "April, late April; a Story." (*Amer. Mercury*, Sept. 1937, XLII, 87–97.)
                      The Web and the Rock. London, Toronto, 1947.
                      You Can't Go Home Again. London, Toronto, 1947.
WOLFE, W. BÉRAN.   *A Woman's Best Years.* London, 1935.
WOLLSTONECRAFT, MARY. *A Vindication of the Rights of Women.* London, 1792.
Woman's Coming of Age. Ed. by S. D. Schmalhausen and V. F. Calverton. New York, 1931.
Women of Colonial and Revolutionary Times. London, 1895–97.
WOOD, BRENDAN.   *Sligo.* Chicago, 1947.
WOOD, MORRISON.   *The Devil is a Lonely Man.* New York, 1946.
Woodhull and Claflin's Weekly.
WOODY, T.   *A History of Women's Education in the United States.* New York, Lancaster, Pa., 1929.
WOOLSON, A. G.   *Woman in American Society.* Boston, 1873.
World Review.
WRIGHT, HENRY C.   *Marriage and Parentage.* 5th thous. Boston, 1858.
WYLIE, P.   *Generation of Vipers.* New York, 1942.
WYSE, F.   *America: its Realities and Resources.* London, 1846.

Yank.
YODER, R. M.   "Be Good! Television's Watching!" (*Sat. Evening Post*, May 14, 1949, CCXXI, 29 ff.)
YORKE, RUTH.   "Every Girl can be Popular with Boys by Obeying These 12 Commandments. . . . Doesn't have to Pet." (*Boston Sunday Post*, Sept. 12, 1937.)
Young (The) Lady's Friend. Boston, 1836.

Young (The) Lady's Parental Monitor. London, 1790.
Young Woman.

ZEIGLER, G. J.   "On the Social Evils, with a Plan for Their Diminu-
                        tion, and a Plea for the Innocent and Helpless."
                        (*Chicago Med. Examiner, 1867*, VIII, 724–30.)
ZOLA, E.   *Nana.* Paris, 1880.

INDEX